MOVING WORDS IN THE NORDIC MIDDLE AGES

ACTA SCANDINAVICA

CAMBRIDGE STUDIES IN THE SCANDINAVIAN WORLD

A series devoted to early Scandinavian culture, history, language, and literature, between the fall of Rome and the emergence of the modern states (seventeenth century) – that is, the Middle Ages, the Renaissance, and the Early Modern period (*c.* 400–1600).

General Editor

Stefan Brink, *University of Cambridge/Uppsala universitet*

Editorial Advisory Board, under the auspices of the Department of Anglo-Saxon, Norse, and Celtic, University of Cambridge

Maria Agren (History), *Uppsala universitet*
Pernille Hermann (Literature), *Aarhus Universitet*
Terry Gunnell (Folklore), *Háskóli Íslands*
Judith Jesch (Old Norse/Runology), *University of Nottingham*
Judy Quinn (Old Norse Literature), *University of Cambridge*
Jens Peter Schjodt (History of Religions), *Aarhus Universitet*
Dagfinn Skre (Archaeology), *Universitet i Oslo*
Jorn Oyrehagen Sunde (Law), *Universitet i Bergen*

Previously published volumes in this series are listed at the back of the book.

Volume 8

MOVING WORDS IN THE NORDIC MIDDLE AGES

Tracing Literacies, Texts, and Verbal Communities

Edited by

Amy C. Mulligan
and Else Mundal

BREPOLS

British Library Cataloguing in Publication Data

A catalogue record for this book is available from the British Library

D/2019/0095/11
ISBN: 978-2-503-57810-1
e-ISBN: 978-2-503-57811-8
DOI: 10.1484/M.AS-EB.5.114326
ISSN: 2466-586X
e-ISSN: 2565-9170

Printed in the EU on acid-free paper

CONTENTS

List of Illustrations

Figures

Graphs

Tables

Introduction

Amy C. Mulligan

'What brings about the great shifts in the world of literature? Often it is when someone seizes upon a simple, overlooked form, discounted as art in the higher sense, and makes it mutate.'[1] Thus began the Swedish literary critic Horace Engdahl's speech celebrating the singer and song-writer Bob Dylan as winner of the 2016 Nobel Prize for Literature, a controversial selection which spurred discussions of what literature really is, and why we value it. Dylan, too, initially baulked at the award and all that its acceptance implied: in his own words, 'the news about the Nobel Prize left me speechless'.[2] Following a fortnight of silence, however, he did accept. Bob Dylan's Nobel Prize, and his own reaction to it, urges us think more broadly about literature, orality, and the range of verbal communities that infuse words with meaning: how do words in dynamic performance, animated tunefully and richly reverberating as song and speech, relate to 'literature' which, per its etymology, has been traditionally seen as comprised of letters (Latin *litterae*) organized upon a page? Words might be written down, yet much of their unique character and power to transform, to mutate into something remarkable, pertains to the way words move through, and are embraced and transformed by, diverse verbal communities.

Dylan's lyrics can be read on the page and will impress as powerful poetry, but we also know that when sung and musically performed, the resultant expe-

[1] Engdahl, 'The Nobel Prize in Literature'.

[2] Dylan, 'If I Accept the Prize? Of Course'.

Amy Mulligan (amullig2@nd.edu) is a Fellow of the Medieval Institute and Assistant Professor of Irish Language and Literature at the University of Notre Dame, Indiana, where she conducts research and publishes on the literatures of medieval Britain, Ireland, and Scandinavia, with particular emphasis on cultural exchange among peoples of the medieval North Atlantic.

Moving Words in the Nordic Middle Ages: Tracing Literacies, Texts, and Verbal Communities, ed. by Amy C. Mulligan and Else Mundal, AS 8   BREPOLS ⬥ PUBLISHERS   (Turnhout: Brepols, 2019)
pp. 1–13   10.1484/M.AS-EB.5.116617

rience is textured to engage and delight multiple senses. Words we encounter as written letters on a page must also be understood as having a dynamic oral/ aural life as well. The same might be said of many types of medieval 'literature'. Indeed, some of the earliest Nordic writers developed their texts to convince the audience of the text's oral character and to ensure that their words moved off the page to participate in an embodied, multidimensional world. We cannot fully recuperate the varied performances of and audience expectations for medieval words. However, the discussions in this book make use of the tools available to us as philologists, linguists, literary and spatial theorists, students of myth and religion, art historians, palaeographers, and scholars of material culture to con- sider how medieval Nordic textual artefacts might have played out in the real world: how the visual, physical, and aural might have shaped and transformed the texts which remain. The essays here examine material texts — historical and literary narratives, full manuscripts and fragments in both Latin and the vernac- ular, runic inscriptions, written correspondence, numbered lists, eddic poems, and French romances translated into Old Norse. Despite their textuality, they all have histories as dynamic, moving words which circulated among living com- munities. While the earliest composers, of Latin histories of the North as well as the vernacular Icelandic sagas, were very much aware of the prestige of writ- ing, their texts still evoke oral performance, using formulae and phrasing that allows the audience to 'hear' the written text coming to life. The introduction of literacy and writing from Christian culture did not cause a move away from oral culture. Rather, Nordic composers created a sophisticated literature whose virtue was continual movement back and forth on the oral-literate spectrum.

Engdahl and the Nobel Committee celebrated Dylan for 'panning poetry gold' from the popular cultural elements around him:

> But what Bob Dylan did was not to return to the Greeks or the Provençals. Instead, he dedicated himself body and soul to 20th-century American popular music, the kind played on radio stations and gramophone records for ordinary people, white and black: protest songs, country, blues, early rock, gospel, mainstream music. He listened day and night, testing the stuff on his instruments, trying to learn. But when he started to write similar songs, they came out differently. In his hands, the material changed. From what he discovered in heirloom and scrap, in banal rhyme and quick wit, in curses and pious prayers, sweet nothings and crude jokes, he panned poetry gold, whether on purpose or by accident is irrelevant; all creativity begins in imitation.[3]

---

[3] Engdahl, 'The Nobel Prize in Literature 2016'.

Like Dylan's transformation of American cultural material, so too the medieval Nordic text-makers discussed in this volume relied upon and in some brilliant ways reinvented Nordic oral and popular culture in their compositions. Using parchment, wooden rune-sticks, epistles, sagas, and histories, they also 'panned gold' from the vast resources at their disposal. And like the medieval Nordic composers using local cultural elements, Dylan himself does not shy from associations with canonical figures, textual forms, or compositional processes. Dylan points out that Shakespeare was as concerned with the often overlooked aspects of performance and getting his words across as he was with lofty literary goals:

> I began to think about William Shakespeare, the great literary figure. I would reckon he thought of himself as a dramatist. The thought that he was writing literature couldn't have entered his head. His words were written for the stage. Meant to be spoken not read. When he was writing Hamlet, I'm sure he was thinking about a lot of different things: 'Who're the right actors for these roles?' 'How should this be staged?' 'Do I really want to set this in Denmark?' His creative vision and ambitions were no doubt at the forefront of his mind, but there were also more mundane matters to consider and deal with. 'Is the financing in place?' 'Are there enough good seats for my patrons?' 'Where am I going to get a human skull?' I would bet that the farthest thing from Shakespeare's mind was the question 'Is this *literature*?'[4]

'Literature' does not always take expected form, and one must remain attuned to the many verbal traditions that inform each text. Indeed, 'A Hard Rain's A-Gonna Fall', performed at the Nobel Prize Ceremony by Patti Smith, eloquently speaks to Dylan's engagement with a long-established literature of prophecy and social commentary. The composition's questioning format ('Oh, where have you been, my blue-eyed son?', 'Oh, what did you see, my blue-eyed son?') and dark answers about a changed landscape on which a deluge will soon fall is Dylan's haunting reinvention of a medieval Anglo-Scottish ballad, 'Lord Randall', infused with biblical flood imagery; it showcases appreciation for and transformation of established literary works. Dylan, like the Nordic composers discussed here, works both within and beyond the canonical tradition, and 'whether on purpose or by accident', these new arts, verbal creations, are part of a conversation with established literary forms. This is germane to the present volume which explores some of the ways that established, literate culture, including Latinate, European models, interacted with local, vernacular, oral traditions, so that some medieval Nordic composers might also be seen as having 'panned poetry gold'.

[4] Dylan, 'Banquet Speech'.

The essays in this volume are written by scholars who were attached to the 'Arrival of Writing' research group at the Centre for Medieval Studies, University of Bergen (2003–12). The authors in this volume intervene by looking at often unconsidered, overlooked sources that were critical in the development of Nordic literacies: letters, lists, urban runic scribbles, manuscript fragments, and women's mourning songs. We also ask questions about some well-established and canonical texts whose literary merits have been long applauded but whose oral, performative aspects, and the nuanced ways they reflect on literacy and orality, still have much to tell us. We examine the interactions of oral and literate culture in the medieval North, and the ways Nordic peoples, especially medieval Norwegians and Icelanders living on the European periphery and away from continental hubs of intellectual, religious, and scribal activity, sought to establish a prestigious literary culture. Finally, we look at the effects of this process as it took place in a society which, previous to the introduction of Christian literacy and writing technologies, had already developed a confident vernacular culture featuring rich narrative, poetic, and legal traditions as well as a runic alphabet.

A main goal of the 'Arrival of Writing' research group was to query the relationships between orality and literacy, particularly in the early stages of the movement of Christian literary practices and technologies to the northern European peripheries. This collection of essays considers the development of literacies in medieval Scandinavia and Iceland, and draws increased scholarly attention to the ways that words are simultaneously dynamic and fossilized, textual and aural, with non-canonical genres often leading the way in highlighting issues of aesthetics, meaning, and the development of textual and literary culture. Our consideration of developing textual traditions has taken into account administrative literacy and practice (epistolary correspondence, informational lists), with a particular emphasis on comparisons between the centre and the periphery on the one hand, and the vernacularization of administrative culture in the later Middle Ages on the other; the relationship between Latin and the vernacular as part of the process of the vernacularization of the written word; and identification of scribal centres throughout the Nordic periphery in order to understand the processes and unique developments evidenced by Nordic book culture, and in a related line of thinking, urban runic writing communities, the Nordic world's popular but much less-considered 'scribal centres'. Finally, researchers considered the travel of texts, literary forms, and traditions from the continent ('centre') to the Nordic countries ('the periphery'). The essays included here are the final fruits of this research.

Moving Words in the Nordic Middle Ages: Tracing Literacies, Texts, and Verbal Communities comprises thirteen detailed case-studies that demonstrate in different ways the power of words to move individuals and to create and mobilize larger social and political communities, through dissemination of texts of all kinds (letters, manuscript fragments, rune-covered objects, historical narratives, poetry, etc.), and their performances. The scholars featured here have attended to the extremely creative ways that the composers add an oral element, as well as an aural element, to enable richer, multi-sensory, imaginative engagement. The essays show that when these words are recorded on a manuscript page or other form of material artefact, they do not become static or fixed. Rather, we find incontrovertible evidence of the ways that the literary practitioners of the medieval North ensured that the written word would continue to speak, to sing, and to engage and transform its varied, and extremely sophisticated, audiences. The essays feature analyses of lesser-studied sources which provide insights into the development of literacy, some of the earliest medieval assessments of writing in the Latin alphabet, and the creation of diverse discursive communities which stimulated thriving systems of medieval Nordic textual production. While one main goal is to consider early bodies of writing that have not been closely examined in analyses of the growth of textual and writing culture in medieval Scandinavia and Iceland, the book also engages with more familiar canonical texts (eddic poetry, king's sagas, sagas of the Icelanders, Old Norse–Icelandic romances, etc.) to bring out new angles by highlighting the complexity of movement back and forth on the oral-literate continuum, and to show the resilience of conceptions of orality in textual representations. While each discussion comprises new, specialist scholarship on Nordic sources, a major goal of this organically linked collection is to highlight what is of global relevance to ongoing dialogues in medieval textual studies regarding writing and appropriation of the Latin alphabet, as well as how textual and intellectual impulses move between centres of European literacy and a remote northern periphery with its incredibly rich (and early) literary culture.

Moving Words in the Nordic Middle Ages opens with the bigger picture of literacy studies and the specifics of the Nordic situation to contextualize the subsequent essays. In 'Literacy Studies: Past, Present, and Future' Leidulf Melve methodologically situates the work of the 'Arrival of Writing' group with a discussion of the state of literacy studies relating to the Middle Ages, with a particular emphasis on key developments over the past two decades. Most important, however, are the issues which remain to be solved: Melve concludes by addressing a few vexing questions informing the direction of recent and future literacy studies, the arguably most important of which is how to

understand and explain multilingual configurations. Study of the Nordic
Middle Ages can reveal much: Latin learning and literacies were productively
absorbed within an already refined vernacular oral literary culture which also
employed a runic alphabet — the confidence with which the Nordic community appropriated the tools of Christian literacy to fit prestigious native
forms can brightly illuminate issues of medieval multilingual configurations
and multi-scripted forms of literacy; this is also addressed in the next essay.
In 'Medieval Nordic Backgrounds: Written Culture in an Oral Society' Else
Mundal provides an overview of key factors which influenced the development
and diffusion of writing in the Nordic Middle Ages. According to the mythological eddic poems, the most important activity of the Old Norse gods was not
struggle with the giants but rather collection of knowledge and its transferral to
humans. This presents a picture of a society poised to embrace the technologies
of Christian culture, with these eddic poems providing models of valorized,
clever knowledge-seekers primed to make the imported tools of literacy and
knowledge preservation their own. Other factors predisposing Nordic society to written culture were, for example, use of runic script, numerous oral art
forms, an administrative culture relying on oral laws applied across wide geographical areas, and (in Iceland more so than in Norway) a social structure that
allowed for social mobility. These are all issues that are pursued in the various
essays, and Mundal provides an overview of the larger cultural and historical
nexus which allowed for these unique Nordic developments.

Aidan Conti takes us to those sources featuring our earliest local
Scandinavian authorial voices and their responses to Christian literate culture.
In 'Creating Absence: The Representation of Writing in Early Histories of the
North' he traces the ways that, as Christianity became firmly entrenched in
Europe's northern periphery, local contingents, often trained abroad, began to
use the new language (Latin) of this religion to graph local populations into a
universal history. Conti looks at three works, each claiming to be the first history of its people: the anonymous *Historia Norwegie* (*c.* 1160–75), Theodoricus
Monachus's *Historia de antiquitate regum norwagiensium* (*c.* 1177–88) and Sven
Aggesen's *Brevis historia regum dacie* (1186–87). Theodoricus's work reveals an
effusive delight in quoting, referencing, and displaying the wonders of writing,
yet recognizes the medium's limitations; the *Historia Norwegie* evinces a more
restrained but no less present learning; and Sven Aggesen eschews the language
of writing, representing the written text as speech (*oratio*) and his readers as listeners (*audientes*). While initially suggesting that Sven's work imagines itself as
a continuation of oral practices of commemoration, its insistence on the silence
of the past and the silence arising from a failure to write in the present effec-

tively usurps the role that oral practices once played. Each text displays remarkably different attitudes towards the authority of the written, the reception of
book learning, and oral forms of collective memory, and we see how these various acts of inscription placed themselves within, and thereby justified, a new
writing practice. Nordic writers worked thoughtfully through oral and literate
traditions, and innovate in some remarkable ways.

Starting a cluster of essays which focus on Norway (and its representation
in saga literature), Åslaug Ommundsen next discusses the material evidence
for scribal multilingualism, and the ways that the tools of Christian learning
were deployed and sustained within the Nordic periphery. Instead of looking
at singular foundational texts, in 'Tracing Scribal Centres in Medieval Norway'
Ommundsen examines the material textual fragments that remain and which
provide rich evidence for a flourishing local literary culture. Medieval book culture was bilingual, and many scribes, if not most, mastered Latin in addition to
their mother tongue, as well as two alphabets. The complexity is represented
at Norwegian scribal centres, with (at least) two languages, two writing systems, and several text-carrying media. However, losses of manuscript sources
(more than 99 per cent of the material) constitute a challenge: only around fifteen Latin and around fifty Old Norse manuscripts (both imported and locally
produced) remain as books from the Norwegian Middle Ages. Nonetheless,
parchment from medieval books later reused as binding material leaves us with
6500 single fragments from medieval manuscripts. Norwegian scribal centres
depended on movement: books and skilled people travelled across borders,
knowledge and technique were passed from one person to another, and fragments show considerable contact with European centres from the eleventh
century onwards. Indeed, peripheral Scandinavian scribal practice illuminates
European textual practices. Small centres of learning like Lom, and the surprising output at the hands of a few scribes, sometimes even a single one, is striking: book culture is institutional yet also highly personal, and these fragments
provide a compelling narrative about the extensive impact of small verbal communities in the medieval North. As Ommundsen argues, these factors all have
important implications for the development of medieval Scandinavia's unique
scribal and book culture.

Continuing along the lines of inquiry established by Conti regarding authorial reflection and rhetorical references to literacy and orality, Jonas Wellendorf
explores the references to the use of written communication in the sagas of
Norwegian kings. 'Letters from Kings: Epistolary Communication in the
Kings' Sagas (until *c.* 1150)' first shows how saga authors readily transformed
written messages into oral ones and vice-versa. Focusing on the letter from King

Ingi to King Sigurðr munnr, styled 'the oldest letter in Norwegian history' and dated to 1139, Wellendorf then argues that this letter should be considered a rhetorical invention. The text of the letter is found in both *Morkinskinna* and *Heimskringla* and is arguably derived from Eiríkr Oddsson's now-lost work *Hryggjarstykki*. While earlier scholarship suggested that Eiríkr Oddsson's pioneering work of Old Norse historiography was modelled on hagiographical texts, Wellendorf makes the case for historiographical models and revises our understandings of the overall ideology of the work and its significance for developments in early vernacular writing.

While Wellendorf looks at the rhetorical work that letters do in the sagas, the next essay by Melve, 'Letters, Networks, and Public Opinion in Medieval Norway (1024–1263)', takes us to administrative correspondence. Playing a prominent role in the literary culture of the Middle Ages, letters — as well as networks and patterns of communication based on letters — arrived rather late in Norway. The first surviving letter is from King Filippus's reign (1207–17), and from the entire thirteenth century only eighty original letters remain. The lack of extant letters poses a tremendous challenge for approaching the emergence of Norwegian written culture, and the pre-thirteenth-century period only provides references to letters from other sources (primarily sagas). Melve analyses the function of letters, patterns of communication, audiences, and networks in this early period and, based initially on quantitative indicators, charts changes in epistolary culture over a period of three hundred years. The evidence indicates that letters involving laity were an important part of Norwegian epistolary culture from the start. Even more striking is the number of references to letters which address public opinion, the large majority of which are contained in lay letters. These quantitative tendencies are, if not confirmed, at least further attested by the references to the laity involved, dialogical deliberation by oral and aural means, and written mediation of letters. Not typically considered a major shaper of literature and literacy in the Nordic Middle Ages, letters were a significant part of writing culture and were a powerful medium that can shed light on how orally and aurally invested writing developed in the Nordic Middle Ages.

We then turn to urban spaces in Norway, specifically the medieval runic inscriptions from Bryggen in Bergen. Like Dylan's songs, which speak of and to a seductive range of human concerns, these runic inscriptions remind us that literacy, and the interface between oral and literate culture, must not be considered the prerogative of 'learned' or traditionally 'literate' groups — some of the most nuanced and innovative treatments of words were performed by ordinary townspeople. In '*Gyrðir á lykil* (Gyrðir owns the key): Materialized Moments of Communication in Runic Items from Medieval Bergen', Kristel Zilmer discusses the surprising diversity of the Bryggen runic corpus and the discursive creativity of the rune-makers and users, specifically as revealed by inscriptions that record personal names. Zilmer advances our understanding of how texts and artefacts act jointly as vehicles of communication, such that, in addition to the content of the message, these verbal assemblages also take a particular material form and outlook that connects with different situational contexts — words move materially, visually, and environmentally. As the runic objects demonstrate, great variability in the meanings attached to the individual runic artefacts becomes possible. They also serve as examples of the functionality and communicative potential of runic writing in the setting of a medieval town. Our own comprehension of literacy and textual culture in the medieval North benefits from consideration of these wider practices, material and urban, taking place outside of the more 'official' sites of learning and literacy.

Lucie Doležalová, in 'Moving Lists: Enumeration between Use and Aesthetics, Storing and Creating', concentrates on one of the most archaic forms of writing: the list. She first considers several lists, both medieval European Latin and Old Norse vernacular lists (*þulur*), linked in different ways to memory, including lists summarizing longer texts, lists for artificial memory, and meditational lists. Doležalová then uses the different ways in which these widespread lists operate and move between memory and paper to illuminate less obvious aspects of medieval storage and management of information. Rather than seeing a passage from one form to another (oral to written), Doležalová's study of lists evidences the idea of the oral-written continuum as a multidimensional space, in which each medium has a meaningful function and provides mutual influences. Following Umberto Eco, Doležalová makes the point that lists, decried as mundane and devoid of imagination, are readable as poetic texts as well as skeletons that privilege personal agency and needs. The argument then turns to the material elements of textual culture and examines in detail what material elements (layout, handwriting, repeated reproduction, etc.) of a list-text reveal. As in Zilmer's essay, here we are urged to remember how the material form of words also shapes how we interact with them, how they move us and our memories.

The next essay, Amy Mulligan's 'Talking Place and Mapping Icelandic Identity in *Íslendingabók* and *Landnámabók*', opens a section on Icelandic writing. Mulligan focuses on the awareness of the Icelandic settlers that taking land was not enough — the act did not become binding, official, or culturally significant, until the act and the new geography could be converted into that powerful verbal currency: words. This essay looks at the sophisticated and nuanced ways that Icelanders, working from a rich oral-literate culture, brought words and story, the importance of 'talking place', to the fore in their national accounts of Icelandic settlement in *Íslendingabók* and *Landnámabók*. The writers of Iceland's settlement myths harnessed the power of words and fused story to landscape in order to create a verbal map which gave a nation of Icelanders an esteemed place in the world. As the Icelanders realized, both the verbal place-worlds and the material geography become more powerful, more persuasive, more Icelandic, when they are fused together, when spatial and narrative practice are intertwined. While other nations created extensive visual maps, we see how the Icelanders used verbal geographies to map a position for themselves in the learned Christian literate world.

Interface dynamics between the oral and the written, and the sophisticated manipulation of the oral within the written by Icelandic writers, is brought into focus when we see how frequently Old Norse writers refer their readers to something related earlier in the text, as Slavica Ranković demonstrates in 'Traversing the Space of the Oral-Written Continuum: Medially Connotative Back-Referring Formulae in *Landnámabók*'. Building on earlier work, Ranković argues that stylistic exploitation of the immediacy of the spoken word achieved through appropriated 'oral' mode varieties of the back-referring formula such as ***sem fyrr var sagt/getit/nefndr/talat*** (as was said/mentioned/named/told before) most likely points to writing as becoming more transparent and internalized as a technology.[5] By contrast, the apparent logical pedantry reflected in the usage of the mirror phrase ***sem fyrr var ritat*** (as was written before/ as already written) suggests a desire to emphasize the special status of writing while also stressing one's own proficiency in a rare and socially desirable skill. It follows, then, that the earlier the text is written, the more prominent the latter attitudes are likely to be than the former, and the ***sem fyrr var ritat*** formula employed more frequently than the oral mode varieties. The evidence from *Landnámabók* supports this hypothesis: in contrast to the sagas of Icelanders, this foundational Icelandic text shows a marked preference for the written mode of the formula, most notably its earliest extant redaction, *Sturlubók*. In this close study of linguistic formulas, Ranković provides insight into some of the ways the earliest vernacular writers understood their role on the oral-literate spectrum, yielding some rich comparisons with the Latin writers Conti discusses who grappled with similar issues and rhetorical devices.

[5] See Ong, *Orality and Literacy*.

In the next essay, Helen Leslie-Jacobsen keeps us in Iceland and considers thirteenth-century developments of oral sources into literate forms. She argues that a long death-song, known well in oral tradition, was not just later interpolation but the very catalyst for the composition of a legendary saga. 'Qrvar-Oddr's *Ævikviða* and the Genesis of *Qrvar-Odds saga*: A Poem on the Move' examines the legendary *Qrvar-Odds saga*, and its likely oral prehistory, to highlight the importance of eddic poetry in formation of the genre of legendary sagas. The argument hinges on the derivation of the body of *Qrvar-Odds saga* from a long poem known as 'the death-song' found at the saga's end. Employment of some of the death-song stanzas in the saga prose suggests it was known in oral tradition as a full poem before it came to be codified. Refuting assertions that much of the death-song is interpolation postdating the saga prose, Leslie-Jacobsen argues that the death-song concluding the saga predates the saga prose, and as such its stanzas form a backbone for the written saga's construction. This discussion reminds us that orality and literacy should not just be seen as teleological: the relationships were ongoing, productive, and simultaneous, even into the thirteenth century. It is important for us, furthermore, to avoid the fallacy of seeing the oral text, the death-song, as a less prestigious or influential form, too popular or non-literary to inform a written saga. Leslie-Jacobsen points out that the song is indeed the backbone of the saga, critical to its structure, and perhaps we ought to accept more fully that medieval composers at the time of the composition of the legendary sagas, when literacy was well established, did not necessarily see orality and literacy as sequential or as oppositional. Rather, like the Nobel Prize Committee, they understand the literary dimensions of song and how literature accrues power by moving from performance to page to performance and back again.

The following essay asks questions about the way in which words move into the sagas, specifically the Norse *riddarasǫgur* of the thirteenth century and later, texts intrinsically linked to French romances and performance (oral and musical) at court. In '"Blood flying and brains falling like rain": Chivalric Conflict Gone Norse', Ingvil Brügger Budal interrogates assumptions about transmission in terms of the changes these verbal compositions underwent as they were 'translated' into Old Norse, with a play on conversion from one language to another, but also relocation (like relics) from one site to another, from France to the Nordic periphery. It is a common assumption that dramatic passages of the Norse *riddarasǫgur* have been given added emphasis in Norse translation, typically by means of expansion or through omission and abbreviation of descriptions, monologues, and other less animated parts of the narrative. Budal examines if, and how, it is possible to measure the emphasis given to specific elements of a text and considers the implications for Norse translation theory and the movement of romances north, through close comparative analysis of three versions of the story of the knight Elie: the only existing French version of the chanson de geste *Elye de Saint Gille* (BnF, MS 25516, *c.* 1280), the oldest Norse version of *Elís saga ok Rosamúndu* (UUB, De la Gardie, 4–7 4°, *c.* 1270), and a later Norse version (Holm Perg fol. 7, late fifteenth century). Budal asks both text-specific and wider methodological questions about the process and ideologies of translation and transmission, geographic, generic, and across the oral-literate continuum, and how we ought to rethink our ways of tracking the movement of words from another vernacular, French, into Old Norse, and the transformations the Norse composers enacted within these texts. Indeed, when the French romances were translated into Old Norse, the translators were required to make some complex decisions. Very early on, the Norse composers were developing these materials for their own uses and tastes — when words moved north, the literary practitioners were also primed to recraft for their audiences — this shows a great deal of confidence in Scandinavian literary traditions, and more local shaping of imported literary forms than previously thought.

Tying together many of the topics raised throughout the collection, Else Mundal provides an overview of the oral-literate continuum in 'From Oral to Written in Old Norse Culture: Questions of Genre, Contact, and Continuity'. This chapter surveys Old Norse oral and written genres and discusses how the arrival of writing and Christian culture transformed discursive forms over time. Some oral genres disappeared without ever having been preserved in writing (for example, female mourning songs); some new genres were introduced with European Christian culture; some originally oral genres (for example, eddic and skaldic poetry) were transcribed, in principle, to preserve oral elements; simultaneously, other genres originating in local Scandinavian oral tradition developed as written literature largely based on European literary models. The arrival of writing also created new roles connected to production and performance of written texts: textual author, copyist, compiler, script-based performer, or dramatic reader, which significantly limited roles for women as narrative practitioners. While the majority of the essays here celebrate the innovative ways in which composers moved along the oral-literate continuum, we also realize that some genres and important oral texts have simply been lost, as have the contributions of the diverse and perhaps unsuspected practitioners who helped shape Nordic literary culture. This chapter provides a view of the landscape of moving words within the Nordic Middle Ages and works to alert us to the pressing issues and implications which scholars must seek to address.

The Scandinavians who awarded the Nobel Prize for Literature to Bob Dylan have asked us to rethink what literature is, what it seeks to accomplish, and to consider the techniques and devices it employs to speak to us. As this volume shows, medieval Nordic practitioners were similarly taken with such questions, and the texts they created demonstrate that they understood how to use words and writing to make objects sing to us, to allow geographic places, static material objects, wooden sticks, and manuscript pages to address us and engage us in their performances. As a result, we can learn much by considering the literacies, texts, and verbal communities of the Nordic Middle Ages.

Works Cited

Dylan, Bob, 'Banquet Speech', <http://www.nobelprize.org/nobel_prizes/literature/laureates/2016/dylan-speech.html> [accessed 9 January 2017]

——, 'If I Accept the Prize? Of Course', Nobel Foundation Press Page, 28 October 2016, <http://www.nobelprize.org/press/#/publications/> [accessed 10 January 2017]

Engdahl, Horace, 'The Nobel Prize in Literature 2016 — Presentation Speech' <http://www.nobelprize.org/nobel_prizes/literature/laureates/2016/presentation-speech.html> [accessed 10 January 2017]

Ong, Walter J., *Orality and Literacy: The Technologizing of the Word* (London: Methuen, 1982)

Literacy Studies: Past, Present, and Future

Introduction

'Literacy is both an urgent practical concern and a metaphor for modernism itself.'[1] This opening passage from *The Cambridge Handbook of Literacy* (2009) encapsulates theoretical and methodical issues that will be dealt with in this essay. Referring to the research field's 'practical concern', the editors David R. Olson and Nancy Torrance highlight the arguably most pervasive theoretical issue of the field, regardless of the emphasis on literacy in contemporary society, or as here, on literacy studies relating to the Middle Ages. From the very start of what is usually considered the 'birth of the discipline of literacy studies' in the 1960s, the field was wrapped in a discussion of the proper way not only to frame questions for research, but also of how to approach the empirical field. Hence, two theories — or schools — appeared: one, called the 'Great Divide Theory', approached literacy in structural terms and claimed, in its radical version, that the written word had cognitive and social implications — an inherent capacity for igniting changes. The Great Divide Theory had evolutionary leanings, positing a more or less unilinear development from (uncivilized) oral society to (civilized) contemporary society — as part of Olson and Torrance's 'modernism'. The second theory, usually referred to as the 'Ideology View', emerged as a reaction to the Great Divide Theory: it insisted that the implica-

[1] Olson and Torrance, 'Preface', p. xiii.

Leidulf Melve (**Leidulf.Melve@uib.no**) is Professor of Medieval History at the University of Bergen. His research interests and areas of publication include intellectual history, historiography, and communication studies.

Moving Words in the Nordic Middle Ages: Tracing Literacies, Texts, and Verbal Communities, ed. by Amy C. Mulligan and Else Mundal, AS 8   BREPOLS ▨ PUBLISHERS   (Turnhout: Brepols, 2019)
pp. 15–36   10.1484/M.AS-EB.5.116618

tions and consequences of the written word did not result from the technology itself but was a result of practical concern — of social use.

Half a century later, the question of approach is still a controversial one. The following is an attempt to discuss the state of literacy studies relating to the Middle Ages by looking particularly at research being undertaken within the last two decades. While the first part ('Past') will address the emergence of the Great Divide Theory and its critics, the second part ('Present') will discuss two more recent historiographical presentations of the field with regard to theoretical and methodical concerns: Christel Meier's retrospective conclusions on the project *Pragmatische Schriftlichkeit*, and Marco Mostert's thoughts on 'New Approaches to Medieval Communication' in the launching of the research project *Pionier Project Verschriftelijking* in 1999. The third part ('Future') will address a few vexing questions in recent and future literacy studies, arguably the most important of which is how to understand and explain multilingual configurations.

Past: The 'Great Divide' and its Critics

If literacy is 'a metaphor for modernism itself', it is difficult to avoid the conclusion that literacy studies as they emerged in the 1950s and in particular the 1960s were responsible for this attachment to modernism.[2] Literacy studies as they appeared in the early 1960s were interdisciplinary in nature, bringing together literature (Walter J. Ong), philology (Eric Havelock), anthropology (Jack Goody and Ian Watt), communication studies (Harold A. Innis, Marshall McLuhan), philosophy (Ernst Cassirer), and history (Carlo Cipolla).[3] This interdisciplinary field conceptualized literacy as a fundamental indicator of modernity, regardless of whether the point of departure was Plato, the printing press, or African tribes. Moreover, the large majority of these contributions also posited a causal relationship between literacy and certain modern cognitive faculties, the most important of which were abstract reasoning, logical deductions, and critical thinking in general. The causal dimension to the field was, on a further note, closely related to the strong structuralist leanings of these early

---

[2] Four names figure prominently in every presentation of the formation of the field of literacy studies: Eric Havelock, Walter Ong, Marshall McLuhan, and Jack Goody. For a retrospective look at the 'birth of the discipline', see Havelock, *The Muse Learns to Write*.

[3] Cassirer, *Language and Myth*; Innis, *The Bias of Communication*; Ong, *Ramus*; McLuhan, *The Gutenberg Galaxy*; Goody and Watt, 'The Consequences of Literacy'; Havelock, *Preface to Plato*; Cipolla, *Literacy and Development in the West*.

studies of literacy. Literacy was, if not always defined as such, at least conceptualized as the most important aspect of communication, determining in essence the mental outlook of agents as well as social groups. Even more important, perhaps, is the extent to which literacy was considered an autonomous force, establishing the environment necessary for the expression or development of not only modern cognitive faculties but also institutions such as capitalism (Cipolla). It is to be noted as well that these studies were first and foremost concerned with literacy, and paid scant attention to orality, effectively creating a 'Great Divide'. As a result, the transition from oral to written society was considered fast, abrupt, and comprehensive — as a result of the technology itself.

The Great Divide Theory was the dominating theory throughout most of the 1960s, but towards the end of the decade the first critical voices appeared. In a pioneering work from 1958, Claude Lévi-Strauss underlined the disciplinary function of literacy. Lévi-Strauss's emphasis on the fact that literacy hardly was a neutral technology but was always immersed in power relations has in retrospect often been considered the beginning of the Ideology View.[4] Similar to the Great Divide Theory, the reaction of the Ideology View was interdisciplinary, but it leaned more towards anthropology than communication studies — at least in its formative period in the 1970s. Since the Ideology View emerged as a reaction to the Great Divide Theory, it is hardly surprising that it took its cues from the Great Divide Theory, offering comprehensive criticism of certain Great Divide features. Inspired by Lévi-Strauss, a number of studies set out to show that the technology in itself did not have cognitive and institutional consequences. Instead, the focus was directed towards the agent — the users of literacy — and the social and ideological context that always circumscribed the act of communication. Hence, by claiming that the technology was neither neutral nor autonomous, advocates of Great Divide — such as Brian Street — accentuated that there were few, if any, differences between orality and literacy.[5]

For all that divides these two schools, they share a negligence of orality: whereas the Great Divide Theory primarily was concerned with literacy, the Ideology View — at least in the 1970s — seems to address orality in order to criticize the dichotomy between orality and literacy, but not for the purpose of understanding orality — and certainly not for reflecting on the transition from orality to literacy. From this point of departure, the 1980s witnessed theoreti-

---

[4] See Lévi-Strauss, *Anthropologie structurale*.

[5] Street, *Literacy in Theory and Practice*.

cal innovation, reflected in approaches that were more interested in bridging the seemingly unsurmountable gap between the Great Divide Theory and the Ideology View. 'Continuum' is a keyword in several of these new approaches, effectively replacing the concern with orality as separated from literacy — either in terms of technology or ideology — with a focus on similarities and, not least, the transition from orality to literacy as a continuum rather than a break. One of the most influential in this respect is Ruth Finnegan, invoking the notion of 'potential' in order to approach orality and literacy — as well as their interrelations. Although she is sceptical towards the Great Divide Theory, Finnegan admits the potential of the written technology. However, this potential is only realized through social use, and the actual implications of the written word vary according to social context.[6]

As for the engagement of medieval studies in literacy theory, it did not really emerge until the 1980s, along with the emergence of mediating approaches. Exceptions do exist, to be sure, including Michael Clanchy's now classic study *From Memory to Written Record* (1978) as well as a handful of minor studies from different fields.[7] Yet it was only in the 1980s that medievalists started to engage with literacy theory, addressing the concerns of the Great Divide Theory and the Ideology View. The large majority of these studies were empirical in nature and established dialogue with theoretical positions only as a point of departure for empirical investigations, such as Rosamond McKitterick's *The Carolingians and the Written Word* (1989).[8] Still, exceptions do exist in this case as well, since the arguably most important theoretical contribution to literacy studies from the ranks of medievalists appeared in 1983 in the form of Brian Stock's theory of textual community. The theory effectively combined a sociological model inspired by Robert Merton's emphasis on the integration of social groups, insights from the Great Divide Theory, and a concern with the users of texts — audiences — in an effort to understand the function of literacy in terms of the emergence of heretical groups in the eleventh and twelfth centuries.[9]

---

[6] Finnegan, *Literacy and Orality*.

[7] Clanchy, *From Memory to Written Record*.

[8] McKitterick, *The Carolingians and the Written Word*.

[9] Stock's empirical cases concentrate on the heretical movements of the early eleventh century in Leutard, Orléans, Arras, and Monforte; on the Pataria as a proto-reform movement; and on the interpretation of the Eucharist from Paschasius Radbertus and Ratramnus of Corbie, to the controversy in the eleventh century involving Berengar of Tours, Hugh of Langres, Durand of Troarn, Lanfranc of Canterbury, and Guitmund of Aversa (Stock, *The Implication of Literacy*, pp. 326–455).

It is Stock's contention that these social groups were held together by their adherence, not so much to a text but to a certain interpretation of a text. This, in turn, introduces the interpreter, basically a literate spokesperson for the group, responsible for disseminating the given interpretation of the text — usually the Scripture — to a wider audience of semi-literates and illiterates by oral and aural communication. The theory has been criticized for the stark asymmetry it seems to advocate, neglecting the dialogue that may be instigated between interpreter and audience. Yet the wide reception of the theory of textual community has shown its flexibility but certainly also confirmed that Stock's notion of 'orality within textuality' highlighted central aspects of the relationship between literacy and orality.

Present: 'New Approaches to Medieval Communication?' and the Pragmatic Turn

The enormous amount of scholarship on different aspects of medieval literacy, in particular since the 1980s ('Present'), renders Marco Mostert's reflections of immense value, since he attempts to extract conclusions and guiding lines from this highly diverse, not to mention complex, research field. Mostert's observations were an attempt to clarify the research agenda for the project *Pionier Project Verschriftelijking*. More in detail, in a tentative effort to answer the question 'New Approaches to Medieval Communication?', five new approaches were deemed important for future research: (1) 'research is centred ever more on the question of the relative importance of writing, seen as part of the whole of medieval forms of communication'; (2) 'Images were clearly meant to convey a message, and used a visual vocabulary, grammar and semantics which are just as difficult to interpret as those of verbal messages. The continued study of their messages provides another promising approach'; (3) 'the study of descriptions of non-verbal and oral communication'; (4) 'the study of the transmission of written texts'; and (5) 'the study of the organization of the texts as it is apparent in their subdivisions and in the lay-out of the manuscript page may suggest psychological changes over the medieval centuries'.[10]

With the exception of his fifth conclusion — that 'may suggest psychological changes' — Mostert's reflections, for all their usefulness, do not address the issue of investigating the implications of literacy. More specifically, he does not deal with one of the most contentious and, indeed, problematic aspects of literacy studies: the alleged cognitive and social implications of the writ-

---

[10] Mostert, 'New Approaches to Medieval Communication?', pp. 35–36.

ten word. From one perspective, Mostert's avoidance of the issue is probably reflecting that medievalists' contributions to the overall discussion of literacy theory first and foremost have challenged the Great Divide Theory, including the theory's emphasis on 'implications'.

If Mostert avoids the question of 'implications' and development, his conclusions are supplemented by Christel Meier's retrospective observations regarding the extremely important research project *Pragmatische Schriftlichkeit im Mittelalter: Erscheinungsformen und Entwicklungsstufen*. This research project, based at the University of Münster (1986–2000), resulted in an impressive number of publications dealing with aspects of pragmatic literacy. The project, and particularly Hagen Keller's definition of the term 'pragmatic literacy' in his introduction to the project from 1992, was a reaction against an overweighted focus on 'who could read and write' in previous research. Keller, as well as other participants in the research project, would by the term 'Pragmatische Schriftlichkeit' signal an emphasis on social use: 'Als pragmatisch verstehen wir dabei alle Formen des Gebrauchs von Schrift und Texten, die unmittelbar zweckhaftem Handeln dienen oder die menschliches Tun durch die Bereitstellung von Wissen anleiten wollen' (We understand as pragmatic all forms of use of writing and texts, which on account of establishment of knowledge contributes to purposeful action or human performance).[11] Needless to say, this focus on social use reflected the mounting criticism of the Great Divide Theory, since it rejected the structural premise that writing had inevitable implications, but rather insisted on investigating the practical use of a given form of communication. While this pragmatic turn, accentuating social use, reflected the current trend in literacy studies in the 1980s, another defining feature of the project — as envisaged by Keller — can hardly be seen as anything other than a reaction against the tendency of depriving the technology of its potential for effectuating social change. Consequently, in Keller's understanding, pragmatic literacy is intimately connected to the extent to which literacy may contribute to a more rational worldview: 'Diese Frage führt uns auf das Problem der "Praxis der Rationalität", wenn ich es einmal so formulieren darf, auf die Frage nach dem geistigen instrumentarium, auf dem die Veränderung der europäischen Kultur seit dem Hochmittelalter beruht' (This question leads to the problem of "the praxis of rationality", since I initially want to formulate it as a question regarding the intellectual instrument that relates to the change of European culture since the high Middle Ages).[12]

---

[11] Keller, 'Pragmatische Schriftlichkeit', p. 1.

[12] Keller, 'Pragmatische Schriftlichkeit', p. 5..

From this point of departure, Meier offers some important conclusions from the project by taking into account what she calls a 'longitudinal view of the evolutionary process of literacy': the eleventh and early twelfth centuries mark new beginnings, reflecting 'an impulse of experimentation'; the late twelfth and the thirteenth centuries represent a phase of consolidation; the late thirteenth and fourteenth centuries display 'a new literate mentality in the practical and technical creation of corpora of texts, and in a transformed relationship to the written text'; the fifteenth and early sixteenth centuries 'display a hitherto unimaginable volume of literature'.[13]

Meier, then, offers a number of conclusions as to how pragmatic literacy should be approached. While some of these conclusions hardly do more than emphasize the need to bring in the historical and social (pragmatic) context,[14] others are of considerably larger interest — both in relation to Mostert's suggestions for new approaches and as points of departure for the discussion of theoretical and methodical aspects of literacy studies below. Meier, in a bold move, contends that the development of literacy in the Middle Ages is dependent on three 'cultural and historical determinants': prevailing multilingualism, the relationship between orality and literacy, and the dichotomy between clergy and laity. Furthermore, and according to Meier, texts should be classified typologically into genre, partly since the criteria for classification correspond closely with the pragmatic aspect of texts (i.e.. the purposes for which the texts were composed), and partly because genre provides clues as to 'the structure and organization of texts and books'.[15] Finally, Meier addresses the long-term implications of literacy: 'Literacy impacts on the whole of society, from top to bottom [...]. The increase and expansion of pragmatic literacy was undoubtedly a decisive impetus in the advance of civilization during the European Middle Ages'.[16]

Aside from the fact that both Mostert and Meier insist on approaching literacy in terms of (pragmatic) use, they diverge on a number of issues. While

---

[13] Meier, 'Fourteen Years', pp. 29–31.

[14] 'Pragmatic literacy in the Middle Ages should be interpreted as a historical process, part of the general expansion and evolution of literacy [...]. Texts are compiled for a variety of uses, and usually in response to external requirements [...]. The aura of dignity of written media — letters, texts and books — vary according to the pragmatic nature of the text' (Meier, 'Fourteen Years', pp. 30–32).

[15] Meier, 'Fourteen Years', pp. 30–31.

[16] The remaining conclusion is: 'The development of literacy in its social to the role of the medium, that is, the instrumental character of the written text and the communication processes triggered by the instrument of writing' (Meier, 'Fourteen Years', pp. 30–32).

Mostert accentuates the 'relative importance of writing', Meier emphasizes the encompassing impact of literacy, reaching from 'top to bottom'. Furthermore, Meier takes Keller's careful polemic against the Ideology View one step further by accentuating the 'decisive impetus' of literacy for 'the advance of civilization'. The contrast to Mostert is formidable indeed, since Meier suggests that (pragmatic) literacy had 'implications' that on one level is strikingly similar to those put forward by advocates of the Great Divide Theory. In both cases, literacy is associated with the emergence of modern civilization. Yet, Meier does not subscribe to the type of technological determinism that at times pervades the Great Divide Theory, for the simple reason that she introduces 'cultural and historical determinants' (multilingualism, the relationship between orality and literacy, and the dichotomy between clergy and laity).

If Meier deserves credit for daring to re-establish dialogue with the Great Divide Theory, her determinants suffer from at least two faults that render them less useful for delineating how (pragmatic) literacy should be approached in the future. For once, the determinants are of such general nature that they fail to even hint at in the ways and extents to which they influence the development of literacy in the Middle Ages. More precisely, they need to be diachronically specified in order to be anything more than a commonsensical description of a communicative infrastructure that applies to the early modern period as much as the Middle Ages. Second, if the intention is to posit causal links — as indicated by the use of terms such as 'development' and 'determinants' — these links need to be specified in terms of different configurations of the aforesaid determinants.

Future: Understanding and Explaining Multilingual Configurations

The point here is not so much to criticize Meier's presentation as to highlight challenges within a research field that has grown to vast interdisciplinary dimensions since its start in the 1960s. So, if we go a bit further and look at the research recently undertaken on Meier's three determinants, we may find that there are reasons why her conclusions are framed in such a general way. Over recent decades, it has become increasingly obvious that it is no longer feasible to deal with medieval literacy as a monolithic entity.[17] Michael Richter may state the obvious when he notes that modern definitions are 'of little relevance for the Middle Ages

---

[17] For a brief summary, see Brockmeier and Olson, 'The Literacy Episteme'.

because of the different cultural and educational contexts'.[18] Yet his reminder is still crucial, bearing in mind the vast proliferation of 'literacies' — such as 'psalter literacy',[19] 'insurgent literacy',[20] and 'bureaucratic literacy',[21] just to name a few.[22] An even more important feature of recent literacy studies, connected indeed to the issue of multiple literacies, is an accentuated unwillingness to approach the subject in dichotomous terms, separating written language from oral vernacular culture. Recent research has effectively destroyed the neat separation of oral and written communication as it was presented by the Great Divide Theory, but has not agreed on what to put in its place. Admittedly, part of the problem is related to (the now disclaimed) tendency in previous scholarship to make a distinction between a 'low' (i.e., vernacular oral) culture and a 'high' (i.e., written Latin) culture. While it is one thing is to emphasize that 'Latin literacy, vernacular literacy, and orality stand in a complex relationship',[23] it is quite another matter to envisage a framework that can be applied for comparative purposes, synchronically as well as diachronically. Colin C. Smith is obviously correct when he notes that 'rather than as composition, the relationship of any vernacular to Latin is best seen as a productive symbiosis'.[24] On a similar note, Marco Mostert and Anna Adamska, in reflecting on the use of the written word in medieval towns, accentuate 'the coexistence of different from and registers of literacy'.[25] One challenge, then, would be to grasp the nature of this 'productive symbiosis'. Furthermore, if it is true that 'medieval vernacular literacy exhibits characteristics of orality in the processes of composition as well as reception',[26] it becomes evident that the task is not only to understand the productive symbiosis between two literacies but also to detect and analyse the oral component. Indeed, the oral component has been

[18] Richter, *The Oral Tradition in the Early Middle Ages*, p. 53.

[19] Brown, 'Latin Writing and the Old English Vernacular'.

[20] Justice, *Writing and Rebellion*.

[21] Clanchy, 'Looking Back From the Invention of Printing'.

[22] The list is continually increasing and a selection includes: passive literacy, verbal literacy, historical literacy, learned literacy, sacred literacy, visual literacy, narrative literacy, rune-literacy, merchant-literacy, citizen literacy, phonetic literacy, comprehension literacy, documentary literacy, vernacular literacy, laymen literacy, and female literacy. For further references and discussion, see Melve, 'European and Scandinavian Research on Literacy'.

[23] Brown, 'Latin Writing', p. 53.

[24] Smith, 'The Vernacular', p. 78.

[25] Mostert and Adamska, 'Conclusion', p. 428.

[26] Bäuml, 'Medieval Texts', p. 39.

found increasingly difficult to understand, primarily because our main access to oral culture is by way of written records. Still, there has also been a tendency, as Slavica Ranković has pointed out, to over-problematize the oral component:

> Radical problematising of the orality of oral literature and the textuality of written literature has [...] led to the point where the validity of the oral-written distinction becomes itself highly questionable; yet somehow, most scholars retract when they reach this point, state that the distinction is still useful and should not be discarded, without necessarily explaining why.[27]

The vital question, then, becomes how the oral culture, or tradition, can be approached. Patrick Geary suggests there are three ways to approach orality: (1) to analyse the conceptual transformation of the oral record; (2) to look for the evidence of oral performance within texts; and (3) to look for descriptions of the encounter between literate and oral modes in medieval texts.[28] While Geary's suggestions certainly are worth taking into account, in particular because of attention to the conceptual level as well as that of performance, they are in many cases hard to put into practice, often resulting either from the scarcity or from the particular character of the sources that provide information on either dimension.

Problems such as these in identifying multilingual configurations at one particular point in time are enhanced when the diachronic dimension is addressed. For once, the trajectory of vernacular literacies seems to be vastly different, varying in terms of period, region, and literary genre — to mention just a few significant factors. For instance, quite a number of studies identify turning points in the relationship between different literacies, for example, when George Hardin Brown concludes that 'it was during the tenth and eleventh centuries that the vernacular truly became more than just a handmaid to the Latin'.[29] The problem is partly that such turning points vary according to the factors mentioned above, for example in terms of whether one is dealing with psalter literacy (as Brown does) or with other fields such as historiography. In the case of the latter, historiography, the same period — the tenth and eleventh centuries — witnessed an upsurge in vernacular historiography in England that followed Latin models closely.[30] Moreover, it is certainly possible to identify

---

[27] Ranković, 'The Oral-Literate Continuum as a Space', p. 70.

[28] Geary, 'Oblivion between Orality and Textuality', p. 115.

[29] Brown, 'Latin Writing', p. 51.

[30] Damian-Grint, *The New Historians of the Twelfth-Century Renaissance*. See also Otter, *Inventiones*.

the first appearance of a number of new vernacular genres in the twelfth and thirteenth centuries, such as biography,[31] the art of memory,[32] *ars dictamis*,[33] poetry,[34] hagiography,[35] prayer books,[36] and, of course, romance.[37] However, it is quite another matter to clarify the further trajectories of these new vernacular forms, including vast regional variations.

Such problems in describing the trajectory of multilingual configurations are probably one reason why there are so few attempts to explain the emergence as well as the development of multilingual configurations. Another reason, not any less important, is related to the dominating role of the Great Divide Theory not only in the early stages of the formation of the discipline but also in setting theoretical and methodical premises for the more recent discussion. The alternative, the Ideology View, was, as mentioned, established as an antithesis to the Great Divide Theory. This was done by denying that the written word had any implications whatsoever, and not by establishing an independent theoretical framework. If we disregard the (usually) postmodern theories (such as those of Foucault and Derrida) used by proponents of the Ideology View to establish their characteristically sceptical and relativist position, the approach is rather under-theorized, especially when it comes to the question of 'implications'.[38] The most consistent and extreme presentation of the Ideology View, that of Brian Street, does not deal with the question of implications at all, and — as mentioned — seems to claim that there are no significant differences between oral and written forms of communication.[39]

[31] Bates, Crick, and Hamilton, 'Introduction'.

[32] Carruthers, *The Book of Memory*.

[33] Camargo, *Ars dictaminis, ars dictandi*.

[34] Dronke, *Poetic Individuality in the Middle Ages*.

[35] Egmond, 'The Audience of Early Medieval Hagiographical Texts'; Head, 'Introduction'; Mulder-Bakker, 'The Invention of Saintliness'.

[36] Saenger, 'Books of Hours'.

[37] Burrow, *Medieval Writers and their Work*; Muir, *Literature and Society in Medieval France*.

[38] 'It [the polarization between autonomous and ideological models of literacy] has also led to certain themes being associated with particular schools of thought, and excluded from others. This is clearly evident in relation to questions about the consequences and utility of literacy as a technology, and its role in progressive forms of social change' (Maddox, 'What Can Ethnographic Studies Tell Us', p. 255).

[39] 'In this context it makes little sense to talk of "literacy", when what is involved are different literacies: and equally it makes little sense to compare the two subjects by distinguishing

Medievalists, when they came to the burgeoning field of literacy studies in the eighties, quickly sided with the Ideology View. Not only did the sceptical and relativistic dimensions to the Ideology View fit the then-current concern with language and power, but the fear of generalization and theory also explains the preference for the Ideology View, then as well as now. In fact, William A. Johnson has talked about this 'intense interest in particulars' as a *Leitmotiv* in current scholarship, reflected in the fact that local variations 'trump generalizing tendencies'.[40] In 1993, Street pleaded for 'some new generalizations about literacy, with the benefit of these new approaches'.[41] Over twenty years later, it is hard to see that 'new generalizations' premised on the Ideology View have been successfully established.[42] It is also true, as Slavica Ranković has emphasized, that the reaction against the Great Divide Theory has 'resulted in the accumulation of isolated data, as well as terminological and conceptual arbitrariness, and, to a certain extent, to scholarly parochialism, too'.[43] In fact, the extensive nature of this research field — involving numerous corpora of texts and oral cultures — makes it virtually impossible to establish general models that take into account every aspect of the process of textualization. However, for more narrowly defined contexts it is certainly worth reflecting upon factors that might impinge on the process of textualization, including multilingual configurations.

Approaching the Problem Anew (1): Bringing Reception Back In

In struggling with the complex relationship between oral and written forms of communication and multilingual configurations, recent research seems to have appropriated the concept of a continuum in an effort to conceptualise the relationship.[44] According to Else Mundal, in addressing the Old Norse culture,

---

between their oral and literate practices when what is involved are different mixes of orality and literacy' (Street, 'Introduction', p. 10).

[40] Johnson, 'Introduction', p. 9.

[41] Street, 'Introduction', p. 3.

[42] Symptomatically, when Street in 2009 reflected on 'the ethnography of reading and writing', he concluded that 'the task of literacy studies in the next phase [...] is to provide rich and complex accounts of literacy practices in the context of such local/global dimensions' (Street, 'Ethnography of Writing and Reading', p. 341).

[43] Rankovic, 'The Oral-Literate Continuum', p. 71.

[44] See, for instance, Thorvaldsen, 'The Eddic Form and its Contexts'; Melve, 'Mapping Public Debates'.

the notion of continuum is used to understand the impact of oral traditions on written texts:

> Most oral art forms are to be found somewhere on a scale between the skaldic poetry where the written form in principle should reflect older oral forms rather closely, and medieval written prose texts which give vague and uncertain information about the oral tradition upon which the written texts build.[45]

The analytical value of such continuum-approaches aside, they are usually of a descriptive nature and are, to my knowledge, not used for explanatory purposes. Explanatory frameworks and approaches are, admittedly, hard to come by. Yet, some do exist, such as those of Joyce Coleman and D. H. Green. From this perspective, it is a bit curious that Mostert, in drawing up the research agenda for the project *Verschrifelijking*, did not mention the importance of constructing theoretical frameworks — or models — that supersede the outdated functionalist frameworks of the Great Divide Theory and the under-theorized the Ideology View. Even the most sophisticated of these efforts — notably Brian Stock's theory of 'textual communities' — have faults resulting from the functionalist residue. Still, Stock's theory is of immense importance, since it was the first (and still the only one) that combined the explanatory value of the Great Divide Theory with a keen sensibility of the role of orality and aurality in the communicative dynamic of the Middle Ages on the one hand, and the importance of audience and reception on the other.[46]

However, along with the increasing awareness of the complexity of the relationship between different forms of communication — their 'plurimedial interplay' — more weight has been placed upon patterns of communication. If the interaction between literacy, aurality, orality, and the vernaculars has been difficult to come to terms with, the complexities related to patterns of communication are no less so. At a basic level, there is the question of how these structures are to be defined. Given the vast variety of communicative situations, it is difficult to agree on common denominators. In some cases, the emphasis is on internal structures. From this perspective, Walter Haug, in his analysis of communication in the early Middle Ages, applies five antitheses in order to identify key patterns: (1) Latin versus vernacular, (2) written versus oral, (3) religious versus secular, (4) clerical versus lay, and (5) learned versus unlearned.[47]

---

[45] Mundal, 'Introduction', p. 2.

[46] Stock, *The Implications of literacy*.

[47] Haug, 'Schriftlichkeit und Reflektion', p. 142.

In other cases, all remnants of structuralism (such as that found in Haug's antitheses) are put aside, and the emphasis is placed on outlining the communicative 'context of reception'. One example is Coleman's typology of 'late medieval English literacies' which consists of 'pragmatic reading', 'religious reading', and 'scholarly professional reading'.[48] More sophisticated and complex is the effort by Dennis Howard Green, distinguishing as he does between three modes of reception with regard to German literature written between 800 and 1300: 'reception by hearing', 'reception by reading', and 'the intermediate mode of reception'. By offering criteria for the different modes of reception, Green establishes a framework that remedies some of the problems resulting from using unspecified terms such as 'written versus oral'. Green is also far more concerned with communicative institutions, at least compared with investigations dealing exclusively with internal evidence of reception. By outlining five 'contexts of reception' — 'court of the secular aristocracy', 'monastery', 'town', 'religious lay community', and 'episcopal court'[49] — Green, in essence, 'establishes a number of centres where, in addition to *illitterati* dependent on listening to a recital, there were also *litterati* present'.[50]

In short, Green's masterly investigation provides important clues as to how patterns of communication can be conceptualized and, not least, explained. Yet, one may ask whether Green's 'contexts of reception' are sufficiently integrated in his own analyses, appearing as they do almost as an appendix adjacent to the book's conclusion. Moreover, Green has also a rather static view on these contexts; it is as though he freezes a moment in time for providing snapshots of the institutions in question. By historicizing and specifying these contexts at crucial moments in their evolutionary trajectory, the dynamic relationship among individual and groups, textual expression, and patterns of communication on the one hand, and the institutionalized environment on the other hand, could have been conceptualized in such a way that Green's 'contexts of reception' not only serve as 'contexts' but also as institutions that, under certain conditions, may structure the reception of a textual expression as well as effect changed in the pattern of communication.[51]

---

[48] Coleman, *Public Reading and the Reading Public*, pp. 89–93.

[49] Green, *Medieval Listening and Reading*, pp. 211–24.

[50] Green, *Medieval Listening and Reading*, p. 211.

[51] For a further discussion of this point, see Melve, 'European and Scandinavian Research on Literacy'.

Approaching the Problem Anew (II): The Comparative Approach

All investigations dealt with thus far have focused on one set of multilingual configurations only; Coleman analyses late medieval English configurations, whereas the focus of Green was German literature in the early and high Middle Ages. In fact, the emphasis on one unit of analysis is a characteristic feature of literacy studies. Pleas for the use of comparison in literacy studies are, needless to say, nothing new. Bryan Maddox, approaching literacy from the point of view of ethnographic studies, claims that 'concern with "general tendencies" suggests a stronger comparative focus in literacy research,'[52] whereas Harvey J. Graff concludes that 'comparative studies' is one of several concerns of what he calls 'new historical literacy studies'.[53] The case for comparison has also been advanced from medievalists, for instance, when Mostert and Adamska stress the need for the study of urban literacy from a comparative perspective.[54] Yet such pleas rarely offer advice on how to go about doing the comparison.[55] Although there has been a slight increase in the number of literacy studies that deal with more than one unit of analysis,[56] most of these investigations focus on one main unit and introduce additional units by analogy, eschewing systematic comparison.[57]

Yet systematic comparison is not always an option; the few extant sources from the Middle Ages, and in particular from the early Middle Ages and from the peripheries of Europe, often render systematic comparisons impossible to undertake. For cases such as these, Jürgen Kocka has argued for 'asymmetrical comparison' — that is, comparison in which one unit is given more weight than other units.[58] In fact, research on the oral tradition in Old Norse socie-

---

[52] Maddox, 'What Can Ethnographic Studies Tell Us', p. 255.

[53] Graff, 'Introduction to Historical Studies of Literacy', p. 19.

[54] Mostert and Adamska, 'Conclusion', p. 430.

[55] Some exceptions do exist; see, for instance, Finnegan's plea for 'middle-range comparison on a fairly modest set of topics' (Finnegan, *Literacy and Orality*).

[56] See Chrisomalis, 'The Origins and Co-Evolution of Literacy and Numeracy', who shows that 'comparative cross-cultural research can shed light on the similarities and differences among social contexts and the constellation of literate and numerate practices used in each' (p. 60).

[57] Hammel, 'The Comparative Method in Anthropological Perspective', p. 146, accentuates that comparisons that use exemplification is trivial and faulty in approach.

[58] However, Kocka does not really provide any firm methodical guiding lines, aside from insisting that the units of comparison need to be carefully selected (Kocka, 'Assymmetrical Historical Comparison', p. 49).

ties exemplifies ways of doing 'asymmetrical comparison', first and foremost by
the dialogue with scholarship on oral formulas and tradition in contemporary
society. Albert Lord's *The Singer of Tales* (1960), investigating Serbo-Croatian
poets and their performance of oral poetry, has constituted a point of departure for comparative investigations of the Old Norse tradition.[59] In summing
up achievements of four decades of research on the oral versus the written, Gísli
Sigurðsson reflects on the use of the comparative method:

> The most important achievement of recent research has thus lain not in the
> counting of formulas and the identification of formalized themes in large bodies
> of ancient texts, but in the possibilities opened up by the so-called comparative
> method, in which data from modern-day field studies are used to plug gaps in our
> fragmentary knowledge from the past [...]. Unfortunately, much research con-
> ducted in the spirit of comparativism has been vitiated by the lumping together of
> societies and literary genres so different that they cannot justifiably be compared
> in any plausible manner, and the method has consequently laid itself upon to criti-
> cism [...]. What we can do, however, is to use new information gathered from living
> oral societies to formulate new questions of the limited sources at our disposal.[60]

Gísli Sigurðsson's reflections are interesting on several accounts. First, his praise
of the comparative method resides in its ability to 'plug in the gaps in our fragmentary knowledge from the past'. This point, often rehearsed in the theoretical discussion on the comparative method,[61] is a vital one indeed, as comparison offers the possibility of compensating for scarcity of sources. What Gísli
Sigurðsson does not mention, however, is that 'modern-day field studies' is only
one of several comparative points of departure. In fact, in order to prevent the
comparison from being 'vitiated by the lumping together of societies and literary genres so different that they cannot justifiably be compared', it is often
necessary to select units of comparison rather close in time and space. At this
point, we encounter yet another aspect of literacy studies, the preference for
nationally defined units of analysis. Gísli Sigurðsson's study is no exception, as
it deals the medieval Icelandic saga and oral tradition very much in isolation
— or to be more precise, the East Fjord district of Iceland. Although it can be
argued that the source material used by Gísli Sigurðsson is so exceptional that

---

[59] For a historiographical view on the subject, see Skafte Jensen, 'The Oral-Formulaic Theory Revisited'.

[60] Gísli Sigurðsson, *The Medieval Icelandic Saga and Oral Tradition*, pp. 41–42.

[61] For perceptive discussions on numerous aspects of the comparative method, see contributions in Haupt and Kocka, *Geschichte und Vergleich*.

it is difficult to find any medieval equivalents, the fact that he does not even discuss the question contributes to solidifying the idea of an Icelandic singularity and exceptionality. This is rather paradoxical, since one of Gísli Sigurðsson's professed aims is to go beyond the old discussion of Book Prose and Free Prose that held Icelandic exceptionality as a more or less acknowledged premise.

A solution here may be to adopt insights from so-called transcultural studies. Basic to this approach is the rejection of all a priori defined frameworks. Instead, the problems and the questions are to be defined through the analysis. The transcultural approach, as presented by Michael Werner and Bénédicte Zimmermann, insists on the need to address 'a multiplicity of possible viewpoints and the divergences resulting from languages, terminologies, categorizations, and conceptualizations, traditions, and disciplinary usages'.[62] Yet, to reject all a priori defined frameworks is probably too drastic a measure, particularly for the Middle Ages which lacked the kind of (global) communicative infrastructure that the advocates of the transcultural approach often take as their point of departure. What could be done, however, is to use Green's above mentioned 'contexts of reception' as the comparative framework: in other words, as transcultural contexts of reception. Needless to say, Green's outlined 'contexts of' — 'court of the secular aristocracy', 'monastery', 'town', 'religious lay community', and 'episcopal court' — are derived from his study of German literature and should, in line with the inductive ideal of transcultural studies, be readjusted in the course of the empirical investigation. Aside from the value of Green's theory on its own terms, as discussed above, within a comparative framework the 'contexts' have three additional functions.

First, it takes into account that vertical lines of communication in the Middle Ages were particularly indebted to mediating institutions in the periphery. Consequently, any 'reception' of a text is contextualized in terms of the relationship between the overall pattern of communication, including multilingual configuration, and the institutional setting — on a local, regional, national, or transnational level — responsible for communicating, and in some cases, instigating dialogue horizontally as well as vertically.

Second, by constructing a framework that also emphasizes communicative institutions, the comparison can more easily deal with the diachronic dimension and not only the synchronic. As for literacy studies, this is most fundamental on account of the (latent) evolutionism that pervades parts of the field. Rather than subscribing to either of the dichotomous views (Great Divide Theory/Ideology View), the question of 'transfer' from orality to literacy as

---

[62] Werner and Zimmermann, 'Beyond Comparison', p. 32.

well as that of the 'implications of literacy' can be approached in terms of an understanding of the communicative institutions ('contexts of reception') in each case. Furthermore, by focusing more on the diachronic dimension, a further advantage of the comparative method is brought to the fore: its potential for explanation. Yet, and in stark contrast to the Great Divide Theory, the comparative method facilitates explanation based on empirical investigations of multilingual configurations and their relationship.

The third advantage of the comparative framework is its potential for bridging the gap not only between the national orientation of literacy studies, but also between different subfields within literacy studies. It is certainly a truism that literacy studies are interdisciplinary, but the specialized nature of many of the subfields have resulted in an interdisciplinarity that in many cases is more apparent than real. In addition, the insistence by the advocates of the Ideology View that the question regarding the transfer from oral to written as well as that of implications can only be investigated by dealing with particulars — that is, unique cases — has resulted in the fact that the common denominator of the Great Divide Theory has been undermined. Hence, it is rather indicative that all the investigations addressed here — those of Coleman, Green, and Gísli Sigurðsson — discuss, and criticize, the Great Divide Theory, but none of them capitalizes on insights from other subdisciplines of literacy studies.

Conclusion

In the previous pages, I have, by addressing a few main concerns of literacy studies in the past and present, highlighted one pertinent issue for future literacy studies: understanding and explaining multilingual configurations. Multilingual configurations are important not only for grasping the transfer from orality to literacy, but also for coming to terms with arguably the most regular communicative environment in the Middle Ages: the coexistence of several written or oral languages. As such, medieval literacy studies could — and perhaps should — establish dialogue with other parts of the field, which also have accentuated the need to deal with modern literacy in terms of 'multiliteracies'.[63]

---

[63] See for instance the observation by Harvey J. Graff: 'Among contemporary scholars of literacy, multiple literacies — dimensions beyond traditional alphabetic or "textual" literacy — the domain of the many proclaimed "new literacies" — from digital and visual to "scientific" and spatial, and beyond — compete for attention and a place on both research agendas and, increasingly, school and university curricula. Claims about both "many" and "new" literacies raise fundamental questions in themselves' (Graff, 'The Literacy Myth at Thirty', p. 647).

Works Cited

Secondary Studies

Bates, David, Julia Crick, and Sarah Hamilton, 'Introduction', in *Writing Medieval Biography 750–1250*, ed. by David Bates, Julia Crick, and Sarah Hamilton (Woodridge: Boydell Press, 2006), pp. 1–13

Brockmeier, Jens, and David R. Olson, 'The Literacy Episteme', in *The Cambridge Handbook of Literacy*, ed. by David R. Olson and Nancy Torrance (Cambridge: Cambridge University Press, 2009), pp. 3–21

Brown, George Hardin, 'Latin Writing and the Old English Vernacular', in *Schriftlichkeit im frühen Mittelalter*, ed. by Ursula Schaefer (Tübingen: Narr, 1993), pp. 36–57

Burrow, J. A., *Medieval Writers and their Work: Middle English Literature and its Background 1100–1500* (Oxford: Oxford University Press, 1982)

Bäuml, Franz H., 'Medieval Texts and the Two Theories of Oral-Formulaic Composition: A Proposal for a Third Theory', *New Literary History*, 16 (1984), 31–49

Camargo, Martin, *Ars dictaminis, ars dictandi* (Turnhout: Brepols, 1991)

Carruthers, Mary J., *The Book of Memory: A Study of Memory in Medieval Culture* (Cambridge: Cambridge University Press, 1993)

Cassirer, Ernst, *Language and Myth* (New York: Dover, 1946)

Chrisomalis, Stephen, 'The Origins and Co-Evolution of Literacy and Numeracy', in *The Cambridge Handbook of Literacy*, ed. by David R. Olson and Nancy Torrance (Cambridge: Cambridge University Press, 2009), pp. 59–74

Cipolla, Carlo M., *Literacy and Development in the West* (Harmondsworth: Penguin, 1969)

Clanchy, Michael T., *From Memory to Written Record: England 1066–1307* (London: Arnold, 1978)

——, 'Looking Back From the Invention of Printing', in *Literacy in Historical Perspective*, ed. David P. Resnick (Washington, DC: Library of Congress, 1983), pp. 7–23

Coleman, Joyce, *Public Reading and the Reading Public in Late Medieval England and France* (Cambridge: Cambridge University Press, 1996)

Damian-Grint, Peter, *The New Historians of the Twelfth-Century Renaissance: Inventing Vernacular Authority* (Woodbridge: Boydell, 1999)

Dronke, Peter, *Poetic Individuality in the Middle Ages: New Departures in Poetry, 1000–1150* (Oxford: Oxford University Press, 1970)

Egmond, Wolfert S. van, 'The Audience of Early Medieval Hagiographical Texts: Some Questions Revisited', in *New Approaches to Medieval Communication*, ed. by Marco Mostert (Turnhout: Brepols, 1999), pp. 41–67

Finnegan, Ruth, *Literacy and Orality: Studies in the Technology of Communication* (Oxford: Blackwell, 1988)

Geary, Patrick J., 'Oblivion between Orality and Textuality in the Tenth Century', in *Medieval Concepts of the Past: Ritual, Memory, Historiography*, ed. by Gerd Althoff, Johannes Fried, and Patrick J. Geary (Cambridge: Cambridge University Press)

Gísli Sigurðsson, *The Medieval Icelandic Saga and Oral Tradition: A Discourse on Method* (Cambridge, MA: Harvard University Press, 2004)

Goody, Jack, and Ian Watt, 'The Consequences of Literacy', *Comparative Studies in Society and History*, 5 (1963), 304–45

Graff, Harvey J., 'Introduction to Historical Studies of Literacy', in *Understanding Literacy in its Historical Contexts: Socio-Cultural History and the Legacy of Egil Johansson*, ed. by Harvey J. Graff and others (Lund: Nordic Academic Press, 2009), pp. 123–31

Graff, Harvey J., 'The Literacy Myth at Thirty', in *Journal of Social History*, spring (2010), 635–62

Green, Dennis Howard, *Medieval Listening and Reading: The Primary Reception of German Literature, 800–1300* (Cambridge: Cambridge University Press, 1994)

Hammel, E. A., 'The Comparative Method in Anthropological Perspective', *Comparative Studies in Society and History*, 22 (1980), 145–55

Haug, Walter, 'Schriftlichkeit und Reflektion: Zur Entstehung und Entwicklung eines deutschsprachigen Schrifttums im Mittelalter', in *Schrift und Gedächtnis: Beiträge zur Archäologie der literarischen Kommunikation*, ed. by Aleida Assmann, Jan Assmann and C. Hardmeier (Munich: Fink, 1983), pp. 141–57

Haupt, Heinz-Gerhard, and Jürgen Kocka, eds, *Geschichte und Vergleich: Ansätze und Ergebnisse international vergleichender Geschichtsschreibung* (Frankfurt: Campus, 1996)

Havelock, Eric A., *Preface to Plato* (Cambridge, MA: Belknap Press of Harvard University Press, 1963)

Havelock, Ernst, *The Muse Learns to Write: Reflections on Orality and Literacy from Antiquity to the Present* (New Haven: Yale University Press, 1993)

Head, Thomas, 'Introduction', in *Medieval Hagiography: An Anthology*, ed. by Thomas Head (New York: Garland, 2000), pp. xiii–xxxix

Innis, Harold A., *The Bias of Communication* (Toronto: Toronto University Press, 1951)

Johnson, William A., 'Introduction', in *Ancient Literacies: The Culture of Reading in Greece and Rome*, ed. by William A. Johnson and Holt N. Parker (Oxford: Oxford University Press, 2009), pp. 1–15

Justice, Steven, *Writing and Rebellion: England in 1381* (Berkeley: University of California Press, 1994)

Keller, Hagen, 'Pragmatische Schriftlichkeit im Mittelalter: Erscheinungsformen und Entwicklungsstufen', in *Pragmatische Schriftlichkeit im Mittelalter: Erscheinungsformen und Entwicklungsstufen*, ed. by Hagen Keller, Klaus Grubmüller, and Nikolaus Staubach (Munich: Fink, 1992), pp. 1–7

Kocka, Jürgen, 'Assymmetrical Historical Comparison: The Case of the German *Sonderweg*', *History and Theory*, 38 (1999), 40–50

Lévi-Strauss, Claude, *Anthropologie structurale* (Paris: Plon, 1958)

Maddox, Bryan, 'What Can Ethnographic Studies Tell Us about the Consequences of Literacy?', *Comparative Education*, 43 (2007), 253–71

McKitterick, Rosamond, *The Carolingians and the Written Word* (Cambridge: Cambridge University Press, 1989)

McLuhan, Marshall, *The Gutenberg Galaxy: The Making of Typographic Man* (Toronto: Toronto University Press, 1962)

Meier, Christel, 'Fourteen Years of Research at Münster into Pragmatic Literacy in the Middle Ages: A Research Project by Collaborative Research Centre 231. Agents, Fields and Forms of Pragmatic Literacy in the Middle Ages', in *Visual Culture and the German Middle Ages*, ed. by Kathryn Starkey and Horst Wenzel (New York: Palgrave Macmillan), pp. 23–39

Melve, Leidulf, 'European and Scandinavian Research on Literacy: Some Methodological Aspects', *NOWELE*, 64/65 (2012), 181–225

——, 'Mapping Public Debates along the Oral-Literate Continuum (1000–1300)', in *Along the Orality-Literacy Continuum: Types of Texts, Relations and their Implications*, ed. by Slavica Ranković, Leidulf Melve, and Else Mundal (Turnhout: Brepols, 2010), pp. 73–100

Mostert, Marco, 'New Approaches to Medieval Communication?', in *New Approaches to Medieval Communication*, ed. by Marco Mostert (Turnhout: Brepols, 1999), pp. 15–37

Mostert, Marco, and Anna Adamska, 'Conclusion', in *Uses of the Written Word in Medieval Towns: Medieval Urban Literacy II*, ed. by Marco Mostert and Anna Adamska (Turnhout: Brepols, 2014), pp. 427–31

Muir, Lynette R., *Literature and Society in Medieval France: The Mirror and the Image, 1100–1500* (New York: St Martin's Press, 1985)

Mulder-Bakker, Anneke B., 'The Invention of Saintliness', in *The Invention of Saintliness*, ed. by Anneke B. Mulder-Bakker (London: Routledge, 2002), pp. 3–23

Mundal, Else, 'Introduction', in *Oral Art Forms and their Passage into Writing*, ed. by Else Mundal and Jonas Wellendorf (Copenhagen: Museum Tusculanum Press, 2008), pp. 1–5

Olson, David R., and Nancy Torrance, 'Preface', in *The Cambridge Handbook of Literacy*, ed. by David R. Olson and Nancy Torrance (Cambridge: Cambridge University Press, 2009), pp. xiii–xx

Ong, Walter J., *Ramus, Method and the Decay of Dialogue: From the Art of Discourse to Art of Record* (Cambridge, MA: Harvard University Press, 1958)

Otter, Monika, *Inventiones: Fiction and Referentiality in Twelfth-Century English Historical Writing* (Chapel Hill: University of North Carolina Press, 1996)

Ranković, Slavica, 'The Oral-Literate Continuum as a Space', in *Along the Orality-Literacy Continuum: Types of Texts, Relations and their Implications*, ed. by Slavica Ranković, Leidulf Melve and Else Mundal (Turnhout: Brepols, 2010), pp. 39–71

Richter, Michael, *The Oral Tradition in the Early Middle Ages* (Turnhout: Brepols, 1994)

Saenger, Paul, 'Books of Hours and the Reading Habits of the Later Middle Ages', in *The Culture of Print: Power and Uses of Print in Early Modern Europe*, ed. by Roger Chartier (Princeton: Princeton University Press, 1989), pp. 141–73

Skafte Jensen, Minna 'The Oral-Formulaic Theory Revisited', in *Oral Art Forms and their Passage into Writing*, ed. by Else Mundal and Jonas Wellendorf (Copenhagen: Museum Tusculanum Press, 2008), pp. 43–52

Smith, Colin C., 'The Vernacular', in *The New Cambridge Medieval History*, v: *c. 1198–c. 1300*, ed. by David Abulafia (Cambridge: Cambridge University Press), pp. 71–81

Stock, Brian, *The Implication of Literacy, Written Language and Models of Interpretation in the Eleventh and Twelfth Centuries* (Princeton: Princeton University Press, 1983)

Street, Brian V., 'Ethnography of Writing and Reading', in *The Cambridge Handbook of Literacy*, ed. David R. Olson and Nancy Torrance (Cambridge: Cambridge University Press, 2009), pp. 329–45

——, 'Introduction: The New Literacy Studies', in *Cross-Cultural Approaches to Literacy*, ed. by Brian Street (Cambridge: Cambridge University Press, 1993), pp. 1–21

——, *Literacy in Theory and Practice* (Cambridge: Cambridge University Press, 1984)

Thorvaldsen, Bernt Øyvind, 'The Eddic Form and its Contexts: An Oral Art Form Performed in Writing', in *Oral Art Forms and their Passage into Writing*, ed. by Else Mundal and Jonas Wellendorf (Copenhagen: Museum Tusculanum Press, 2008), pp. 151–62

Werner, Michael, and Bénédicte Zimmermann, 'Beyond Comparison: *Histoire croisée* and the Challenge of Reflexivity', *History and Theory*, 45 (2006), 30–50

Medieval Nordic Backgrounds:
Written Culture in an Oral Society

Else Mundal

Introduction

In the early phases of literacy studies, scholars were mostly occupied with
changes in society caused by the arrival of writing. This included changes that
were both common to all societies and culturally specific manifestations due
to the new medium of writing being used for distinct purposes. The transition
from oral to written was labelled 'the great divide', emphasizing the differences
between oral and written cultures, yet subsequent scholarship has also emphasized that the two overlapped. The arrival of writing did not mean an end to a
previous oral culture; the two existed side by side and influenced each other,
and there was an oral-written continuum.[1]

There is no doubt that literate societies share certain traits: it is also obvious that societies might employ the new technology of writing differently and
thereby promote the development of new cultural variations. There are, however, discrepancies among various literate cultures that are difficult to explain

---

[1] For an overview of this debate, see the first part of Melve's article, 'Literacy Studies: Past,
Present and Future' in this volume.

Else Mundal (else.mundal@lle.uib.no) is Professor Emerita of Old Norse Philology in the
Department of Linguistic, Literary, and Aesthetic Studies, at the University of Bergen. From
2003–12 she was the leader of the Arrival of Writing research group at the Centre for Medieval
Studies, University of Bergen.

Moving Words in the Nordic Middle Ages: Tracing Literacies, Texts, and Verbal Communities, ed. by
Amy C. Mulligan and Else Mundal, AS 8   BREPOLS 🕮 PUBLISHERS   (Turnhout: Brepols, 2019)
pp. 37–60   10.1484/M.AS-EB.5.116619

as the result of divergent choices in how to use the new technology of writing.[2] It is, for instance, obvious that there were variations from one culture to another regarding how large a part of the population learnt to read and write, and there were probably also differences as to how literacy spread among diverse social classes and as to how many women became literate. It is striking that in some geographical areas literacy was confined to Latin, while in other areas, the vernacular was employed in many contexts. In some cultures, the written medium was used mainly for administration, both by the Church and the king, and of course to write texts that were needed by the Church, and perhaps also texts that the king could use to promote his own interests, but nevertheless, writing was not used in wider circles in society. In other cultures, however, it seems that the writing and production of literature also spread to milieux beyond Church and court.

These variations can hardly be explained as the results of diverging choices. It is more likely that they are caused — at least partly — by differences in the oral culture that was previously there, and it is logical that the consequences of the arrival of writing could vary from one society to another. Differences in choice of language, in the development of a written literature, and in the development of an administration using written text and communication must be seen in connection with the oral culture that was previously in place.

The aim of this essay is to identify factors in Old Norse oral culture — and combinations of factors — that might have promoted the development of literacy.[3] This case study of Old Norse society should also have some relevance

---

[2] A scholar who has emphasized differences alongside similarities in oral traditions from different cultures is John Miles Foley. See for instance his books *Traditional Oral Epic* and *The Singer of Tales in Performance*.

[3] The explanation of the flourishing literature in Old Norse culture, and especially in Iceland, has always been a topic of fascination for Old Norse scholars. In the beginning of saga research, the view was that most written texts had previous oral equivalents, and the factors that explained the strong written literature were more or less the same as those that explained the oral tradition: plenty of time in the long winter evenings, aristocratic settlers who were proud of their history, and a certain genetic disposition, the national soul (*folkeånd*). Later, Sigurður Nordal (1952), with a certain amount of humour, pointed at plenty of time alongside a plentiful supply of vellum as the main factors with which to explain the rich written culture in medieval Iceland (Sigurður Nordal, 'Time and Vellum'). Certain factors connected to the Icelandic Church and the Christianization of Iceland have also been emphasized as favourable for cultural growth. Walter Baetke (1956) argued that the explanation was found in the organization of the Icelandic Church. This Church was not an institution outside or above the farmer society, but formed part of this society, and thereby became a lever for cultural growth

for the study of other medieval societies because the factors that promoted — or counteracted — the spread of literacy and the use of writing for various purposes must have been more or less similar in all European cultures. However, the strength with which the different factors worked in a certain society — and the combinations of factors found in disparate societies — may have led to varying types and degrees of literacy in different cultures. The focus here is on the factors in preliterate Old Norse society that promoted the spread of literacy in the period when written culture was first introduced. These factors are, however, at least partly identical to those that later influenced the development of written culture in the society where the oral and the written existed side by side in an oral-written continuum.

It is a fact that Iceland, which had a much smaller population than Norway, Sweden, and Denmark, developed a much stronger culture of literacy than the other Scandinavian-speaking countries. Iceland shared many cultural traits with Norway, from where the majority of the Icelandic settlers came, but there may also have been differences between the countries that can partly explain the dissimilarities in their cultural developments. Furthermore, there may also have been divergences between Iceland and Norway (the western Old Norse area) on the one hand and Sweden and Denmark (the eastern Old Norse area) on the other. In the following I will first draw attention to some factors that are common to the whole Scandinavian-speaking area, and thereafter concentrate on factors that are specific to the Norwegian-Icelandic area or Iceland in particular.

The Attitude towards Knowledge in Old Norse Mythology

The attitude towards the importance of knowledge in an oral society is a factor that may have directed the development of later written culture. There are certain characteristics connected to Old Norse culture indicating that knowledge and learning were at the culture's core. Good sources for the view of knowledge in the oral period are the mythological eddic poems. Extant, written forms of these poems are only preserved in Iceland, but there is reason to believe that

---

for the whole society (Baetke, *Über die Entstehung*, especially the seventh and last chapter). Kurt Schier, in an article from 1991 ('Anfänge und erste Entwicklung') pointed to the peaceful conversion to Christianity in Iceland, which secured continuity and stability in society, and a tolerant attitude towards the heathen past as providing a very good base for the development of a literate culture. This, combined with the strong positions of the Benedictines with their taste for writing and learning, resulted in a flourishing written culture.

many of them, or most of them, were also known in Norway and to some extent also in the rest of Scandinavia.[4] The view of knowledge reflected by these poems is therefore characteristic of the full western Old Norse area and likely the entirety of Scandinavian culture.

When reading introductions to Old Norse mythology and religion, it is very easy to get the impression that the main activity of the Old Norse gods was to fight another group of mythological beings, the giants. In the fullest and most detailed source, Snorri's *Edda*, the fight between the gods and the giants is in fact a very central and dominating subject. In the eddic mythological poems, which were Snorri's main sources when he compiled his *Edda*, however, another activity provided the focus. This is the gods' untiring attempt to collect knowledge and memories of the past as well as prophecies about the future, and these same poems also make it clear that the gods shared their knowledge with the humans. The difference between Snorri's *Edda* and his sources is of course one of degree, since both the struggle against the giants and the gods' attempts to collect knowledge are found in both places.[5] Several reasons might account for the difference. As Snorri's *Edda* functions as a textbook for skalds, a retelling of myths about the struggles between gods and giants formed a necessary basis for the understanding of many kennings. The myths containing stories about fights between gods and giants were perhaps more amusing and had a higher entertainment value than stories about the gods collecting and transmitting knowledge. Furthermore, it is possible that in this particular source from Christian times, the fight between the gods and the giants is focused upon and given space because Old Norse religion is interpreted in the light of the Christian religion and the fight between good and evil.

The exact number of eddic mythological poems is a question of definition.[6] The poem *Hávamál*, as we know it today, should rather be considered a collection of poems instead of one poem. Two poems, *Grógaldr* and *Fjǫlsvinnsmál*, are sometimes edited together as one poem under the title *Svipdagsmál*, and it is a matter of contention whether these poems should be regarded as mythological or heroic poems — most scholars count them among the heroic poems. One poem, *Hrafnagaldr Óðins* or *Forspjallsljóð*, is most likely a young pastiche and is normally not counted among the genuine mythological poems. This leaves us with thirteen mythological eddic poems.

[4] See Mundal, 'From Oral to Written in Old Norse Culture' in this book.

[5] On knowledge in eddic poetry, see Quinn, 'Liquid Knowledge'.

[6] A good introduction to and comments on eddic poems is found in *Eddukvæði* I and II, edited by Jónas Kristjánsson and Vésteinn Ólason.

If we take a look at the preserved mythological poems an astonishing picture of the importance of knowledge emerges. Six out of thirteen poems — that is, nearly half of the poems, or more than half if *Hávamál* is counted as more than one poem — in one way or another deal with collection or transmission of knowledge. In *Vǫluspá*, Óðinn questions a *vǫlva* to obtain knowledge about both the past and the future. In *Hávamál*, Óðinn gives advice and shares his knowledge with humans. He also relates how he himself obtained wisdom by self-sacrifice. Knowledge of runes was part of this wisdom. *Vafþrúðnismál* tells of how Óðinn travelled to the world of giants to question the giant Vafþrúðnir and collect knowledge from him. In *Grímnismál*, Óðinn shares his knowledge about the world of gods and giants with a worldly prince. *Rígsþula* relates how the god Rígr/Heimdallr became the father of three human sons, one by a slave woman, one by a farmer's wife, and one by a highborn woman. After some years, the god returned to share his knowledge with his highborn son. Knowledge of runes was part of this wisdom. In *Hyndluljóð*, the goddess Freyja questions the giantess Hyndla and makes her reveal genealogical information. In addition to these mythological poems, parts of the eddic poem *Sigrdrífumál* should also be mentioned. Sigrdrífa is a *valkyrja* and can be counted both as a mythological and a heroic figure, and the knowledge she passes on is not, in principle, different from the type of knowledge that Óðinn passes on to humans.

According to Old Norse mythology, the giants possessed more knowledge than the gods because they belonged to an older race and remembered more than the gods; this is why the gods questioned the giants when collecting knowledge. The giants had, however, quite a different attitude towards wisdom than the gods. While the gods shared their knowledge with humans, the giants were not interested in disbursing their memories, and they answered questions only reluctantly.

The importance given to collecting and transmitting knowledge in Old Norse mythology reflects the high value placed on wisdom and its preservation in Old Norse culture.[7] What seems to be distinct is that the importance of knowledge is clearly linked to and motivated by its role in Old Norse mythology. There are no clear parallels to the gods' search for knowledge in the mythology of neighbouring peoples. Old Norse mythology is unique in

---

[7] The positive evaluation of knowledge and wisdom in Old Norse culture documented in Old Norse mythology is also clearly expressed in several other ways in Old Norse sources. Words meaning 'wise' are positive bynames (as in the Ari *fróði* and Sæmundr *fróði*), and in descriptions of people in written sources, both of men and women, words with the same meaning are frequently used.

this respect. In the late Finnish *Kalevala* poems, and especially in the Irish and Welsh material, it can be difficult to distinguish gods and goddesses from heroes and heroines, and also to differentiate motifs and stories that may be rooted in mythology from those rooted in heroic literature. In any case, the collection and transmission of knowledge was not the main activity of the gods or heroes in these neighbouring cultures. That this interest is so dominant in Old Norse mythology emphasizes the special status of knowledge in the culture. This very positive evaluation of knowledge in Old Norse preliterate culture formed a firm foundation for the development of a strong written culture.

The Use of the Runic Alphabet

In all parts of Scandinavia the runic script had been in use for centuries before the Latin alphabet and writing on parchment were introduced by the Church. Runes may have been used for slightly divergent purposes in different geographical areas. Memorial inscriptions on impressive erected stones are most typical for the area around Uppsala in Sweden, and multiple types of inscriptions reflecting everyday life are found in several towns; especially rich are the finds in the Norwegian town of Bergen.[8] However, there is enough evidence to show that runic script was used throughout Scandinavia and the new areas where people from Scandinavia, especially Norway, settled in the Viking period. If knowledge of the runic script formed a basis for later literacy in the Latin alphabet, this basis existed throughout Scandinavia and in the new settlements as well.[9]

Quite a lot of the preserved runic inscriptions date from the time following Christianization and the introduction of the Latin alphabet. For instance, all of the runic sticks from the Bryggen excavations in Bergen are late, and the suggestion that writing in the Latin alphabet even advanced writing in runes cannot be ignored.[10] But even if that should be the case, the use and knowledge of runic writing in pre-Christian Scandinavian countries must have been widespread — probably with local variations both as to how extensively runes were used and for what purposes. What knowledge of runic script in pre-Christian Scandinavian oral culture meant for the development of the later written culture in the Latin alphabet is an interesting question. In principle, writing and

---

[8] See Zilmer's article in this volume.

[9] A good overview of different types of runic inscriptions is found in Seim, 'Runologi'.

[10] See Hagland, 'Høgmellomalderens bruk av runer'.

reading were the same in both alphabets; therefore, it is logical that knowledge of runes was a factor that facilitated introduction of the Latin alphabet. In other words, the more people there were who knew how to use runes, the more people there were who could become literate in the new forms of written culture.

It is difficult to know how large a percentage of the population was skilled in runes, and the sources point in different directions. That the word *rún* (mostly used in pl. *rúnar*) also has the meanings 'secret', 'whispering/hidden conversation', and 'sorcery', indicates that this knowledge was not common. There are, however, other sources that seem to take for granted that people in Old Norse society knew runes. An often quoted passage is found in the *Older Frostathing law* IV, 43: this paragraph gives instructions about how a man who has been injured and had his tongue cut out shall act to point out the perpetrator. He shall go to the thing, and if he sees the man who cut out his tongue, he shall point his axe handle at him. If he does not see him at the thing, he shall write his perpetrator's name in runes if he knows runes. The law text sees it as a possibility that the victim might not know runes, but since writing his name in runes is depicted as the standard way of identifying a criminal absent from the thing, it appears that knowledge of runes was rather common. Furthermore, the great number of runic inscriptions in some milieux and the great differences between them concerning form, function, and content (see Zilmer's article in this book) indicate that the rune carvers consisted of a large and heterogeneous group of people. One may also ask what the point of erected rune stones was if only very few people were able to read them.

It is important to consider who in society knew runes. Was this knowledge widespread only among the upper strata of society, and how was runic knowledge gendered? Runic monumental stones were no doubt erected by people belonging to an upper stratum of society. The engravings of inscriptions seem to have been done by professionals, and stone-carving was men's work. But there may have been exceptions regarding women's involvement, even at a professional level. One Swedish runestone from Hälsingeland (Hs 21) mentions Gunnborga as the runemaster.[11] Although the carving of runes on stones seems to have been the work of male professionals, this does not mean that knowledge of how to use runes was limited to male specialists belonging to the upper

---

[11] The inscription is edited in Åhlén, 'Runinskrifter i Hälsingland', pp. 47–48. The verb used for making the runes is *fá* (paint). That could of course mean that someone else carved them and she painted them.

classes. To carve runes on a wooden stick with a little knife was a cheap activity which could be done by anyone — men and women alike — who possessed the skill. From medieval runic inscriptions it seems clear that many women had learned how to write and read runes. From the preliterate period, the sources are scarcer, but there are after all a number of sources which demonstrate that it was taken for granted that at least some women knew runes. In the eddic poem *Sigrdrífumál* it is a female figure who shares her wisdom in runes with the hero of the poem, Sigurðr Fáfnisbani. In the poem *Atlamál*, Guðrún carves runes to send a message of warning to her brothers, but they are defaced by the messenger. Kostbera, Hǫgni's wife, was, however, able to decipher them. The poem states: 'Kend vas Kostbera | kunni skil rúna' (Kostbera had been taught | she understood runes). *Egils saga* depicts Egill's daughter Þorgerðr carving Egill's poem *Sonatorrek* on a *kefli* (a piece of wood) in runes. This saga is of course a thirteenth-century source, but it shows how people living at that time thought such things could have happened in the preliterate period. The evidence does not allow us to draw firm conclusions about women's runic skill in Old Norse society, but there are a few sources, such as those mentioned above, which indicate that many women were no less skilled in runes than men. Women's knowledge of runes is of importance in our understanding of how this knowledge spread in society, since women bore the main responsibility of child-rearing and in that capacity would have transmitted a significant amount of information to the next generation (see below).

System of Government

All of the Scandinavian countries, as well as the settlements established by Scandinavians, developed some type of oral administrative framework. The form and extent of oral laws are unknown, but they did exist. Laws were given and judgements passed by regional assemblies or things (*þing*) where originally all free men (and at least in Norway, women running a farm) could meet,[12] and oral formulas were used in many different situations to make an act or an agreement legally valid. Many of the rules for legal procedures as we know them from later written laws do, in all likelihood, build on those originating in this earlier oral culture. There was also a territorial army (*leiðangr*), a warning system that involved lighting a fire at raised elevations in case of attack, and communica-

---

[12] In Norway the regional things became things where only representatives from a region met. We do not know exactly when this happened, but probably in the tenth century.

tion between the ruler and his men took place by direct contact or by sending messengers. In the Scandinavian kingdoms it seems that the king, in the time prior to Christianization and the arrival of writing in the Latin alphabet, had placed himself at the top of an already-developed administrative structure and gradually changed it to serve his purpose. Nonetheless, laws still had to be accepted by the thing, and the relationship between the ruler and his subjects was understood as a sort of contract. This is even the case in the Christian sections of the law. The laws determined what the farmers had to do, and breaking the law meant having to pay fines. However, the laws also dictate what these farmers should expect from the Church in return, and if the representatives of the Church did not fulfil their obligations, they too would have to pay fines.

In societies with strong links between administrative structures in oral and written times, and with a powerful class of farmers to be taken into consideration, we should expect that the vernacular would be employed as an administrative language at the time when writing was first put to use, especially in areas where this society of farmers was party to the case. In the whole of Scandinavia as well as in the Scandinavian settlements elsewhere, social organization in the preliterate period was such that we should expect the vernacular to be the administrative language. There are, however, differences between Norway and Iceland on the one hand, and Sweden and Denmark on the other. In both places the laws were written down in the vernacular, but while laws in Norway and Iceland were written down very early, in Norway this took place most likely in the last quarter of the eleventh century and in Iceland in the winter 1117/18. The laws of Sweden and Denmark were put into writing much later. Both Church and King used Latin when corresponding with figures outside the Scandinavian-speaking areas, but while letters in Iceland and Norway with local addressees were written in the vernacular, in Sweden and Denmark Latin was used in such letters for a long time.[13]

The writing down of laws in Norway and Iceland was so early that it might have made a considerable contribution to the formation of a solid basis for the later written culture in the vernacular. The much stronger position of the vernacular in the writing of letters in Norway and Iceland in comparison to the neighbouring countries may also partly be the result of the position (and prestige) the vernacular had already achieved as the language of written laws.

---

[13] For more on this topic see Melve, 'Letters, Networks and Public Opinion in Medieval Norway, 1024–1263', and Wellendorf, 'Letters from Kings: Epistolary Communication in the Kings' Sagas (until *c.* 1150)', in this book.

It is difficult to say to what degree these differences in administrative use of the vernacular, between Norway and Iceland on the one hand and Sweden and Denmark on the other, are connected to cultural or structural variations in their respective oral societies. It has been suggested that the early use of the vernacular as an administrative language in Norway should be seen in connection with the consolidation of the Norwegian state taking place earlier than in the two other countries.[14] Whether Norway really underwent consolidation earlier than Denmark is a matter of discussion, and an early consolidation of the Norwegian state does not explain why Iceland followed Norway in the use of the vernacular for administrative purposes.

It was of course practical in many ways to have laws, and all types of legal documents, in writing. A letter from the king read aloud to the addressees could make a greater impression than the words of a messenger, and to be seen as literate would probably lend honour to the king and his administration. From *Íslendingabók*, we can see that the writing of laws in Iceland was accompanied by a simultaneous major revision of the laws. If the same thing happened in Norway, the king could have viewed the process of transcribing the laws as his opportunity to exert influence over them. In the laws as we have them, fines are used more frequently in Icelandic and Norwegian laws than in Swedish and Danish,[15] and that is certainly a factor that would have interested both the king in Norway and the Norwegian and Icelandic Church, since they often received money from the fines. Whichever conditions led to early writing down of laws in Norway and Iceland, they also promoted later writing in the vernacular.

Education, Schools, and Centres of Writing

The ability to obtain knowledge and transfer it to the next generation was a skill crucial to all oral societies to enable their culture to survive and to grow. Practical knowledge about how things should be done in everyday life was vital, and new generations would learn such skills by working with and imitating the adults. In Old Norse society, where there were sharp divisions between men's and women's work, young boys would learn practical knowledge from men as did young girls from women. However, transmission of wisdom such as the

---

[14] For a thorough discussion of this topic, see Bagge, *From Viking Stronghold to Christian Kingdom*, especially the chapters 'Justice, Law and Power' and 'Royal and Ecclesiastical Administration'.

[15] See Imsen, 'Straff'.

knowledge of the past, oral art forms, family traditions and genealogy, and the writing and reading of runes, were less divided along gender lines. In Old Norse society, as in other societies, it was women's responsibility to care for children. To what degree did women's care and concern for the children's upbringing also include education in topics such as those just mentioned? We do not know much about this, but the Icelandic sources occasionally mention that children or young people were taught by their mothers or other women.[16] Since women were mainly responsible for child-rearing, the level of their knowledge dictates a great deal regarding the basic education of children.

In Christian times, young boys were sent to schools to be educated for the priesthood. In European Christian societies, schools and education were in the hands of Church institutions such as episcopal sees and convents, and centres of writing were connected to the same institutions as well as to the courts of kings and princes. This was also the case in the Scandinavian kingdoms. Iceland had no king, and here the development of centres of writing was therefore slightly different. The Norwegian king Óláfr Tryggvason was admittedly given the honour of having Christianized Iceland, but in reality it was Icelandic chieftains who took the lead in the Christianization process and in Church organization. The absence of a king may even have given more scope for the chieftains — and perhaps have opened the way for a competition between them — to build their private churches and work to establish the Icelandic Church. Chieftains and powerful farmers had churches erected on their farms, and in some cases they were educated and ordained as priests in their own churches. The first Icelandic bishopric, Skálholt, was established in 1056 on the farm of the chieftain elected bishop, and monasteries were also founded by men belonging to the same influential and wealthy families. The two bishoprics (Hólar was established in 1106) and the monasteries became important centres of writing and learning. Thus far Iceland followed the normal pattern, but there were also differences. As early as in the eleventh century, some chieftains who had built churches on their farms set up schools there as well.[17] These schools played a very important part in the cultural life of the country. Another Icelandic special arrangement must also be mentioned. Probably as a consequence of the introduction of tithes, many

[16] In *Þorláks saga byskups in elzta*, ch. 6, it is recorded that the bishop in his youth was taught *ættvísi ok mannfræði* (genealogy and knowledge about people) by his mother. In *Eiríks saga rauða*, ch. 4, there is a description of a cultic ritual, and as part of it a woman performs a poem which she says she had learned from her foster-mother.

[17] Examples of such early centres of learning are Haukadalr and Oddi where Ari fróði and Snorri Sturluson respectively were educated.

chieftains who had built churches on their farms transferred their churches, including the farms, to a foundation in which the church owned itself. The previous owner could, however, continue to live on the farm and secure himself and his heirs control over the church and its income. These institutions, which were called *staðir*, would be small — though sometimes larger — church centres with several clerics.[18] Schools were occasionally connected to these institutions, and some of them developed into important centres of writing and learning, such as Reykholt in Snorri's time, but even the less important *staðir* would host a number of learned and literate people.

The schools on chieftains' farms have often been mentioned as unique to Iceland. On one hand they were, but on the other hand they can perhaps be seen as not so exceptional when compared to the other centres of learning in Iceland: like the first bishopric, the convents, and *staðir*, these schools were established by men belonging to the chieftain class, and what was taught at the chieftains' farm schools was not necessarily very different from what was taught at a bishopric's school.

What was specific to Iceland, however, was that the establishment of schools at chieftains' farms and the foundation of the many *staðir* all over Iceland — in addition to the 'normal' schools connected to bishoprics and monasteries — resulted in many small milieux where there were a number of people who could read and write. Many were so small that they should perhaps not be called centres of writing, but they may still have been influential. Multiple small centres of writing dispersed throughout the country could spread literacy among the population more effectively than a handful of big centres few and far between.

In the many small literary milieux that developed in Iceland in a rural society, there may have been an inclination to use the vernacular more often and in more situations than in schools connected to important ecclesiastical centres. As Guðrún Nordal has convincingly argued, skaldic poetry could replace Latin poetry in schools in Iceland, most likely from early on.[19] This shows, of course, the strong position of skaldic poetry in Icelandic society, and the use of skaldic poetry instead of Latin poetry as well as the scientific interest in the vernacular demonstrated by the author of the *First Grammatical Treatise* as early as around the middle of the twelfth century, show the strong position of the vernacular.

---

[18] Concerning the Icelandic institution *staðr*, see Magnús Stefánsson, *Staðir og staðamál*, esp. ch. 11, 'Den islandske staden'. A discussion of how a *staðr* should be defined is found in Benedikt Eyþórsson, 'History of the Icelandic Church'.

[19] Guðrún Nordal, *Tools of Literacy*, especially the chapter 'Dróttkvætt and the Study of Grammatica'.

The use of the vernacular in schools should probably be seen in connection with the type of schools — small, learned milieux in a rural society. It is difficult to say what is cause and what is effect, but in any case, the strong position of the vernacular in schools would in all likelihood result in a spread of literacy extending beyond Latin's orbit, and would build a solid foundation for the development of a literature in the vernacular.

Recruitment to the Clergy

Clergy were important to the spread of literacy everywhere, yet in Iceland there may have been special conditions associated with the clergy that promoted the spread of literacy.

The Norwegian *Older Gulathing law* (ch. 15) states that priests should no longer be beaten for an infraction; rather, they should pay a fine instead. Since only slaves could be beaten in Old Norse society, this statement in the law has been interpreted as saying that in the earliest Christian period many priests were recruited from the class of slaves, but that later this practice ended. In a letter from the pope in 1078, the pope asked King Óláfr kyrri to send young men of good families to Rome for education,[20] and it is obvious that at least church leaders later came from leading families, but we know very little of the social background of ordinary priests.

The sources are richer for Iceland. Priests recruited from among slaves in the earliest Christian period are not mentioned in Icelandic sources, yet this cannot be ruled out since it happened in Norway. From later written sources we know that young men from leading Icelandic families studied abroad as early as in the eleventh century: Ísleifr, who became the first bishop in Skálholt (1056), had studied at Herford (Saxen); and Sæmundr fróði, who was born in 1056, studied in France, most likely in Paris. After returning home, he founded a centre of learning at his farm in Oddi. Icelandic sources, for example bishops' sagas and *Sturlunga saga*, give the impression that several priests in Iceland were recruited from the mightiest families in society. However, the literary sources focus much more on the chieftains and the upper strata of society than on poor farmers and ordinary priests, and therefore the sources may give the impression that the number of priests from chieftain families was higher than it really was.

There is a list containing forty names of priests, ten from each quarter of the country, dating from the time of Ari fróði. The list has the heading: 'Þessi

---

[20] See *Regesta Norwegica I*, ed. by Gunnes, no. 50, p. 40.

eru nǫfn nǫkkura presta kynborinna íslenzkra' (These are the names of some highborn Icelandic priests).[21] It is difficult to say exactly what the word *kynborinn* means here. Originally the meaning was 'freeborn', but in Ari's time and later the meaning was more that of 'highborn' or 'of good family'. The exact meaning is unclear, and it is likely that the list also includes priests from the families of big farmers. The wording of the heading indicates that the list of highborn priest is not complete, and the fact that the list mentions exactly ten priests from each quarter points in the same direction. The total number of priests who were regarded as from good families may therefore have been a little higher than forty. We do not know the total number of priests in Iceland in Ari's time, but we know that bishop Páll in Skálholt (bishop 1195–1211) estimated the need of priests in his bishopric to be 190.[22] The number of priests in Hólar bishopric must have been at least half of the number in the southern bishopric. Even if we take into consideration that the number of priests had increased in the period between Ari fróði and Bishop Páll, and that the number of highborn priests in Ari's time was higher than forty, it seems safe to conclude that the majority of Icelandic priests were not highborn, and among those most were probably sons of ordinary farmers, neither wealthy nor very poor. Such individuals could, for example, work as priests at a farmer-owned church, and they would be paid for their work.

There was in Iceland, however, also a third group of priests. A church-owner could make a contract with a young man, or with his family if the young man was under sixteen years old. The church-owner would agree to pay for his education and as repayment the young man was required to do lifetime service as priest for that church-owner. These priests were called *kirkjuprestar* (church priests), and in reality they shared much with slaves and could be brought back in the same way as other slaves if they tried to run away. Lowborn and poor, they were born free; that we can see from the fact that the church-owner had to make a legal contract with them. These priests are never mentioned in the sagas, only in Icelandic laws from the Free State period, and we do not know how many they were or in which period they were found.[23]

Even though it is impossible to say how great a percentage of Icelandic priests were highborn, lowborn, or from the middle stratum of society, we know

---

[21] The manuscript containing the list is printed in *Diplomatarium Islandicum* I, no. 29, pp. 185–86.

[22] *Páls saga byskups*, ed. by Ásdís Egilsdóttir, p. 313.

[23] For more about these priests, see Mundal, 'At læra prest til kirkju'.

enough to say that priests were recruited from all levels of society. This may be important for the spread of literacy. Highborn priests had honour and social standing beforehand, and becoming a priest would probably not add much to this, though learning would have given an advantage. Since there would always be competition between chieftain families, to have educated men among the members of a family could easily become a factor that generated competitive 'pressure' on other families of the same social standing to see to it that young men in the family were educated.

The fact that many chieftains and rich farmers were educated priests likely added to the honour of the clergy, and this must have made education attractive to young men — and their families — who wanted to rise in society. Sons of ordinary farmers could improve their own social standing, as well as the social standing of their family, by becoming priests. The lowborn did not have much honour to gain by becoming priests, but the interesting question concerning these priests is what it meant for the spread of literacy when the lowest-born members of society became literate. They may have taught family members and other lowborn people how to read and write. However, the ways a lowborn priest's literacy affected the members of the church-owner's family and other people in the surroundings is a more important question. Is it possible that the lowest-born household member's literacy would exert pressure and motivate those around him to become literate?

Social Mobility

Social differences and the possibilities for social mobility — or lack thereof — in a certain culture may have been one of the factors that could influence the development of later written culture. Did a society open to social mobility make learning attractive to a larger part of the population than a society in which social mobility was restricted?

Both Norway and Iceland were socially hierarchical, but both societies were to some degree open to social mobility, Iceland probably more so than Norway. One indication of this is that while Norwegian society was divided into different social groups by law, an Icelander's social standing was negotiable.

According to the Norwegian laws, the number of social groups, as well as the terms for them, varied from one district of the country to another. If we take the Norwegian *Older Gulathing law* as an example, we find the slave at the bottom of society with no, or very few, legal rights. The position of the freed slave was slightly better, and the position of the freed slave's offspring even better again. The standard for comparison of legal status (and rights) in society was that of the *bóndi*, or fully free farmer, and at the top of this farmer society was the *hǫldr*, who belonged to a family that had owned the land they occupied for a long period of time. The different status of social groups is reflected, for instance, in the size of fines and compensations. The normal compensation that a freed slave was entitled to if he were attacked or wounded was, according to the *Older Gulathing law*, 6 *aurar*, with his son entitled to 1 *mǫrk* (1 *mǫrk* = 8 *aurar*), the *bóndi* to 12 *aurar*, and the *hǫldr* to 3 *merkr* (*merkr* is pl. of *mǫrk*). In the laws of eastern Norway, the *Older Eiðsivathing law* and the *Older Borgarthing law*, of which only the Christian section of the laws are preserved, the social group above descendants of slaves, that of the fully free farmers, was not divided into two: there was only one group called *hǫldar* (pl. of *hǫldr*). In the *Older Frostathing law*, farmer society was divided into two as in the *Older Gulathing law*, with the upper strata referred to as *hǫldar*, and the lower as *árbárnir menn*. Between the fully free farmers and the descendants of slaves there was a group called *rekspegnir*. We do not know for certain who they were, though one possibility is that they were nomadic Sami. In the Norwegian laws, there was also a social group above the farmer society, the *lendrmenn*, in the service of the king. Their social standing, as measured by the size of fines and compensations, was twice as high as the position of the *hǫldr*. Money and time could help to improve one's social standing. A slave could be given freedom, or he could buy freedom for himself, and thereby improve his social status. His offspring could buy themselves a farm — if they were lucky — and after some generations obtain the status of a *bóndi*. Some generations later it would even, in theory, be possible to climb to the top of farmer society and become a *hǫldr*.

In Icelandic society there were, according to the law of the Free State, no social divisions above the group consisting of slaves' descendants. The personal right (*fullrétti*), the compensation a man would get if attacked or wounded, would be the same for all free men, and there was only one standard *mannbót*, 'the compensation for killing a free man'. However, in reality, as in the descriptions of society in the written sagas from the thirteenth century, the compensation would vary from one case to another, and could consist of both two and three *mannbœtr* (pl. of *mannbót*). The amount of compensation for some of the saga heroes of the past may have been exaggerated to increase their honour. There is, however, no reason to doubt this general picture: namely, that Icelanders' honour and social status were to a high degree determined individually, and that factors other than family background — for instance, a person's skills and capability — would determine social status.

Before the time of Christianization and the arrival of writing, the king had represented an institution that could offer improved social status to its followers, both Norwegians and Icelanders, for the court of the Norwegian king was open both to his own countrymen and to the Icelanders. The *lendrmenn* who took land as a fief from the king in return for their services, would, as we have seen, manage to climb to the very top of society — only the earl, and in Christian times the bishop, would be above them, and over the earl and bishop again, the king. The *lendrmaðr* obtained his position as a personal reward for service to the king. That can clearly be seen from the fact that the social status of the *landrmaðr*'s son, if he did not become a *lendrmaðr* himself, would be that of the *hǫldr*. The personal right of the king's *stallari*, 'the leader of the king's court', would be the same as that of the *lendrmaðr*, the personal right of a *skutilsveinn* would be identical to that of the *hǫldr*, and even in cases where the personal right of a man would not change (for instance if a *hǫldr* became a *skutilsveinn*) there would be honour to gain by becoming a member of the king's court.

There were also men in the king's service whose social status was rather low: namely, the king's *ármaðr*. The meaning of the word is 'servant', and the *ármaðr* is in a few places mentioned in the laws in connection with slaves. Both this fact and the descriptions of *ármenn* in kings' sagas seem to support the theory that these men in the king's service, whose main task in the beginning was probably to run the king's farm, were recruited from among the lower strata of society. However, even if the social status of the *ármaðr* in the king's service never became a high one, it is of no doubt that to go into the service of the king would improve a poor man's social status considerably, and the status of the *ármaðr* was probably improving during the Middle Ages until the *sýslumaðr* took over his administrative functions.

A person's abilities and skills may also have helped him to rise in society. To be a good *skáld*, for instance, was something that could provide entrance to the circles around the king.

To enter into the king's court or the king's service would offer the opportunity for social climbing in addition to the possibilities that existed within farmer society. These possibilities were primarily open to Norwegians but also to Icelanders. It is, however, difficult to say how much social mobility the highly competitive positions in the king's service may have led to. A son of a *lendmaðr* would probably have better chances than others to become a *lendrmaðr*, and an *ármaðr* would never climb very high, but in the circles around the king and in the king's service there would be possibilities for some social advancement, especially in periods with political struggle. However, the number of persons who would be able to improve their social position by joining the court or by going into the king's service would be relatively low.

The Church offered a new possibility for social climbing. After Christianization, a great number of new priests were needed. Later, when the monasteries were established, monks — and some nuns too — would go to these institutions for a life very different from the one they knew before, and as the Church and the king started to build up their administration, a great number of clerics were needed. As already argued, men belonging to the upper strata of society would probably not significantly improve their social standing by entering the Church, and for some priests (*kirkjuprestar*) becoming a priest would not mean social advancement. However, for the majority of priests the Church would offer a possibility of social climbing, and the more open a society was to social mobility the higher it would be possible to climb. What would be required of all those in the service of the Church was that they learn Latin and how to read and write. The fact that learning made social climbing a realistic possibility for many people in a society open to social mobility would make literacy attractive and promote its diffusion in society.

The Importance of Oral Genres and Art Forms

It is reasonable that a society in which a number of oral art forms flourished in the preliterate period was more likely to develop a rich literary culture with thriving centres of writing than societies with a poorer oral culture. The oral culture, and not only the oral culture that existed before the arrival of writing but the oral culture that continued to exist in an oral-written continuum, formed a reservoir in which the writer could find subject matter and inspiration. The co-existence of the two cultures supported each other.

Eddic poetry is preserved only in Icelandic manuscripts, but there are reasons to believe that this poetry was known in Norway, and at least partly in the rest of Scandinavia.[24] Skaldic poetry was included in kings' sagas both in Iceland and in Norway, and even though skaldic tradition was especially strong in Iceland, skaldic stanzas written on rune sticks found in excavations at Bryggen in Bergen in the 1970s show us that skaldic poetry continued to flour-

---

[24] The eddic poem *Hávamál* is quoted by the Norwegian skald Eyvindr Finnsson in his memorial poem to Hákon inn góði, *Hákonarmál*; A stanza in eddic metre is found on the rune stone from Rök (Östergötland) from the ninth century; motifs known from the poems about Sigurðr fáfnisbani are found both on Norwegian church doors and on picture stones from other parts of Scandinavia; and finally motifs from both heroic and mythological eddic poems are found in ballads in the Scandinavian countries, something that indicates that the two genres overlapped in time.

ish in Norway longer than previously believed. Skaldic poetry was an extremely demanding oral genre and bears witness to a high intellectual level in Old Norse society, which in itself formed a good basis for a written culture. Oral tradition about kings, probably supported by skaldic stanzas, must have existed in Norway, Iceland, and Denmark, and most likely in Sweden even though Swedish tradition is documented to a lesser degree through later written works. The *fornaldarsǫgur* (sagas about the ancient past) were written in Iceland, but oral tradition of the same type as that which the authors of the *fornaldarsǫgur* built on must have existed in the rest of Scandinavia, especially in Norway, since some Scandinavian ballads share many motifs with this saga genre.[25]

Both Saxo Grammaticus, the author of the Danish Latin chronicle *Gesta Danorum*, and Theodoricus, the author of the Norwegian Latin chronicle *Historia de antiquitate regum Norwagiensium*, both writing in the late twelfth century, mention in their introductions that they had access to traditions from Icelanders, who knew more than others about the old days. Even though oral art forms that could have formed a good basis for a later written culture probably existed throughout Scandinavia, Icelanders seem to have had a special reputation as bearers of tradition. Finally, there is one type of tradition that for good reason was unique to Iceland: the tradition of settling a new land and forming a new nation, which stimulated the generation and dissemination of new narratives about the past, as I will discuss below. It is still worth noting that even though the existence of oral art forms might be an important basis for a rich written culture later on, there is nothing which indicates that the cultivation of oral genres would automatically lead to a later, rich written culture.

Remembering the Past in New Settlements

In all oral societies it must have been important to remember the past. However, in a new settlement like Iceland, remembering the past was in all likelihood even more significant than it had been in the old homeland. The settlers' search for roots was mentioned as important for the development of oral tradition, which later formed the basis for written literature already in the early phases of saga research. History has, however, shown that searching for roots is very common in a society of settlers, and this old idea may still be valid.

Departure from the place where the family had lived from time immemorial and settlement in a new location far from the old homeland was a break in his-

---

[25] See Liestøl, *Norske trollvisor*.

tory, a great divide that was much easier to remember than most other events in the history of a family or a people. Most importantly, this epoch-making event resulted in a large number of stories about the settlers in Iceland that had to be told to new generations.

How important the knowledge of the past was for the Icelanders and their self-awareness is clearly expressed in a text that was probably part of the introduction to an older, lost version of *Landnámabók*:

> Þat er margra manna mál, at þat sé óskyldr fróðleikr at rita landnám. En vér þykjumsk heldr svara kunna útlendum mǫnnum, þá er þeir bregða oss því, at vér séim komnir af þrælum eða illmennum, ef vér vitum víst várar kynferðir sannar[26]
>
> (People often say that writing about the settlement is irrelevant learning, but we think we can better meet the criticism of foreigners when they accuse us of being descended from slaves or scoundrels, if we knew for certain the truth about our ancestry.)

This statement (also discussed in Mulligan's chapter below) of the importance of knowing about the settlement and the past has consequences extending far beyond *Landnámabók*. The whole genre of the sagas of Icelanders also deals with the settlement, and if it was necessary to write about it in the thirteenth century, it was also necessary to tell about it in the oral period.

One further factor might have had an impact on whom oral tradition was attached to and about whom sagas were later written. In the Scandinavian kingdoms, important events that formed the history of the people were in most cases attached to kings, and probably earls. The Old Norse settlements in the Orkneys were ruled by earls, and here sagas about the earls were eventually produced. Iceland was not ruled by kings or earls, and this lack of a ruling dynasty may have made it easier to attach stories, and later written sagas, to chieftains and farmers who, in the absence of a king, became the bearers of the history of the new settlement. The same can be said about the Faroe Islands. The history of the islands as we have it in *Færeyinga saga* is the history of two of the most important families on the islands. The saga is in all likelihood written in Iceland, but the author must have built on Faroese tradition.

---

[26] *Landnámabók*, ed. by Jakob Benediktsson, pt 2, p. 336, note. The text is preserved in the young manuscript Þórðarbók from the seventeenth century, and Þórðarbók takes its text from a manuscript of the Melabók redaction (Melabók was written in the late thirteenth century). The Melabók introduction from which the quotation on writing about settlement was most likely taken, originally came from the now lost Styrmisbók composed early in the thirteenth century, in the same period during which many sagas of Icelanders were written.

The absence of a king may also partly explain why there were sagas written about the bishops in Iceland. Two of the early sagas about Icelandic bishops were written about bishops venerated as saints, Jón and Þorlákr, and their sagas are written as legends. Later sagas about Icelandic bishops were most likely inspired by the bishop legends. Owing to the absence of a king, the Icelandic bishoprics were state-bearing institutions, which made the bishops suitable subjects for written texts. In Adam of Bremen's *Gesta Hammaburgensis ecclesiae pontificum*, Book IV, ch. 36, the author says that the Icelanders regarded the bishop as their king, and in the bishop-saga *Hungrvaka*, ch. 5, it is written of Bishop Gizurr that he was both king and bishop of the country as long as he lived. In Ari fróði's *Íslendingabók*, which is the first history of Iceland, there is no doubt that the Church is presented as the state-bearing institution, and the bishops may therefore have served as the focus for narratives in more or less the same way as a king in a kingdom.

Conclusion

It is not possible to single out one factor that was more decisive for the development of written culture than others. The cultural milieu favourable for a development of a rich written culture which put oral genres into writing, adopted European genres and developed new ones, as occurred in Iceland in particular, seems to have been the result of a fortunate combination of many factors. The full Scandinavian-speaking area was characterized by certain cultural traits that must have been favourable for the development of written culture, but the factors that are specific to Iceland, the many small centres of learning and spread of writing throughout the country, priests recruited from all social levels, a society relatively open to social mobility, and the fact that Iceland was a society of settlers, are factors that in combination with others may have started a cultural growth unparalleled in any other medieval rural community. The early writing down of laws in the vernacular may have promoted the use of the vernacular in other contexts, and the spread of literacy in society among people who did not read Latin generated a demand for literature in the vernacular.

Works Cited

Primary Sources

Diplomatarium Islandicum – Íslenzkt fornbréfasafn I, ed. by Jón Sigurðsson, 16 vols (Kaupmannahöfn: Hið íslenzka bókmentafélag, 1857–72)

Eddukvæði, ed. by Jónas Kristjánsson and Vésteinn Ólason, Íslenzk fornrit, 2 vols (Reykjavík: Hið íslenzka fornritafélag, 2014)

Egils saga Skalla-Grímssonar, ed. by Sigurður Nordal, Íslenzk fornrit, 2 (Reykjavík: Hið íslenzka fornritafélag, 1933)

Eiríks saga rauða, ed. by Einar Ól. Sveinsson and Matthías Þórðarson, Íslenzk fornrit, 4 (Reykjavík: Hið íslenzka fornritafélag, 1935)

Gesta Hammaburgensis ecclesiae pontificum, ed. by Bernhard Schneidler *Hamburgische Kirchengeschichte = Magisteri Adam Bremensis Gesta Hammaburgensis ecclesiae pontificum* (Hannover: Hahn, 1917)

Historia de antiquitate regum Norwagiensium, ed. by Gustav Storm, Monumenta historica norvegiæ: Latinske kildeskrifter til Norges historie i middelalderen (Kristiania: Brögger, 1880)

Hungrvaka, in *Biskupa sögur II*, ed. by Ásdís Egilsdóttir, Íslenzk fornrit, 16 (Reykjavík: Hið íslenzka fornritafélag, 2002), pp. 1–43

Íslendingabók; Landnámabók, ed. by Jakob Benediktsson, Íslenzk fornrit, 1 (Reykjavík: Hið íslenzka fornritafélag, 1968)

Older Borgarthing law = Den ældre Borgarthings—eller Vikens Christenrett, in *Norges gamle Love indtil 1387 I*, ed. by Rudolf Keyser and Peter A. Munch (Christiania: Chr. Gröndahl, 1846), pp. 337–72

Older Eidsivathing law = Den ældre Eidsivathings Christenret, in *Norges gamle Love indtil 1387 I*, ed. by Rudolf Keyser and Peter A. Munch (Christiania: Chr. Gröndahl, 1846), pp. 373–406

Older Frostathing law = Den ældre Frostathings-Lov, in *Norges gamle Love indtil 1387 I*, ed. by Rudolf Keyser and Peter A. Munch (Christiania: Chr. Gröndahl, 1846), pp. 119–258

Older Gulathing law = Den ældre Gulathings-Lov, in *Norges gamle Love indtil 1387 I*, ed. by Rudolf Keyser and Peter A. Munch (Christiania: Chr. Gröndahl, 1846), pp. 1–118

Páls saga byskups, in *Biskupa sögur II*, ed. by Ásdís Egilsdóttir, Íslenzk fornrit, 16 (Reykjavík: Hið íslenzka fornritafélag, 2002), pp. 295–332

Regesta Norvegica I, ed. by Erik Gunnes (Oslo: Norsk historisk Kjeldeskrift-institutt, 1989)

Saxo Grammaticus, *Gesta Danorum*, ed. by Karsten Friis-Jensen and Peter Zeeberg, 2 vols (Copenhagen: Det Danske Sprog-og Litteraturselskab & Gads Forlag, 2005)

Snorri Sturluson, *Edda. Prologue and Gylfaginning*, ed. by Anthony Faulkes (London: Viking Society for Northern Research/University College of London, 1988)

——, *Edda. Skáldskaparmál*, I: *Introduction: Text and Notes*, ed. by Anthony Faulkes (London: Viking Society for Northern Research/University College of London, 1998)

Sturlunga saga, ed. by Örnólfur Thorsson, 3 vols (Reykjavík: Svart á hvítu, 1988)
Þorláks saga byskups in elzta, in *Biskupa sögur II*, ed. by Ásdís Egilsdóttir, Íslenzk fornrit, 16 (Reykjavík: Hið íslenzka fornritafélag, 2002), pp. 45–99

Secondary Studies

Åhlén, Marit, 'Runinskrifter i Hälsingland', *Hälsinglands bebyggelse före 1600, Bebyggelse-historisk tidskrift*, 27 (1994), 33–49
Baetke, Walter, *Über die Entstehung der Isländersagas*, Sitzungsberichte der Sächischen Akademie der Wissenschaften zu Leipzig, Philologisch-historische Klasse, 98.6 (Berlin: Akademie, 1956)
Bagge, Sverre, *From Viking Stronghold to Christian Kingdom: State Formation in Norway, c. 900–1350* (Copenhagen: Museum Tusculanum Press, 2010)
Benedikt Eyþórsson, 'History of the Icelandic Church, 1000–1300: Status and Research', in *Church Centres: Church Centres in Iceland from the 11th to the 13th Century and their Parellels in Other Countries*, ed. by Helgi Þorláksson (Reykholt: Snorrastofa, 2005), pp. 19–69
Foley, John Miles, *The Singer of Tales in Performance*, Voices in Performance and Text (Bloomington: Indiana University Press, 1995)
——, *Traditional Oral Epic: The 'Odyssey', 'Beowulf', and the Serbo-Croation Return Song* (Berkeley: University of California Press, 1990)
Guðrún Nordal, *Tools of Literacy: The Role of Skaldic Verse in Icelandic Textual Culture of the Twelfth and Thirteenth Centuries* (Toronto: University of Toronto Press, 2001)
Hagland, Jan Ragnar, 'Høgmellomalderens bruk av runer — ekte tradisjon frå nordisk fortid, eller kyrkjeleg inspirert renessansefenomen?', in *Den nordiske renessansen i høymiddelalderen*, ed. by Jón Viðar Sigurðsson and Preben Meulengracht Sørensen, Tid og tanke, 6 (Oslo: Historisk institutt, Universitetet i Oslo, 2000), pp. 37–46
Imsen, Steinar, 'Straff', *Kulturhistorisk leksikon for nordisk middelalder*, 21 (supp.) (1977), 318–25
Liestøl, Knut, *Norske trollvisor og norrøne sogor* (Kristiania: Norlis, 1915)
Magnús Stefánsson, *Staðir og staðamál: Studier i islandske egenkirkelige og beneficialrett-slige forhold i middelanderen*, Skrifter, 4 (Bergen: Historisk institutt, Universitetet i Bergen, 2000)
Mundal, Else, 'At læra prest til kirkju: Islandske prestar i ufridom', in *Kyrklig rätt och kyrklig orätt — Kyrkorättsliga Perspectiv: Festskrift till professor Bertil Nilsson*, ed. by Martin Berntson and Anna Minara Ciardi, Bibliotheca Theologiae Practicae, 97 (Uppsala: Artos, 2016), pp. 277–88
——, 'Íslendingabók vurdert som bispestolskrønike'. *Alvíssmál*, 3 (1994), 63–72
Quinn, Judy, 'Liquid Knowledge: Traditional Conceptualisation of Learning in Eddic Poetry', in *Along the Oral-Written Continuum: Types of Texts, Relations and their Implications*, ed. by Slavica Ranković with Leidulf Melve and Else Mundal, Utrecht Studies in Medieval Literacy (Turnhout: Brepols, 2010), pp. 183–226

Schier, Kurt, 'Anfänge und erste Entwicklung der Literatur in Island und Schweden: Wie beginnt Literatur in einer schriftlosen Gesellschaft?', in *Schriften der Sudetendeutschen Akademie der Wissenschaften und Künste*, Forschungsbeiträge der Wissenschaftliche Klasse (München: Verlaghaus Sudetenland, 1991), x, 103–49

Seim, Karin Fjellhammer, 'Runologi', in *Handbok i norrøn filologi*, ed. by Odd Einar Haugen, 2nd edn (Bergen: Fagbokforlaget Vigmostad & Bjørke, 2013), pp. 128–93

Sigurður Nordal, 'Time and Vellum', *Annual Bulletin of the Modern Humanities Research Association*, 24 (1952), 15–26

CREATING ABSENCE:
THE REPRESENTATION OF WRITING
IN EARLY HISTORIES OF THE NORTH

Aidan Conti

I n the absence of first-hand accounts and ethnographic observation, it is difficult to estimate the extent to which the introduction of Roman writing led to or was perceived to have led to a transformation in ways of thinking and social roles in Europe's northern periphery.[1] Nevertheless, recent research indicates a demonstrable pattern in the way in which writing practices and literary production developed after the adoption of Christianity in Northern and eastern Central Europe in the years around the turn of the first millennium. As Christianity became firmly entrenched — that is, after the nominal adoption of the religion, the subsequent importation of practices, books, and culture (sometimes coming together in the form of translations of Christian stories and teaching) — local contingents, often trained abroad, began to compose myth and legend-creating works in the new language of religion that graphed a local people into the universal fold, at the same time bolstering the credentials of the

---

[1] Much contemporary work refuses to posit a direct link between literacy per se and cognitive and social change. Scribner and Cole (*The Psychology of Literacy*, esp. pp. 218 and 132) found that literacy was not a prime mover in social change, but rather education, that is, the application of literacy towards particular social aims. Indeed, it is often difficult literacy from its social institutions; for example, schooling is (most often) a literate institution (see Olson, *The World on Paper*, esp. p. 44).

Aidan Conti (aidan.conti@uib.no) is Professor of Medieval Latin in the Department of Linguistic, Literary, and Aesthetic Studies at the University of Bergen.

Moving Words in the Nordic Middle Ages: Tracing Literacies, Texts, and Verbal Communities, ed. by Amy C. Mulligan and Else Mundal, AS 8   BREPOLS 🖳 PUBLISHERS   (Turnhout: Brepols, 2019)
pp. 61–80   10.1484/M.AS-EB.5.116620

ecclesiastical institutions that bridged the two worlds.[2] As part of this process, in the second half of the twelfth century three works — two from Norway and one from Denmark — claim to represent the first attempts to write the history of the polities from which they emerge: namely the anonymous *Historia Norwegie* (from the third quarter of the twelfth century, possibly between 1160 and 1175),[3] Theodoricus Monachus's *Historia de antiquitate regum Norwagiensium* (written between 1177 and 1188, believably in 1177–78),[4] and Sven Aggesen's *Brevis historia regum dacie* (from 1186 to 1187).[5] As self-styled first attempts at histories of their respective peoples and royal lines, these works offer early opportunities to hear local authorial voices, and not surprisingly a fair amount of scholarship has probed their accuracy, reliability, erudition, and aims.[6] Taking a different tack, this essay will examine how these voices employ (or do not employ) the rhetoric of writing and, in looking at the role of writing in the individual works, will endeavour to suggest the different attitudes towards the reception of Latin writing in the north.

Such an approach to reading these works does not posit a great transformation, divide, or distinction between oral and written culture which has long been recognized as untenable. However, the rhetoric on writing in the works themselves, especially the self-awareness of being 'first', suggests tensions

---

[2] On this phenomenon, see Mortensen, 'Sanctified Beginnings and Mythopoietic Moments'. On the development and interaction between native and imported works from a formalist point of departure, see the various incarnations of publications by Itamar Even-Zohar under 'polysystem studies'.

[3] *Historia Norwegie*, ed. by Ekrem and Mortensen. Subsequent references cite by book and section number.

[4] Theodoricus Monachus, *Historia de antiquitate regum Norwagiensium* ed. by Gustav Storm. Subsequent references cite chapter number following by page and line numbers in parentheses. Egil Kraggerud's new editon (2018) of Theodoricus appeared too late to be taken into consideration for this publication, but will undoubtedly serve as the reference text for the future.

[5] Sven Aggesen, *Brevis historia regum dacie*, ed. by Martin Claurentius Gertz. Subsequent references cite by chapter number (with page numbers in parentheses) from the X-version.

[6] For an overview of Theodoricus, see Bagge, 'Theodoricus Monachus: Clerical Historiography', as well as the survey in the introduction to the translation by McDougall and McDougall in Theodoricus Monachus, *An Account of the Ancient History of the Norwegian Kings*, pp. vii–xxx. Recent overviews on these issues in Sven Aggesen and the *Historie Norwegie* can be found in a comparison of the two works in Mortensen, '*Historia Norwegie* and Sven Aggesen'. Further details on the *Historia Norwegie* can be found in Mortensen, 'Introduction'. A thorough account of Sven's life and works is found in Christiansen, 'Introduction'. A recent reassessment of Sven Aggesen's work can be found in Münster-Swendsen, 'The Making of the Danish Court Nobility'.

between contemporary written forms of commemoration and the previous oral practices that these written histories claim to replace, as we will see. While much of the rhetoric strikes us as commonplace and formulaic, when read in juxtaposition, the ways each of these works represents writing reveal striking differences in the way the cultural work of 'writing' could be positioned with respect to the oral. In this light, writing can be received and portrayed as a new form of monumental building, a prescriptive authority that abnegates oral practices, or an open invitation to new hermeneutic horizons.

Naturally, the *Historia Norwegie*, Theodoricus Monachus's *Historia de antiquitate regum Norwagiensium*, and Sven Aggesen's *Brevis historia regum dacie* represent part of a larger constellation of Latin writing in these regions in a period which includes Ælnoth's *Gesta Swegnomagni et passio Kanuti*, the anonymous *Passio Olavi*, the *Profectio Danorum*, and, of course, Saxo's *Gesta Danorum*, all of which form a part of a broader literary sphere that includes the vernacular and less literary production. However, as self-fashioned pioneering endeavours, the *Historia Norwegie*, Theodoricus, and Sven Aggesen can be seen as a distinct subset, even without invoking generic classifications, be they modern or medieval. Of the three, in their preserved states, Theodoricus's work appears most ambitious in length at over fifty pages in its modern edition.

Sven Aggesen's work is about half as long as is the extant part of the *Historia Norwegie*. However, the intended length of the fragmentary *Historia Norwegie* is difficult to ascertain; its scope may have been fairly grand, and it may have been as long as, if not longer than, Theodoricus's work.[7] Comments on writing in all three works are largely found in the prefaces in which the enterprise is explained and justified. Theodoricus's *Historia*, however, persistently evokes writing and its hermeneutic role, giving the work the appearance of greater literary aspiration, but also thereby providing more detailed commentary about writing, its relation to authority and questions of access thereto. For this reason, the *Historia de antiquitate regum Norwagiensium* receives somewhat more attention than Sven Aggesen and the *Historia Norwegie* in the following treatment.

An initial reading of the *Historia Norwegie* exposes many of the commonplace tropes found not only in historical writing but medieval composition more broadly. The address to the dedicatee, the otherwise unidentified Agnellus, evokes familiar themes:

> Tu igitur, o Agnelle, iure didascalico mi prelate, utcumque alii ferant hec mea scripta legentes non rhetorico lepore polita, immo scrupulosis barbarismis implicita,

---

[7] See Mortensen, 'Introduction', p. 10.

gratanter, ut decet amicum, accipito. Neque enim laudis auidus ut cronographus existo, neque uituperii stimulos ut falsidicus exorreo, cum nichil a me de uetustatis serie nouum uel inauditum assumpserim, sed in omnibus seniorum asserciones secutus. Si quid uero nostris temporibus memorie dignum accidisse repperi, hoc ipse addidi, quoniam multorum magnificencias cum suis auctoribus ob scriptorum inopiam a memoria modernorum cotidie elabi perspexi.

(However much, then, others who read this document of mine may say it is unpolished and lacks the charm of eloquence, or indeed accuse it of being tangled up in jagged, barbaric expressions, you, Agnellus, who have been set over me with a teacher's authority, receive it graciously as befits a friend. I do not thirst for fame as a historian, nor do I shudder at the smarts inflicted by those who might brand me a liar, since I have incorporated on my own account nothing new or unheard of from earlier ages, but have followed the statements of my elders in every respect. If I have discovered any happening of our own times worth remembering, I have inserted that fact myself, since I have observed that many men's splendid feats, together with their performers, sink daily into oblivion among our contemporaries owing to the shortage of written records.)[8]

In reiterating the generic concerns of the widespread medieval humility *topos*, the anonymous expresses misgivings that the reader knows have already been set aside, at least to the extent that the work has been completed: 'ad quod poscor, uolens nolens aggredi temptabo' (willing or not I will endeavour to undertake what is demanded).[9] Compelled by the demand, the anonymous text lays out the historic method of the work. It positions itself as writing (which is less obvious than one might think, as we will see in the case of Sven Aggesen), that is, 'mea scripta', at the same time as it identifies oral sources by acknowledging that events from earlier ages follow the spoken statements of elders, 'seniorum asserciones'.

Such oral statements serve the author well enough to buttress the present historical enterprise; nevertheless, according to this rhetorical disposition, contemporary wonders and their authors are at risk of slipping from memory due to the lack of written records ('ob scriptorum inopiam'). This incongruity, whereby former events have been remembered through statements of elders, while contemporary matters risk being forgotten if entrusted to those very same forms of communal memory, stands without further comment; indeed, the very fact that this sleight of hand does not evince some remark suggests its uncontro-

---

[8] *Historia Norwegie*, Prol. 7–9. The translation is Peter Fisher's. In the following, translations by others are noted; otherwise the translations are mine.

[9] *Historia Norwegie*, Prol. 2.

versial nature. While undertaking a written history of the Norwegians is a project which demands authorial self-effacement due to its boldness, there simply is no question that writing is the appropriate medium for this new monument.

Moreover, despite the effort to suggest that nothing new has been added — 'nichil a me de uetustatis serie nouum uel inauditum' — , there is some recognition of the writer's creative role when the recreation of the genealogy of rulers is evoked ('rectorum genealogiam retexere').[10] The reweaving suggests that the writer must select which strands will be included and which will be omitted; the process of narrativization requires a display of some judgement. Yet while one imagines that this weaving grants writing a particular type of authority, that is, one coming from discernment rather than appointment, on the whole it is striking that explicit recourse to written authority is sparse throughout the work. The *Historia* cites Cicero in its opening sentence: 'Tullius in philosophie tractatu suo laudans amicitiam […]'.[11] Later, the text invokes Solinus, although as the editors note, the information more likely comes from Honorius Augustodunensis's *Imago Mundi*, in a rather heavy-handed reference to the written nature of the source: 'in libro suo […] scripsit […] unde scriptum est').[12]

The rather overt naming of Solinus (Honorius) and Cicero notwithstanding, by and large the *Historia Norwegie* does not proclaim its learning or sources aloud. Rather, we can discern certain poetic turns of phrase ultimately deriving from classical poets, but probably known to the anonymous as school adages or common lines. For example, in the presentation of Sami paganism, towards the

---

[10] *Historia Norwegie*, Prol. 3: 'Est enim mihi imperito grauis sarcina situm latissime regionis circumquaque discribere eiusque rectorum genealogiam retexere et aduentum christianitatis simul et paganismi fugam ac utriusque statum exponere' (It is a serious imposition on one as unpractised as myself to be obliged to describe the full extent of this wide-flung region, to recreate the genealogy of its rulers and to reveal both the arrival of Christianity and the expulsion of heathendom, with the present situation of each). The translation is Peter Fisher's.

[11] *Historia Norwegie*, Prol. 1. Admittedly, the citation of Cicero is based on editorial conjecture (one that is eminently acceptable). Nevertheless, it is clear that if not Cicero, the text cites an authority, presumably written and relatively well known at this point.

[12] *Historia Norwegie*, 8. 13: Dixit namque Solinus in libro suo, quem de mundi mirabilibus scripsit, abyssum profundissimam in ipsa terra existere (unde scriptum est: rupti sunt fontes abyssi magnæ); iuxta quam speluncas propatulas uentos aquatica spiracione conceptos in se continere, qui sunt spiritus procellarum (For in his book on the wonders of the universe Solinus has said (*literally:* has written) that there is a vast, yawning pit in the earth itself (whence it is written: 'the fountains of the great deep were broken up'); that by the side of this, unobstructed hollows contain windows engendered by watery exhalations, and these form the breath of storms). The translation is Peter Fisher's.

end of his incantations the magician is 'spumans ora' (foaming at the mouth), a turn of phrase that employs poetic syntax (that is the Greek or poetic accusative in *ora*) as well as diction reminiscent of, but not directly from Vergil.[13] Similarly, when the *Historia* relates wording parallel to that found in Adam of Bremen, there is no explicit reference.[14] And while there are arguments that the author drew on a lost version of Ari's *Íslendingabók*, the *Historia* does not recognize this openly. Rather, the work relies on the foundation of literate and literary schooling, but allows this learning to be assumed rather than announced. As the recent edition notes, 'the narrator appropriates authoritative language rather than quotes it [...]. The technique is more monumental and unified than that of e.g. Theodoricus who often yields the floor to ancient or medieval authorities'.[15] The *Historia Norwegie* presents an example of monumental writing in which the building materials are largely hidden from view so as to allow the structure in its entirety, rather than its method and construction, to impress.

In rather stark contrast to the understated — but ever-present — literate background of the *Historia Norwegie*, Sven Aggesen's compendium places itself in a rather different relation to assessments of oral and written forms of commemoration. Like contemporaries, the *Brevis historia* underscores the primacy of his historical endeavour, but whereas the *Historia Norwegie* noted the lack of writers, Sven's *Historia* reports studying the books of the ancients and recognizing in turn that the achievements of Danish rulers have been consigned to permanent silence:

> Cum ueterum in codicibus contemplatione numerosa priscorum gesta stilo conscripta elegantissimo crebro perspicabar, diurnis suspiraui gemitibus, nostrorum regum seu principum immanissima gesta eterno deputari silentio.
>
> (Often, as I was studying the books of the ancients and the numerous deeds of early times recorded in the most elegant language, I daily lamented in sighs that the mightiest achievements of our own kings and chiefs were consigned to perpetual silence.)[16]

---

[13] See Ekrem and Mortensen, 'Commentary', p. 123 (note to *Historia Norwegie* 4. 19). Similarly, *lippis et tunsoribus liquido apparet* is a medieval school adage based on Horace (see Ekrem and Mortensen, 'Commentary', p. 140, on *Historia Norwegie* 13. 10); and the philosophical passage on the limits of human understanding (*Historie Norwegie* 8. 19–20) has parallels in earlier, near contemporary thought, but does not cite authorities (see Ekrem and Mortensen, 'Commentary', p. 132).

[14] See Ekrem and Mortensen, 'Commentary', p. 111 (on *Historia Norwegie*, Prol. 8).

[15] Mortensen, 'Introduction', p. 27.

[16] Sven Aggesen, *Brevis historia regum dacie*, Proemium (p. 94).

This first sentence, which implicitly ties historical writing to 'giving voice' and overcoming the 'silence' to which Danish rulers had been consigned, marks an important rhetorical gesture, the elaboration of which is continued throughout the work. In many places where one might expect references to writing, the *Brevis historia* uses language that avoids words for the act of writing, such as *scribo*, *exaro*, and writing matter, for example *liber*, *scripta*, *schedulae*. In deliberating whether to write the work, the authorial voice talks not of writing but handing things over to memory, and again reiterates the threat of silence:

> Diu itaque mens mihi fluebat in biuio, utrumnam, notam non declinans arrogantie, stilo licet illepido regum genealogias regnorumque successiones sub compendio memorie commendarem, aut sub silentio cuncta preterirem.
>
> (And so for a long time my mind was going in two directions: Should I accept the mark of arrogance and commend to memory an abridgement of the successive reigns and genealogies of our kings in my own style however unpolished, or should I let them all pass away into silence?)[17]

The notion that the past has been consigned to silence and will remain silent without writing appears perhaps more ironic in this case given that Sven acknowledges that his ability to ascertain historical matters relies on his questioning of older individuals:

> Sed, ut ait Martianus, 'ne incomperta falsitatem admiscere uideatur assertio', et ne fabulose uidear historiam enarrare, quantum ab annosis et ueteribus certa ualui inquisitione percunctari, compendiose perstringam.
>
> (But as Martianus says, 'an unascertained statement must not appear to mingle with falsehood', and lest I should seem to relate history as fable, I will briefly touch on matters to the degree that I have been able to ascertain them by questioning the aged and old.)[18]

In addressing concerns about the verification and trustworthiness of sources, the concern is not that one might *write* incorrect history, but rather that one appears to *relate* history as fable: 'fabulose uidear historiam enarrare'. Similarly, as the preface draws to its close, we are told that those whose deeds deserve remembrance will be recalled to memory ('ad memoriam [...] reuocare'), and that the author's speech or tale ('nostra oratio') will recreate ('retexat') the legendary Skjold. In using the verb *retexere* Sven uses language similar to the

---

[17] Sven Aggesen, *Brevis historia regum dacie*, Proemium (p. 94).

[18] Sven Aggesen, *Brevis historia regum dacie*, Proemium (p. 94).

Historia Norwegie when it reconstructed genealogies. But the rhetorical context in which each reweaving or reconstruction occurs differs dramatically. Whereas the *Historia* works within a written framework, referring to 'mea scripta', Sven frames his work in oral discourse describing it as 'nostra oratio.[19]

The casting of the historical enterprise as a speech-act, as opposed to inscription, persists in Sven's well-known reference to Saxo's contemporaneous and similar endeavour.

> Quorum gesta plenarie superfluum duxi recolere, ne crebrius idem repetitum fastidium pariat audientibus, cum, illustri archipresule Absolone referente, contubernalis meus Saxo elegantiori stilo omnium gesta executurus prolixius insudabat.

> (I have deemed it superfluous to recount their deeds in full (that is, the deeds of the five sons of Sven Estridsen who were kings), lest the frequent repetition cause aversion for my listeners, for the noble Archbishop Absalon informed me that my colleague Saxo was labouring to describe at greater length the deeds of them all in a more elegant style.)[20]

While *audientibus*, 'for listeners', has been translated as 'readers' (and one imagines that the work had readers), Sven's rhetoric maintains the representation of his work as *oratio*.[21]

It is tempting to see Sven's decision to cast his work in terms of speech as a gesture that embraces oral commemoration and portrays Sven's written work as a continuation of such a tradition, albeit in a different medium. However, Sven's work explicitly depicts the past as silence, refuting previous methods of commemoration, and suggests that if history is not written it disappears. The

---

[19] Sven Aggesen, *Brevis historia regum dacie*, Proemium (pp. 94–95): 'eos ad memoriam conabor reuocare, illorum gestis modicam impendens operam [...] Illum igitur <nunc> nostra retexat oratio, quem priscorum annositas iugi primum commendauit memorie' (I will try to recall to memory those men, to whose deeds I find the task appropriate [...]. And so our tale will recreate the man whom forebears of old first commended to eternal memory).

[20] Sven Aggesen, *Brevis historia regum dacie*, 10 (p. 124).

[21] Christiansen (*The Works of Sven Aggesen*, p. 65) translates 'lest they should be repeated together and weary my readers'. A supplementary point of comparison might be mentioned in the portrayal of king as law giver. The *Brevis historia* recounts that Harald Hen was the first to confer laws to the Danes. By contrast, in creating a true legendary law-giving king, we might expect him to have committed these laws to writing in the manner that the *Passio Olavi* takes pains to note of its namesake. Sven's work may avoid such a presentation of Harald for other reasons: namely, Harald's legacy in Denmark not as universally acclaimed as Olav's in Norway and the law not universally accepted. Nonetheless, it is remarkable that Sven again avoids writing about writing.

silencing of early commemorative forms is all the more striking when read in light of the statements of Sven's contemporary, Saxo, who not only recognizes that the feats of ancestors had been popularized in vernacular song, but that these were inscribed again in the letters of their own language on rocks and stones:

> Nec ignotum uolo Danorum antiquiores conspicuis fortitudinis operibus editis glorie emulatione suffusos Romani stili imitatione non solum rerum a se magnifice gestarum titulos exquisito contextus genere ueluti poetico quodam opere perstrinxisse, uerumetiam maiorum acta patrii sermonis carminibus uulgata lingue sue literis saxis ac rupibus insculpenda curasse.

> (I should like it to be known that Danes of an older age, filled with a desire to echo the glory when notable braveries had been performed, alluded in the Roman manner to the splendour of their nobly wrought achievements with choice compositions of a poetical nature; not only that, but they engraved the letters of their own language on rocks and stones to retell those feats of their ancestors which had been made popular in the songs of their mother tongue.)[22]

While Saxo maintains the need for a literary memorial, the recognition of previous forms for the commemoration of notable deeds appears markedly more generous than Sven's seemingly deliberate denial. Indeed, by construing his work as speech, Sven effectively usurps the role of oral commemoration while casting a new form, written history, in traditional clothing.

Sven's rhetoric of orality is almost entirely reversed in Theodoricus's *Historia de antiquitate regum Norwagiensium*, where the references to writing and the written abound. Although Theodoricus affects less modestly than his contemporaries in his prologue (a fuller statement of modesty and request for readers' forgiveness can be found at the conclusion of the work), his opening expresses common ideas in the assiduous inquiry of living sources. However, in this case he acknowledges the poetic works of Icelanders as a reliable source:

> Operæ pretium duxi, vir illustrissime, pauca hæc de antiquitate regum Norwagiensium breviter annotare, et prout sagaciter perquirere potuimus ab eis, penes quos horum memoria præcipue vigere creditur, quos nos Islendinga vocamus, qui hæc in suis antiquis carminibus percelebrata recolunt.

> (I have deemed it worthwhile, noble sir, to write down in brief these few details concerning the ancient history of the Norwegian kings, as I have been able to learn by assiduous inquiry from the people among whom in particular the remembrance

---

[22] Saxo Grammaticus, *Gesta Danorum*, Pr.1.3 (1, 6).

of these matters is believed to thrive — namely those whom we call Icelanders, who preserve them as much celebrated themes in their ancient poems.)[23]

By referring to these poetic works as 'antiqua carmina' (ancient songs/poems), Theodorius invokes their oral performance. So while the lack of writers has effaced the memory of great deeds, Theodoricus recognizes that these deeds can be learned from oral sources. Indeed, Theodoricus seems to present his work as a record for posterity, stating 'dignum putavi hæc, pauca licet, majorum nostrorum memoriæ posteritatis tradere' (I have thought it proper to record for posterity these relics of our forefathers, few though they are).[24] In this, we see less an effacement of earlier forms, but a continuation. The justification for putting these records into writing arises 'quia pæne nulla natio est tam rudis et inculta, quæ non aliqua monumenta suorum antecessorum ad posteros transmiserit' (because almost no people is so rude and uncivilized that it has not passed on some monuments of its predecessors to later generations).[25] While this statement does impose a civilized/uncivilized division with respect to written and oral discourse, nonetheless it is a transparent imposition; in Theodoricus's world the expectations and demands for creating lasting monuments require written rather than oral sources.

The way in which Theodoricus positions written commemoration within a civilizing phenomenon is seen in the way in which he notes the lack of writers, framing this expression within a quotation attributed to Boethius. Explaining the decision to begin the history with the ascension of Harald Fair-Hair, Theodoricus states:

> Sed quia constat nullam ratam regalis stemmatis successionem in hac terra extitisse ante Haraldi pulchre-comati tempora, ab ipso exordium fecimus: non quia dubitaverim etiam ante ejus ætatem fuisse in hac terra viros secundum præsens sæculum probitate conspicuos, quos nimirum, ut ait Boetius, clarissimos suis temporibus viros scriptorum inops delevit opinio.

> (Because it is clear that no established succession of the royal line existed in this land before the time of Haraldr Fair-hair, I have begun with him; and I have not done this because I doubted that before his day there were in this land men, who by the standards of the present age, were distinguished by their prowess, since cer-

---

[23] Theodoricus Monachus, *Historia de antiquitate regum Norwagiensium*, Prol. (p. 4. 7–11). The translation is that of McDougall and McDougall (*Theodoricus Monachus*, p. 1).

[24] Theodoricus Monachus, *Historia de antiquitate regum Norwagiensium*, Prol. (pp. 4, 13–15).

[25] Theodoricus Monachus, *Historia de antiquitate regum Norwagiensium*, Prol. (pp. 4, 11–13).

tainly, as Boethius says, 'reputation without authors has effaced those men who were very famous in their own times'.)[26]

Moreover, as Theodoricus notes the dearth of writers as part of the effacement of former deeds further on in the prologue, he clearly signals that the statement reiterates the quotation from Boethius: 'sed ut diximus illorum memoriam scriptorum inopia delevit' (but as we have said a dearth of writers has effaced any memory of them).[27] In other words, while the writing of a Norwegian history is novel, observing an absence of writers or written material is not. Theodoricus announces its commonness by saying it twice and letting us know that such statements are as old as antiquity. Consequently, while the enterprise itself might be something new from a local point of view, it stands on the firmament of authoritative written models.

Similarly, the frequent digressions, which have made the work so tedious for many modern readers, have been added, according to Theodoricus, in the manner of ancient historians: 'more antiquorum chronographorum').[28] While the number of these digressions differs based on the criteria used to count them, there are in the neighbourhood of fifteen, ten of which occupy more than half a chapter.[29] Of these ten, the longest seven digressions dominate the chapters in which they are found and cluster towards the second half of the work. Indeed, the entire seventeenth chapter, marking the halfway point of the book's thirty-four chapters, is a digression on Charybdis. Many of these can be read typologically, such as the story of Jovian's (331–64) re-confirmation of imperial Christianity after the rule of Julian the apostate (331/32–363), which parallels

---

[26] Theodoricus Monachus, *Historia de antiquitate regum Norwagiensium*, Prol. (Storm, p. 3. 15–20); translated by McDougall and McDougall (*Theodoricus Monachus*, p. 1). Note that the quotation itself is disputed. Kraggerud ('Theodoricus Scrutinized') argues against *opinio*, stating that 'scriptorum inops [...] oblivio' (oblivion without recourse to written records), the actual Boethius quotation, is what Theodoricus read. Karlsen and Vatsend ('On Theodoricus Monachus') support *opinio*. Kraggerud ('Boëthius and the Preface of Theodoricus') reiterates support for *oblivio*. For the present discussion, it is important that Theodoricus cites Boethius, less the accuracy of the citation or the citation itself.

[27] Theodoricus Monachus, *Historia de antiquitate regum Norwagiensium*, Prol. (Storm, p. 4. 10–12).

[28] Theodoricus Monachus, *Historia de antiquitate regum Norwagensium*, Prol. (Storm, pp. 4, 16–17).

[29] One count is twelve (Bagge, 'Theodoricus Monachus: Clerical Historiography', p. 116); another is fifteen, but with recognition that the number could vary (Mortensen, 'Det 12. århundredes renæssance i Norge', p. 31).

Óláfr Tryggvason's rule after Hákon jarl, and the examples of *ambitio* in the chapter-long screed (Chapter 26) that relate to Norwegian politics by dealing with conflicts between close relatives.[30] The exception to this typological reading is the discussion in Chapter 20 of the reckoning of time. Almost all of these longer digressions refer to their written background — not always in terms of sources behind the digression, but also in terms of literary justification for taking up a subject not immediately germane to the narrative. The exceptions to this are, interestingly, the three digressions involving medieval figures: the two digressions which evoke Charlemagne, one in Chapter 23 describing the battle against the Langobards on behalf of the pope, the other in Chapter 30 listing the portents that foretold his death; the third exception is the digression on Otto II's (973–78) generosity to churches. But even these three exceptions give a central role to writing. We find an extended reference to the *Roman History* in Chapter 25 amidst chapters on the reign of Magnús inn góði (Chapters 24–27). Additionally, in the two digressions evoking Charlemagne, we see writing in the letter of the pope to the emperor and also in the portents of Charlemagne's death, wherein the ruler's name was written along the top of a wall in golden letters so large that anyone standing below could read them with great ease. In short, in all of these digressions, which represent critical moments of interpretation, writing figures prominently and frequently dominates the hermeneutic excursus.

The focus on writing and the role it plays in the correct interpretation of events reveals itself at all turns in Theodoricus's work which names at least a dozen other works and/or authors. As we have seen, the *Historia Norwegie* by contrast names two authors (Cicero and Solinus), Saxo Grammaticus only three (Bede, Paul the Deacon, and Dudo of Saint-Quentin).[31] Moreover, Theodoricus includes around twenty quotations, a handful from the Bible, another from various usually religious authorities but also Horace, Ovid, Proba (whom he cites as Vergil), and nine (or perhaps more accurately eight) from Lucan.[32]

---

[30] Bagge, 'Theodoricus Monachus: Clerical Historiography', pp. 118–20.

[31] Friis-Jensen notes that all three of these authors wrote histories of peoples who can be considered descended from the Danes (Saxo Grammaticus, *Gesta Danorum*, I, 21 n. 4). I am grateful to Richard Cole for this reference.

[32] In one case, Theodoricus quotes three lines from Lucan (*De bello civili*, VII.552–54 at the end of Chapter 34), and then introduces a quotation from the same passage by adding it appears elsewhere (*alio loco*) in Lucan, when the following quotation is separated by only one line in the *Bellum civile*. It has been suggested that the unawareness that these two quotations

These abundant references and citations, and the acknowledged self-aware-ness of the work's place within written, and so learned, ecclesiastical and elite tradition, have earned Theodoricus a reputation as more ambitious than con-temporaries; this can easily give the impression that the goal of such a dis-play of learning was the proscription of other media of authoritative knowl-edge. However, for all its literary qualities, the *Historia de antiquitate* does not present writing as an unqualified or unimpeachable authority. The work undermines its own authority with its mistakes in the citation of its sources: the *Historia* also highlights the variability of opinion in written authorities by detailing rather lengthy debates and discussions relating to the interpreta-tive hurdles that accompany book learning. Theodoricus minces no words, for example when considering the calculation of the number of years from the beginning of the world:

> Sciendum vero est, in libris nil adeo corruptum ut supputationem numerorum, tum maxime vitio scriptorum, tum etiam minori industria calculantium, et ideo, ut in primis diximus, hunc numerum annorum nolumus præjudicare certiori, semper et ubique præcaventes contentiones, in his præcipue quæ contra fidem non sunt.

> (It should be understood that in books nothing is as garbled as the calculation of numbers, especially through the fault of scribes, but also through lack of diligence on the part of those doing the reckoning. Therefore, as I stated at the outset, I do not wish to present this count of years as preferable to one which may be more certain. For always and everywhere I seek to avoid strife, especially in such matters as are not at odds with faith.)[33]

In other words, at issue are not just inherent problems in the transmission of texts but also the problems represented by those who fail to apply the appro-priate critical modes of discernment to the texts they are supposedly equipped to study. Even Origen, he notes elsewhere, although a worthy commentator ('nobilis tractator') on scripture, erred regarding the alternation of ages, and moreover — 'proh dolor!' — intermingled many worthless passages from the books of philosophers which conflict with sound doctrine.[34]

---

are from the same passage indicates that Theodoricus did not have first-hand knowledge of the poem. See McDougall and McDougall, 'Notes', p. 115 n. 329, and Hanssen, 'Theodoricus Monachus and European Literature', p. 88.

[33] Theodoricus Monachus, *Historia de antiquitate regum Norwagiensium*, 20 (pp. 42, 10–14); translated by McDougall and McDougall (*Theodoricus Monachus*, pp. 31–32).

[34] Theodoricus references Origen's *Peri arkhon* (*de principiis*) in this case.

Another somewhat more elaborate discussion of wrong teaching in books comes in Chapter 26, the digression on ambition, which itself includes an interior digression on canonical works with reference to the so-called *Decretum Gelasianum*:

> Et quia hujus regis mentionem fecimus, quæso ne onerosum videatur lectori, si pauca de Romana historia excerpta hic ponantur propter illam scripturam, quæ fertur de exaltatione sanctæ crucis, in qua quibusdam veris multa falsa interlita sunt, propter quod a sancta Romana ecclesia non recipitur. Gelasius namque papa, vir doctissimus et magnæ auctoritatis in ecclesia Dei, compendioso sermone secernit apocryphas scripturas a sacro canone, dicens: 'non egere ecclesiam Dei falsitatis comprobatione, quæ ab ipsa veritate Deo fundata est'. [...] Ponit idem Gelasius inter apocrypha passiones apostolorum præter solius Andreæ, librum de infantia Jesu, librum de nativitate beatæ Mariæ, itinerarium Clementis, evangelium secundum Thomam, evangelium secundum Bartholomæum et multa alia, quæ longum est enumerare. Sed jam videamus, quomodo illa scriptura de exaltatione sanctæ crucis conveniat veritati Romanæ historiæ.

> (And since I have made mention of this king, I pray that it will not seem burdensome to the reader if a few selections for the *Roman History* are added here as they are found in the work which is called 'On the exaltation of the Holy Cross', a book in which many streaks of falsehood appear among some true details and which for that reason, is not accepted by the holy Roman Church. For Pope Gelasius, a man of great learning and authority in God's Church, distinguishes in a brief sermon the apocryphal writings from the sacred canon, saying that God's Church has no need of support from falsehood, for it is founded by God, who is truth itself [...]. This same Gelasius includes among the apocrypha the passions of the apostles (except that of Andrew alone), the book of the infancy of Jesus, the book about the birth of the blessed Mary, the itinerary of Clement, the gospel according to Thomas, the gospel according to Bartholomew, and many other texts which it would take a long time to enumerate. But let us now see how this treatise, 'On the exaltation of the Holy Cross' accords with the truth of the *Roman History*.)[35]

Because Theodoricus intends to rehearse passages from *De exaltatione crucis* and accord them with the *Roman History* — probably Paul the Deacon's or Landulf Sagax's expansion of Eutropius's *Breviarium historiae Romanae* — in a gesture of full disclosure he admits that *De exultatione* has many streaks of falsehood among its true details, and is consequently non-canonical. As far as we know the exaltation of the Holy Cross is not in the *Decretum*, but *De*

---

[35] Theodoricus Monachus, *Historia de antiquitate regum Norwagiensium*, 26 (p. 52. 6–p. 54. 14); translated by McDougall and McDougall (*Theodoricus Monachus*, p. 41).

inventione crucis is.[36] Assuming that a confusion or conflation of titles lies at the heart of the misstatement, it seems likely that Theodoricus believed that the *Decretum*'s findings on the *Inventio* apply to the *Exaltatio*, namely, that some Catholics read it, but like other recent works it must be examined so that only what is correct is taken from it.[37] In other words, those who access the text must show critical judgement in interpreting it. In this light, Theodoricus doesn't commend the reading of non-canonical writing, but he may be displaying the very type of discernment he finds lacking in those who write calculations (although this display somewhat paradoxically appears based on a conflation of titles). Namely, the text assures that it maintains the judgement to know what one can take from the sources, unlike those who garble the ages of the world.

The confusion found in books also informs the *Historia*'s treatment of the place of Óláfr Haraldsson's baptism. Some say he was baptized in Oppland at the age of three, others suggest England, and Dudo suggests Rouen. That there can be such confusion is excused by Theodoricus via — it should come as no surprise now — recourse to a similar problem regarding baptism in a written text of some authority, namely, Jerome's discussion concerning Constantine's place of baptism:

> Nec mirum de Olavo hoc contigisse in illa terra, ubi nullus antiquitatum unquam scriptor fuerit, cum idem scribat beatus Hieronymus de Constantino magno filio Constantii et Helenæ, quod quidam dicant eum Bithyniæ baptizatum fuisse in ultima senectute, alii Constantinopoli, quidam Romæ a beato Sylvestro papa, et adhuc sub judice lis est quis verius scripserit.

> (Nor is it any wonder that this could have happened with regard to Óláfr in that land where there has never been a chronicler of ancient events, when the blessed Jerome writes the same thing concerning Constantine the Great, son of Constantius and Helena. He notes that some say that he was baptized in Bithynia in advanced old

---

[36] See McDougall and McDougall, 'Notes', p. 100.

[37] 'Item scriptura de inventione crucis et alia scriptura de inventione capitis beati Iohannis Baptistae novellae quidem relationes sunt et nonnulli eas catholici legunt; sed cum haec ad catholicorum manus advenerint, beati Pauli apostoli praecedat sententia: "omnia probate, quod bonum est tenete"' (Likewise the writings on the finding of the cross and certain other novel writings on the finding of the head of the blessed John the Baptist are romances and some of them are read by catholics; but when these come into the hand of catholics, the saying of Paul the blessed apostle should be <considered> first: "prove all things, hold fast to what is good"'); *Das Decretum Gelasianum*, ed. by Dobschütz, iv. 4.

age, others at Constantinople, some at Rome by the blessed pope Sylvester. Who has written more truthfully is 'a matter still before the court'.)[38]

The writing of history, while it may represent a method for ensuring in Theodoricus's eyes the commemoration of events and hence a people, does not necessarily settle all the questions of interpretation that the study of the past raises. Theodoricus's work demonstrates that this has always been the case: namely, that the certainty some believe adheres to the permanence of writing is refuted in the very writings on which the notion of Christian writing is based.

This qualification in the use of written material also informs our reading of the one passage in which Theodoricus has been seen to assert the unequivocal authority of writing vis-a-vis oral tradition, namely, the reckoning of Haraldr Hárfagri's rule. Theodoricus posits 862 based on his assessment of Icelandic accounts,[39] but does not pronounce in favour of this date over one more certain, relating that it is difficult to arrive at the truth in such matters where no written authority provides assistance (*nulla optilatur scriptorum auctoritas*). Given the problems noted elsewhere in written calculations of time and the lack of concord in some written accounts, Theodoricus's statement may imply that written sources are unclear, or that those he used cannot be considered *auctoritates*.[40] It need not suggest that he had no written sources or that he disparages ultimately orally-derived information. Rather, much like the way in which the assessment of Óláfr's baptism indicates that such problems of dating for Theodoricus are not intrinsic to one medium and absent in another, the statement may simply indicate that his use of written sources does not allow a firm commitment to one date or another.

---

[38] Theodoricus Monachus, *Historia de antiquitate regum Norwagiensium*, 13 (p. 23. 3–8); translated by McDougall and McDougall (*Theodoricus Monachus*, p. 17).

[39] Theodoricus Monachus, *Historia de antiquitate regum Norwagiensium*, 1 (p. 6. 11–p. 7. 2): 'Sed quia valde difficile est in hujusce ad liquidum veritatem comprehendere, maxime ubi nulla opitulatur scriptorum auctoritas, istum numerum nullo modo volumus præjudicare certiori, si reperiri valet, considerantes illud apostoli ad Timotheum: geneologias et infinitas quæstiones devita, et alibi: Si quis contentiosus est, nos hujusmodi consuetudinem non habemus' (But because it is exceedingly difficult to arrive at the pure truth in such matters, especially where no written authority provides assistance, I by no means wish to pronounce in favour of this date rather than a more certain one, if one can be found, since I keep in mind the words of the apostle to Timothy: "Shun genealogies and endless questions"; and elsewhere; "If any man seem to be contentious, we have no such custom"') (*Theodoricus Monachus*, trans. by McDougall and McDougall, p. 5).

[40] See Bagge, 'Theodoricus Monachus: The Kingdom of Norway'.

By the time the *Historia Norwegie*, Sven Aggesen's *Brevis historia*, and Theodoricus's *Historia de antiquitate regum* were written in the second half of the
twelfth century, Latin writing was a well-established practice.[41] As a result, these
works do not witness or assess the introduction of a new technology or mode of
communication. Nonetheless, the rhetoric of writing, however formulaic, situates these works within competing and also coeval social structures that dictate
and determine who or what sort of people have the place of interpreting what
is right and wrong, acceptable or taboo, historical and fabulous. Obviously, the
twelfth century did not possess or elaborate the same theoretical models and
understanding of literacies and writing as those found in present-day scholarship. In other words, the medieval world did not have the same ideological
frameworks for understanding development, progress, and hence the assumptions that underpin approaches that extol the 'cognitive consequences' (and
one might add social consequences) of literacy. In this light, it is perhaps fair
to imagine that societies that were in the process of adapting more complex
literate practices understood that literacy is always contested, both in its definition and its practice. Indeed, the formulaic language as it appears in a range of
'first' histories suggests this tension between staking out written practices of
common cultural commemoration and their interaction with oral networks of
communication. Taken to a logical conclusion, we might say that it is impossible to imagine a traditional society in which texts are addressed solely to *readers*
rather than to both readers and listeners, those who experience the 'text' in written and aural forms. Nonetheless, the ways in which these written forms represent the status of writing in their rhetoric about writing/reading and speaking/
hearing allows us to see how this contested space was negotiated. In the prefaces and discussions of these works, we see different authors and audiences 'taking hold' of the new social practice and depicting its role in shaping identities,
institutions, and commemoration in these lands.[42] The claim to primacy that
characterizes these three works bespeaks a common attitude towards writing as
the legitimate medium for commemorative endeavour and a common acceptance of all the attendant changes, by this time believingly consolidated, that
are related to shifts in who holds the right to legitimate interpretations of the
past. Writing, then as now, was an activity that played an important role in self-

---

[41] See Haugen, 'The Development of Latin Script I; Karlsen, 'Katalogisering av latinske
membranfragmenter'.

[42] On this idea of locals 'taking hold' of literate practices in the process of becoming literate, see the effective summary of ethnographic literacy studies by Street, 'Ethnography of Writing and Reading'.

defining a people, its mores, and morals. Against this common attitude, however, the rhetoric of writing in these works reveals rather different dispositions towards this 'new' world of learning and hermeneutic authority. In this respect, Sven's work appears most prescriptive. By putting new wine into old bottles, appropriating the language of orality to written works, Sven's history silences an oral past and its present. The *Historia Norwegie* presents an impersonal and arguably inscrutable monument, impressing more than inviting. Theodoricus's history appears rather more magnanimous despite its adamant grounding in the written world. While Theodoricus's work effectively circumscribes access to interpretive roles by requiring reading, it acknowledges that this skill does not in itself assure legitimate authority. The written word can be debated, accepted, or cast aside. Its authority is dependent, contingent on scribes and readers, not inherent to its medium. The insistent quotations and references suggest a desire to share with local peers what must have seemed like, to paraphrase Miranda's exclamation in *The Tempest*, a brave new world that has such knowledge in it. Indeed, Theodoricus's recourse to writing does not prohibit discussion but seems to invite debate in a new spirit.

Works Cited

Primary Sources

Das Decretum Gelasianum de libris reipiendis et non recipiendis, ed. by Ernst von Dobschütz (Leipzig: Hinrichs, 1912)

Historia Norwegie, ed. by Inger Ekrem and Lars Boje Mortensen, trans. by Peter Fisher (Copenhagen: Museum Tusculanum Press, 2003)

Saxo Grammaticus, *Gesta Danorum: The History of the Danes*, ed. by Karsten Friis-Jensen, trans. by Peter Fisher, 2 vols (Oxford: Oxford University Press, 2015)

Sven Aggesen, *Brevis Historia Regum Dacie*, in *Scriptores Minores Historiæ Danicæ Medii Ævi*, ed. by Martin Claurentius Gertz, 2 vols (Copenhagen: Gad, 1917–18), i, 94–141 (X-version)

Theodoricus Monachus, *An Account of the Ancient History of the Norwegian Kings*, trans. by Ian McDougall and David McDougall, Viking Society for Northern Research, 11 (London: Viking Society for Northern Research, 1998)

——, *Historia de antiquitate regum Norwagiensium*, in *Monumenta Historica Norvegiæ: Latinske Kildskrifter til Norges Historie i middelalderen*, ed. by Gustav Storm (Kristiania: Brøgger, 1880), pp. 1–68

Secondary Studies

Bagge, Sverre, 'Theodoricus Monachus: The Kingdom of Norway and the History of Salvation', in *Historical Narratives and Christian Identity on a European Periphery: Early History Writing in Northern, East-Central, and Eastern Europe (c. 1070–1200)*, ed. by Ildar Garipzanov (Turnhout: Brepols, 2011), pp. 71–90

Bagge, Sverre, 'Theodoricus Monachus: Clerical Historiography in Twelfth-Century Norway', *Scandinavian Journal of History*, 14 (1989), 113–33

Christiansen, Eric, 'Introduction', in *The Works of Sven Aggesen, Twelfth-Century Danish Historian*, trans. by Eric Christiansen, Viking Society for Northern Research, 9 (London: Viking Society for Northern Research, 1992), pp. 1–30

Ekrem, Inger, and Lars Boje Mortensen, 'Commentary', in *Historia Norwegie*, ed. by Inger Ekrem and Lars Boje Mortensen, trans. by Peter Fisher (Copenhagen: Museum Tusculanum Press, 2003), pp. 107–53

Hanssen, Jens S. Th., 'Theodoricus Monachus and European Literature', *Symbolae Osloensis*, 27 (1949), 70–127

Haugen, Odd Einar, 'The Development of Latin Script i: In Norway' in *The Nordic Languages: An International Handbook of the North Germanic Languages*, ed. by Oskar Bandle and others, 2 vols (Berlin: De Gruyter, 2002), i, 824–32

Karlsen, Espen, 'Katalogisering av latinske membranfragmenter som forskningsprosjekt: Del 2', in *Arkivverkets forskningsseminar Gardarmoen 2003*, Rapporter og retningslinjer, 16 (Oslo: Riksarkivet, 2003), pp. 58–88

Karlsen, Espen, and Kyrre Vatsend, 'On Theodoricus Monachus' Use of Late Classical Authors', *Collegium Medievale*, 16 (2003), 239–63

Kraggerud, Egil, 'Boëthius and the Preface of Theodoricus', *Historia — opinio* versus *oblivio* once again', *Collegium Medievale*, 18 (2005), 144–47

——, 'Theodoricus Scrutinized', *Collegium Medievale*, 11 (1998), 119–26

Olson, David, *The World on Paper: The Conceptual and Cognitive Implications of Writing and Reading* (Cambridge: Cambridge University Press, 1994)

McDougall, David, and Ian McDougall, 'Introduction', in *An Account of the Ancient History of the Norwegian Kings*, trans. by Ian McDougall and David McDougall, Viking Society for Northern Research, 11 (London: Viking Society for Northern Research, 1998), pp. vii–xxxi, 55–115

Mortensen, Lars Boje, 'Det 12. århundredes renæssance i Norge: Teodorik Munk og Romerriget', in *Antikken i norsk litteratur*, ed. by Øivind Andersen and Asbjørn Aarseth (Bergen: Nordisk institutt, Universitetet i Bergen, 1993), pp. 17–35

——, '*Historia Norwegie* and Sven Aggesen: Two Pioneers in Comparison', in *Historical Narratives and Christian Identity on a European Periphery: Early History Writing in Northern, East-Central, and Eastern Europe (c. 1070–1200)*, ed. by Ildar Garipzanov (Turnhout: Brepols, 2011), pp. 57–70

——, 'Introduction', in *Historia Norwegie*, ed. by Inger Ekrem and Lars Boje Mortensen, trans. by Peter Fisher (Copenhagen: Museum Tusculanum Press, 2003), pp. 8–47

——, 'Sanctified Beginnings and Mythopoietic Moments: The First Wave of Writing on the Past in Norway, Denmark, and Hungary, c. 1000–1300', in *The Making of Christian Myths in the Periphery of Latin Christendom (c. 1000–1300)*, ed. by Lars Bje Mortensen (Copenhagen: Museum Tusculanum Press, 2006), pp. 247–73

Münster-Swendsen, Mia, 'The Making of the Danish Court Nobility: The "Lex castrensis sive curiae" of Sven Aggesen Reconsidered', in *Statsutvikling i de nordiske rikene i mellomalderen*, ed. by Sverre Bagge and others (Oslo: Dreyers forlag, 2012), pp. 257–79

Scribner, Sylvia, and Michael Cole, *The Psychology of Literacy* (Cambridge, MA: Harvard University Press, 1981)

Street, Brian, 'Ethnography of Writing and Reading', in *The Cambridge Handbook of Literacy*, ed. by David Olson and Nancy Torrance (Cambridge: Cambridge University Press, 2009), pp. 329–45

Tracing Scribal Centres
in Medieval Norway

Åslaug Ommundsen*

Manuscripts owned by churches and religious institutions in medieval Norway may be all but lost, but through a stroke of luck they have not all disappeared without trace. The parchment that constituted the pages of medieval books was strong and durable, and once their texts were no longer of consequence or interest, the parchment could be utilized as protective covers for paper, a far more brittle material. Consequently, in Norway, as all over Europe, post-medieval paper leaflets and archival material were bound with leaves or scraps of parchment from medieval manuscripts.

In Scandinavia there are approximately fifty thousand single fragments from medieval books, preserved mainly as passengers on account books of the sixteenth and seventeenth centuries.[1] The *c.* 6500 Norwegian fragments have been

* I would like to thank Michael Gullick and Gisela Attinger, the editors of this volume and the Arrival of Writing group, and the anonymous peer reviewer, for invaluable help and advice during the writing of this chapter.

[1] For more about the Nordic fragment collections, see Ommundsen and Heikkilä, *Nordic Latin Manuscript Fragments*. The largest holder is Riksarkivet (the Swedish National Archives) in Stockholm with *c.* 22,700 fragments (see <https://sok.riksarkivet.se/MPO>). Kansalliskirjasto (the Finnish National Library) in Helsinki counts *c.* 9400 leaves, displayed in an online searchable database (<http://fragmenta.kansalliskirjasto.fi>). A rough estimate for

Åslaug Ommundsen (aslaug.ommundsen@uib.no) is Professor of Medieval Latin Philology at the University of Bergen, and her primary research and publication areas are manuscript studies and palaeography. Following her time at the Centre for Medieval Studies in Bergen as a doctoral candidate and post-doctoral fellow, Ommundsen led the international research project 'From Manuscript Fragments to Book History', funded by the Bergen Research Foundation and the University of Bergen.

Moving Words in the Nordic Middle Ages: Tracing Literacies, Texts, and Verbal Communities, ed. by Amy C. Mulligan and Else Mundal, AS 8   BREPOLS 🕮 PUBLISHERS   (Turnhout: Brepols, 2019)
pp. 81–112
10.1484/M.AS-EB.5.116621

estimated to represent roughly 1000–1200 different books, and these provide a vivid sketch of the medieval book corpus as far as genre, format, date, and origin are concerned.[2] These fragmentary 'phantom books' supplement around twelve to fifteen surviving Latin manuscripts with a Norwegian provenance or origin and around fifty manuscripts in Old Norwegian. Together these form important source material for ecclesiastical history as well as scribal and literary activity in Norwegian towns and institutions. The diversity of the books represented in the fragment collections make them a valuable means of understanding contacts with religious houses and centres of learning abroad, as well as witnesses to local scribal culture.

Book fragments are the obvious starting point for any investigation into scribal centres in Scandinavia, and they should be seen in light of surviving manuscripts, other historical sources, surviving literary texts, and archaeological material. This is particularly true for Norway, with its poor transmission of complete manuscripts. The current chapter considers how we may use fragments in the study of early book and scribal culture, and provide some examples of specific identifications that exemplify how one may trace scribal centres in medieval Norway.

The Oldest Books

In Norway, as in other Scandinavian countries, most of the surviving fragments are from liturgical books in Latin, books that would have been considered of little value after the Protestant Reformation in 1536/37. Although the practice of reusing old parchment leaves had already begun in the Middle Ages, the royal officials of early modern times took the reuse of manuscript parchment

---

Det Kongelige Bibliotek (the Royal Danish Library) <http://www.kb.dk/da/nb/materialer/haandskrifter/HA/e-mss/flh.html> and the Rigsarkivet (the Danish National Archives) in Copenhagen is about ten thousand fragments, while the Icelandic public collections in Copenhagen and Reykjavik hold *c.* 750 fragments, the ones with musical notation available online <https://www.ismus.is>, <https://handrit.is>.

[2] About six thousand fragments are held in Riksarkivet (NRA; the National Archives of Norway) in Oslo; around five hundred are divided among various public archives, museums, and libraries. Regarding the estimates of 1000–1200 book units, Thorsten Eken suggested already in 1963 that Riksarkivet in Oslo held fragments from about 1200 Latin codices (Eken, *Gammalnorske membranfragment i Riksarkivet*, p. xiii). The latest overview of Latin book units after the completion of the research project 'From Manuscript Fragments to Book History' (2012–17) shows 1199 units (unpublished, counted September 2017). The number will probably decrease, but Eken's estimate seems remarkably good.

to new heights: old and useless service books were gathered, dismembered, and reused at different levels in the royal administration, from local bailiffs to more centrally placed governors.[3] Since bailiffs and governors harvested the same manuscripts for parchment over several years or even decades, the fragment collections to some extent represent a huge jigsaw puzzle of 'reconstructable' manuscripts (although most of them still in very fragmentary form). Around 1660, the supply of medieval manuscripts, liturgical or otherwise, appears to have run out.

Liturgical books are not generally considered flag-bearers of learning and literacy. Still, there is general consensus regarding the primary role played by these books as Christianity and book culture first spread to the outer margins of Europe in the tenth century: liturgical books were the first to be imported in larger numbers. They were also the first books to be copied locally, and this was taking place by the eleventh century.[4] The urgent need to supply service books to the growing number of parish churches from the early twelfth century onwards seems to have kept local scribes very active until the early fourteenth century.[5]

A high proportion of the material in Scandinavian fragment collections seems to be from books which were used in parish churches, books which have a poor survival rate elsewhere in Europe. Perhaps surprisingly, a large number of the books used and kept in Norwegian churches at the time of the Reformation appear to have been of a considerable age,[6] and the fragment material in Riksarkivet in Oslo includes fragments from several books dating back to the

---

[3] For more information about binding practices, see Pettersen, 'From Parchment Books to Fragments'.

[4] See Karlsen, 'Katalogisering av membranfragmenter', pp. 64–68. See also Mortensen, 'Sanctified Beginnings and Mythopoietic Moments', pp. 252–54.

[5] The material indicates a decline in production *c.* 1300, presumably because of a certain saturation of the market, cf. Karlsen, 'Liturgiske bøker i Norge inntil år 1300', p. 151.

[6] The age of the fragment material corresponds with surviving church inventories: two inventories from the early fourteenth century, one from Hålandsdalen (1306, DN 21.7) and one from Ylmheim (1320s, DN 15.8), list psalters referred to as *forn* (old). The inventory of the bishop's chapel in Bergen from 1408 (DN 15.42) describes some books as unbound and *illafaren* (in a bad state) and one psalter as *fordærwadh* (damaged); see Ommundsen, 'Books, Scribes and Sequences', I, 74–75. The variable age, state, and content of the books in Norwegian churches is also described by Archbishop Erik Valkendorf in his prefaces to the first printed missal and breviary of Nidaros from 1519. Not only is there a general shortage of books, he states, but many books in daily use are 'ancient' and 'hardly legible' (*Missale Nidrosiense* and *Breviarium Nidrosiense*).

eleventh century and even earlier. A large part of the materials are from manuscripts written before 1300.

In this context, it is important to remember that the circumstances of the 'surviving' book units may have been very different in the sixteenth century compared to the eleventh, twelfth, and thirteenth centuries. In all likelihood, several of the oldest books were already fragmentary by the sixteenth century. Based on the few surviving liturgical books, we may assume that many of the dismembered manuscripts were composites: that is, books consisting of leaves and quires formerly belonging to separate manuscripts. As bindings succumbed to wear and tear over the centuries, some leaves and quires fell out and were lost. Remaining quires were rebound, perhaps multiple times, often together with more recent manuscript material, which was considered useful and complementary by the book's user. With this in mind, we should, strictly speaking, be talking about our reconstructed entities as 'codicological units' rather than 'reconstructed manuscripts'. How the volumes actually appeared and what they contained are lost to us. Nevertheless, the archival bindings from the sixteenth and seventeenth centuries are witnesses to the very beginning of Norwegian book and scribal culture in the late eleventh and early twelfth centuries and to its development in the following centuries.

It is likely that cathedrals and monasteries were active users and producers of books from the beginning, arranging to bring books and scribes to Norway and to establish the first Norwegian scriptoria. The first permanent bishops' sees on the Norwegian mainland, Trondheim, Selja/Bergen, and Oslo, would meet the requirements necessary for the earliest scriptoria: a degree of stability, access to resources, including books to be used as exemplars, and knowledgeable people who were skilled and experienced in book production. The first monasteries, Nidarholm by Trondheim (*c.* 1100), Selja off the western coast (*c.* 1100 or slightly earlier), and Munkeliv in Bergen (*c.* 1110)[7] likely each had some kind of scriptorium to produce books for their own use, although whether any of them made books for others is not yet clear. Though probably not until well into the thirteenth century, book production may eventually have passed from ecclesiastical institutions to secular workshops also in Norway; at present, however, this is uncertain.

---

[7] According to Matthew Paris, Nidarholm was founded by King Knútr in 1028, while the twelfth-century author Theodoricus monachus names Sigurðr Ullstrengr, a local nobleman, as founder, which would date the monastery to 1100; Gunnes, 'Klosterlivet i Norge', p. 51.

The source material indicates that local books were produced under rather variable conditions and circumstances. In some cases we appear to be talking about book-producing individuals more or less connected to a larger environment; in other cases we can see the contours of a more closely knit scriptorium, although it is difficult to identify any environment that has been stable over any length of time. The term 'scriptorium', although it could also be a physical place, is most commonly understood as a unit of two or more people working simultaneously over a period of time, ideally with a degree of continuity over at least two generations.[8] In this chapter the less specific term 'scribal centre' is used to denote a large or small community of people skilled in producing books, including scribes who wrote texts, scribes who supplied musical notation and artists who decorated the work of both the text and music scribes. These communities would likely have also included parchmenters and bookbinders.

Losses, Reuse, and New Lease of Life

A broad study of scribal culture in Norway faces several challenges, the greatest of which is the extent to which the source material has been lost, not only the majority of historical documents but also well over 99 per cent of the manuscript leaves.[9] As durable as parchment is, it could certainly not survive everything to which it was subjected. Not all reuse of parchment was as gentle as archival bindings: many interesting texts have been exploded in fireworks and been baked along with pies, and are consequently lost for good.[10] A large number of manuscript leaves were not reused at all but simply tossed away or used for kindling fires on cold, dark winter nights.[11] The estimated loss of *c.* 99

---

[8] The term 'scriptorium' has several levels of meaning: see, for example, Mazal, 'Skriptorium'. See also Bell, 'Cistercian Scriptoria in England'.

[9] Since *c.* 1000–1200 of an estimated 10,000–12,000 books are represented in the fragment material, we may have remnants of *c.* 10 per cent of the books. However, since no more than a few fragments are left from each book, the losses of material in total climb to well over 99 per cent; cf. Ommundsen, 'Books, Scribes and Sequences', I, 80. For a more recent discussion around survival and losses, see also Karlsen, 'Latin Manuscripts of Medieval Norway', pp. 33–36.

[10] Old manuscripts were in 1634 collected to be used in the fireworks at Prince Christian's wedding; Brunius, 'Från mässböcker til munkepärmar', p. 16. A tale involving a book page under a Christmas pie, as well as a poem describing the fate of written pages bottoming tarts and cheesecakes, are referred to in Smith, 'Preface', p. xii.

[11] As late as in the 1930s a maid in Viggiona in northern Italy was observed lighting the fire with a leaf from an Ambrosian antiphoner; Baroffio, 'Colligere fragmenta ne pereant', by n. 63.

per cent of the leaves is therefore a realistic one, whether one counts from the medieval period, when books were lost to fire, shipwreck, or simple wear and tear, or whether the count is based on manuscripts which existed at the time of the Reformation. It is not only in Norway that the survival rates are bad. Though Italy possesses bountiful extant manuscripts, it has been estimated that for every entire book that once existed, on average only between 0.1 and 1 per cent remain today.[12]

There were, no doubt, also original texts among the leaves of the numerous lost manuscripts, and we can only speculate about how many original works have vanished. In Norway, with its limited population, locally written narratives and records were not likely to be kept in multiple copies, with perhaps just one or two copies serving community needs. A number of Norwegian works have survived by the skin of their teeth. Some are transmitted in a single copy only, on randomly surviving fragments from Norwegian books.[13] Even a central composition like the sequence for Saint Óláfr, *Lux illuxit*, survive in only three copies in the Norwegian fragment material, none of the fragments containing the sequence in complete form.[14] Thankfully, there are multiple surviving copies in our neighbouring countries, thirty-five in Sweden alone.[15] In other cases, too, we can be grateful to foreign copyists for the survival of Norwegian-made texts, which are lost without trace in Norway itself.[16] Some

---

[12] For example, out of an estimated 25,000 missals in Italy *c.* 1350, a few hundred remain complete; Baroffio, 'Colligere fragmenta ne pereant', p. 680.

[13] *Itinerarium in terram sanctam*, describing a journey from Bergen to the Holy Land, was found (with lacunae) on late thirteenth-century fragments (NRA, Nor. fragm. 92) and edited in Storm, *Monumenta Historica Norvegiae*, pp. 163–68. The liturgical Office for the Holy Blood of Nidaros was preserved on a set of fragments in the Royal Library in Copenhagen (MS Add 47 fol.) and is edited in Attinger and Haug, *The Nidaros Office and the Holy Blood*.

[14] See Ommundsen, 'Books, Scribes and Sequences', I, 243 (NRA, Lat. fragm. 418, Lat. fragm. 986, and Lat. fragm. 932).

[15] Based on search in the MPO (Medeltida PergamentOmslag) database of 'Lux illuxit' (September 2017).

[16] One example is the sequence for Saint Hallvarðr, patron saint of Oslo, *Lux illuxit*, discovered by Georg Reiss among Icelandic fragments in the Arnamagnæan Collection (Copenhagen, AM 241b IV fol.); Reiss, *Musiken ved den middelalderlige Olavsdyrkelsen i Norden*, pp. 44–52. Another example is *Historia Norvegie* from the second half of the twelfth century, surviving in Scotland in a copy from *c.* 1510. The copy was part of the Dalhousie papers, since 2007 kept in the Scottish National Archives. The text was edited in 2003, in *Historia Norvegie*, ed. by Ekrem and Mortensen. A third example, *Fundatio Lysensis*, was copied in Denmark in the seventeenth-century from a scroll that later burned in the 1728 Copenhagen fire. The text

central medieval texts are left to us primarily through their inclusion in early printed books.[17]

As frustrating as the thought of lost works may be, the huge losses of the thousands of books with known texts — liturgical books, patristic authors, canon law, and so forth — are for a study of this kind almost as lamentable, since a medieval book conveys so much more than its text. It provides physical evidence of particular scribes' style of writing, their training and level of competence, and their access to good writing implements and materials. The palaeographical and codicological evidence contained in each individual fragment makes every little scrap of parchment important.

Building upon the work of earlier scholars, one of the first tasks, therefore, in the study of medieval book culture in Norway is to survey, date, and localize the material that has survived. The lack of a systematic catalogue was for a long time a big challenge for research, preventing the inclusion of the fragment material in broader surveys of cultural history.[18] A major project was launched in 2002 to enter the around six thousand fragments in Riksarkivet in Oslo into a digital database, a task that was completed in 2016.[19] Since the official database would clearly be a time-consuming project, in 2007 Michael Gullick drew up a handlist of the fragments in Riksarkivet, which he generously made available for others. Gullick's handlist presented all the fragments in a file along with basic information (estimated date, origin, etc.) and observations, giving

was edited by Storm, *Monumenta Historica Norvegiae*, pp. 169–72. For the function of the text itself, see France, 'Cistercian foundation narratives in Scandinavia'.

[17] Theodoricus Monachus's history of the Norwegian kings was discovered in Lübeck and printed in Kirchmann, *Commentarii historici duo hactenus inediti* in 1684. Egil Kraggerud's new edition *Theodoricus* appeared after this chapter had gone through the editorial process; as a result, it could not be taken into consideration, but will undoubtedly serve as the reference text for the future. Another example is the liturgical Office of Saint Sunnifa, patron saint of Bergen, where the text was preserved in the printed *Breviarium Nidrosiense* (1519) and edited in Storm, *Monumenta Historica Norvegiae*, pp. 283–89. The music is lost.

[18] In a book from 2001 on learning and ideas in medieval Norway, Sverre Bagge acknowledged the importance of the fragment material and pointed out the need for a systematic review and identification of its content; see Bagge, *Da boken kom til Norge*, p. 80.

[19] The digital database project at Riksarkivet in Oslo was initiated as a collaborative project between the Centre for Medieval Studies at the Norwegian University of Science and Technology in Trondheim and Riksarkivet in Oslo, and was funded by the Norwegian Research Council in the period 2002–06. The Norwegian database was built on the same template as the MPO project in Sweden in order to make the two catalogues compatible. All fragments were entered by 2016, but the database is yet to be available on the internet.

all interested scholars a valuable starting point. At the University of Bergen, our fragment research has used Gullick's handlist as a point of departure. One outcome of the fragment research here is complementary digital databases and tools, both under construction and already published, including a display of 'reconstructed' virtual manuscripts.[20] The intention is to make the fragment collections more accessible to scholars and the interested public, and provide more knowledge about the books in Norwegian churches, institutions, and collections.

Foreign Impulses and Local Initiatives

The religious communities that emerged in eleventh- and twelfth-century Norway did not necessarily include Norwegian-speaking individuals from the time of their foundation. Local funders of bishops' sees and religious houses — whether kings, noblemen, or bishops — looked abroad for the experience and know-how required to establish and run major religious institutions and to tutor promising locals. The efforts were apparently crowned with success. The activity of the first century of literacy was immense: liturgical books were copied, laws were committed to writing, basic religious texts were studied and selected pieces translated, documents were drawn up and letters written, to mention a few things.

Insofar as bishops took responsibility for the supply of books to parishes, the environs of cathedrals are important, particularly Trondheim, Selja/Bergen, and Oslo which were established as permanent bishop's sees during the reign of Óláfr kyrri (r. 1067–93).[21] As see of the archdiocese of Nidaros from 1152/53

---

[20] See <www.fragment.uib.no>. This site was part of the project 'From Manuscript Fragments to Book History' (2012–17), funded by Bergen Research Foundation and the University of Bergen. In time it will be linked to the site which constitutes the research data management of the project mentioned above, with the assistance of the University of Bergen Library. This data set will subsequently be linked with yet another online initiative, <https://fragments.app.uib.no>, an online illustrated inventory with nearly one thousand fragments (from 194 'phantom books') [both websites accessed 27 January 2019].

[21] The two smaller bishoprics on the Norwegian main land, Stavanger and Hamar, were established *c.* 1120 and 1152/53 respectively. Regarding doubts whether the formal transition of the bishop of western Norway from Selja to Bergen was done with the move of the bishop to Bergen in the 1090s or the translation of Sancta Sunnifa in 1170, see Ommundsen, 'The Cults of Saints in Norway before 1200', p. 79. The conclusion here is that the use of *Bergensis* and not *Seliensis* in official sources from the early twelfth century onwards (including the papal concession to the arch see of Nidaros in 1152/53) shows that Bergen was the official bishop's see in

and home to the shrine of Saint Óláfr (d. 1030), Trondheim was an important pilgrimage site. Bergen, a crucial trade centre and the preferred town of the kings until *c.* 1300, had numerous churches and religious institutions both in the town and its vicinity. Oslo was the largest town in the east, and from the early twelfth century onwards, Oslo cathedral housed the shrine of a local saint, Hallvarðr, further enhancing the status of the bishop's see.[22] Archaeological finds such as wax tablets and styli, rune sticks, and various inscribed items testify to the scribal activity in these towns.[23]

To copy already existing books, liturgical or otherwise, was altogether more widespread than original composition of texts. Not only was there from the beginning a great demand for liturgical books for church services, but the bishops' sees and larger religious communities also needed to be equipped with books covering anything from basic Latin grammar to patristic texts and homiletic guidebooks. To provide a quickly expanding church organization with the appropriate number of books in a relatively short amount of time must have been a formidable task for book-producing communities which were still relatively young. The goal was apparently achieved through a combination of imported books and local production efforts, and the highly international make-up of the first religious institutions influenced the corpus of books brought in as well as the style of writing and character of locally made books.

The fragments of eleventh-century manuscripts confirm to a high degree that Norway's first scribal centres had a strong international presence. The fragments to some extent corroborate what can be gleaned from other sources: namely, that England played a dominant role in the education and guidance of the first clergy-members. The English influence was certainly strong and has been most thoroughly studied;[24] however, Germans also contributed to

---

western Norway long before 1170, and presumably from the 1090s. Still, Selja continued to be an important religious centre and pilgrimage site throughout the Middle Ages.

[22] Saint Hallvard was apparently still in Lier in the 1070s, at the time of Adam of Bremen. He was moved any time between then and 1137, when his shrine according to Snorri was rescued from Oslo cathedral; Snorri Sturluson, *Heimskringla*, ed. by Bjarni Aðalbjarnarson, pp. 26–28. A high level of ecclesiastical activity shortly after 1100, with several churches built in stone, including Oslo Cathedral, is probably the back-drop for the move.

[23] Surprisingly few styli have been found in Bergen, although they may have been registered under different names, as there was an example of in 2011 when a stylus was identified among the items found in the foundations of St Mary's convent in Bergen. Cf. Ommundsen, 'Å skrive med stil'.

[24] See, for instance, Gullick, 'A Preliminary Account of the English Element' and 'A Preliminary List of Manuscripts'. See also Watson, *The English Contribution*.

Norwegian book production from an early date.[25] In the twelfth century a certain French influence is also distinguishable in the remaining Norwegian manuscript material.[26]

The convergence of European influences is not only visible through the palaeographical and codicological evidence provided by the fragments, but also in their contents and in a liturgical ordinal which probably reflects the ordinal of Nidaros cathedral.[27] The liturgical material certainly displays great variation, and the ordinal was itself highly eclectic.[28] One example is the repertory of sequences (a particular liturgical genre sung after the Alleluia in Mass on feast-days) which combines sets of German and Anglo-French sequences that normally are not found together. While the German sequences are relegated to less important days, the English and French sequences are preferred for major feast days. One possible explanation is that a wave of Anglo-French sequences overtook an older German repertory in the mid- to late twelfth century.[29]

Nidaros's status as archbishopric in 1152/53 seems to have fuelled ambitions further. Historical narratives in Latin and the vernacular were written, and several liturgical songs and offices were composed — these formed part of a growing Norwegian national identity and sense of self from around the middle of the twelfth century,[30] about a century after the first liturgical books are believed to have been copied on Norwegian soil. Much of the activity focused on Saint Óláfr, *rex perpetuus Norwegie*, as the figurehead of the Norwegian Church and the archbishopric of Nidaros. Furthermore, the activity in Trondheim seems to have spurred similar campaigns to promote Sunnifa in Bergen and Hallvarðr in Oslo.[31] The new works, such as liturgical offices, songs, and new redactions of local saints' legends, must have been followed by a

---

[25] Karlsen, 'Fragments of Patristic and Other Ecclesiastical Literature', pp. 218–19.

[26] See Myking, 'The French Connection'.

[27] Regarding the Nidaros ordinal, see discussion in a forthcoming publication: Marner, 'Liturgical Change and Liturgical Plurality'. Astrid Marner questions the notion that the edited ordinal is a testimony to a conscious effort *c.* 1200 to complete and distribute one liturgical rite to the whole archbishopric of Nidaros; cf. Gjerløw, *Ordo Nidrosiensis*.

[28] See, for instance, the publications of Gjerløw: *Ordo Nidrosiensis* and *Antiphonarium Nidrosiensis*.

[29] Kruckenberg, 'Making a Sequence Repertory', pp. 31–32.

[30] Lars Boje Mortensen refers to the middle of the twelfth century as one of Norway's 'mythopoietic moment', where intense creative activity shaped local group identities in a changing world; see Mortensen, 'Sanctified Beginnings and Mythopoietic Moments', pp. 267–69.

[31] Ommundsen, 'The Cult of Saints', pp. 88–90.

surge in the copying of books, the only means of circulating this new material. These scribal and literary activities were two aspects of the same movement and goal: to equip Norway and Nidaros with the tools necessary to practise religion at a level on par with the rest of Europe.

While it is natural to look to activities in the largest towns and bishops' sees, it is important to keep in mind that a scribal centre or centre of learning need not be urban, and the book-producing farms of Iceland remind us of the productivity of active individuals or groups in smaller places. In Norway it is worth mentioning a place like Lom, where the walls of the local stave church are covered in runic inscriptions, and the floorboards have not only revealed fragments of liturgical books, a unique parchment scroll containing the sequence of Thomas Becket, *Aquas plenas*, and numerous rune sticks, but also a bifolium from Donatus's *Ars minor* (a basic Latin grammar). None of these books can be shown to have been written in Lom, but it is remarkable that so much material is gathered there, and it merits further investigation. Runic writing in general is also an interesting aspect of medieval scribal culture, and the presence of prayers on rune-sticks, with Latin words spelled out in runes, makes it clear that some of these were carved by individuals with at least a basic knowledge of Latin grammar and orthography.[32] In other words, literate people engaged with writing in several forms, and they may have enjoyed various degrees of mastery in the Latin language as well as the runic script. The (at least) two languages, two writing systems (the Latin alphabet and runes), and several text-carrying media from parchment to wood, form part of the multi-layered complexity represented at Norwegian scribal centres.

Mapping the Scribes

With Norway's limited number of inhabitants and relatively few urban centres, it may seem strange that scribal and literary activities in the largest Norwegian towns and bishops' sees are relatively unmapped. However, none of the book collections in Norwegian towns or institutions have survived, and the flukes

---

[32] One example is a *peperit*-charm (a type of birth prayer) spelled out in perfect Latin in runes found on a rune-stick predating 1332 (Bergensnummer: B073, NIYR-nummer: 631). It is edited in Liestøl and Johnsen, *Norges Innskrifter*, VI.1, pp. 50–55. More than sixty variants of the *peperit*-charm have been found throughout Europe, often in the context of practical or medical handbooks. Several of the rune-sticks in Bergen have their contents in Latin, whether religious prayers (most commonly *Ave Maria* and *Pater noster*) or songs. There are also popular quotes, like *Amor vincit omnia*, or even examples of European goliardic songs.

of survival among written works and manuscripts often lack known dates and institutional affiliation. Furthermore, in most cases the authors and scribes remain elusive figures. Assembling groups of fragments together often depends upon the identification of peculiar or distinctive features in the work of individual scribes. This type of 'visual memory', or the ability to quickly recall or recognize something that one has seen before, may not be the most scientific working method, but it is at the moment the best we have to link fragments to each other.

To get any closer to understanding the activity in Norwegian scribal centres, it is necessary to look at the Latin and Old Norse material as two sides of the same coin. For those of us studying the palaeography of Latin books, it is particularly useful to give the vernacular manuscripts and fragments due attention, especially as much vernacular material can be localized by philological and linguistic evidence in a way that Latin material cannot.

When moving in on the level of individual scribes, one should keep in mind that the study of Norwegian scribal centres will always depend on a broad overview, both of the available source material and of European manuscript culture in general, since the 'local' to a considerable degree depends on the movements of books and scribes from other places. In the case of manuscripts, any small group of manuscripts can only be understood from a broad knowledge of many other manuscripts. And it is important to familiarize oneself with related fragment and manuscript collections, particularly in the Nordic countries where contact has been close and books have been exchanged both before and after the Reformation.

The first systematic effort in Norway to map the distribution of books and scribes to specific towns and institutions goes back to Didrik Arup Seip (1884–1963). Dealing mainly with vernacular manuscript material, he evaluated the regional affiliation of scribes on the basis of the Old Norse dialects discernible in the text samples.[33] Seip also mentions a few manuscripts in Latin with a possible Norwegian origin.[34] As far as the Latin liturgical material was

---

[33] Seip identified fourteen hands divided between eight manuscripts for the period before *c.* 1225, and placed the first four manuscripts (with four hands) in Nidaros and the last four manuscripts (with ten hands) in Bergen. For the periods after 1225, the number of vernacular manuscripts is considerably higher; cf. Seip, *Palæografi*.

[34] For the time before 1225 Seip suggests two Latin books which may have been written in Norway: GkS 1347 4° (a Gospel book) and NkS 32 8° (a liturgical book); cf. Seip, *Palæografi*, p. 6. While NkS 32 8° was presumably written in Norway, the Gospel book GkS 1347 4° was written in England in the 1130s ; see <http://www.kb.dk/permalink/2006/manus/237/eng/>

concerned, Seip dared not venture further into the matter but admitted that some liturgical books may have been written in Norway.[35]

Lilli Gjerløw (1910–98), who worked with the fragments throughout her career, identified further material featuring Norwegian scribes to be added to Seip's lists. Although Gjerløw's primary concern was medieval liturgy, she also had a remarkable eye for individual scribes. In her edition of the Nidaros ordinal from 1968, she presents some of her scribal identifications, linking Latin fragments to some of the important books in the vernacular.[36] She also supplemented Seip's lists of Norwegian hands from before 1225 with three items from the liturgical material.[37] Being very aware of the historical context, she often considered not only the most likely *origin* of a particular manuscript but also its most likely secondary provenance — that is, in which Norwegian bishopric it was used before ending up as a cover or in a binding.[38] Gjerløw considered material from across the Middle Ages, including the very earliest fragments dating to the eleventh century.[39]

The mobility of books and scribes is clearly visible in the whole corpus of fragments, and different European influences are immediately evidenced in the locally produced material. The lack of uniformity seems to be one characteristic trait of early Norwegian scribal centres, and so far we have seen no sign of large environments of near-identical hands or long stable lines of development. Scribes clearly trained in different traditions are found working together.[40]

[accessed 27 January 2019]. It is, however, commendable that Seip took into account the Gospel book itself: the property list written on the last quire of this book has captured the attention of Old Norse scholars to such a degree that the list is sometimes presented as a fragment from a separate Old Norse book rather than as part of an existing Latin book. For Latin books between 1225 and 1300, see Seip, *Palæografi*, p. 68.

[35] Seip, *Palæografi*, p. 68.

[36] Gjerløw, *Ordo Nidrosiensis Ecclesiae*, pp. 34–38.

[37] Gjerløw, 'Missaler brukt i Bjørgvin bispedømme', p. 112.

[38] In addition to 'Missaler brukt i Bjørgvin bispedømme', see also Gjerløw, 'Missaler brukt i Oslo bispedømme'.

[39] For more about Gjerløw's efforts and the research history of Norwegian fragments, see Karlsen, 'Introduction', pp. 15–19; Edwards, 'A Memoir of Lilli Gjerløw'; and Dverstorp, 'Lilli Gjerløw — a Bibliography'.

[40] For instance, a missal from the second half of the twelfth century, believed to be a Norwegian product, features two collaborating scribes, one writing in an Anglo-French manner, the other in a German style (Gjerløw's Mi 42, NRA, Lat. fragm. 751). For the change in hands, see Lat. fragm. 751.1–4ᵛ.

Norway in the twelfth and thirteenth century did not seem to have scriptoria resembling the large Carolingian scriptoria of the eighth and ninth century. When we do find similarities either in style or in single features of script, decoration, or musical notation, we form groups.[41] These often fall into the following categories:

1. fragments from the same book;

2. fragments from different books but involving the same scribe(s) or music scribes;

3. fragments from books written in a similar style or featuring the same decorative elements, which may or may not be connected to the same milieu.

The identifications under the second category are particularly relevant in this context. The more books which can be shown to originate from the same environment, the higher the chance that they represent local production rather than import, and the more information one is able to extract about the environment in which the books were made. There are particularly numerous defined groups among manuscripts dating to the decades before and after 1200. This may be coincidental, but it may also indicate a particularly high activity at this time combined with a 'high' survival rate. What follows is a list of various constellations for the time around 1200, indicating scriptoria or scribal centres in larger towns or smaller places:

1. One scribe seemingly working alone;

2. Two or more scribes working together, either on equal footing or in a hierarchy;

3. One or more text scribes working with one or more music scribes.

Two Norwegian scribes who stand out as remarkable individuals are 'the Benedict scribe' and 'the Homily Book scribe'.[42] Both scribes are named for their works in the vernacular, although they also copied liturgical books in Latin.

---

[41] For a more thorough discussion regarding methods for reconstructing books from fragments, see Gullick, 'Reflections on Nordic Latin Fragment Studies', pp. 24–30.

[42] The most valuable work on these two scribes has been done by Michael Gullick and has been published in both Norwegian and English: Gullick, 'Skriveren og kunstneren bak homilieboken', was amplified and expanded in Gullick and Ommundsen, 'Two Scribes and One Scriptorium Active in Norway ca. 1200'.

While the Benedict scribe most likely worked in Trondheim *c.* 1175–1200, the Homily Book scribe was based in a Bergen scriptorium a bit later, probably *c.* 1200–25.

The Benedict scribe, who copied the Rule of Benedict in Old Norse translation (see Figure 1), has been identified in as many as seven different books.[43] This number is highly unusual for Norwegian conditions and indicates that his production was substantial. His connection to Trondheim is supported both by the Old Norse dialect of the Rule and by the Trondheim provenance of the seventeenth-century accounts bound using his books (Figure 2)

The Benedict scribe seems to have worked mainly alone — at least there is no obvious identification of other scribes or artists in his works. The initials in his manuscripts appear to be his own, with distinct decorative features,

Figure 1. The fragments from an Old Norse translation of the Rule of Benedict show a skilled scribe, although not necessarily connected to a Benedictine monastery. Oslo, Riksarkivet, Nor. fragm. 81a. Printed with permission. Figure printed at actual size.

---

[43] NRA, Nor. fragm. 81ᵃ.1–5. Gullick identified the Benedict scribe in fragments from two antiphoners and a breviary-missal in Riksarkivet in Oslo and in two composite liturgical books, Thott 110 8° and NkS 133 f 4°, in Det Kongelige Bibliotek in Copenhagen. The two antiphoners are NRA, Lat. fragm. 934.1–6 (Gjerløw's Ant 39) and NRA, Lat. fragm. 889.1–5 (Gjerløw's Ant 43), while the breviary-missal is NRA, Lat. fragm. 137.1–6 + 320.1 + Box 45.37 (Gjerløw's Br-Mi 1). A leaf from a sixth liturgical book, another antiphoner, was then discovered by the author among the Latin fragments in Den Arnamagnæanske Samling in Copenhagen (AM Acc. 7 no. 56).

Figure 2. Several of the Latin fragments by the Benedict scribe, such as this fragment from an antiphoner (Gjerløw's Ant 39), were used to bind accounts from Trondheim. Oslo, Riksarkivet, Lat. fragm. 934.3ʳ. Printed with permission. Figure printed at actual size.

and the music notation may well be too, although this is as of yet uncertain. Given that he copied the Rule of Benedict one would think that he belonged to a monastic house, but the liturgical books from his hand indicate otherwise.[44] One prayer in a partially preserved sacramentary written by him includes a reference to the relics of Saint Óláfr 'resting in this very church'. This has previously been dismissed as too general to be a significant piece of information.[45] However, it is most likely that the prayer in fact refers to Óláfr's body, not a random Óláfr relic. In that case, the prayer was meant to be said in Nidaros cathedral, where Óláfr's shrine was kept. Since the book is by far his most modest book, with initials only partially filled in, it was probably written for his own personal use. This means that the Benedict scribe may possibly have been a canon at the Trondheim cathedral chapter or at the near-by Augustinian house of Elgeseter, using his sacramentary for services in the church. If so, he lived in the environs of Nidaros cathedral during the turbulent times of Archbishop Eiríkr Ivarsson (1188–1213), and was possibly already there at the time of Archbishop Eysteinn Erlendsson (1158/59–88). If the Benedict scribe was in

[44] This breviary-missal came from an Augustinian house according to Lilli Gjerløw, since it was made for an institution with both a prior and an abbot which did not follow the monastic liturgy; Gjerløw, *Ordo Nidrosiensis*, p. 84.

[45] Fæhn, *Manuale Norwegicum*, p. xliii.

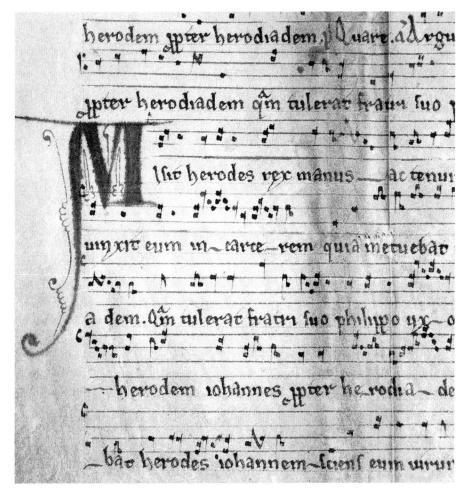

Figure 3. The Homily Book scribe made his own initials and also mastered music notation, as shown in this section from a fragmentarily preserved antiphoner (Gjerløw's Ant 7). Oslo, Riksarkivet, Lat. fragm. 1018.11. Printed with permission. Figure printed at actual size.

fact a member of one of the country's largest religious communities, it is all the more remarkable that he seems to have been more or less self-sufficient and working alone.

Another scribe, whose affiliations and identity has been much discussed, is the Homily Book scribe.[46] He seems to have worked *c.* 1200–25, less than a

---

[46] Until recently leaves from his hand had been interpreted as those of four different scribes. Fragments from a missal and antiphoner which Lilli Gjerløw in 1968 identified as

generation later than the Benedict scribe, and possibly had a similar position in the cathedral chapter in Bergen or a nearby Augustinian house. The source material indicates, however, that he related to his environment in a more active way. In addition to his 'own' books (see Figure 3), among them the oldest preserved manuscript in Old Norse, the Homily Book scribe contributed to the production of books written by other scribes, supplying musical notation, rubrics, and initials.[47] The other identified scribes, three in number, were probably affiliated to the same institution as the Homily Book scribe and were possibly being trained by him. All in all, there is evidence of five or six books from the Homily Book scribe's scriptorium: two in Old Norse (the Old Norwegian Homily Book and a translation of Honorius's *Gemma animae* from which four leaves survive, bound together with the Homily Book) and three or four liturgical books in Latin, two of which have the Homily Book scribe as the main scribe.[48]

Since the Homily Book scribe mastered music, it is likely that he acted as cantor in his institution, an office which would also have responsibility for the upkeep of liturgical books. How large a proportion of locally produced books were in fact made under the supervision of the cantor or by himself (with or without others to assist him) is uncertain.

Both these scribes reveal something about their background through their handwriting: the Benedict scribe writes in a rounder, more formal style, perhaps slightly old-fashioned for his time, while the Homily Book scribe is more dynamic and less formal in his way of writing. Both scribes are skilled, experienced, and clearly talented scribes, highly influenced by English models or teachers. They worked in centres with a good supply of fundamental writing implements, as well as access to good-quality pigments. With their diligence and skill, they were no doubt of great benefit to their respective communities.

---

closely related to the Homily Book, were interpreted as the product of a fifth scribe. Michael Gullick has argued convincingly that these 'five scribes' are in fact one and the same, see Gullick and Ommundsen, 'Two Scribes and One Scriptorium Active in Norway ca. 1200'.

[47] Identified by Michael Gullick and Gisela Attinger.

[48] The Homily Book is in Copenhagen (AM 619 4o) while the missal fragment (NRA, Lat. fragm. 764) and the antiphoner fragments are in Oslo (NRA, Lat. fragm. 959; Lat. fragm. 1018; Lat. fragm. 1039; Lat. fragm. 1043 a and b). For a reconstruction of the antiphoner, see <www.fragment.uib.no> [accessed 27 January 2019].

Other Constellations of Scribes and Artists c. 1200

Where we can say that the Benedict scribe, so far at least, represents the 'lone wolf', albeit in a large community in Trondheim, the Homily Book scribe is the 'supervisor' and 'team player' in Bergen. (This picture is, of course, open to modification with more source material.) There are other examples of groups working together around the same time, just before or after 1200, although it is more difficult to identify a specific town or institution. The following three groups of fragments have not yet been published in the way that the works of the two previous scribes have, since there is still a way to go in the analysis of the material and coming closer to establishing the historical context. Their hands are not identified in Old Norse material like those of the Benedict and Homily Book scribes; however, the very number of fragments from different manuscripts connected to the same scribal centre through overlapping scribes suggests a Norwegian origin for all three groups, and this is at least not contradicted by the style of the scribes or quality of the parchment.

The third 'group' (that is, third after the Benedict and Homily Book scribe) consists of two collaborating scribes who each wrote an antiphoner with musical notation around 1200 'in the same clumsy style' (see Figure 4).[49]

The initials and rubrics in both manuscripts were added by the same person, and so was the music notation.[50] The fragments are all in the same suede-like parchment.[51] It therefore seems safe to say that the two books were made in the same place. Both antiphoners follow secular — that is, not monastic — liturgy. There may be a link with English Augustinians through an antiphon

---

[49] The two manuscripts (Gjerløw's Ant 20 and Ant 30) were connected long ago by Lilli Gjerløw because of their initials; see Gjerløw, *Antiphonarium Nidrosiensis*, p. 35. Ant 20 consists of NRA, Lat. fragm. 765.1–3 and Nasjonalbiblioteket (the Norwegian National Library), fragm. 13 (unknown provenance). The leaves are 34 cm tall, written space 26.5 cm, and there are fourteen lines to the page. Ant 30 originally consisted of NRA, Lat. fragm. 420.1–18 (eastern Norway). The leaves are 36 cm tall, and the written space is 23.5 × 16 cm, with fifteen lines. In 2010 Gisela Attinger discovered two new fragment-units (NRA Lat. fragm. 1026.1–6 and Lat. fragm. 737) featuring the same scribe as Ant 30. Lat. fragm. 1026.1–6 (northern Norway) has a written space of 25.3 × 16 cm and fourteen lines, i.e., similar to Ant 20 and Lat. fragm. 737 (Bergen 1631) has a written space 25.1 cm tall and counts fifteen lines, like Ant 30. The character of the fragments makes it difficult to determine with certainty which fragments belong together, and whether the antiphoners could have been part of one unevenly constructed book.

[50] This was probably the scribe of Ant 30.

[51] A characteristic of Scandinavian parchment according to Gullick, 'Preliminary Observations'.

Figure 4. The style of this antiphoner (Gjerløw's Ant 20) and others may suggest book production by less experienced scribes, perhaps dictated by the needs of their institution. Oslo, Riksarkivet, Lat. fragm. 765.2ʳ. Printed with permission. Figure printed at actual size.

Figure 5. This text scribe of this antiphoner (Gjerløw's Ant 88) is also identified in other books, including in a marginal addition in a book written by someone else (see Figure 6). Oslo, Riksarkivet, Lat. fragm. 1012.4–5. Printed with permission. Figure printed at actual size.

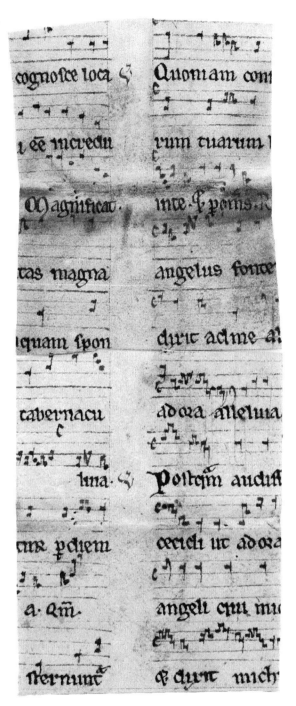

for the Assumption of Mary in one of the antiphoners, and it has been suggested that the antiphoner could come from a community of Augustinian canons.[52] Unfortunately, the provenances of the accounts do not point in a clear geographical direction to the place where these antiphoners were made: some accounts come from the western coast, some from the east and others from the north.[53] When we see that the earliest account bindings for both Ant 20 and 30 are for Hardanger and Halsnøy (1615), it is tempting to suggest a connection with the Augustinian canons at Halsnøy, but, as things stand at the moment, this is pure conjecture. What we can read from the evidence, however, is that none of these scribes share the skill and experience of the Benedict or Homily Book scribe. Since the

[52] Gjerløw, *Antiphonarium Nidrosiensis*, p. 82.

[53] NRA, Lat. fragm. 765.1–3 were taken from accounts concerning Hardanger og Halsnø 1615.

spes mortaliū · celsi to
nantis unice · caueq;
ꝯplet iugmis. a dgr
tam surgentibz · erur
gat ex mens soba · fla
elanseq; inlaudem dei ·
gꝵes ꝛependat debitas ·
iā ꝛefulget lucifer/
sparsāq; luce nunciat.
cadit caligo nochiū · lur
scā nos illuminet.
uensq; nūis sensibz · noc
aethꝛa ꝛepellat scdi · ōiꝗ
fine diei · ꝓgata ser
uet pectoꝛa. uelica
tā ꝑmū fides · radicet
altius sensibz. sedā spes
congaudeat · ꝗ maioꝛ
ꝺꝛtat caritas. eoꝑꝛi

Audiuim tuum ꝺo[...]
In tympano & choro
Laudare ꝺ. In maꝛ
terna
ꝯordie dei nostꝛi in
iꝗ conspectu angelo[...]
abi deus meus.
me ꝗ ꝯgnouisti mꝛ

Figure 6. The marginal addition supplied in this antiphoner (Gjerløw's Ant 37) shows that it was used in an institution with at least one active scribe (cf. Figure 5). Oslo, Riksarkivet, Lat. fragm. 1048.3–4. Printed with permission.

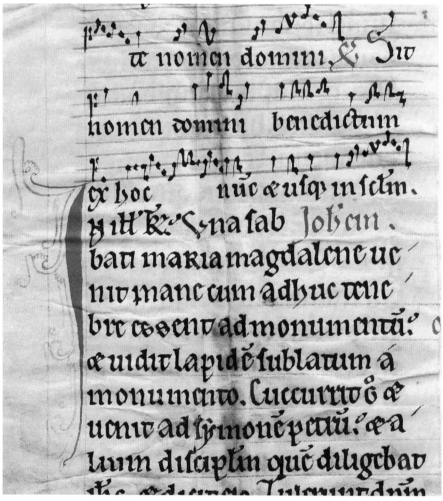

Figure 7. A fragment from a missal (Gjerløw's Mi 31) features one of the
four scribes in this group, along with the music scribe. Oslo, Riksarkivet,
Lat. fragm. 480.1. Printed with permission. Figure printed at actual size.

antiphoners have a certain awkwardness about them, one wonders whether the
scribes in this case were a cantor and a collaborator in a religious institution,
doing their best to fulfil their duties and supply a book needed at their own
institution, rather than commission it from others.

A fourth group, this time with three distinguishable individuals, can be
identified in fragments from one or two antiphoners and one missal featur-

ing one text scribe and two music scribes writing *c.* 1200–25.[54] The regional or institutional affiliation is unknown, but the antiphoners were used to bind account books from northern Norway. It is an unusual group of fragments, since we have evidence not only of the books produced by the scribe himself (see Figure 5), but also his addition into the margins of an older manuscript probably made somewhere else (see Figure 6).[55]

Although there is only one text scribe present, there are two different, seemingly contemporary, music scribes. This suggests a larger environment, less dependent on a single cantor or priest. Since all the fragments were used to bind archival material from northern Norway, it seems likely that they were collected in bulk from the same institution to be used as bindings in the north. It is of course possible that different liturgical books, or parts of these, were bound together in a composite volume at the time, and thus came as one manuscript to the bailiff or whoever was in charge of the bindings in which the fragments were used *c.* 1620. In any case, the text scribe demonstrates the active role that could be taken in updating and adapting older manuscripts to suit the needs of one institution at a given time.

I will briefly mention a fifth group consisting of four text scribes and one music scribe, which constitutes a proper scriptorium and a rather large scribal community in a Norwegian context. The music scribe, identified and recognized by the musicologist Gisela Attinger, ties together five or six (fragmentary) manuscripts from *c.* 1200.[56]

Where the manuscripts were made and the scriptorium situated is unclear, although the provenance of the bindings points to eastern Norway.[57] The generally high quality of the four text scribes (see Figures 7 and 8) and the fact

---

[54] Lat. fragm. 1012.4–5 (Vardøhus 1621); Lat. fragm. 1038 (Vardøhus 1622); Lat. fragm. 1055 (Vardøhus 1620). Ant 37 (unnumbered + Lat. fragm. 1048) (Lofoten 1619). The scribe and music scribe listed in this fourth group were identified in 2010 by the present author and Gisela Attinger.

[55] Two antiphoners (Lat. fragm. 1012.4–5 and Lat. fragm. 1038.1–2) and one missal (Lat. fragm. 1055). The music scribes appear to be different. There are several additions in the margin of Gjerløw's Ant 37, but the one relevant here is in NRA, Lat. fragm. 1048. It was identified by Gisela Attinger.

[56] Three missals (Mi 31 and 31b, and Mi 89/Mi 139), two graduals (Gr 46 and Gr 46b), and a breviary (Lat. fragm. 502.3–4).

[57] While fragments from the larger missal were reused in account books from all over southern Norway, the other four books were used to bind accounts from eastern Norway: Mi 89/139 (Tønsberg and Robygdelag in the period 1620–40); Gr 46 (Tønsberg 1617–19); Gr 46b (Akershus 1619) Breviary (Lat. fragm. 502.3–4) (Fredrikstad 1622–23).

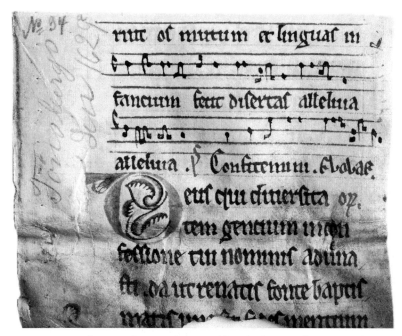

Figure 8. A fragment from another missal (Gjerløw's Mi 139) is associated
with the group via its music scribe. Oslo, Riksarkivet, Lat. fragm. 494.3.
Printed with permission. Figure printed at actual size.

that the books are completed with music notation and decorated with multi-
coloured initials, indicates a large, well-organized community. Hopefully we
will in time find a clue to identify where the scribes lived and worked.

These are several questions it may be useful to put to larger fragment groups
of local affiliation. How do the individuals relate to each other, and how large
would a 'typical' Norwegian scriptorium be? How many of the distinguished
book producing groups can be located with some certainty? To compare groups
of (presumed) local scribes working around the same time is a useful exercise,
and can be done for other periods within the Middle Ages.

Conclusion

One general conclusion that can be drawn about the Norwegian material from
fragment studies at their current level is that stylistic variation among scribes is
considerable. The number of active scribes in Norway *c.* 1200 was probably not
very high, and the ones we have evidence of display variable skills and different

regional influences in their work. Both single scriptoria and the institutions in a larger scribal centre would be manned with people with different backgrounds and different talents, normally in a size range from one to five active individuals. It is also likely that the levels of book production varied over time, depending on the number and skill of those present in such places at any one time.

The five groups of fragments presented above, testifying to different scribal communities, may appear to be assembled from chance finds and identifications, and to a certain extent they are. Where we have a starting point in the work of other scholars, it is easier also to 'programme' one's own visual memory to recognize features of specific scribes. For example, in the case of the Norwegian Homily Book scribe, three features were used for connecting several fragments: the general aspect of the scribe's hand, his repertory of decorative elements, and the character of his musical notation.[58] This way of working is, of course, not infallible: changing quality in pens and parchment, and different book formats may obscure similarities; furthermore, deciding what may be the significant detail (or details) to memorize or make note of is not always easy. And leafing through thousands of fragments is also time-consuming, although connections and identifications occur frequently enough to show the usefulness of a good visual memory combined with careful note taking.

In manuscript studies we assume that it is possible to some degree to say something about scribes, their models, and contact through the styles of their handwriting. By focusing on the materiality and uniqueness of manuscripts and manuscript fragments, one can, among other things, extract information about international contacts and collaboration.

A study of scribal centres is in other words just as much about the actual *books* as about the texts. This is by no means an exact science, and sometimes we are bound to be bewildered and sometimes wrong. Our attempts to contextualize and place pieces of written evidence in time and space may seem like a frustrating exercise. It seems to be a prerequisite for many aspects of medieval studies to first accept, and even embrace, chaos: scribes would move between countries, and would to some extent also move between languages — write in the vernacular one day and in Latin the next — as well as translate textual content from one language to the next. In addition, they could sometimes move between different writing systems, seemingly belonging to two different spheres: the Latin alphabet and the runes.

---

[58] Even after we thought that no more fragments were to be found, the Homily Book scribe was recognized in yet another fragment (NRA, Lat. fragm. 959) by Gisela Attinger in 2017.

One feature of fragment research is that the best work is done in interdisciplinary and international groups — scholars often know best the style of writing in the region they come from. Also, research often moves one step at a time: a discovery made by one scholar is added on to by others until firmer conclusions can be drawn, as shown in the examples of the Benedict scribe and the Homily Book scribe. At the same time, this makes fragment studies an almost unending 'work in progress'. Earlier assumptions and results need to be constantly adjusted and amended, and in some cases, corrected. It is therefore always tempting to delay publication, but perhaps the key is instead to overcome the fear of presenting imperfect and unpolished research results, in order to benefit from useful feedback from others in the next stages. Digital databases and internet presentations are particularly apt for discussing and investigating manuscripts preserved in the form of fragments, especially fragments scattered across different collections. Also, a digital presentation of the manuscript is none the worse for the lack of a binding, and no fragments need to be physically moved. Using digital tools it may be possible to leaf through the remains of our 'phantom books' as a unified whole (albeit with lacunae) long after they were destroyed, from anywhere in the world.[59] Fragments can only benefit from more exposure.

The scribal centres in Norway, on the edge of Europe, may be considered small in a European context. The long production lines and unified styles may not be their strength. However, we catch glimpses of individual scribes, working alone or in groups, who played a role in their respective communities. As much as medieval written culture was institutional, and followed broad international lines, it was also personal. Talented individuals could dominate an environment, making it flourish. Still, when institutions were as small as the Norwegian ones and so dependent on resourceful individuals, they became vulnerable: times of high-quality book production could be followed by periods of less activity (or possibly, periods when not-so-skilled people carried too much responsibility).

When working with Latin fragments and manuscripts and the environments that produced them, it is important to maintain a broad perspective on the culture of writing: literature should be seen in connection with liturgy, text composition with the copying of books, manuscripts with diplomas, Latin with Old Norse, Latin letters with runes. Then we will get a fuller and richer image of the scribal centres in the northernmost parts of Europe, what connects them with the rest of Europe, and what separates them.

---

[59] See for instance <fragment.uib.no>, as mentioned above [accessed 27 January 2019].

Works Cited

Manuscript Sources

Copenhagen, Den Arnamagnæanske Samling
    AM Acc. 7 no. 56
    AM 241b IV fol.
    AM 619 4°
Copenhagen, Det Kongelige Bibliotek
    Add 47 fol.
    GkS 1347 4°
    NkS 32 8°
    NkS 133 f 4°
    Thott 110 8°
Oslo, Riksarkivet (NRA)
    Box 45.37
    Lat. fragm. 137.1–6
    Lat. fragm. 320.1
    Lat. fragm. 418
    Lat. fragm. 420.1–18
    Lat. fragm. 502.3–4
    Lat. fragm. 737
    Lat. fragm. 751
    Lat. fragm. 764
    Lat. fragm. 765.1–3
    Lat. fragm. 889.1–5
    Lat. fragm. 932
    Lat. fragm. 934.1–6
    Lat. fragm. 959
    Lat. fragm. 986
    Lat. fragm. 1012.4–5
    Lat. fragm. 1018
    Lat. fragm. 1026.1–6
    Lat. fragm. 1038
    Lat. fragm. 1039
    Lat. fragm. 1043 a and b
    Lat. fragm. 1055
    Lat. fragm. 1048
    Nor. fragm. 81[a], 1–5
    Nor. fragm. 92
    Oslo, Nasjonalbiblioteket, fragm. 13

Primary Sources

DN 15 = *Diplomatarium Norvegicum* 15 (of 22 vols to date), ed. by C. R. Unger and H. J. Huitfeld-Kaas (Christiania: Malling, 1896–1900)

DN 21= *Diplomatarium Norvegicum* 21 (of 22 vols to date), ed. by Hallvard Magerøy (Oslo: Norsk historisk kjeldeskrift-institutt)

Historia Norwegie, ed. by Inger Ekrem and Lars Boje Mortensen, trans. by Peter Fisher (Copenhagen: Museum Tusculanum Press, 2003)

Theodoricus Monachus, *Historia de antiquitate regum Norwagiensium*, in *Commentarii historici duo hactenus inediti, alter de regibus vetustis Norvagicis, alter de profectione Danorum in terram sanctam, circa annum MCLXXXV susceptam, eodem tempore ab incerto autore conscriptus, cura olim et opera viri clarissimi Johannis Kirchmanni, Lubec., nunc primum editi ab hujus nepote Bernh. Casp. Kirchmanno J.U.D, Amsterdam*, ed. by B. C. Kirchmann (Amsterdam, 1684), pp. 1–76

Theodoricus, *De antiquitate regum Norwagiensium/On the Old Norwegian Kings*, ed. by Egil Kraggerud (Oslo: Novus, 2018)

Snorri Sturluson, *Heimskringla*, ed. by Bjarni Aðalbjarnarson, Íslenzk fornrit, 26–28, 3 vols (Reykjavík: Hið íslenzka fornritafélag, 1941–51)

Secondary Studies

Attinger, Gisela, and Andreas Haug, *The Nidaros Office and the Holy Blood: Liturgical Music in Medieval Norway* (Trondheim: Tapir, 2004)

Bagge, Sverre, *Da boken kom til Norge*, Norsk idéhistorie, 1 (Oslo: Aschehoug, 2001)

Baroffio, Giacomo, 'Colligere fragmenta ne pereant: Il recupero dei frammenti liturgici italiani', *Rivista liturgica*, 88 (2001), 679–94

Bell, David N., 'Cistercian Scriptoria in England: What They Were and Where They Were', *Citeaux*, 57 (2006), 45–67

Brunius, Jan, 'Från mässböcker till munkepärmar', in *Helgerånet*, ed. by Kerstin Abukhanfusa and others (Stockholm: Carlssons Bokförlag, 1993), pp. 15–22

Dverstorp, Nils, 'Lilli Gjerløw — a Bibliography', in *Latin Manuscripts of Medieval Norway: Studies in Memory of Lilli Gjerløw*, ed. by Espen Karlsen (Oslo: Novus, 2013), pp. 387–90

Edwards, Owain Tudor, 'A Memoir of Lilli Gjerløw and her Contribution to Norwegian Liturgical Research', in *Latin Manuscripts of Medieval Norway: Studies in Memory of Lilli Gjerløw*, ed. by Espen Karlsen (Oslo: Novus, 2013), pp. 361–80

Eken, Thorsten, ed., *Gammalnorske membranfragment i Riksarkivet: B. 1, 1–12 Lovtekster* (Oslo: Riksarkivet og Selskapet til utgivelse av gamle norske håndskrifter, 1963)

France, James, 'Cistercian Foundation Narratives in Scandinavia in their Wider Context', *Citeaux*, 43 (1992), 119–60

Fæhn, Helge, *Manuale Norwegicum* (Oslo: Norsk historisk kjeldeskrift-institutt, 1962)

Gjerløw, Lilli, *Antiphonarium Nidrosiense Ecclesiae* (Oslo: Norsk historisk kjeldeskrift-institutt, 1979)

——, 'Missaler brukt i Bjørgvin bispedømme fra misjonstiden til Nidarosordinariet', in *Bjørgvin bispestol: Byen og bispedømmet*, ed. by P. Juvkam (Bergen: Universitetsforlaget, 1970), pp. 73–128

——, 'Missaler brukt i Oslo bispedømme fra misjonstiden til Nidarosordinariet', in *Oslo bispedømme 900 år*, ed. by Fridtjov Birkeli and others (Oslo: Universitetsforlaget, 1974), pp. 73–142

——, *Ordo Nidrosiensis ecclesiae* (Oslo: Norsk historisk kjeldeskrift-institutt, 1968), pp. 34–38

Gullick, Michael, 'A Preliminary Account of the English Element in Book Acquisition and Production in Norway before 1225', in *Latin Manuscripts of Medieval Norway: Studies in Memory of Lilli Gjerløw*, ed. by Espen Karlsen (Oslo: Novus, 2013), pp. 103–21

——, 'A Preliminary List of Manuscripts, Manuscript Fragments and Documents of English Origin or the Work of English Scribes in Norway Datable to before 1225', in *Latin Manuscripts of Medieval Norway: Studies in Memory of Lilli Gjerløw*, ed. by Espen Karlsen (Oslo: Novus, 2013), pp. 123–97

——, 'Preliminary Observations on Romanesque manuscript fragments of English, Norman and Swedish origin in the Riksarkivet (Stockholm)', in *Medieval Book Fragments in Sweden*, ed. by Jan Brunius (Stockholm: Royal Academy of Letters, History and Antiquities 2005), pp. 31–82

——, 'Reflections on Nordic Latin Fragment Studies — Past and Present — Together with Three Case Studies', in *Nordic Latin Manuscript Fragments: The Destruction and Reconstruction of Medieval Books*, ed. by Åslaug Ommundsen and Tuomas Heikkilä (London: Routledge, 2017), pp. 24–65

——, 'Skriveren og kunstneren bak homilieboken', in *Vår eldste bok*, ed. by Odd Einar Haugen and Åslaug Ommundsen (Oslo: Novus, 2010), pp. 77–99

Gullick, Michael, and Åslaug Ommundsen, 'Two Scribes and One Scriptorium Active in Norway ca. 1200', *Scriptorium*, 66.1 (2012), 25–54

Gunnes, Erik, 'Klosterlivet i Norge: Tilblivelse — økonomi — avvikling', *Foreningen til norske fortidsminnesmerkers bevaring. Årbok* 1987 (141), 49–84

Heikkilä, Tuomas, and Åslaug Ommundsen, 'Piecing together the Past: The Accidental Manuscript Collections of the North', in *Nordic Latin Manuscript Fragments: The Destruction and Reconstruction of Medieval Books*, ed. by Åslaug Ommundsen and Tuomas Heikkilä (London and New York: Routledge, 2017), pp. 1–23

Karlsen, Espen, 'Fragments of Patristic and Other Ecclesiastical Literature', in *Latin Manuscripts of Medieval Norway: Studies in Memory of Lilli Gjerløw*, ed. by Espen Karlsen (Oslo: Novus, 2013), pp. 215–69

——, 'Introduction', in *Latin Manuscripts of Medieval Norway: Studies in Memory of Lilli Gjerløw*, ed. by Espen Karlsen (Oslo: Novus, 2013), pp. 13–26

——, 'Katalogisering av membranfragmenter som forskningsprosjekt, del 2', *Riksarkivaren: Rapporter og retningslinjer. Arkivverkets forskningsseminar* 16 (Gardermoen: Riksarkivaren, 2003), 58–88

——, 'Latin Manuscripts of Medieval Norway: Survival and Losses', in *Latin Manuscripts of Medieval Norway: Studies in Memory of Lilli Gjerløw*, ed. by Espen Karlsen (Oslo: Novus, 2013), pp. 27–39

——, 'Liturgiske bøker i Norge inntil år 1300 — import og egenproduksjon', in *Den kirke-historiske utfordring*, ed. by Steinar Imsen (Trondheim: Tapir, 2005), pp. 147–70

Kruckenberg, Lori, 'Making a Sequence Repertory: The Tradition of the Ordo Nidrosiensis Ecclesiae'. in *The Sequences of Nidaros: A Nordic Repertory and its European Context*, ed. by Lori Kruckenberg and Andreas Haug (Trondheim: Tapir, 2006), pp. 5–44

Liestøl, Aslak, and Ingrid Sannes Johnson, *Norges innskrifter med de yngre Runer*, VI.1: *Bryggen i Bergen* (Oslo: Norsk Historisk Kjeldeskrift-Institutt, 1980)

Marner, Astrid, 'Liturgical Change and Liturgical Plurality in the Province of Nidaros: New Light on the *Ordo Nidrosiensis Ecclesiae*', in *Bishop Jón Halldórsson of Skálholt and his Influence on Icelandic Literature*, ed. by Gunnar Harðarson (Reykjavík, forthcoming).

Mazal, Otto, 'Skriptorium', *Lexicon des Mittelalters*, 7 (2002), 1993–97

Mortensen, Lars Boje, 'Sanctified Beginnings and Mythopoietic Moments: The First Wave of Writing on the Past in Norway, Denmark, and Hungary, c. 1000–1230', in *The Making of Christian Myths in the Periphery of Latin Christendom (c. 1000–1300)*, ed. by Lars Boje Mortensen (Copenhagen: Museum Tusculanum Press, 2006), pp. 247–73

Myking, Synnøve, 'The French Connection: Manuscript Fragments of French Origin and their Historical Context' (unpublished PhD thesis, University of Bergen, 2016)

Ommundsen, Åslaug, 'Books, Scribes and Sequences in Medieval Norway', 2 vols (unpublished PhD thesis, University of Bergen, 2007)

——, 'The Cults of Saints in Norway before 1200', in *Saints and their Lives on the Periphery*, ed. by Haki Antonsson and Ildar Garipzanov (Turnhout: Brepols, 2010), pp. 67–94

——, 'Å skrive med stil — stylus frå Nonneseter gjenoppdaga i museets magasin', *Bergen museums årbok* (2011), 51–55

Ommundsen, Åslaug, and Tuomas Heikkilä, eds, *Nordic Latin Manuscript Fragments: The Destruction and Reconstruction of Medieval Books* (London: Routledge, 2017)

Pettersen, Gunnar I., 'From Parchment Books to Fragments: Norwegian Medieval Codices before and after the Reformation', in *Latin Manuscripts of Medieval Norway: Studies in Memory of Lilli Gjerløw*, ed. by Espen Karlsen (Oslo: Novus, 2013), pp. 41–65

Reiss, Georg, *Musiken ved den middelalderlige Olavsdyrkelsen i Norden*, Videnskapsselskapets Skrifter, 2: Hist.-filos. Klasse. 1911, 5 (Kristiania: Videnskapsselskapet, 1912)

Sanness Johnsen, Ingrid, and James E. Knirk, *Norges Innskrifter med de yngre Runer*, VI.2: *Bryggen i Bergen* (Oslo: Norsk Historisk Kjeldeskrift-Institutt, 1990)

Seip, Didrik Arup, *Palæografi. B. Norge og Island*, Nordisk Kultur, 28B (Uppsala: Bonnier, 1954)

Smith, Margaret M., 'Preface', in *Interpreting and Collecting Fragments of Medieval Books*, ed. by Linda L. Brownrigg and Margaret M. Smith (London: Anderson-Lovelace, 2000), pp. xi–xv

Storm, Gustav, *Monumenta Historica Norvegiae* (Kristiania: Brøgger, 1880)

Watson, Matilda, 'The English Contribution to the Emergence of Manuscript Culture in Eleventh-Century Norway and Sweden' (unpublished PhD thesis, University of Cambridge, 2015)

LETTERS FROM KINGS:
EPISTOLARY COMMUNICATION IN THE KINGS' SAGAS (UNTIL *c.* 1150)

Jonas Wellendorf

Most would agree that the breakthrough of textual culture in Norway and the development of literate mentalities occurred over the course of the twelfth century. Latin and vernacular manuscript fragments testify to ecclesiastical use of the newly imported technology of writing for liturgical, literary, pastoral, and practical purposes.[1] Direct evidence of secular uses of the same technology, be they practical or literary, are — aside from the laws — harder to come by for this early period.[2] Indirect testimonies in the form of references to letters sent between members of the secular elite can be

---

[1] The oldest locally produced Norwegian Latin fragments are dated to the late eleventh century (see Karlsen, 'Om innholdet', pp. 64–70).

[2] The oldest is a letter by King Philippús Símonarson to the people of Morsdal. The letter is not dated, but it must have been written during Philippús's reign (1207–17) (*DN* I, 3; *RN* I, 398). According to Hreinn Benediktsson, *Early Icelandic Script*, p. 16, the earliest known document might date from 1083. The original of this document (if authentic) has not been preserved, and it is only known through later copies (printed in *Grágás* I, 2, 197 and *DI* I, 64). Rindal, 'Dei eldste norske kristenrettane', p. 110, maintains that Norwegian laws were written already in the early eleventh century, writing: 'Dei eldste lovene kan såleis vere skrivne ned i fyrste halvdelen av 1000-talet' and 'det [er] grunn til å tru at den norske kristenretten går så langt tilbake som til ca. 1020', but few scholars accept such an early date.

Jonas Wellendorf (wellendorf@berkeley.edu) is Associate Professor of Old Norse in the Department of Scandinavian at the University of California, Berkeley, and director of the Program in Medieval Studies. His research focuses on the interface between vernacular Old Norse literature and the Latin tradition.

Moving Words in the Nordic Middle Ages: Tracing Literacies, Texts, and Verbal Communities, ed. by Amy C. Mulligan and Else Mundal, AS 8   BREPOLS PUBLISHERS   (Turnhout: Brepols, 2019)
pp. 113–141   10.1484/M.AS-EB.5.116622

found in narrative sources like the kings' sagas, but certainty about the historical truth of such accounts is often hard to achieve. Writers of kings' sagas can be
considered historians and their compositions viewed as accounts of past events
that have taken place, but their works differed from those of modern historians
in that they did not necessarily endeavour to present factual accounts of events
combined with analytical interpretations. Rather, they strove to present their
analysis in narrative form. They did so by fashioning plausible accounts of minor
events to explain major events in a manner that was satisfying and in agreement
with their general interpretation of the course of events. *Heimskringla*, which
reworks and develops many anecdotes told in earlier kings' sagas, provides clear
examples of this. These anecdotes often take the form of elaborate scenes that
suspend the grander panoramic narrative.[3]

This tendency to combine the factual and the non-factual and to interpret
a core set of historical facts or events by means of fictional narration poses significant problems for those who attempt to use kings' sagas as direct sources
for historical incidents or processes, such as, for instance, the development of
secular uses of literacy. Scholars working on the sagas are often acutely aware of
these problems and exhibit due caution in many cases, but some saga episodes
and scenes are still considered factual rather than plausible. This essay will focus
on one such case. Scholarly consensus holds that a letter of 1139 from King Ingi
krókhryggr 'hunchback' (d. 1161) to King Sigurðr munnr 'mouth' (d. 1155),
quoted in the kings' sagas *Morkinskinna* and *Heimskringla*, reflects an actual
historical letter. Because it is impossible to determine the letter's historicity or
lack thereof with any certainty, I will consider the letter of 1139 first in the
light of other letters quoted in the major kings' sagas dealing with the eleventh
and early twelfth centuries. Then I will consider the text of the letter and its
function as a component of *Morkinskinna* and *Heimskringla*. The final section
will consider the question of the origin of the letter and outline what this can
tell us about the secular uses of writing in the mid-twelfth century in Norway.

Before this the enigmatic and now-lost text *Hryggjarstykki* should be introduced. It is clear from references in *Morkinskinna* and *Heimskringla* that this
text was written by a certain Eiríkr Oddsson.[4] It is generally thought that the

---

[3] See Meulengracht Sørensen's analysis in 'Historiefortælleren Sturla Þórðarson' of Sturla
Þórðarson's description of the battle of Ǫrlygsstaðir and the events that led up to this in *Íslendinga saga*.

[4] *Heimskringla* contains a handful of references to an Eiríkr Oddsson (*Hrk* III, 313 and
317–19) and mentions that he wrote a book called *Hryggjarstykki* (*Hrk* III, 318). *Morkinskinna* also contains a reference to a piece of writing by Eiríkr Oddsson (*Msk* II, 185), but the

text of the letter of 1139 derived from *Hryggjarstykki* as well. In his mono-
graph on *Hryggjarstykki*, Bjarni Guðnason considered the letter of 1139 to be
among the few written sources Eiríkr Oddsson had at his disposal in the mid-
twelfth century when composing the text.[5] Bjarni Guðnason characterized it
as a 'letter marking a watershed moment', as 'the oldest letter in the history of
Norway of which the content has been preserved', and as a 'significant historical
source to the domestic conditions in Norway in 1139'.[6] These views of Bjarni
Guðnason have by and large been accepted, and both the recent authoritative
Íslenzk fornrit edition of *Morkinskinna* and the fairly recent English translation refer without comment to Bjarni Guðnason's work.[7] This now-lost work is
so obscure that certainty about the content, style, sources, and size is unlikely to
be attained. Even the exact meaning of the title *Hryggjarstykki*, perhaps 'backbone piece(s)', remains a matter of conjecture.[8]

Bjarni Guðnason labelled *Hryggjarstykki* 'the first saga' and dated it to
around 1150. He argued that Eiríkr Oddsson used the genre of hagiography as
his narrative model and structured *Hryggjarstykki* accordingly. He argued further that *Hryggjarstykki* should be seen as a saga of Sigurðr slembir (or slembi-
djákn) (d. 1139) and that its purpose was to advocate the sanctity of this failed

---

text itself is not named. The text of the *Hulda-Hrokkinskinna* compilation also refers to *Hryggjarstykki*, but it betrays no first-hand knowledge of the *Hryggjarstykki*, and the text in this
part of the compilation mainly derives from *Heimskringla* (*Hulda*, ed. by Louis-Jensen, p. 26).

[5] Bjarni Guðnason, *Fyrsta sagan*, p. 73.

[6] Despite his views on the significance of the letter, Bjarni Guðnason does not think that
the exact wording of the letter is the original, but its subject matter is: 'Bréf þetta, sem nefnt er
rit, í *Msk.* og *Fsk.*, er tímamótabréf. Það er elst bréfa, sem geymst hefur að efni til, í sögu Noregs,
og í annan stað merk söguleg heimild um innanlandsástandið í Noregi í 1139' (Bjarni Guðnason, *Fyrsta sagan*, p. 73).

[7] See *Msk* II, 200 n. 1, and *Morkinskinna*, trans. by Andersson and Gade, p. 463. See also
Bagge, *From Viking Stronghold to Christian Kingdom*, pp. 244–45, who is inclined to see the
letter as authentic. Scholars of the earlier twentieth century were more divided in their opinion
on the authenticity of the letter. Kválen, *Den eldste norske kongesoga*, pp. 162–64, uses inverted
commas every time he refers to the letter in order to signal that he thinks it is inauthentic, while
Agerholt, *Gamal brevskipnad*, II, 639–40, holds that the content is authentic while the wording
might have been changed, but he also adds: 'endå um ein sogeskrivar skulde ha laga brevet frå
1139 (eller òg laga det heilt um), høyrer det likevel med millom dei eldste me kjenner'.

[8] The most recent discussion of the title appears to be a brief article by Sverrir Tómasson
from 1979 (reprinted with a few additional notes in 2011). The latest contribution to scholarship on *Hryggjarstykki* is by Mundal, 'Sagaskrivarane og Bergen' from 2014.

pretender to the Norwegian throne.[9] Danielsson, in the latest substantial contribution to the discussion on *Hryggjarstykki*, has since then undermined many of Bjarni Guðnason's central claims, to the extent that Bjarni Guðnason's central point concerning the attempts to have Sigurðr sanctified 'ter sig [...] helt grundlös'.[10] Concerning the letter, Danielsson finds it impossible to ascertain whether or not the letter was a part of *Hryggjarstykki*, although he suspects that it was not (I will return to this below).

Letters in Kings' Sagas

Old Norse chroniclers or saga writers of the late thirteenth and fourteenth centuries relied, sometimes to a great extent, on documentary material. Sturla Þórðarson (d. 1284) appears to have had access to a wealth of written documents in Bergen when composing his saga about King Hákon Hákonarson around 1263, and he refers frequently to these letters throughout the saga.[11] No fewer than 130 letters are mentioned, but Sturla only quotes — or claims to quote — directly from these letters on two occasions.[12] None of the letters he quotes or refers to appear to be preserved independently. Even if it is therefore impossible to verify Sturla's epistolary claims, the circumstances under which he wrote, the nature of the information derived from the putative letters, and our knowledge of the royal chancery at the time of writing make it likely that Sturla Þórðarson did indeed have access to material of this kind when composing the saga of King Hákon Hákonarson. In the fourteenth century, the authors of the sagas of Bishop Árni of Skálholt (*Árna saga*) and Bishop Lawrence of Hólar (*Lárentíus saga*) used a similar method when writing about the bishops, and in some cases, the existence of documents referred to in the sagas is confirmed by documents preserved independently of the sagas.[13] While documentary sources thus provided saga writers of the late thirteenth and fourteenth century with rich and valuable source material, saga writers of earlier periods do not appear to have had a comparable amount of written material at their disposal. They do

---

[9] Bjarni Guðnason, *Fyrsta sagan*, p. 158.

[10] Danielsson, *Sagorna om Norges kungar*, p. 288.

[11] See Bjørgo, 'Om skriftlige kjelder'.

[12] These letters can be found in *Hákonar saga Hákonarsonar*, ed. by Þorleifur Hauksson, Sverrir Jakobsson, and Tor Ulset, I, 195 and 312.

[13] See *Biskupa sögur III*, ed. by Guðrún Ása Grímsdóttir, pp. xlii–xliii and lxxxviii–xciii

nevertheless occasionally refer to letters, and the texts of some of these letters are also quoted in the course of the saga narratives.

Saga writers were well aware of the fact that the earliest Norse kings reigned before parchment literacy had been introduced into Scandinavia, at a point in time when writing, excepting shorter messages carved in runes, was not commonly used in the Norse world. Saga writers would presumably have considered it anachronistic to represent a ninth-century king such as Haraldr hárfagri (fair-hair) sending royal writs to his subordinates. If Haraldr hárfagri had a message to communicate to someone, he was therefore depicted sending messengers rather than written messages.[14] Similarly, the Old Norse gods are not depicted as being literate in the Roman alphabet; should we believe the Eddas, not even runic literacy appears to have been widespread among the gods, even though Óðinn is said to have found the runes. In the reign of St Óláfr (d. 1030), the point in time when it was acceptable for a kings' saga to represent a Norwegian king actively taking advantage of the technology of writing had apparently not yet arrived.[15] *Heimskringla* depicts Óláfr as the recipient of a sealed letter from Knútr inn ríki (Canute the Great), king of England and Denmark, but Óláfr's response takes the form of an oral rather than a written message. Historians date this putative letter of King Knútr to 1024–26.[16] While it is thus appropriate for a kings' saga to show King Knútr making use of the technology of writing, the same cannot be said of his Norwegian contemporary Óláfr Haraldsson. As soon as Knútr's messengers met with King Óláfr in Túnsberg, they produced the letter and explained its message. Óláfr, on the other hand, gave an oral reply. The messengers left, it is said, and 'váru eigi ørendi fegnir' (were not pleased with the result of their errand).[17] It should

---

[14] For example, *Hkr* I, 96.

[15] *Fagrskinna* is unique in portraying the dying Hákon góði (the good) (d. 961) as sending a letter (*bréf*) to the sons of Gunnhildr, his nephews and adversaries (*Fsk*, pp. 94–95). According to *Historia de antiquitate regum Norwagiensium*, p. 29, St Óláfr had laws written down: 'Leges patria lingua conscribi fecit juris et moderationis plenissimas, quæ hactenus a bonis omnibus et tenentur et venerantur' (He [St Óláfr] had laws replete with justice and equity committed to writing in the native language: and to this day these are upheld and venerated by all good men), (transl. McDougall and McDougall, p. 21). However, the majority tradition holds that Óláfr merely 'laid down the law' (*máttu leggja landsrétt*, Sighvatr Þórðarson, *Hkr* II, p. 73), 'established' or 'organized' the law (*setti* and *skipa*, *Hkr* II, p. 73; *setti*, *Legendariske saga*, p. 28), 'gave' the law (*gaf*, *Legendariske saga*, p. 35), etc.

[16] *RN* I, 25.

[17] *Hkr* II, 224; *Heimskringla*, trans. by Finlay and Faulkes, II, 149.

be mentioned that it was King Óláfr's refusal to give in to the demands of King Knútr and to turn over the rule of Norway to him, not Óláfr's failure to provide a written response, that caused the envoys' displeasure.[18]

Representations of letter-sending kings in England (even a Scandinavian one) were clearly not considered anachronistic by saga writers,[19] and *Heimskringla* also mentions that Knútr's wife Emma at one point succeeded in laying her hands on the seal of the king and used it to send forged letters to Denmark without his knowledge.[20] In Norway, however, the kings were represented as sticking to the old ways.

In the reign of Magnús góði (the good) (r. 1035–47), the son of St Óláfr, letter-sending appears for the first time in the three major kings' sagas representations of the activities of a Norwegian king.[21] *Morkinskinna* refers to one sealed letter from Magnús góði to Kálfr Árnason that promises him pardon and safe conduct if he will give his support to Rǫgnvaldr, who has been appointed earl over the Orkneys (*Msk* 43).[22] *Orkneyinga saga* relates the same incident, but the message from the king is ambiguously referred to as *orð* (words), which can refer to a written message as well as an oral one.[23] *Heimskringla* gives a rather different account of Kálfr Árnason's reconciliation with the Norwegian king (which, in this case, is Haraldr harðráði, r. 1046–66). The Norwegian king makes an oral agreement with Kálfr's brother Finnr Árnason, who in turn communicates the agreement to Kálfr. As in the case of *Orkneyinga saga*, it is impossible to

---

[18] Terje Spurkland, 'Þeir báru fram bref', p. 63, has studied this episode, which is recounted in a number of kings' sagas, from a literacy perspective, and concludes that the account in *Heimskringla* reflects a phase in Norwegian history at which letters had a primarily symbolic function, giving legitimacy and authority to messages that were primarily delivered orally. Spurkland further argued that the accounts of the same episode in *Fagrskinna* and *Flateyjarbók* bear witness to a more developed stage in the development of a literary mentality — in a response to Spurkland, Jan Ragnar Hagland, '*Segia fra* eller *rita*', (2002) argued the opposite.

[19] Knútr inn ríki had an effective administrative system at his disposal in England, and there can be no doubt that the use of writing was an integral element of his government as a fair number of authentic charters and letters issued by Knútr have been preserved (catalogued by Sawyers in *Anglo-Saxon Charters*, and discussed by Keynes, 'Cnut's Earls').

[20] *Hkr* ii, 275; also in *Fsk*, p. 203.

[21] According to *Fagrskinna*, Hákon sent a letter to the Eiríkssons as he lay dying (*Fsk*, pp. 94–95).

[22] Kálfr Árnason had part in the killing of Magnús' father, St Óláfr, at Stiklastaðir, and the sagas therefore depict his relationship with Magnús as somewhat strained.

[23] 'Hann sendi orð Kálfi Árnasyni' (he sent words to Kálfr Árnason) (*Orkneyinga saga*, ed. by Finnbogi Guðmundsson, p. 65).

determine whether the author of *Heimskringla* wished to represent the central message to Kálfr in the Orkneys as a written message or an oral one; the word used is *orðsending* (message) (*Hkr* III, p. 132).[24] It would be tempting to argue that *Heimskringla* is consciously vague as to the medium of the Norwegian king's message, had it not represented Magnús góði sending a letter on an earlier occasion. Not content with merely mentioning the letter, *Heimskringla* even gives the text of Magnús's letter as a direct extended quotation.

The major episode involving epistolary communication in the reign of Magnús the good involves the English king Játvarðr (Edward the Confessor, d. 1066). The prelude to this epistolary exchange is that Magnús and Hǫrða-Knútr 'Hartha-Cnut', son and successor of Knútr inn ríki as king of Denmark (r. 1035–42) and England (1040–42), famously had agreed that if either died without an heir, the other would inherit the kingdom. After Hǫrða-Knútr's death, Magnús took over the Danish part of Hǫrða-Knútr's kingdom while Játvarðr was taken as king in England. Magnús then writes to Játvarðr and demands that he surrender his royal authority to Magnús. *Morkinskinna* and *Fagrskinna* both mention Magnús's letter and report its content.[25] *Heimskringla* on the other hand, is not satisfied with just referring to what it contains, and quotes the body of the letter: 'En þat stóð a bréfum með kveðjusending Magnúss konungs: "Þér munuð spurt hafa einkamál þau, er vér Hǫrða-Knútr gerðum með oss"' (And this is what was included in the letters along with King Magnús's greetings: 'You will have heard of the special agreements that Hǫrða-Knútr and I have made between ourselves').[26]

In all three texts, the English king responds to Magnús's demands by enumerating how his claim to the English throne had been slighted repeatedly after the death of his father (Aðalráðr/Æthelred the Unready in 1016) and how oth-

[24] *Hkr* III, 132. 'Finnr Árnason, bróðir hans, gerði orð Kálfi ok lét segja honum einkamál þau, er þeir Haraldr konungr hǫfðu við mælzk [...]. En er Kálfi kom sjá orðsending, þá [...]' (His brother Finnr Árnason sent word to Kálf and had him told of the private agreement that he and King Haraldr had entered into together][...]. And when this message reached Kálfr, then he [...]' (*Heimskringla*, trans. Finlay and Faulkes, III, 79).

[25] '[Magnús sendi] menn með bréfum til Englands vestr, á fund Játvarðs góða [...]. En á þeim bréfum var sú orðsending at [...]' (Magnús sent men with a letter to England in the West, to Játvarðr the Good [...]. The letter contained the message that [...]) (*Msk* I, 77). '[Magnús sendi] menn með bréfum <vestr> til Englands á fund Játvarðar konungs, ok var sú orðsending í bréfum, at [...]' (Magnús sent messengers with a letter to King Játvarðr in England in the West, and the message in the letter was that [...]) (*Fsk*, p. 216). At this point the *Morkinskinna* text is from the younger part of *Flateyjarbók*.

[26] *Hkr* III, 65; *Heimskringla*, trans. Finlay and Faulkes, III, 39.

ers have ascended to the throne instead of him — first his brother Jatmundr/ Edmund, then his stepfather Knútr, then his second brother Haraldr, and finally Hǫrða-Knútr, yet another brother. As a conclusion, Játvarðr mentions that it is unlikely he will raise an army to defend his kingdom should Magnús desire to subjugate England by force. Softened by the story of Játvarðr's great tribulations (*mikla hǫrmung*), Magnús completely abandons his claim to the English throne.[27] There is a clear, and not necessarily coincidental, parallelism between Magnús's correspondence with Játvarðr on the one hand and Knútr's earlier correspondence with Óláfr on the other. Besides this, Játvarðr's response functions as a brief recapitulation of recent English history, and the episode serves to illustrate how Magnús turns from iniquity to righteousness when prompted; a characteristic that on another occasion had earned him the sobriquet inn góði 'the good'.

Both *Morkinskinna* and *Fagrskinna* quote Játvarðr's somewhat naively written response, while *Heimskringla* represents Játvarðr responding orally. Magnús's messengers then return to Norway and inform King Magnús of the English king's answer.[28] Each of the three kings' sagas then present the interaction between the two kings in a unique modal combination. For clarity, the various configurations of the demand of the Norwegian king and the response of the English king are presented in the following table.

	Morkinskinna	*Fagrskinna*	*Heimskringla*
Magnús to Játvarðr	content of letter summarized	content of letter summarized	letter quoted
Játvarðr to Magnús	letter quoted	direct speech	direct speech

The differences in the accounts of the exchange of messages between the kings show how the three sagas readily substitute one communicative medium for another, transforming oral messages into written ones and vice versa — the messages transcend the media through which they are delivered while the core meaning remains unaffected. The differences between these two modes of communication are apparently no bigger than the difference between direct and reported speech, and the boundary between the two modes can be crossed at will.[29]

---

[27] *Msk* I, 79.

[28] English historical sources confirm that Magnús claimed England but not that the story of Játvarðr's difficulties made him renounce his claim. Rather, Magnús continued to be seen as a threat to the English until his death in 1047 (Bugge, *Små bidrag til Norges historie*, pp. 5–10). See also Barlow, 'Edward'.

[29] One can observe a similar mechanism in other genres. The longest version of the Mar-

The kings' sagas' accounts of another event that occurred in the reign of Magnús underline this point. When Haraldr Sigurðsson returned from his long journey and Magnús refused to give up half his kingdom, Haraldr banded with the Danish earl Sveinn Úlfsson, and the two harried Zealand. King Magnús naturally felt threatened by this assault on his sovereignty and, according to *Morkinskinna*, sent messengers with a *leyndarbréf* (secret letter) to Haraldr inviting him to peace talks.[30] In *Heimskringla*'s account of the same episode no letters are mentioned, but messengers travel 'in the greatest secrecy'.[31] Again it is clear that the specific oral or written form of the message is less important to the saga authors than the message's contents and that sagas' interpretation of history allows for the substitution of one mode of communication for the other. The important thing is that Magnús and Haraldr eventually became co-rulers.

In the course of the following hundred years, the kings' sagas contain few references to any literary and epistolary activities of the Norwegian kings. The most elaborate piece of information, given in *Morkinskinna*, is that Haraldr harðráði laid his hands upon the seal of the Danish king by chance. With the help of this seal, he forged a letter in the name of the Danish king that he sent to all Norwegian landed men (*lendir menn*) in order to test their fidelity to the Norwegian king (i.e., himself) — a test not all of them passed.[32]

This assortment of episodes, which the kings' sagas represent as transpiring before 1139, demonstrates that as soon as 'the age of writing' (*ritǫldin*) was believed to have been inaugurated at some point in the reign of Magnús góði (r. 1035–47), saga authors could insert letters in their accounts as well as extract them. This reduces the possibility of distinguishing between historical and fictional letters on the basis of saga material and internal evidence alone.[33]

---

ian legend about Theophilus, e.g., includes a long letter from an archbishop (*Mariu saga*, ed. by Unger, pp. 403–04), while the shorter versions (pp. 65–69, 1080–90, and 1090–1104) have no such letter.

[30] *Msk* I, 123.

[31] *Heimskringla*, trans. by Finlay and Faulkes, III, 56. 'Þetta mál fór mjǫk af hljóði'; *Hkr* III, 95–96. This episode is not related in *Fagrskinna*.

[32] *Msk* I, 211–14. In addition, in one *þáttr* in *Morkinskinna* the Icelander Stúfr requests a letter with the seal of King Haraldr harðráði (*Msk* I, 292), and in another one King Eysteinn Magnússon offers to write a sealed letter for the Icelander Ívarr Ingimundarson — an offer the Icelander declines (*Msk* III, 104).

[33] The editor of *Regesta Norvegica* I, Erik Gunnes, acknowledges this problem in his preface (*RN* I, p. 10) but the regest nevertheless dutifully records many of the letters mentioned

King Ingi's Letter of 1139

Bjarni Guðnason has called King Ingi's letter of 1139 'the oldest Norwegian letter whose content has been preserved'. In the previous section, it was argued that it is virtually impossible to distinguish between historical and non-historical letters in the kings' sagas that deal with the eleventh and early twelfth century. Consequently, this section will treat King Ingi's letter as an *element* of the sagas that quote text of the letter, that is, *Morkinskinna* and *Heimskringla*, rather than as a *source* of these sagas.

According to the kings' sagas, the letter was sent from King Ingi, who was in the Vík area in south-eastern Norway to King Sigurðr munnr, who was in Þrándheimr. The letter was sent at a point in time when the pretender Sigurðr slembir, accompanied by the blinded, maimed, gelded, and deposed King Magnús blindi, was raiding along the Norwegian coast. Sigurðr slembir and Magnús blindi then withdrew to Denmark, but they were expected to return to Norway. In the letter, King Ingi asks Sigurðr, his brother and fellow king, to come to his assistance and help defend Norway.

All the major kings' sagas that cover this period of time tell about the events that unfolded around Sigurðr slembir in the 1130s. The most elaborate treatment is found in *Morkinskinna*, but *Heimskringla* and *Fagrskinna* also recount episodes in which Sigurðr slembir plays an important part, with *Gesta Danorum* written by the Danish historian Saxo Grammaticus, who probably completed his work around 1208,[34] also mentioning some of the events. Sigurðr slembir claimed that he was a son of King Magnús berfœttr 'barelegs' (r. 1093–1103). Sigurðr's mother, Þóra Saxadóttir, was the sister of King Magnús berfœttr's lawful wife. Sigurðr slembir was fostered by a priest in southern Norway and had received the ordination of a deacon. In 1136 according to saga chronology, he seeks out his (putative) half-brother King Haraldr gilli (r. 1130–36) in Norway and claims co-regency. The counsellors of the weak Haraldr gilli recognize that Sigurðr slembir is a threat to both their own position and the general peace of the kingdom, and they convince the king that Sigurðr slembir needs to be done away with. Sigurðr is captured but manages to flee to Denmark. He returns to Norway incognito, assassinates King Haraldr gilli in Bergen, and flees town. Meanwhile in the eastern part of Norway, Ingi, one

in the kings' sagas. Of Magnús's three letters, mentioned above, only the exchange with the English king is recorded in *RN* (ɪ, 31 and 32).

[34] Friis-Jensen, 'When Did Saxo Finish his *Gesta?*'.

of Haraldr gilli's sons, is taken to the king in eastern Norway, while another son of Haraldr, Sigurðr munnr, is taken as king by the Þrœndir. The two new kings were both toddlers at the time. Sigurðr slembir travels to the monastery at Níðarhólmr in the Þrándheimr fjord, where he forcibly frees Magnús, a former king and an illegitimate son of King Sigurðr Jórsalafari, from the monastery. Magnús had been blinded, maimed, and gelded when he was deposed by Haraldr gilli, and he became known under the name Magnús blindi (the blind). Together Sigurðr slembir and Magnús blindi make a failed attack on the king's residence in Þrándheimr. The following summer, Sigurðr and Magnús blindi attack and kill one of King Ingi's retainers in southern Norway. King Ingi pursues some of Sigurðr slembir and Magnús's men, while the two make for northern Norway, where they spend the winter. The following spring they sail south, all the way to Víkin, and along the way they attack and kill a number of important allies of the Norwegian kings. King Ingi attempts to put an end to the killing and harrying by sending out a group of men on the ship Hreinninn (the reindeer). But the king's men return *við lítinn orðstír* (having gained little renown).[35] Sigurðr slembir and Magnús blindi sail south to Denmark. It is at this point that King Ingi sends the 'first Norwegian letter of which the contents have been preserved' to King Sigurðr munnr. In the letter, King Ingi urges King Sigurðr munnr to come to his assistance in southern Norway. *Morkinskinna* and *Heimskringla* present similar texts of the letter, and in both sagas King Sigurðr munnr decides to join his brother. It is mid-October when Sigurðr slembir and Magnús blindi return to Norway with a fleet of thirty ships, more than half of them Danish. The Norwegian kings meet them with a large fleet, and at Martinmas (November 11) they engage in battle, with the Norwegian kings gaining victory. The already maimed, blinded, and crippled Magnús blindi falls in battle while Sigurðr slembir is captured and tortured to death. His dead body is hung in a tree, but a priest brings it to a nearby church, and Danish friends of Sigurðr slembir move his corpse to Álaborg in Denmark, where he is buried in the church of St Mary.

The summary above is based on *Morkinskinna*, but *Fagrskinna* and *Heimskringla* relate many of these events as well — *Fagrskinna* is rather brief, while *Heimskringla* is more elaborate. Saxo recounts some of the dramatic highlights in his *Gesta danorum*, but as a consequence of his Danish perspective his account focuses on events that involved the Danes. Consequently he has more

---

[35] *Msk* II, 198; *Hkr* III, 313.

to report on Sigurðr slembir and Magnús blindi than on the Norwegian kings, and he makes no mention of the letter.

At this point it will be expedient to present the complete text of the rather short letter as it is given in *Morkinskinna*.[36]

> **1** Ingi konungr sendir kveðju Sigurði brœðr sínum ok hans ráðuneyti, [Sáða-Gyrði, Ǫgmundi svipti], Óttari birtingi, ok ǫllum lendum mǫnnum hans ok svá hirðmǫnnum ok húskǫrlum, vinum okkrum, búǫndum ok búþegnum ok allri alþýðu, sælum ok veslum, ungum ok gǫmlum, Guðs ok sína.
>
> **2** Vandræði okkur eru ǫllum mǫnnum kunnig í þessu landi ok svá œska sú, er þú ert fimm vetra gamall en ek þriggja vetra, ok megum ekki at hafask nema vit njótim vina okkarra ok góðra manna, en vinir mínir þykkjask við vandræði komnir, en þér ok yðrir vinir hafið kyrrsæti ok hóglífi. **3** Gørið nú svá vel at þér sœkið til míns fundar sem fjǫlmennstir, ok verum báðir saman, hvatki er í gørisk. **4** Nú er sá okkarr vinr mestr er til þess heldr at vit sém sem sáttastir ok jafnhaldnir af ǫllu, en með því at þér afrœkizk ok gørið eigi fara, sem þér hafið fyrr gǫrt, af nauðsynligri orðsendingu minni, skaltu við því búask at ek mun gera lið á hendr þér, ok skipti þá Guð með okkr, því at eigi þykkjumsk vér standask mega at hafa fjǫlmenni með oss sem vér þurfum við ótta þenna, en þú tekr landskyldir allar hálfar við oss í Nóregi.
>
> **5** Lifið í Guðs friði.

> (**1** King Ingi sends his brother Sigurðr and his counselors, Sáða-Gyrðr, Ǫgmundr sviptir, Óttarr birtingr, and all his district chieftains as well as his retainers and housecarls, our friends, the farmers, and tillers and all the people, rich and poor, young and old, God's greeting and his own.
>
> **2** Our difficulties are known to all in this land, and also our youth, since you are five years old and I am three, so that we are capable of no initiative unless we have the benefit of our friends and men of good will. But my friends think that they are in a poor position while [you and] your friends live in ease and tranquility. **3** Now do me the favor of joining me with as many men as possible, and let us stick together, come what may. **4** Our greatest friends will be those who do the most to ensure that we remain on good terms and are held in equal esteem. But should you refuse and fail to come, as you have done before, at my urgent request, then you should be prepared for me to march against you. God may then decide between us, for we do not think that we have the necessary forces to meet this threat as long as you do no more than collect half the revenue in Norway.
>
> **5** Fare you well in God's peace.)

---

[36] *Msk* ɪɪ, 199–200; *Morkinskinna*, trans. by Andersson and Gade, p. 382. I have numbered the sentences for ease of reference.

The letter can be divided into three parts (protocol: 1, main text: 2–4, and eschatocol: 5), and includes many of the elements one expects to see in a medieval
Norse letter.[37] The protocol (1) contains the *intitulatio* in which the sender names
himself and gives his position, the *inscriptio* in which the recipients are mentioned, and the *salutatio* in which the recipients are greeted. The most conspicuous element of this protocol is the unusually detailed *inscriptio* in which King Ingi
not only greets his brother (though without using his royal title) but virtually everyone, moving gradually from the closest circle around his brother[38] to the populace in general (rich and poor, young and old). Despite the many recipients, the
main text of the letter addresses Sigurðr munnr directly, using the singular pronoun *þú* (you) as well as the polite plural *þér* (ye) when addressing Sigurðr munnr
and forms of the dual pronoun *vit* (we two) when referring to the two kings.[39]
The eschatocol (5) contains a brief *apprecatio* (concluding wish) but neither date
nor *subscriptio* (i.e., signature/monogram). The main body of the letter (2–4) is
more loosely structured, but it can be divided into a *narratio* (2) that explains the
background to the message, a *dispositio* (3) where the king's decision is stated, and
a *sanctio* (4) describing the consequences of disregarding the *dispositio*. The structure of the text shows that whoever wrote the letter was thoroughly familiar with
the conventions of letter writing in medieval Norway (and elsewhere).

The general message of the letter is that Sigurðr munnr should come to the
assistance of King Ingi, but the central rhetorical theme of the letter is friendship. The kings rely on their friends, and they themselves should stand together
(as friends) no matter what happens (*hvatki er í gørisk* or 'come what may')
(2). Therefore, those who facilitate the solidarity of the kings are their greatest friends (4). However, if the kings do not stick together, their friendship
will turn to enmity since Ingi will march on Sigurðr munnr if he fails to send
support (3). Curiously, no mention is made of the immediate cause of letter. It is merely stated that Ingi's 'friends think they are in a poor situation',
while Sigurðr munnr and his 'friends live in ease and tranquility' (2). It is thus
taken for granted that the people in Þrándheimr are fully up to date on the latest movements of the pretenders to the throne, Sigurðr slembir and Magnús

---

[37] See Agerholt, *Gamal brevskipnad*, and, more briefly, Jørgensen, 'Diplomer, lover og
jordebøker', pp. 257–61, for an outline and exemplification of the standard elements of medieval Norwegian letters.

[38] According to *Hkr* III, 303, Sáða-Gyrðir was Sigurðr munnr's foster-father.

[39] In some cases, it is difficult to determine whether *þér* refers to Sigurðr munnr alone
or whether it includes the circle around Sigurðr as well, but *þér ok yðrir vinir* (you and your
friends) in 2 is a clear case of the use of the polite plural.

blindi. This complicated situation is simply referred to as *vandræði okkur* (our difficulties). This reticence is even more conspicuous when contrasted with the specificity with which the *narratio* enumerates the facts that the circle around the king in Þrándheimr must have been very well aware of: namely, that the two Norwegian kings are mere children at this point in time. Sigurðr is five years old and Ingi, who sent the letter, is only three. The consequences of the young age of the kings should also be well known to the immediate recipients of the letter in Þrándheimr — namely, that the kings have to rely on their friends and men of good will — but the letter writer seemingly found it necessary to explain this as well.

The *sanctio* contains a reference to an earlier occasion in which Sigurðr munnr has failed to come to the assistance of Ingi, though it is unclear what this refers to. It might allude to Ingi's hostile encounters with Magnús blindi and his Swedish and Danish supporters, or it might be a reference to the failed attempt to capture Sigurðr slembir. However, none of the sagas mention that Ingi requested the assistance of Sigurðr munnr at any point prior to the sending of the letter. The original recipients of the letter, however, might well have known what Ingi had in mind when he complained about Sigurðr munnr's failure to send support.

The final threat of the *sanctio*, that Ingi will march against Sigurðr munnr should he fail to come to Ingi's assistance, is perhaps best regarded as an empty threat. If the present *vandræði* (difficulties) were really so serious that Ingi needed the help of his brothers in the south, it is unlikely that he commanded the necessary forces to launch an expedition against his brother Sigurðr munnr in the north.

Heimskringla cites the letter as well. Considering the general instability of medieval texts, and in particular the variance of epistolary texts illustrated above, it should be no surprise that the text of the letter in *Heimskringla* differs from that of *Morkinskinna* at many points. It is only the concluding *sanctio* (5) that is completely identical in the two texts. However, the differences are quite small, and they are mainly found at the level of word order and choice. The most significant difference is perhaps that *Heimskringla* spells out the precarious economic aspect of the situation more clearly than *Morkinskinna* does. Maintaining a standing force is expensive, and Ingi writes in *Heimskringla* that he will not carry this burden alone as long as Sigurðr munnr collects half the revenues of Norway:

> Eigi megum vér hafa lengr svá búit, at sitja með svá miklum kostnaði ok fjǫlmenni sem hér þarf fyrir ófriðar sakir, en þú tekr hálfar allar landskyldir ok aðrar tekjur í Nóregi.

(we cannot go on any longer with things as they are, staying with such great expanse and large numbers as a necessary here because of the hostility, while you are taking half of all the land dues and other revenues in Norway.)[40]

With *Heimskringla* in mind, it is possible to read the text in *Morkinskinna* in the same way,[41] although the translation of Andersson and Gade (as quoted above) is the most obvious. However, the purely economic motivation given in *Heimskringla* is inconsistent with the introductory information on the occasion of the letter as given in *Heimskringla* (and with other words in *Morkinskinna*):

Víkverjar ok Bjǫrgynjarmenn mæltu, at þat var ósómi, er Sigurðr konungr ok vinir hans sátu kyrrir norðr í kaupangi, þótt fǫðurbanar hans fœri þjóðleið fyrir útan Þrándheimsmynni, en Ingi konungr ok hans lið sát í Vík austr við háskann ok varði landit ok hafði átt margar orrustur.

(The Víkverjar and Bjǫrgynjarmenn said it was a disgrace that King Sigurðr and his friends sat doing nothing north in Kaupangr, though the slayers of his father were sailing the high seas outside Þrándheimsmynni, and King Ingi and his troops were staying east in Vík in danger and defending the land and had fought many battles.)[42]

The greatest friend of the two kings (cf. 4) turns out to be Óttarr birtingr.[43] In a speech delivered in response to the letter, he recommends that Sigurðr munnr travel south with reinforcements, even though the tone of Ingi's letter is rather harsh. The king agrees, and he wants to travel down 'fara at hitta Inga bróður minn (to meet Ingi my brother) as soon as possible.[44] In what appears to be a slightly ironical tone, *Morkinskinna* then states:

[40] *Hkr* III, 314–15; *Heimskringla*, trans. by Finlay and Faulkes, III, 193.

[41] The last part of 4 could there be translated as follows: 'eigi þykkjumsk vér standask mega at hafa fjǫlmenni með oss sem vér þurfum við ótta þenna, en þú tekr landskyldir allar hálfar við oss í Nóregi' (we do not think that we have the necessary means to have a standing host such as we need to meet this threat as long as you collect half the revenue in Norway).

[42] *Hkr* III, 314; *Heimskringla*, trans. by Finlay and Faulkes, III, 192–93. *Morkinskinna* appears to have had a passage to a similar effect, but a few words are illegible in the manuscript.

[43] Óttarr birtingr is later described as being a great supporter of Ingi: 'En Sigurðr konungr var ekki vinr hans ok þótti hann allt hallr vera undir Ingi konung, mág sinn' (But King Sigurðr was not a friend to him and thought that he was biased in favor of his kinsman King Ingi) (*Msk* II, 212; *Morkinskinna*, trans. by Andersson and Gade, p. 388).

[44] *Msk* II, 200.

Síðan mælti hverr þeira í orða stað annars, sem vanði þeira er til, ok tǫlðu um tǫlur langar, bæði Gyrðr ok Qgmundr ok margir aðir lendir menn, on þó kom í sama stað niðr sem Óttarr haddi mælt fyrir ǫndverðu.

(one after the other spoke to the same effect, as is often done. Both Gyrðr and Qgmundr and many other district chieftains made long speeches, but it all amounted to what Óttarr had already said at the outset.)[45]

So they travel south — and in the ensuing battle against Sigurðr slembir, Magnús blindi, and their men, the Norwegian kings are victorious.

It was stated above that friendship is a key theme of the letter, and it seems that the kings' reliance on friends and men of good will is the general theme of this part of Norwegian history as it is described in the kings' sagas. When the rightful kings are unable to govern, their friends and men of good will should hold the reins of the kingdom for them. Before Ingi and Sigurðr munnr come of age, Norway is effectively governed by a group of good-willed noblemen, and the same was the case during the (brief) reign of the weak Haraldr gilli. With the help of the men of good will, internal peace prevails in Norway and threats, such as the ones caused by Sigurðr slembir and Magnús blindi, are dealt with successfully.

Because the men of good govern in the names of the kings, it is to be expected that the letter is written in the name of the three-year-old Ingi and not of his guardians. Similarly it is addressed to the five-year-old Sigurðr, and not to his guardians, although they are actually the ones making the decisions. The sagas provide many parallel examples where acts are attributed to kings even though it is obvious that the kings did not perform them in person. One clear example is provided by Kolli inn prúði's praise poetry in honour of King Ingi:

Unnuð austr fyr Mynni / oddhríð, ok brátt síðan, / hilmir, fekk und hjalmi, / hrafns verðar lið sverðum. / Lǫgðuð ér, en eirar / ǫrr synjaði brynju, / ungr varðir þú, þengill, / þitt land, saman randir.[46]

(You fought a battle East outside Mynni, and soon after, king, the helmet clad host gave the raven food with their swords. You placed shield against shield, and the energetic ruler showed the byrnie no leniency. Young, you defended your land.)

This stanza looks like a fairly commonplace praise poem in which the king is praised for his martial prowess and energy, but the words take on a different

---

[45] *Msk* II, 200; *Morkinskinna*, trans. by Andersson and Gade, p. 382.
[46] *Msk* II, 181.

meaning when the stanza is considered in the context of *Morkinskinna*, the text in which it is transmitted. When the battle by Mynni was fought, Ingi was even younger than when he 'wrote' the letter, and *Morkinskinna* describes how the chieftain Þjóstólfr Álason carried the infant king in a sling during the battle. As a result of the hard fight, Ingi was crippled for life.[47] It is thus clear that it was not King Ingi in person who 'showed the byrnie no leniency', defended his kingdom, and performed the deeds referred to by the poet. It was the office of the king, rather than the person of the king, that acted.

The men of good will around King Ingi and Sigurðr are responsible for maintaining peace in the kingdom, and serious difficulties do not arise before the good men around the kings die:[48]

> Þeira brœðra fór allt vel í milli meðan fóstrar þeira lifðu, ok hǫfðu þeir eina hirð, Ingi konungr ok Sigurðr, en Eysteinn einn sér. En þá er þeir ǫnduðusk, Gyrðr ok Ámundi, Þjóstólfr ok Óttarr birtingr, Ǫgmundr sviptir ok Ǫgmundr, sonr Kyrpinga-Orms, bróðir Erlings skakka [...] en er þeir váru allir andaðir þá skildu þeir Ingi konungr ok Sigurðr konungr hirðina bráðliga. Sigurðr var ofstopamaðr mikill ok óeirðar um alla hluti, þá er hann óx upp, ok svá var Eysteinn konungr bróðir hans, ok var þat nær nǫkkvi, en allra var hann fégjarnastr. Ingi konungr var lítt heill; hann var hryggbrotinn, ok svá visnaði fótr hans annarr at hann gekk mjǫk haltr, en hann var þó vinsæll mjǫk við alþýðu.

> (The brothers got on well as long as their foster fathers were alive. King Ingi and Sigurðr had a combined retinue, and Eysteinn a separate one.[49] [One after the other] Gyrðr, Ámundi, Þjóstólfr, Óttarr birtingr, Ǫgmundr sviptir, and Ǫgmundr Kyrpinga-Ormsson, Erlingr skakki's brother, died [...]. When they were all dead, King Ingi and King Sigurðr quickly separated their retinues. King Sigurðr was altogether a very overbearing and contentious man in his youth, and his brother Eysteinn was not very different except that he was also a very covetous man. King Ingi was in poor health. His back was crooked [*hann var hryggbrotinn*] and one foot was withered so that he was very lame, but still he was popular with the people.)[50]

---

[47] *Msk* II, 180–81. A similar argument can be made for *Heimskringla*, even though this saga only preserves the first *helmingr* of the stanza (*Hkr* III, 305).

[48] At this point a third king, Eysteinn, who is yet another son of Haraldr gilli, has arrived from the west.

[49] Eysteinn became co-regent with Ingi and Sigurðr in 1142 some years after the death of Sigurðr Slembir and Magnús blindi. He ruled until his death in 1157.

[50] *Msk* II, 221; *Morkinskinna*, trans. by Andersson and Gade, p. 392, slightly modified by the author.

The picture of the kingdom of Norway painted by *Morkinskinna* is then one in which the nobility plays a particular important role in maintaining peace in the kingdom and peace between the kings. One gets a similar impression from *Heimskringla* even if the happy concord between the kings is described in less positive terms: 'var þeira samþykki til nǫkkurrar hlítar' (there was a fairly reasonable concord between them [the kings]).[51] Unrest and serious conflicts between the kings do not break out until after the magnates' deaths. The kings themselves do not change, but when no longer held in check by the magnates, Sigurðr munnr's and Eysteinn's bad characters are unrestrained, and civil war breaks out. This eventually leads to the death of Sigurðr munnr in 1155 and Eysteinn's death two years later. Ingi is more favourably depicted in the sagas. *Heimskringla* also stresses that he relied heavily on his chieftains when it comes to government,[52] and when Ingi's end draws near, *Heimskringla* even makes him repeat what he wrote in the letter to Sigurðr munnr many years before about the importance of being able to rely on trustworthy and benevolent advisors: 'Ek má ekki at fœrask, ef ek missi þeira manna, er brjóst eru ok rǫskvastir eru ok lengi hafa verit fórstjórar fyrr mér ok mínu ríki' (I cannot do anything if I lose the men who are my shield and are the most valiant and have long been in charge of me and my kingdom).[53] A few years afterward in 1161, Ingi was killed by the supporters of Hákon herðibreiðr (the broadsouldered), a fourteen-year-old illegitimate son of Sigurðr munnr.

---

[51] *Hkr* III, 330; *Heimskringla*, trans. by Finlay and Faulkes, III, 203. See also *Ágrip* (*Ágr*, pp. 51–52).

[52] '[Ingi] var blíðmælt ok dæll vinum sínum, ǫrr af fé ok lét mjǫk hǫfðingja ráða með sér landráðum, vinsæll við alþýðu, ok dró þat allt saman mjǫk undir hans ríki ok fjǫlmenni' ([Ingi] was cheerful of speech and pleasant with his friends, generous with wealth, mostly letting leading men make decisions about the government with him, popular with ordinary people, and all of this very much attracted power and followers to him) (*Hkr* III, 331; *Heimskringla*, trans. by Finlay and Faulkes, III, 204).

[53] *Hkr* III, 358; *Heimskringla*, trans. by Finlay and Faulkes, III, 222. Bjarni Guðnason, *Fyrsta sagan*, p. 22, points out that Ingi here uses the unusual expression *at fœrask* that was also used in the *Heimskringla* text of the letter of 1139: 'Megum vit ekki at fœrask nema þat, er vit njótum vina okkarra ok góðra manna' (We can undertake nothing except what we do with the help of our friends and kind people) (*Hkr* III, 314; *Heimskringla*, trans. by Finlay and Faulkes, III, 193).

Origin of the Letter and Rhetorical Invention

Having studied the letter as a component of *Morkinskinna* (and *Heimskringla*), it is now time to enter the realm of speculation and turn to the origin of the letter. As mentioned in the introduction, the four most important texts that describe the dealings of the Norwegian kings with Sigurðr slembir and Magnús blindi are *Morkinskinna*, *Fagrskinna*, *Heimskringla*, and Saxo Grammaticus's *Gesta Danorum*. In some cases one can observe verbatim or near-verbatim agreements between the texts, and these are normally accounted for by positing a common source utilized by all four texts: namely, *Hryggjarstykki*.[54] This relatively simple textual situation is however complicated by the fact that none of the vernacular texts are independent of one another[55] and that none of them are believed to retain the text of *Hryggjarstykki* unchanged; Bjarni Guðnason is also uncertain as to whether Saxo Grammaticus had direct access to *Hryggjarstykki*. *Morkinskinna* is considered the best witness to *Hryggjarstykki*,[56] even though it is thought unlikely that the many stanzas from Ívarr Ingimundarson's *Sigurðarbálkr* contained in *Morkinskinna*'s section on Sigurðr slembir were in *Hryggjarstykki*.[57] Danielsson presents and discusses all the passages in *Heimskringla* and *Morkinskinna* that are explicitly connected with Eiríkr Oddsson (the author of *Hryggjarstykki*) or his informants. He rejects Bjarni Guðnason's suggestion that *Hryggjarstykki* was the saga of

[54] Bjarni Guðnason, *Fyrsta sagan*, pp. 32–66.

[55] *Heimskringla* can be shown to have relied on *Morkinskinna*- and *Fagrskinna*-text in other passages.

[56] Hallberg, '*Hryggjarstykki*', analysed the ratio of present and preterite verb forms in *Morkinskinna*'s section on Sigurðr slembir. He found that the percentage of verbs in the present tense in this part of *Morkinskinna* was remarkably low in comparison with other parts. This led him to support the idea that *Morkinskinna* in this section incorporates another text relatively unchanged and that this text was *Hryggjarstykki*. On the basis of the same analysis, Hallberg argued that a description of Sigurðr's visit to Þorgils Oddason's farm Saurbœr in Iceland (only found in *Morkinskinna*; *Msk* II, 173–75) was not a part of *Hryggjarstykki*. This passage has a much higher percentage of verbs in the present tense than the surrounding text (Hallberg, '*Hryggjarstykki*', pp. 118–19). A weak point in Hallberg's analysis is that it ignores that the many stanzas of *Sigurðarbálkr* quoted in this section of *Morkinskinna* were inserted at a later point in time and that changes must have been introduced into the surrounding prose text as well — if only to introduce the stanzas. He does exclude verbs of utterance followed by direct speech and the stanzas, but his analysis is too mechanical to account for other the introductions to the stanzas and other changes.

[57] Neither is it considered likely that they were in the so-called 'Oldest *Morkinskinna*'; see the discussion in *Morkinskinna*, trans. by Andersson and Gade, pp. 46–56.

Sigurðr slembir on the grounds that this identification contradicts the explicit statement about the content of Eiríkr Oddsson's work in *Morkinskinna*,[58] and that the role of Sigurðr slembir is not that prominent in the passages of the kings' sagas where Eiríkr Oddsson's work is referred to. One can add that none of the identified informants of Eiríkr Oddsson were on Sigurðr slembir's side in the conflict: one is a landed man of the kings, another a victim of Sigurðr's harrying, a third a sister of a later archbishop, and a fourth a retainer of King Ingi.[59] The fifth and last informant mentioned was not involved in the conflict at all but was a provost in Denmark.[60] Danielsson rightly finds it impossible to ascertain whether or not the letter was a part of *Hryggjarstykki*. However, on the basis of an *en passant* notice in *Heimskringla* that King Sverrir had something written about Ingi's role in the death of Eysteinn,[61] Danielsson suggests that the letter was part of this otherwise unknown text, which could have contained the letter of Ingi and speeches modelled on those of *Sverris saga*.[62] This suggestion must remain conjectural as it can neither be proved nor disproved, but one consequence of this suggestion is that the letter might be regarded as a rhetorical invention inspired by *Sverris saga* — and hence a text dating to the turn of the early thirteenth century rather than the mid-twelfth century.

It was above argued that *Morkinskinna* and *Heimskringla* both stress the importance of the magnates around the kings, King Ingi in particular, and the magnates' role in maintaining peace and stability in the kingdom. This particular ideological stance may be derived from *Hryggjarstykki*.[63] Even though the

---

[58] *Morkinskinna* records: 'Nú er at segja frá sonum Haralds konungs, Inga ok Sigurði, sem sagt hefir vitr maðr ok skynsamr, Eiríkr Oddsson' (Now the story turns to the sons of King Haraldr, Ingi and Sigurðr, according to the account of the wise and discriminating man Eiríkr Oddsson) (*Msk* II, 185; *Morkinskinna*, trans. by Andersson and Gade, p. 375).

[59] The *lendrmaðr* of the kings was Hákon magi (*Msk* II, 185; *Hkr* III, 319), the victim is Einarr Laxa-Pálsson (*Hrk* III, 313, cf. *Msk* II, 198), the sister is Guðríðr Birgisdóttir (*Hkr* III, 317, cf. *Msk* II, 206), and the retainer is Hallr Þorgeirsson (*Hkr* III, 318–20, cf. *Msk* II, 208–10). See also Danielsson, *Sagorna om Norges kungar*, p. 288.

[60] Ketill, a provost of the church of Mary in Álaborg, told Eiríkr that Sigurðr slembir was buried there (*Hkr* III, 320). Ketill does not appear to have been personally involved in any of the events described so far and did not become provost in Álaborg until after 1145 (Jensen, 'Sanctus Ketillus'), six years after Sigurðr slembir's death.

[61] *Hkr* III, 345–46.

[62] Danielsson, *Sagorna om Norges kungar*, p. 287. *Sverris saga* occasionally quotes letters (pp. 14, 69–70, 217–18). (Page numbers following mention of *Sverris saga* are to the edition of Þorleifur Hauksson.)

[63] If the importance of the men of good will was indeed the particular theme of *Hryg-*

explicit reference to Eiríkr Oddsson's work (quoted in n. 58) states that Eiríkr wrote about the kings, the kings are not particularly active in the passages that certainly derive from *Hryggjarstykki* (i.e., those, where Eiríkr or his informants are explicitly mentioned). This is a natural consequence of their young age. The men of good will around the kings must have been in charge of the actual government, decision-making, and warfare.

One can see that this representation of history reflects a particular ideological stance that is by no means self-evident and all-pervasive by comparing briefly with Saxo Grammaticus's descriptions of the three kings in *Gesta Danorum*. Saxo makes no mention of the men of good will surrounding the kings and explains all the misfortunes that befall the Norwegian kings as results of their own personalities. Their personalities in turn are determined by the (un)lawfulness of their births. Ingi is favourably characterized as 'perfectly fitted out with every kind of rectitude' but is unsuccessful because he is cursed with two brothers, one 'spattered with the blemishes of avarice' the other 'covered with the filth of lechery'.[64] Saxo explains the degenerate characters of Ingi's brothers by the fact that they, in contrast to Ingi, are born outside of a lawful marriage:

> E quibus Ingo dumtaxat iusto matrimonio ortus fratribus, quorum alter Noruegica, alter Hiberniensi pellice editus fuerat, ut ingenuitatis, ita et morum ornamentis prestabat.[65]

> (Of Haraldr's sons, it was only Ingi who sprung out of a rightful marriage, of the others, one was the offspring of a Norwegian mistress, the other of an Irish. As he excelled through the nobility of his birth, thus he excelled through the ornament of moral behaviour).

One might also contrast the theme of *Hryggjarstykki* with that of *Sverris saga* where Sverrir, who has the makings of a true king[66] and acts of his own accord,

---

gjarstykki, *Ágrip*, which also stresses that relative peace prevailed in the realm as long as the advisors of the kings were alive (*Ágr*, pp. 51–52), is likely to have relied on *Hryggjarstykki* as well. Unfortunately, *Ágrip* is very fragmentary at this point, and the two texts are not normally discussed in conjunction. In fact, Indrebø, 'Nokre merknader', p. 61, criticizes Bjarni Aðalbjarnarson for disregarding *Hryggjarstykki* in his discussion of the sources of *Ágrip*.

[64] Ingi (Ingo): 'omnibus honestatis numeris instructissimus'; Sigurðr (Siuardus): 'auaritie maculis respersus'; Eysteinn (Ostenus): 'luxurie sordibus obsitus' (Saxo Grammaticus, *Gesta Danorum*, § 14.29.6).

[65] Saxo Grammaticus, *Gesta Danorum*, § 14.29.6

[66] Ármann Jakobsson, 'Sinn eiginn smiður', pp. 120–25.

is juxtaposed with the much less kingly Magnús Erlingsson, who to a great extent has to rely on the advice of his father, Erlingr skakki.

The image of *Hryggjarstykki* sketched here then agrees with — but does not rely on — Sverrir Tómasson's suggestion that the title of *Hryggjarstykki* should be interpreted as 'backbone' and that it refers to the role of the chieftains in society.[67] In *Heimskringla*'s representation, King Ingi himself refers to the men of good will around him as his *brjóst* (breast), as discussed above. *Brjóst* is often used in this figurative sense in Old Norse,[68] but one can add that a king like Ingi who is described as literally having a broken back (*hryggbrotinn*) will benefit immensely from having an external backbone.[69]

Since classical antiquity historians have routinely included speeches and letters in their works, with the Greek historian Thucydides (*c.* 460–00 BCE) famously stating that 'my method in this book has been to make each speaker say broadly what I supposed would have been needed on any given occasion, while keeping as closely as I could to the overall intent of what was actually said'.[70] Letters appear to have received a treatment similar to that of speeches, and scholars usually consider the letters included in Thucydides' history plausible rather than historical. Later historians followed Thucydides' lead and likewise included plausible speeches and letters in their works. Of particular importance for the Middle Ages are the widely read works of the Roman historian Sallust (d. *c.* 35 BCE)[71] which would also have been familiar to some

---

[67] Sverrir Tómasson, '*Hryggjarstykki*', has suggested, with reference to the *Speech against the bishops* where earls and chieftains are referred to as the *hryggr* 'back' of society, that the title *Hryggjarstykki* should be interpreted as 'backbone' and that this then referred to the role of the chieftains in society.

[68] See *ONP* s.v. *brjóst*, 9.

[69] *Ágr*, p. 53; *Fsk*, p. 335; *Msk* II, 221. Or backbones. Old Norse *stykki* is a neuter, and it is therefore impossible to determine whether the word is singular or plural.

[70] Thucydides, *The Peloponnesian War*, trans. by Hammond, p. 22.

[71] Sallust's longest work, the *Historiae*, is primarily known through quotations by other authors. In addition, four speeches and two letters had been excerpted from the work and copied in a single manuscript of the ninth century (Città del Vaticano, BAV, Vat. Lat. 3864) together with all the speeches from his works on the Jugurthian war, the Catiline conspiracy, and other material. Clearly, the one who made this compilation considered the letters and the speeches birds of a feather. Scholars today also generally consider the letters of the *Historiae* rhetorical inventions; for examples of recent scholarship, see Adler, *Valorizing the Barbarians*, pp. 17–35, and Meyer, 'Allusion and Contrast', the latter on Thucydides as well as Sallust. Seminal works on rhetorical invention in ancient historiography are Wiseman, *Clio's Cosmetics*, pp. 1–53, and Woodman, *Rhetoric in Classical Historiography*, pp. 1–116.

readers in the Old Norse world in their original Latin form or in the vernacular reworking found in *Rómverja saga*.[72] Sallust's quotation of C. Manlius's message to the general Marcius Rex in *De coniuratione Catilinae* 33 is interesting in this regard. In the Latin original, the message is delivered in the form of a speech by C. Manlius's legates to Marcius Rex, but in the Old Norse version, the speech has been transformed to a written letter.[73] The substitution of one medium for another does not change the general contents of the message. Neither has, as far as the fragmentary nature of the Old Norse version in AM 595 a–b 4° allows us to determine, the text of the speech/letter been adapted to a letter format in the Old Norse version.

Since the invention of letters was a standard part of the rhetorical technique of historiography, there is no need to assume with Danielsson that the author of the letter from Ingi to Sigurðr was inspired by *Sverris saga* (see above). He simply followed the conventions of the genre of historical writings. Historians operated with a two-layer model. At the foundation of their works were the givens that were considered as (and might well be) historical facts, such as the expeditions of the kings and their battles. Snorri famously refers to these givens in his discussion of his poetic sources the prologue to *Heimskringla*: 'Tǫkum vér þat alt fyrir satt er í þeim kvæðum finnsk um ferðir þeira eða orrustur', because 'engi myndi þat þora at segja sjálfum honum þau verk hans, er allir þeir, er heyrði, vissi, at hégómi væri ok skrǫk, ok svá sjálfr hann' ('We regard as true

---

[72] This text has traditionally been dated to the late twelfth century. In her recent edition Þorbjörg Helgadóttir argued that the parts that make up *Rómverja saga* were translated in stages in the second half of the twelfth century; *Rómverja saga*, I, pp. cxciv–cxcv). Wellendorf, '"Ancient Traditions" in *Sverris saga*', pp. 16–17, argues that the main argument for such an early date of *Rómverja saga* is invalid. See also the two letters included in the work on the Jugurthian war, which provide good examples of this reworking technique in Þorbjörg Helgadóttir's edition, which gives both the Old Norse and the Latin texts of the letters (*Rómverja saga*, II, 8 and 24–25). For another example, see *Alexanders saga*, ed. by Finnur Jónsson, p. 19, in which a letter from the Persian king Darius to Alexander the Great is cited.

[73] Latin: 'C. Manlius ex suo numero legatos ad Marcium Regem mittit cum mandatis huiusce modi: "Deos hominesque testamur"' (C. Manlius sent some of his followers as to King Marcius with instructions to the following effect: 'We swear by gods and men') (*Cat* 32.3–33,1). Old Norse: 'Er þetta var tíðenda í Rómaborg sendi Gaius Manlius bréf Quinto Marcio konungi með þessum orðum: "Heyr þú ræðismaðr, vér sverjum bæði fyrir guð ok men at [...]"' (*Rómverja saga*, ed. by Þorbjörg Helgadóttir, II, 185) (While this happened in Rome, Gaius Manlius sent a letter to King Quintus Marcius with these words: 'Listen, commander, we swear by gods and men that [...]'). It is possible that the Old Norse translator simply mistook the speech of Manlius's legates for a letter (in which case he would not have been the first, cf. Williams, 'Manlius' *mandata*').

everything that is found in those poems [i.e. skaldic poems in praise of kings] about their expeditions and battles', because 'no one would dare to tell him [the king] to his face about deeds of his which all who listened, as well as the man himself, knew were falsehoods and fictions).[74] However, factual information, such as that found in skaldic poems, does not suffice for a broad saga narrative and, in Snorri's view, gives no interpretation of history. In addition to these bare facts, Snorri mentions *fornar frásagnir* (old accounts) he has heard from well-informed men. He explicitly states that he cannot vouch for the veracity of this information, but he knows that *some* men of learning have regarded similar stories as true.[75] Turning this material into a saga requires elaboration, and it is at this point rhetorical invention enters the picture. The primary purpose of this invention is to flesh out the facts in a plausible manner. The historian/saga writer will have known what happened and where, but not necessarily how. If he succeeded in explaining how something happened in a plausible, pleasing, and convincing fashion, the result might in turn become a given for the audience and the next generation of saga writers. In the end, it is therefore impossible to decide with certainty whether King Ingi's letter is historical. The differing texts of the letter given by *Morkinskinna* and *Heimskringla* show that saga authors were happy to develop their material where they found that improvement was needed.

I began with some considerations on the breakthrough of the practical application of the technology of writing for secular purposes among leading Norwegians. The saga accounts cannot help us determine the stage of development reached in 1139 and thus cannot be said to mark the watershed moment Bjarni Guðnason referred to. But since medieval historians strove for plausibility, it can show us that the audience of the text would have considered it plausible that this mode of communication was used at this point in time. Now, if the letter really was a part of *Hryggjarstykki*, it is unlikely that it would have been written long after Ingi's death (in 1161), and this means that it is indeed likely that Norwegian kings and magnates had begun to use the new technique of literacy for practical purposes in Ingi's days.[76]

---

[74] *Hkr* i, 5, cf. *Hkr* ii, 422; *Heimskringla*, trans. by Finlay and Faulkes, i, 3–4.

[75] 'En þótt vér vitim eigi sannendi á því, þá vitum vér dœmi til at gamlir frœðimenn hafa slíkt fyrir satt haft' (*Hkr* i, 4) (But even though we do not know the truthfulness of this, we know examples of old men of learning have considered similar things true).

[76] In this connection, it might be of interest to note that Gelting, 'Saxo Grammaticus in the Archives', has argued that Saxo could rely on well-ordered royal archives from *c.* 1158 when composing *Gesta Danorum*. The earliest royal Danish document whose text is preserved,

Hryggjarstykki belongs to the oldest layer of Old Norse prose writings. This pioneering work would have been written at a point in time when the conventions governing the writing of kings' sagas had not yet been fixed. In this early phase of saga writing, authors could not rely on the historiographical conventions that only developed gradually in the course of the following decades. Eiríkr Oddsson would therefore have had to look elsewhere for models when fashioning his work. Bjarni Guðnason has suggested, as mentioned above, that Eiríkr Oddsson chose the hagiographical genre as his model. This might well have been the case, although the contours of *Hryggjarstykki* that emerge from a comparison of the relevant episodes in the kings' sagas and Saxo Grammaticus's *Gesta Danorum* only vaguely resemble the earliest Old Norse representatives of the hagiographical genre, such as *Passio Olavi* (in Latin and in the vernacular), *Mattheus saga*, *Placidus saga*, and *Blasius saga* (to mention the earliest preserved Norwegian forays into that genre). This study of the letter of 1139 suggests that Eiríkr's guiding framework is that of the genre of historiography, with its inserted speeches and letters, as it had been practised in the West since antiquity.[77] The works of Sallust were known in the North already at an early stage and could have provided a model in this respect, but *Hryggjarstykki*'s author could also have had many other historiographical models.

St Knud's charter to the Cathedral in Lund from 1085, is, however, much older. On Saxo's use of letters, see also Riis, *Einführung in die 'Gesta Danorum'*, 79–93.

[77] This, of course, does not preclude that Eiríkr also drew on hagiographical models, and the two genres also overlapped in some respects.

Works Cited

Primary Sources

Ágr — *Ágrip af Nóregskonunga sǫgum*, in *Ágrip af Nóregskonunga sǫgum* — *Fagrskinna: Nóregs konunga tal*, ed. by Bjarni Einarsson, Íslenzk fornrit, 29 (Reykjavík: Hið íslenzka fornritafélag, 1985), pp. 1–54

Alexanders saga, ed. by Finnur Jónsson (Copenhagen: Gyldendalske boghandel, 1925)

Biskupa sögur III, ed. by Guðrún Ása Grímsdóttir, Íslenzk fornrit, 17 (Reykjavík: Hið íslenska fornritafélag 1998)

Cat — *C. Sallusti Crispi Catilina, Iugurtha, Historiarum fragmenta selecta, appendix Sallustiana*, ed. by L. D. Reynolds (Oxford: Oxford University Press, 1991)

DI I — *Diplomatarium Islandicum - Íslenzkt fornbréfasafn* I, ed. by Jón Sigurðsson, 16 vols (Kaupmannahöfn: Hið íslenzka bókmentafélag, 1857–72)

DN I — *Diplomatarium Norvegicum* I, ed. by Christian A. Lange and Carl R. Unger, 22 vols to date (Christiania: Malling, 1847–)

Fsk — *Ágrip af Nóregskonunga sǫgum* — *Fagrskinna: Nóregs konunga tal*, ed. by Bjarni Einarsson, Íslenzk fornrit, 29 (Reykjavík: Hið íslenzka fornritafélag, 1985), pp. 55–373

Grágás: Islændernes lovbog i fristatens tid, ed. by Vilhjálmur Finsen, 4 vols (Copenhagen: Brødrene Berlings Bogtrykkeri, 1852–83)

Hákonar saga Hákonarsonar, ed. by Þorleifur Hauksson, Sverrir Jakobsson, and Tor Ulset, Íslenzk fornrit, 31–32, 2 vols (Reykjavík: Hið íslenzka fornritafélag, 2013)

Historia de antiquitate regum Norwagiensium, ed. by Gustav Storm, Monumenta historica norvegiæ: Latinske kildeskrifter til Norges historie i middelalderen (Kristiania: Brögger, 1880)

Hkr — Snorri Sturluson, *Heimskringla*, ed. by Bjarni Aðalbjarnarson, Íslenzk fornrit, 26–28, 3 vols (Reykjavík: Hið íslenzka fornritafélag, 1941–51)

Hulda: Sagas of the Kings of Norway, 1035–1177; Manuscript no. 66 fol. in the Aramagnæan Collection, ed. by Jonna Louis-Jensen (Copenhagen: Rosenkilde and Bagger, 1968)

Legendariske *saga* = See *Olafs saga hins helga*

Mariu saga: Legender om Jomfru Maria og hendes Jertegn, ed. by C. R. Unger (Christiania: Brögger & Christie, 1871)

Morkinskinna: The Earliest Icelandic Chronicle of the Norwegian Kings (1030–1157), trans. by Theodore M. Andersson and Kari Ellen Gade, Islandica, 51 (Ithaca: Cornell University Press, 2000)

Msk — *Morkinskinna*, ed. by Ármann Jakobsson and Þórður Ingi Guðjónsson, Íslenzk fornrit, 23–24, 2 vols (Reykjavík: Hið íslenzka fornritafélag, 2011)

Olafs saga hins helga: Efter pergamenthaandskrift i Uppsala Universitetsbibliotek, Delagardieske samling nr. 8^{II}, ed. by Oscar Albert Johnsen (Kristiania: Jacob Dybwad, 1922)

ONP — *Ordbog over det norrøne prosasprog*, 3 vols to date (Copenhagen: Den arnamagnæanske kommission, 1989–)

Orkneyinga saga, ed. by Finnbogi Guðmundsson, Íslenzk fornrit, 34 (Reykjavík: Hið íslenzka fornritafélag, 1965)

RN I — *Regesta Norvegica*, I: *822–1263*, ed. by Erik Gunnes (Oslo: Kjeldeskriftfondet, 1978)

Rómverja saga, ed. by Þorbjörg Helgadóttir, 2 vols (Reykjavík: Stofnun Árna Magnússonar í íslenskum fræðum, 2010)

Saxo Grammaticus, *Gesta Danorum*, ed. by Karsten Friis-Jensen, Oxford Medieval Texts (Oxford: Oxford University Press, 2015)

Snorri Sturluson, *Heimskringla*, trans. by Alison Finlay and Anthony Faulkes, Viking Society for Northern Research, 3 vols (London: University College London, 2011–15)

Sverris saga, ed. by Þorleifur Hauksson, Íslenzk fornrit, 30 (Reykjavík: Hið íslenzka fornritafélag, 2007)

Theodoricus Monachus, *An Account of the Ancient History of the Norwegian Kings*, trans. by Ian McDougall and David McDougall, Viking Society for Northern Research, 11 (London: Viking Society for Northern Research, 1998)

Thucydides, *The Peloponnesian War*, trans. by Martin Hammond (Oxford: Oxford University Press, 2009)

Secondary Studies

Adler, Eric, *Valorizing the Barbarians: Enemy Speeches in Roman Historiography* (Austin: University of Texas Press, 2011)

Agerholt, Johan, *Gamal brevskipnad: Etterrøkjingar og utgreidingar i norsk diplomatikk*, 2 vols (Oslo: J. Chr. Gundersen Boktrykkeri, 1928–32)

Ármann Jakobsson, 'Sinn eiginn smiður: Ævintýrið um Sverri konung', *Skírnir*, 179.1 (2005), 109–39

Bagge, Sverre, *From Viking Stronghold to Christian Kingdom: State Formation in Norway, c. 900–1350* (Copenhagen: Museum Tusculanum Press, 2010)

Barlow, Frank, 'Edward [St Edward; *known as* Edward the Confessor] (1003x5–1066)', *Oxford Dictionary of National Biography* (Oxford: Oxford University Press) <http://www.oxforddnb.com/view/article/8516> [accessed 14 November 2017]

Bjarni Guðnason, *Fyrsta sagan*, Studia Islandica, 37 (Reykjavík: Bókaútgáfa menningarsjóðs, 1978)

Bjørgo, Narve, 'Om skriftlege kjelder for *Hákonar saga*', *(Norsk) Historisk Tidskrift*, 46 (1967), 185–229

Bugge, Alexander, *Små bidrag til Norges historie paa 1000-tallet*, Videnskapsselskapets skrifter, 2: Hist.-Filos. Klasse 1914.2 (Kristania: Jacob Dybwad, 1914)

Danielsson, Tommy, *Sagorna om Norges kungar: Från Magnús góði till Magnús Erlingsson* (Södertälje: Gidlunds förlag, 2002)

Friis-Jensen, Karsten, 'When Did Saxo Finish his *Gesta Danorum*? A Discussion of its *Terminus ante quem*', in *The Creation of Medieval Northern Europe: Essays in Honour of Sverre Bagge*, ed. by Leidulf Melve and Sigbjørn Sønnesyn (Oslo: Dreyer, 2012), pp. 316–21

Gelting, Michael H., 'Saxo Grammaticus in the Archives', in *The Creation of Medieval Northern Europe: Essays in Honour of Sverre Bagge*, ed. by Leidulf Melve and Sigbjørn Sønnesyn (Oslo: Dreyer, 2012), pp. 322–45

Hagland, Jan Ragnar, '*Segia frá* eller *rita*, *lesa* eller *heyra* i kongesagalitteraturen — fri variasjon, eller ulike perspektiv på overgang frå "orality" til "literacy"?', *Arkiv för nordisk filologi*, 117 (2002), 85–96

Hallberg, Peter, '*Hryggjarstykki*: Några anteckningar', *Maal og Minne* (1979), 113–21

Hreinn Benediktsson, *Early Icelandic Script: As Illustrated in Vernacular Texts from the Twelfth and Thirteenth Centuries*, Íslensk handrit, Series in Folio, 2 (Reykjavík: Manuscript Institute of Iceland, 1965)

Indrebø, Gustav, 'Nokre merknader til den norröne kongesoga', *Arkiv för nordisk filologi*, 54 (1938–39), 58–79

Jensen, Brian Møller, 'Sanctus Ketillus', in *Medieval Nordic Literature in Latin*, ed. by Stephen Borgehammar and others) <https://wikihost.uib.no/medieval/index.php/Sanctus_Ketillus> [accessed 14 November 2017]

Jørgensen, Jon Gunnar, 'Diplomer, lover og jordebøker', in *Handbok i norrøn filologi*, ed. by Odd Einar Haugen (Bergen: Fagbokforlaget, 2013), pp. 250–301

Karlsen, Espe, 'Om innholdet i samlingen av latinske membranfragmenter i Riksarkivet', *Arkivverkets forskningsseminar — Gardermoen 2003*, Rapporter og retningslinjer, 16 (2003), 58–88

Keynes, Simon, 'Cnut's Earls', in *The Reign of Cnut: King of England, Denmark and Norway*, ed. by Alexander R. Rumble (London: Leicester University Press 1994), pp. 43–88

Kválen, Eivind, *Den eldste norske kongesoga* (Oslo: [n. pub.], 1925)

Meulengracht Sørensen, Preben, 'Historiefortælleren Sturla Þórðarson', in *Sturlustefna: Ráðstefna haldin á sjö alda ártíð Sturlu Þórðarsonar sagnaritara 1984*, ed. by Guðrún Ása Grímsdóttir and Jónas Kristjánsson, Rit 32 (Reykjavík: Stofnun Árna Magnússonar, 1988), pp. 112–26

Meyer, Elizabeth A., 'Allusion and Contrast in the Letters of Nicias (Thuc. 7.11–15) and Pompey (Sall. *Hist.* 2.98M)', in *Ancient Historiography in its Contexts: Studies in Honour of A. J. Woodman*, ed. by Christina S. Kraus, John Marincola, and Christopher Pelling (Oxford: Oxford University Press, 2010), pp. 97–117

Mundal, Else, 'Sagaskrivarane og Bergen', in *Fragment frå fortida*, ed. by Øystein Brekke and Geir Atle Ersland (Oslo: Dreyer, 2014), pp. 174–99

Riis, Thomas, *Einführung in die 'Gesta Danorum' des Saxo Grammaticus* (Odense: University Press of Southern Denmark, 2006)

Rindal, Magnus, 'Dei eldste norske kristenrettane', in *Religionsskiftet i Norden: Brytninger mellom nordisk og europæisk kultur 800–1200 e.Kr.*, ed. by Jón Viðar Sigurðsson and others, Occasional Papers, 6 (Oslo: Senter for studier i vikingetid og nordisk middelalder, 2004), pp. 103–37

Sawyer, Peter, *Anglo-Saxon Charters: An Annotated List and Bibliography* (London: Royal Historical Society, 1968)

Spurkland, Terje, "'Þeir báru fram bréf ok segja ørendi þau sem fylgðu": Om brevveksling i middelalderen', *Den nordiske renessansen i høymiddelalderen*, ed. by Jón Viðar Sigurðsson and Preben Meulengracht-Sørensen, Tid og Tanke, 6 (Oslo: Historisk Institutt, 2000), pp. 45–61

Sverrir Tómasson, 'Hryggjarstykki', in *Tækilig vitni: Greinar um bókmenntir gefnar út í tilefni sjötugsafmælis hans 5. apríl 2011*, ed. by Svanhildur Óskarsdóttir (Reykjavík: Stofnun Árna Magnússonar í íslenskum fræðum and Hið íslenska bókmenntafélag, 2011), pp. 54–61

Wellendorf, Jonas, "'Ancient Traditions" in *Sverris saga*: The Background of an Episode in *Sverris saga* and a Note on the Dating of *Rómverja saga*', *Journal of English and Germanic Philology*, 113.1 (2014), 1–17

Williams, Kathryn F., 'Manlius' *Mandata*: Sallust *Bellum Catilinae* 33', *Classical Philology*, 95.2 (2000), 160–71

Wiseman, T. P., *Clio's Cosmetics: Three Studies in Greco-Roman Literature* (Leicester: Leicester University Press, 1979)

Woodman, A. J., *Rhetoric in Classical Historiography: Four Studies* (London: Croom Helm, 1988)

Letters, Networks, and Public Opinion in Medieval Norway (1024–1263)

Leidulf Melve

Introduction

Letters played a prominent role in the literary culture of the Middle Ages. No less so in medieval Norway, although letters — as well as networks and patterns of communication based on letters — arrived rather late in Norway. In fact, the first surviving letter is from King Filippus's reign (1207–17), perhaps from 1210,[1] and from the entire thirteenth century only eighty original letters have survived.[2] As Sverre Bagge has pointed out, everything issued in Norway from 1000 to 1570 amounts to just a few decades' worth of what was issued by the English royal chancery during the 1200s.[3] Needless to say, references to letters go further back: the first might be a letter of Norwegian origin from 1043, allegedly a letter from the Norwegian king Magnús inn góði (Magnus the

---

[1] *Diplomatarium Norvegicum*, ed. by Lange and Unger, I, 3.

[2] Larger number of the letters only appears after 1280. According to Agerholt, over 150 original royal letters and letters from dukes exist from the period between 1280 and 1387 (Agerholt, *Gamal brevskipnad*, p. 622). In addition, over 180 have survived in copies. See also Holm-Olsen, *Med fjærpenn og pergament*; Melve, *Med ordet som våpen*; Hagland, *Literacy i norsk seinmellomalder*.

[3] Bagge, *Cross and Scepter*, pp. 141–42.

Leidulf Melve (Leidulf.Melve@uib.no) is Professor of Medieval History at the University of Bergen. His research interests and areas of publication include intellectual history, historiography, and communication studies.

Moving Words in the Nordic Middle Ages: Tracing Literacies, Texts, and Verbal Communities, ed. by Amy C. Mulligan and Else Mundal, AS 8   BREPOLS ☙PUBLISHERS   (Turnhout: Brepols, 2019)
pp. 143–164   10.1484/M.AS-EB.5.116623

Good) (1035–47) to the English king Edward the Confessor (1042–66).[4] The first reference to a letter addressed to a Norwegian recipient is from between 1024 and 1026 — from the Danish king Canute the Great (1018–35) to the Norwegian king Haraldr harðrádi (1015–66).[5]

The lack of extant letters poses a tremendous challenge in terms of approaching the emergence of written culture in medieval Norway. What we are left with, at least with respect to the epistolary dimension, are references to letters contained in other sources, largely the sagas. These references are of different kinds: in the majority of cases, the sender and recipient are specified, and on occasion we are briefly informed about the letter's content. In other cases the content of the letter is paraphrased, whereas in yet other cases the letter in question is quoted verbatim. The authenticity of these references has been discussed at length, without any agreement being reached. There are reasons for contending that letters quoted verbatim — at least the earliest ones — may be rhetorical constructions. However, even if the content of the letter — as reported in the sagas — is considered a construction, this does not necessarily undermine the authenticity of the reference to the letter as such. My general impression is that the references should be considered authentic, whereas the verbatim quotes come across as a bit too polished in order to be taken at face value. In any case, the question of authenticity is of minor relevance for the following discussion of the early epistolary culture in Norway: even if authenticity is questionable, investigation can still provide indicators of how the authors of the sagas — considered the most important narrative sources of medieval Norway — regarded the form and function of letters, patterns of communications, audiences, and networks in the period prior to that of the first extant letters in the thirteenth century. In addition to delineating and discussing general distribution patterns according to clerical and lay letters, I will also provide examples of the complex interaction of oral, aural, and written communication, particularly in the context of attempts to appeal to public opinion.

---

[4] The letter is referred to in Snorri's *Heimskringla*, in *Fagrskinna*, and in *Flateyjarbók*. For a discussion, see Spurkland, 'Þeir báru fram bréf', p. 56.

[5] On this letter with further references, see Terje Spurkland, 'Þeir báru fram bréf'; Hagland, 'Segia frá eller rita'.

Table 1. Letters 1024–1263: some general tendencies.

	1024–1263	1024–1177	1177–1202	1202–63
Total number of references	374	40	57	277
Clerical letters	159	24	37	98
Lay letters	215	16	20	179
References to letters relating to public opinion	37	8	6	23
Clerical letters	12	5	4	3
Lay letters	25	3	2	20

Letters 1024–1263: Some General Tendencies[6]

In total there are 374 references to letters relating to the Norwegian realm in the period 1024–1263.[7] Clerical letters — letters sent from an individual, a group, or an institution — amount to 42.5% of the total, whereas lay letters are responsible for 57.5% of the total number of references. The period 1024–1263 is divided into three sections, on account of changes in the distribution pattern corresponding with the rule of Sverrir Sigurðsson (1177–1202) and Hákon Hákonarson (1202–63). If the 374 references are distributed within our three periods, a first quantitative upsurge takes place in Sverrir's reign; the fifty-seven references from the period 1177–1202 account for a vast increase compared to only forty references in the entire period 1124–77. While this hardly comes as a surprise, it is of interest to note that the distribution patterns between clerical and lay letters are rather similar, approximately 60% clerical to 40% lay letters.

If Sverrir's reign marks the first upsurge of references to letters, the period under Hákon Hákonarson constitutes something of a revolution. Notwithstanding the longevity of Hákon's reign, the 277 references compared to fifty-seven under

---

[6] The overview includes only letters which have a Norwegian provenance and/or addressee. Admittedly, Norway is a slippery unit, particularly at the end of this period. For the sake of simplicity, I will use the term 'the Norwegian realm' to refer to an evolving unit that in the period under scrutiny included these units: the Orkneys, Shetland, the Hebrides, Man, Ireland, Faroe Islands, Iceland, Greenland, Jämtland, and Härjedalen.

[7] All types of letters are included, regardless of how they are referred to in the sources and regardless of how they are categorized. In the *Regesta Norvegica*, several terms are applied, such as *epistolum*, *privilegium*, *responsum*, and *rescriptum*. The three last mentioned refer largely to papal correspondence which does survive — either in original or in later copies. I should also mention that all English translations are my own.

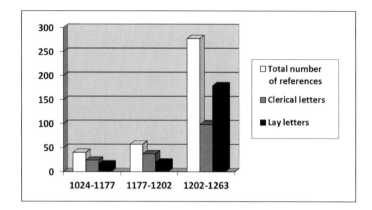

Graph 1.
Clerical and
lay letters.

Sverrir amount to almost six times as many references. The distribution pattern between clerical and lay references changes as well. Whereas references to clerical letters predominate in the period up till 1177, in the subsequent period under Hákon references to lay letters accounts for 64.6% of the total. In short, the 179 references to lay letters, the majority of which are to royal letters, are responsible for the overall distribution pattern: lay letters outnumber clerical letters.

The significant presence of lay letters in our first period (1024–1177) is a forceful reminder that not even in the early development of epistolary culture did the alleged clerical monopoly of written culture exclude lay contributions. If more recent research on non-Scandinavian diplomatics — particularly on the Carolingian period — has emphasized that lay segments played a more important role in this respect, the view of the Church's predominant role in introducing the written word in the newly Christianized North has gone virtually unquestioned. The parallel existence of two written languages, Latin and Old Norse, has too easily led to an imposition of a cultural dichotomy: Old Norse as a lay language and Latin as the language of the Church. The vast increase of letters in the reign of Hákon, not to mention the predominance of lay letters, seems to indicate that the laity played an important role in the emergence of an epistolary culture in Norway.

Aside from the total number of references to letters, the quantitative overview also deals with references to letters addressing public opinion. Needless to say, it is notoriously difficult to come to terms with public opinion in a medieval context, both in terms of terminology and as a phenomenon recognized by contemporaries. However, in this case, I attempt to delineate public opinion in accordance with what Charles W. Connell suggested some years ago: in order to understand the form and function of medieval public opinion, it is

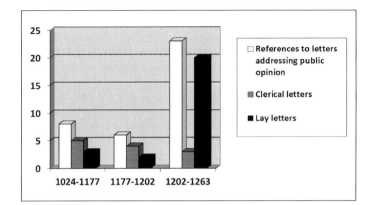

Graph 2.
Letters addressing
public opinion
(1024–1263).

important to 'move away from the focus on political questions in order to try to determine the identity of particular publics and to try to understand issues of greatest importance to those publics'.[8] Connell is also presenting sound advice in terms of how to study medieval public opinion, accentuating as he does the means of communication, the influence of networks, the distinction between audience and publics, and the ways the medieval world understood the potential value of public opinion.[9]

My attempt to delineate the form and function of public opinion from references to Norwegian medieval letters takes as its basic point of departure reference to letters that either are addressed to or sent from lay groups. Consequently, all of these references have a collective addressee or sender, and all concern a lay audience. Thirty-seven references, or 9.8% of the total, fall into this category. Of these thirty-seven references, only twelve (3.2%) are to clerical letters, whereas twenty-five (6.6%) are to lay letters. If we distribute these thirty-seven references according to our three periods, some rather interesting tendencies appear. In the earliest period (1024–1177) eight out of forty references are of this kind (18.5%). The subsequent period, Sverrir's reign (1177–1202), only contains six such references, amounting to a mere 10.5% of the total of fifty-seven references.[10]

---

[8] Connell, 'A Neglected Aspect', p. 55. See also Boas, *Vox populi*; Menache, *The Vox Dei*; Melve, '"Even the very laymen are chattering about it"'.

[9] Connell, 'A Neglected Aspect', p. 55.

[10] This difference is less surprising than it may appear, since — as will be seen below — five of these eight references appear between 1164 and 1174, in other words, in the years leading up to Sverre's reign (our second period).

It should also be underscored that references to clerical letters predominate in the first as well as in the second period: five out of the eight references to letters addressing public opinion between 1024 and 1177 and four out of the six in Sverrir's reign have a clerical sender. This pattern changes in the reign of Hákon. Contrary to what one might have expected, only twenty-three out of 277 references fall into the category 'letters addressing public opinion' (8.3%). Whereas the majority of these references in the two first periods are found in letters sent by clerics, in the reign of Hákon only three of twenty-five references to letters that involve public opinion are from clerical hands. In other words, close to 87% of these references are found in lay letters.

Aural Communication, Networks, and Public Opinion (1024–1177)

Admittedly, the letters addressing public opinion in the period 1024–1177 do not contain much information in terms of communication and networks. The correspondence between King Valdemar I of Denmark (1157–82) and the aristocracy of Trøndelag is an exception, since the two sources that refer to the letters — Snorri's saga of Magnús V Erlingsson (1156–84) and *Fagrskinna* — provide information that in consort details the act of communication. The sources are not independent (Snorri knew *Fagrskinna*) but they nonetheless emphasize different communicative features of the incident. The description in *Fagrskinna* is the more detailed, stating that

> komu til Þrándheims menn Danakonungs með bréfum. Fluttu þeir bréfin fyrir ríkismenn ok vingjafar með, er Danakonungr hafði sent þeim[11]
>
> (men from the Danish king came to Trondheim with letters; they gave the letters to powerful men, together with gifts of friendship that the Danish king had sent them.)

Snorri's description, however, provides more information on the communicative context, since he stresses the role of the mediator:

> Þessari orðsending fylgði bréf ok innsigli Danakonungs ok þat með at þeir bœndrnir skyldu senda í mót sín bréf ok innsigli[12]
>
> (This oral message was accompanied by letters with the seal of the Danish king and a request that the men [from Trøndelag] should send sealed letters in return.)

---

[11] *Fagrskinna*, ed. by Bjarni Einarsson, p. 351.

[12] Snorri Sturluson, *Heimskringla*, ed. by Bjarni Aðalbjarnarson, III, 401.

Table 2. Letters addressing public opinion (1024–1177).

Date	Sender	Recipient(s)
1056	Adalbert of Bremen	People in Iceland and Greenland[13]
1056–72	Adalbert of Bremen	People in Iceland[14]
1164	King Valdemar I of Denmark	Powerful men of Trøndelag[15]
1165	Powerful men of Trøndelag	King Valdemar I of Denmark[16]
1167	From Norway	King Valdemar I of Denmark[17]
1171	Pope Alexander III	Kings, chieftains, and the other Christians in the realms of the Danes, the Norwegians, the Swedes, and the Goths[18]
1173–74	Archbishop Eysteinn	The bishops, chieftains, and people of Iceland[19]

The two sources also differ in their description of the answer given by the powerful men of Trøndelag. *Fagrskinna* mentions that 'Margir skipuðusk hér vel við ok gøra í móti jartegnum hans bréf' (Many were convinced by this [the argument of the Danish king], accepted it, and replied with letters)[20] Snorri, however, refers to the double form of communication — oral as well as aural: 'Þeir gerðu svá ok urpusk flestir vel undir orðsending Danakonungs' (They did so [namely, replied to the Danish letter with a sealed letter], and the majority received this oral mediation from the Danish king favourably).[21]

There are good reasons for following Snorri's description when it comes to his outline of the combination of oral and aural communication. Not only does it accord with the function of the mediator as we know it from numerous other sources (Old Norse as well as Latin), but the act of communication — involving lay people unable to read — would be jeopardized without oral mediation

---

[13] Adam of Bremen, *Gesta Hammaburgensis*, ed. by Buchner, Schmale, and Goetz, p. 486.

[14] *Byskupa sögur*, ed. by Guðni Jónsson, I, 5.

[15] *Fagrskinna*, ed. by Bjarni Einarsson, p. 180; Snorri Sturluson, *Heimskringla*, ed. by Bjarni Aðalbjarnarson, III, 631.

[16] *Fagrskinna*, ed. by Bjarni Einarsson, p. 180; Snorri Sturluson, *Heimskringla*, ed. by Bjarni Aðalbjarnarson, III, 632.

[17] Saxo Grammaticus, *Gesta Danorum*, ed. by Friis-Jensen and Munch, I, 338.

[18] Vandvik, *Latinske dokument*, p. 82.

[19] *Diplomatarium Islandicum*, ed. by Jón Sigurðsson, I, no. 38.

[20] *Fagrskinna*, ed. by Bjarni Einarsson, p. 351.

[21] Snorri Sturluson, *Heimskringla*, ed. by Bjarni Aðalbjarnarson, III, 401.

Table 3. Letters addressing public opinion (1177–1202).

Date	Sender	Recipient(s)
1177	King Sverrir	The people of Telemark[22]
1178	Archbishop Eysteinn	The people of Iceland[23]
1180–81	The landed men of King Magnús	King Sverrir[24]
1189	Pope Clemens	All clerics in Norway[25]
1196	Pope Celestine III	King Sverrir and the people of Norway[26]
1198	Pope Innocent IV	The chieftains and people of Iceland[27]

of the content of the letter. According to Snorri, Erlingr obtains the letter, and then convenes the people of Trøndelag at an assembly (*þing*) and there he accuses them of treason. When the people reject the accusation outright,

> Þá stóð upp kaplín Erlings ok helt upp bréfum mǫrgum ok innsiglum ok spurði, ef þeir kenndi innsigli sín þar, þau er þeir hǫfðu sent um várit Danakonungi[28]
>
> (Erlingr's chaplain then stood up and displayed several letters and seals, asking whether they recognized their own seals — the same seals as they last spring had sent to the Danish king).

The description in *Fagrskinna* is very similar, emphasizing also the function of the letter — or, rather, the seal — as proof of treason, but adds that 'Váru þá bréf upp lesin ok sǫgðu svá at þeir bundusk í þat ráð at drepa konung ok Erling' (the letters were now read out loud and stated that they had committed themselves to kill the king and Erlingr).[29]

What, then, does this correspondence reveal of networks of epistolary communication? Aside from providing the communicative context for the relatively high number of letters addressing public opinion in the form of oral communication, two additional points should be emphasized. First, it shows that

[22] *Sverris saga*, ed. by Þorleifur Hauksson, p. 20.

[23] *Byskupa sögur*, ed. by Guðni Jónsson, I, 54.

[24] *Sverris saga*, ed. by Þorleifur Hauksson, pp. 79–80.

[25] Vandvik, *Latinske dokument*, p. 84.

[26] *Sverris saga*, ed. by Þorleifur Hauksson, p. 193.

[27] Vandvik, *Latinske dokument*, p. 116.

[28] Snorri Sturluson, *Heimskringla*, ed. by Bjarni Aðalbjarnarson, III, 402.

[29] *Fagrskinna*, ed. by Bjarni Einarsson, p. 353.

communication relying on a combination of oral, aural, and written dissemination of letters adapted easily to existing political institutions. In this case, the local assembly constitutes the focal point, not only for oral promulgation of the letter but also for oral deliberation with public opinion. Moreover, these networks, in which letters acted as agents for mobilization, were vertical as well as horizontal, providing for new configurations of political alliances. Second, the network of communication described in the dialogue between King Valdemar and the people of Trøndelag is rather exceptional, since it is a very early example of dialogical deliberation involving public opinion. In comparison, the extensive corpus of letters from the Becket Controversy in the 1160s contains numerous invocations of public opinion, but not a single shred of evidence from the perspective of those holding the opinion targeted by the two parties.[30]

Aural Communication, Networks, and Public Opinion (1177–1202)

Sverrir's reign lacks references to the type of dialogical interaction that was seen in the previous period between King Valdemar and the people of Trøndelag. Yet in this period too there are examples of the inclusion of public opinion in networks based on letters. As related in *Sverris saga*,

> Eftir þat sendi hann bréf sín í Nóreg á Þelamǫrk, því at þeir váru rangsáttir við Magnús konung ok Erling jarl, ok hét hann þeim nǫkkurum réttarbótum ef þeir snerisk til hans[31]

> (He [Sverrir] then sent his letters to Telemark in Norway, because the people there were in disagreement with King Magnús and Erlingr jarl; he promised them a fair trial if they would change sides.)

While the saga is silent on oral mediation of the content of the letter, its function in the escalation of the conflict indicates that its content was diffused to the receiving end:

> Ok er hann kom þar spurði hann at Hrútr ok átta tigir manna váru komnir af Þelamǫrk ok vel vápnaðir; váru komnir at þeiri orðsendingu ok bréfum er fyrr var nǫkkut af sagt at hann hafði sent á Þelamǫrk[32]

---

[30] See Melve, "'Even the very laymen are chattering about it'".

[31] *Sverris saga*, ed. by Þorleifur Hauksson, p. 20.

[32] *Sverris saga*, ed. by Þorleifur Hauksson, p. 15.

(At this place [Soknedalen] the king was told that as a result of the letter he had sent there, Hrútr together with 80 men, all well-armed, had arrived from Telemark.)

If the dialogue between Valdemar and the powerful men of Trøndelag displays the importance of epistolary networks in conflict resolution, Sverrir's letter to the people of Telemark is a rare example of mobilization of public opinion by means of epistolary communication. Still, the two cases display subtle differences regarding the conceptualization of the authority of the written word. Whereas the dialogue between Valdemar and the powerful men of Trøndelag hinges on a combination of oral, aural, written, and symbolic communication (the seal), in Sverrir's dealings with the people of Telemark the letter is at the centre stage — to the extent that the author of the saga highlights the letter as singlehandedly being responsible for the mobilization of public opinion. With this in mind, the letter of 1180–81 from the landed men of King Magnús to Sverrir provides another example of the role of letters in mediating between segments of public opinion and the king:

En þat bjó í þessu máli at allir lendir menn Magnús konungs hǫfðu sent Sverri konungi leyndarbréf ok leituðu til hans griða ok fullkominnar vináttu. Þessi bréf hafði konungr í pung sér[33]

(The truth was that all the landed men of King Magnus had sent secret letters to King Sverrir and pleaded for mercy and true friendship, and these letters the king carried in his purse.)

Still, in none of these cases can the authority of the written word be separated from the oral and symbolic aspects of the act of communication. Too often, oral and symbolic communication have been considered antithetical to the authority of the written word, rather than discrete, yet integral, parts of a process of communication that involved illiterate and semi-literate audiences. The spurious letter from Pope Celestine III to King Sverrir and the people of Norway from 1096 exemplifies this communicative complexity. The context is well known, revolving around Sverrir's struggle with the Church and his effort to remedy the effects of his excommunication (1194) with regard to public opinion:

En nǫkkurri stundu síðarr komú danskir menn ok fluttu Sverri konungi bréf ok innsigli páfans [...]. Sverrir konungr lét bréf þessi lesa á kor uppi ok sýna þar páfans innsigli ok bréf. Stóð þat á bréfum at þegar er páfinn vissi it sanna, at konungri mælti réttara en erkibyskup, þá leysti páfinn hann ok allt ríki hans frá ǫllum stórmælum.[34]

---

[33] *Sverris saga*, ed. by Þorleifur Hauksson, pp. 79–80.

[34] *Sverris saga*, ed. by Þorleifur Hauksson, p. 193.

(A bit later, some Danes came to King Sverre and brought to him a sealed letter from the pope [...]. King Sverre had the letter read out in the choir, displaying the papal seal. In the letter, it was stated that as soon as the pope had learned the truth — that the king was more right in his claims than the archbishop — the pope released him and his entire realm from excommunication.)

These passages should be analysed both in terms of the communicative scenario they outline and in relation to their function in *Sverris saga*. As for the first, the author depicts a process of communication in which symbolic and aural communication enhance the authority of the written word; symbolic communication, in the form of the seal, secures the authenticity of the letter in the front of an audience, whereas aurality mediates the content of the Latin letter to an audience of illiterates. Consequently, the authority of the letter is only invoked when it is communicated to the intended audience, since the letter would have been worthless as a political weapon in Sverrir's fight against his opposition without it being disseminated to a wider public. However, and contrary to the attempts to conflate form and content ('the medium is the message'), the epistemological point of departure is still the written content of the letter without which the communicative scenario — including symbolic and aural communication — would not have taken place. This impression is strengthened if we address the function of these passages in the saga: to emphasize the victory of Sverre. In *Sverris saga*, these are the only passages that deal with the final release of the oath, indicating the extent to which the author structures his narrative so as to give authority to the papal letter.

Aural Communication, Networks, and Public Opinion (1202–63)

The reign of Hákon has been regarded as a period in which 'it was common to write letters, also in order to present information that made the letter worthless after it had reached its recipient'.[35] Evidence of what has also been called 'a new epoch'[36] is usually found in the saga of Hákon, containing no less than 130 references to letters — of which two are quoted in full. As mentioned above, the predominantly clerical initiatives to address public opinion during the reign of Sverrir are replaced by an effort on Hákon's part to address a wider public opinion which had a significant lay component. It is fair to say that the so-called 'Civil War' involving Hákon and Skúli Bárðarson in a struggle for the throne,

[35] Bjørgo, '*Om skriftlege kjelder for Hákonar saga*', p. 219.
[36] Bagge, 'Administrative Literacy in Norway', p. 374.

Table 4. Letters addressing public opinion (1202–1263).

Date	Sender	Recipient(s)
1204	King Guðþormr Sigurðarson and Duke Hákon	The people of Trøndelag[37]
1207–08	The birkebeiner party	Bishop Nikolas of Oslo[38]
1217	Bishop Hávarðr of Bergen, and the lendmenn of Gulatingslagen	The people of Trøndelag[39]
1217	Skúli Bárðarson	People 'north and south in the country' as well as in Sweden[40]
1207–17	King Filippus	The people of Morsdal [Mossedal][41]
1224	King Hákon	The people of Viken[42]
1224	The people of the Hebrides	King Hákon[43]
1226	'Men from the north'	King Hákon[44]
1227	King Hákon	The peasants of Värmland[45]
1239	King Hákon	The people of Inn-Trøndelag[46]
1239	Skúli Bárðarson	The people of Bergen[47]
1239	Skúli Bárðarson	Jämtland and Sweden[48]
1246	Pope Innocent IV	All clerical and lay people, as well as public opinion in Norway and Sweden[49]
1247	King Hákon	All his *lendmenn*, lawspeakers, and *hirð*, and the most prominent peasants in the realm[50]

[37] *Soga om birkebeinar og baglar*, ed. by Magerøy, II, 19.

[38] *Soga om birkebeinar og baglar*, ed. by Magerøy, II, 113.

[39] *Hákonar saga Hákonarsonar*, ed. by Mundt, p. 15.

[40] *Hákonar saga Hákonarsonar*, ed. by Mundt, p. 18.

[41] *Diplomatarium Norvegicum*, ed. by Lange and Unger, I, no. 3.3.

[42] *Hákonar saga Hákonarsonar*, ed. by Mundt, p. 61.

[43] *Hákonar saga Hákonarsonar*, ed. by Mundt, p. 60.

[44] *Hákonar saga Hákonarsonar*, ed. by Mundt, p. 69.

[45] *Hákonar saga Hákonarsonar*, ed. by Mundt, p. 79.

[46] *Hákonar saga Hákonarsonar*, ed. by Mundt, p. 102.

[47] *Hákonar saga Hákonarsonar*, ed. by Mundt, p. 111.

[48] *Hákonar saga Hákonarsonar*, ed. by Mundt, p. 114.

[49] *Diplomatarium Norvegicum*, ed. by Lange and Unger, I, no. 31.25.

[50] *Hákonar saga Hákonarsonar*, ed. by Mundt, p. 138.

Date	Sender	Recipient(s)
1247	King Hákon and Cardinal Wilhelm of Sabina	The people of Iceland[51]
1252	King Hákon	The people of Northern Iceland[52]
1257	Archbishop Laurentius of Uppsala	The people of Hälsingland and Jämtland[53]
1260	King Hákon	The people of Iceland[54]
1263	King Hákon	All *lendmenn*, *sysselmenn*, *hirð*, men at court, peasants, and farmers in the diocese of Hamar[55]
1263	King Hákon	The people of Caithness[56]
1219–63	King Hákon	All men in Viken[57]

provides the context for these efforts to appeal to public opinion. In fact, all references to letters addressing public opinion between 1204 and 1246 appear in the context of the Civil War. It is only towards the end of his reign that new subjects appear, first and foremost subjects relating to legal issues and taxation in particular.[58]

From the perspective of focusing on letters as instigators of dialogue with public opinion, the context of the references indicates a new concern with ensuring that information reached the intended audience. When Sturla Þórðarson in 1224 refers to a letter from Hákon to the people of Viken, he stresses that

Kongur liet þa giora bref og liet bædi fara hid efra og hid ytra austur j Vijkena og bad men gæta sijn[59]

---

[51] *Hákonar saga Hákonarsonar*, ed. by Mundt, p. 144.

[52] *Sturlunga saga*, ed. by Gudbrand Vigfusson, II, 118.

[53] *Diplomatarium Suecanum*, ed. by Liljegren, I, no. 444.

[54] *Hákonar saga Hákonarsonar*, ed. by Mundt, p. 182.

[55] *Norges gamle Love*, ed. by Munch and Keyser, I, 462–63.

[56] *Hákonar saga Hákonarsonar*, ed. by Mundt, p. 195.

[57] *Norges gamle Love*, ed. by Munch and Keyser, I, 459–60.

[58] The Swedish case offers a parallel: according to Larsson, the reign of Magnus III of Sweden (1275–90) marked a turning point, since wider social groups in peripheral areas were included into the ambit of the written word (Larsson, *Svenska medeltidsbrev*).

[59] *Hákonar saga Hákonarsonar*, ed. by Mundt, p. 61.

(The king sent letters both with ship and over land and asked them to be on their guard.)

Along with this concern for securing the dissemination of information, letters achieve new functions, becoming objects of deceit and treason. In 1239, for instance, Skúli allegedly replaced a letter to the bishop — reporting the debts owed by people in Bergen — with a different letter:

> Ok er innſigla ſkyllde let hertugi ſkípta ok hafde klerkur aunnur ſuðr hakon konungr komz at brefum þessvm, varð viſſ allz þes falſ ſem a uar til hanſſ ok hanſ manna.[60]

> (But when the letter was to be sealed, the duke replaced it, and the cleric travelled south with a different letter. King Hákon was able to get hold of letters, and thus was informed about the betrayal against him and his men contained in it [the letter].)

The pattern of communication is much the same in the thirteenth century compared to the previous period: public opinion continues to be addressed by the political and ecclesiastical elite, but initiatives on the part of public opinion are largely found wanting. The only reference to a letter from a lay group representing public opinion in this period is from the people in the Hebrides to Hákon in 1224, noting that 'Og marger Sudureyingar / og hofdu til Hakonar kongs / morg bref vmm Naudsyniar landa þeira' (many men from the Hebrides brought letters to King Hákon about the hardship of their countrymen).[61] From this perspective, the act of communication is monological rather than dialogical, since letters are used to rally public opinion for support — usually in times of crisis. The most significant new feature of the epistolary culture in the reign of Hákon is not the use of oral and aural communication, but rather the extent to which written communication in the form of letters becomes integrated in institutions based on face-to-face interactions. The description in *Sverris saga* of a papal letter being read out from the choir of the church is the only reference to dialogical interaction by the use of already-established institutions in the previous period. In the period 1202–63, by contrast, letters make their inroads into three already established institutions: the *leiðangr*, the gathering of the *hirð*, and the *þing*.

The use of the *leiðangr* as an institution of communication is addressed in *Hákonar saga Hákonarsonar*, the context being that the people of Trøndelag in 1227 responded to a letter by means of oral communication. Evidently, the king

---

[60] *Hákonar saga Hákonarsonar*, ed. by Mundt, pp. 111–12.

[61] *Hákonar saga Hákonarsonar*, ed. by Mundt, p. 60.

was so in need of supplies and men that the called for the *leiðangr*, sent letters, and demanded the mobilization of all men in Trondheim, only to discover that the peasants claimed to have no duty to deliver according to these demands.[62] A second institution, the gathering of the *hirð*, was the site of oral deliberation as well, at least according to a reference to a letter from Bishop Hávarðr of Bergen to the people of Trøndelag:

> Hann hafdi Bref fra Havardi / er þa var Biskups-efni j Biorgvin kosenn epter anndlat Marteinns Biskups / og fra lendumm monnum j Gulaþinngs-logumm / þa er Dagfinnur var nykomenn til Bæarenns var Blaasid til hyrdstefnu / og var þar Bref vplesid[63]

> (He [Dagfinnr the Lawman] brought a letter from Hávarðr, bishop elect in Bergen, elected after the death of Bishop Marteinn and from landed men from the county of Gulating. Immediately after Dagfinnr had arrived in the town, a gathering of the *hirð* was convened, and the letter was read aloud.)

The third institution in which different forms of communication interact to establish dialogical deliberation is addressed in the reference to a letter from King Hákon to the people of Iceland (1260):

> Hann hafdi adr um fumarit fpurtt af jflandi at gizur iall hafdi litin huga lagtt at flytia mal hanf uid iflendzka. Uoru þa gior ut bref med þeim ok kuad kongr at huerffu mikinn fkatt hann uilldi hafa at landinu ok fuo huad iall fkylldi hafa. Med þeffum brefum for iuar arnliotar-fon ok pall linfauma hirdmenn kongf þeir komu ut fyrir alþingi [...] þa uoru flutt bref hakonar kongs ok uar þar mikel manndeilld aa huerffu þeim uar tekid.[64]

> (He [Hákon] had previously in the summer heard from Iceland that Gizurr jarl had done little to argue his cause amongst the Icelanders. Letters were then dispatched to him [Gizurr] and the King declared how high the taxes were which he wished to have from the country, and what the earl [Gizurr] was to have [as his share]. The *hirðmenn* of the king, Ívarr Arnljótarson and Páll línsauma, brought these letters along; they arrived in Iceland before the alþing and travelled quickly to the *þing* [...]. The letter of Hákon was read out, but there was disagreement as to how it should be received.)

---

[62] *Hákonar saga Hákonarsonar*, ed. by Mundt, p. 102.

[63] *Hákonar saga Hákonarsonar*, p. 15.

[64] *Hákonar saga Hákonarsonar*, ed. by Mundt, p. 182.

In this case, dialogical interaction with public opinion is secured by the combination of oral, aural, and written forms of communication at an institution originally premised on and operated through oral deliberation. Significantly, the letter is at the centre of attention — not the oral mediation of the letter by the king's *hirðmenn*. If signs of the increasing authority of the written word can be found during Sverrir's reign, in the thirteenth century the letter as the point of departure for assembly deliberation is surely a new and rather forceful indicator of the extent to which the written word now is at the centre of dialogue with public opinion.

The evidence, scarce as it may be, indicates that letters addressed to public opinion received new functions in the reign of Hákon — at least compared to those in the previous period. Arguably, the most important of these new functions is the role of letters in secret gatherings involving public opinion. To a modern observer, the link between 'secret gatherings' and 'public opinion' may seem contradictory. In a medieval context, however, the private-public division is not only drawn differently from the modern conceptualization of these categories, but the fact that these categories defy neat classification results in several possible configurations of the private-public relationship.[65] One of these configurations is exemplified in *Böglunga sögur* for the years 1207–08, which notes not only that letters were sent between the earl and bishop Nikolas, but also that he held secret gatherings with the most powerful peasants.[66] If letters in this case seem to be the point of departure for secret oral deliberation, in other cases letters are responsible for making public that which had taken place in (secret) oral deliberations. In the reference to a letter from 1217 sent by Skúli, we are told:

> Enn jall var alla þessa stunnd j Radagiordumm vid vine sijna / og sendi Bref bædi sudur og nordur j landed / var þad flestumm monnum okunnugt hua daa þeim var / þuiat faa voru konginum synnd[67]

> (Throughout, the earl held deliberations with his friends, and sent letters both south and north in the country. Not many knew what was written in these letters, and few of them were shown to the king.)

---

[65] On the numerous issues that may be relevant in order to define public and private in the Middle Ages, see Firey, *A Contrite Heart*, p. 1; Symes, *A Common Stage*, pp. 127–28.

[66] *Soga om birkebeinar og baglar*, ed. by Magerøy, II, 113–14.

[67] *Hákonar saga Hákonarsonar*, ed. by Mundt, p. 18.

Yet, the best example of the complex interaction between different forms of communication is contained in the reference to King Hákon's letter to the people of northern Iceland from 1252. The context is a meeting at Höfðahólar, convening the so-called *bændr* of the district — Þorleifr of Garðar and Egill of Reykjaholt in particular. The people of the district were present as well, and according to *Sturlunga saga*, Óláfr Þórðarson rose, spoke, and demanded that the gathered men give proper reception to the letters and messages from such a noble lord as King Hákon.[68] Then, the king's representative Þorgils Bǫðvarsson stood up and replied:

> Þat er mönnum kunnigt, at ek hefi stefnt fund þenna. En þat er fyrir þá sök, at ek em skyldaðr til í dag at reka konungs örendi. Man hér lesit vera konungs-bréf. Bið ek, at men gefi hér til gótt hljóð, ok hyggi síðan at svörum.[69]

> (Everyone knows that I have called this meeting, and for this reason — that I am bound today to deliver the king's message — the king's letter will now be read out here, and I ask that all give it a good hearing and afterwards remember their oaths.)

Thereafter we are told that Þorgils held the letter in his hand, looked at the seal, and then bade Þorleifr choose someone to read it if he would, which Þorleifr refused on the grounds that few there on that day could give an answer to the king.[70] According to the saga, many men supported Þorleifr's position that the king did not deserve to have any voice in the decision about Snorri Sturluson's inheritance.[71] In the end Þorgils responded:

> 'Vita skulu þér Þorleifr, at ek ætla at láta lesa hér í dag konungs-bréf, tvau eðr þrjú, opinberlega svá at þèr heyrit; ok skal ek eigi myrða þetta konungsbréfit, þóttú hafir myrt þau konungs-bréf er til þín hafa send verit; ok má vera, at þú eigir því hér at svara í dag, ok þurfir eigi til annarra svörum at víkja'. Þorleifr drap þá niðr höfði, ok svaraði öngu; ok vóru hans tillögur fár í hávaða. Lét Þorgils þá lesa bréf konungs; ok görði [þat] Þórðr Hitnesingr. En er bréfit var lesit, þá tóku men eigi skjótt til svara. Þá mælti Óláfr Þórðarson: 'Þat er siðr hæveskra manna, at þegja eigi á móti konungs örendum; en flestir munu hér meta svör við Þorleif'. Þorleifr segir: 'Eigi mun ek halda hérad fyrir konungi, ok eigi reisa flokk í móti þeim sem í sezt' [...]. Þaðan frá urðu þar eingin mótmæli berlega, enda ekki skörulegt já-orð. Þá lét Þor-

---

[68] *Sturlunga saga*, ed. by Gudbrand Vigfusson, p. 118.

[69] *Sturlunga saga*, ed. by Gudbrand Vigfusson, p. 118.

[70] *Sturlunga saga*, ed. by Gudbrand Vigfusson, p. 118.

[71] *Sturlunga saga*, ed. by Gudbrand Vigfusson, p. 118.

gils lesa konungs-bréf þat er Þorleifi var sent. Var hann mjök ávítaðr um þat er hann hafði brotið bréf konungs[72]

('You will find, Þorleifr, that I intend to have two or three of the king's letters read publicly here today so that you will hear them; nor will I keep secret this letter from the king, even though you have kept secret those letters from the king which have been sent to you. And it may be that you will have to give an answer here today without considering any other forms of reply'. Þorleifr lowered his head and made no other reply; after this he made few comments which were audible. Þorgils had the king's letter read — Þórðr hítnesingr read it. When the letter had been read men were in no hurry to respond. Then Óláfr Þórðarson said, 'It is not the custom of courteous men to remain silent before the king's messengers, but most men here want to leave the answer to Þorleifr'. Þorleifr replied, 'I will not withhold the district from the king nor will I raise forces against those who take possession of it' [...]. From now on there was no downright opposition, but no outright assent either. Þorgils had the king's letter, which had earlier been sent to Þorleifr, read aloud. Þorleifr was severely reprimanded because he had ignored the letter.)

These passages offer tantalizing insight into medieval assembly politics, since they provide a glimpse into the secret phase of the deliberation. Specifically, the narration describes the role of letters not only in combination with other forms of communication, but more crucially, their significance in dialogical deliberation which challenged the divide between the private, or secret, and the public side of medieval political culture. From the very start, letters are depicted as representing the public side of the private-public divide, since it is Þorgils's intention 'to have two or three of the king's letter read publicly here today'. At the same time, the written word — in the form of letters — is given two additional functions within the deliberation. On the one hand, the written word is established as the point of departure for the dialogue, partly through its constructed publicness, and partly by an attempt to give the letters additional authority on account of the fact that they contain a 'seal'. On the other hand, and perhaps of greater significance, is the extent to which the publicness and authority of the written word is related to the assembly setting in which public opinion is a part of the dialogue and hence receives a political function in the dialogue.

Consequently, letters provide the point of departure for deliberation, and public opinion is presented as the final court of appeal. With this in mind, the concluding words of Þorgils ('You will have to give an answer here today') are a powerful indicator of the force of public opinion, and so is Þorleifr's reaction — he 'lowered his head and made no other reply'. While symbolic communi-

---

[72] *Sturlunga saga*, ed. by Gudbrand Vigfusson, p. 119.

cation certainly is at play here — the lowering of one's head appears in other descriptions of assembly proceedings as well — the narration keeps the written word at the centre of attention. In fact, the letter once again becomes the point of departure for deliberation when Þórðr Hítnesingr reads it out loud. The dialogue is then resumed, but emphasis is redirected to the contentious subject — the king's demands — eschewing the previous focus on formalities relating to the private-public divide. However, the force of public opinion is strongly present in this phase of deliberation as well, powerfully exemplified in the fact that Þorleifr is required to respond to the demands presented in the letter. This time, however, the letter has a more prominent symbolic function; it is read aloud once again, serving to highlight that there 'was no downright opposition' as well as Þorleifr's defeat.

Admittedly, it is impossible to ascertain whether this Icelandic example of assembly deliberation actually happened as it is presented in the saga. However, other indicators of the new functions of the epistolary culture during the reign of Hákon attest to the reliability of the description. In a comparative perspective, continental evidence of what may be called the textualization of assembly politics is noticeable from the last decades of the eleventh century.[73] In these cases as well, the process of textualization is first and foremost noticeable in the extent to which texts of different types gradually set the premise for deliberation regarding both procedure as well as dialogue over contested points. But whereas the continental evidence — from the eleventh and twelfth centuries at least — either stems from ecclesiastical assemblies or from secular assemblies with a prominent ecclesiastical element, the example analysed above indicates that textualization of assembly politics was a feature of lay assemblies in medieval Norway and Iceland as well. As such, the concern with the laity in assembly politics resonates with a new feature of the reign of Hákon: attempts to influence public opinion by the use of the written word.

Conclusion

The lack of surviving Norwegian letters for the period prior to the thirteenth century renders any effort to deal with the early epistolary culture in Norway riddled with difficulties. This investigation, addressing references to letters in the saga literature, is no less so — assuming as it does that the large majority of the references are authentic. From this point of departure, I have attempted to

---

[73] See Melve, 'Assembly Politics'.

chart, based initially on quantitative indicators, changes in the epistolary culture over a period of three hundred years. The emerging tendencies are rather
striking. On account of the high percentage of references in the saga material
to letters of lay provenance, I conclude that letters involving the laity were an
important aspect of Norwegian epistolary culture from the outset. Less surprising is the significant change that apparently takes place in the reign of Hákon,
coinciding with the survival of the earliest extant letters of Norwegian provenance. For the first time, references to lay letters outnumber clerical letters,
reflecting the new administrative apparatus of Hákon's reign. Yet, even more
striking is the number of references to letters which address public opinion,
the large majority of which are contained in lay letters. These quantitative tendencies, if not confirmed, are at least further attested by references to the laity
being involved in dialogic deliberation by oral, aural, and written mediation of
letters. On a further note, the numerous ways in which oral, aural, and written
forms combined in order to instigate dialogue is another forceful reminder of
the extent to which public opinion could be mobilized by means of letters in
the age of manuscripts.

Works Cited

Primary Sources

Adam of Bremen, *Gesta Hammaburgensis ecclesiae pontificum*, ed. by Rudolf Buchner, Franz-Joseph Schmale, and Hans-Werner Goetz, Ausgewählte Quellen zur deutschen Geschichte des Mittelalters (Darmstadt: Wissenschaftliche Buchgesellschaft, 2000)

Byskupa sögur, ed. by Guðni Jónsson, 3 vols (Akureyri: Íslendingasagnaútgáfan, Haukadals-útgáfan, 1981)

Diplomatarium Islandicum – Íslenzkt fornbréfasafn I, ed. by Jón Sigurðsson, 16 vols (Kaup-mannahöfn: Hið íslenzka bókmentafélag, 1857–72)

Diplomatarium Norvegicum I, ed. by Christian A. Lange and Carl R. Unger (Christiania: Malling, 1847)

Diplomatarium Suecanum, ed. by J. G. Liljegren, 6 vols (Stockholm: Norstedt, 1829–1946)

Fagrskinna, ed. by Bjarni Einarsson, Íslenzk fornrit, 29 (Reykjavík: Hið íslenzka fornri-tafélag, 1984)

Hákonar saga Hákonarsonar, ed. by Marina Mundt (Oslo: I kommisjon hos Forlags-sentralen, 1977)

Norges gamle Love indtil 1387, ed. by Rudolf Keyser and Peter A. Munch, 5 vols (Christiania: Gröndahl, 1846–95)

Saxo Grammaticus, *Gesta Danorum*, ed. by Karsten Friis-Jensen and Peter Zeeberg, 2 vols (Copenhagen: Det Danske Sprog-og Litteraturselskab & Gads Forlag, 2005)

Soga om birkebeinar og baglar, ed. by Hallvard Magerøy, 2 vols (Oslo: Solum forlag og kjeldeskriftfondet, 1988)

Sturlunga saga, ed. by Gudbrand Vigfusson, 2 vols (Oxford: Clarendon Press, 1878)

Snorri Sturluson, *Heimskringla*, ed. by Bjarni Aðalbjarnarson, Íslenzk fornrit, 26–28, 3 vols (Reykjavík: Hið íslenzka fornritafélag, 1941–51)

Sverris saga, ed. by Þorleifur Hauksson, Íslenzk fornrit, 30 (Reykjavik: Hið íslenzka forn-ritafélag, 2007)

Secondary Studies

Agerholt, Peter Johan, *Gamal brevskipnad: Etterrøkjingar og utgreidingar i norsk diplo-matikk*, I: *Formelverket i kongebrev på norsk 1280–1387* (Oslo: J. C. Gundersen bok-trykkeri, 1929)

Bagge, Sverre, 'Administrative Literacy in Norway', in *Along the Oral-Written Continuum: Types of Texts, Relations and their Implications*, ed. by Slavica Ranković, Leidulf Melve, and Else Mundal (Turnhout: Brepols, 2010), pp. 371–95

——, *Cross and Scepter: The Rise of the Scandinavian Kingdoms from the Vikings to the Reformation* (Princeton: Princeton University Press, 2014)

Bjørgo, Narve, 'Om skriftlege kjelder for *Hákonar saga*', *Historisk tidsskrift*, 46 (1967), 185–229

Boas, George, *Vox populi: Essays in the History of an Idea* (Baltimore: Johns Hopkins University Press, 1969)

Connell, Charles W., 'A Neglected Aspect of the Study of Popular Culture: "Public Opinion" in the Middle Ages', in *Folk Life in the Middle Ages*, ed. by Edvard Peters (= *Medieval Perspectives: Publications of the Southeastern Medieval Association*, 3.2 (1991)), pp. 38–66

Firey, Abigail, *A Contrite heart: Prosecution and Redemption in the Carolingian Empire* (Leiden: Brill, 2009)

Hagland, Jan Ragnar, *Literacy i norsk seinmellomalder* (Oslo: Novus, 2005)

——, 'Segia frá eller rita, lesa eller heyra i kongesagalitteraturen — fri variasjon, eller ulike perspektiv på overgang frå "orality" til "literacy"?', *Arkiv för nordisk filologi*, 117 (2002), 85–96

Holm-Olsen, Ludvig, *Med fjærpenn og pergament. Vår skriftkultur i middelalderen* (Oslo: Cappelens Forlag, 1990)

Larsson, Inger, *Svenska medeltidsbrev: Om framväxten av ett offentlig skriftbruk innom administration, förvaltning och rättsutövning* (Stockholm: Sällskapet Runica et Mediævalia, 2001)

Melve, Leidulf, 'Assembly Politics and the "Rules-of-the-Game" (c. 650–c. 1150)', *Viator*, 41 (2010), 69–90

——, '"Even the very laymen are chattering about it": The Politicisation of Public Opinion, 800–1200', *Viator*, 44 (2013), 25–48

——, *Med ordet som våpen: Tale og skrift i vestleg historie* (Oslo: Samlaget, 2001)

Menache, Sophia, *The Vox Dei: Communication in the Middle Ages* (Oxford: Oxford University Press, 1990)

Spurkland, Terje, 'Þeir báru fram bréf ok segja ørendi þau sem fylgðu: Om brevveksling i middelalderen', in *Den nordiske renessansen i høymiddelalderen*, ed. by Jón Viðar Sigurðsson and Preben Meulengracht Sørensen (Oslo: Historisk institutt, Universitetet i Oslo, 2000), pp. 47–63

Symes, Carol, *A Common Stage: Theater and Public Life in Medieval Arras* (Ithaca: Cornell University Press, 2007)

Vandvik, Eirik, *Latinske dokument til norsk historie* (Oslo: Det Norske Samlaget, 1959)

GYRÐIR Á LYKIL (GYRÐIR OWNS THE KEY): MATERIALIZED MOMENTS OF COMMUNICATION IN RUNIC ITEMS FROM MEDIEVAL BERGEN

Kristel Zilmer

Introduction

Runic inscriptions on a variety of loose objects found in medieval Scandinavian towns are important sources for the study of medieval communication and textual culture, in particular as evidence of the practice of literacy in an urban setting. Inscriptions from Bryggen, Bergen's medieval wharf, are perhaps most widely known among this material. Prior to the excavations launched following the 1955 fire, only some eight medieval inscriptions from the area had surfaced.[1] Until that point, the Norwegian medieval runic material was dominated by finds from ecclesiastical contexts, many directly connected to church buildings. Currently, over 650 runic finds from Bergen are registered, most of which are dated to the twelfth, thirteenth, and fourteenth centuries, though some artefacts date to the fifteenth century and a few may be even younger. Together with hundreds of inscriptions from other towns, they have reshaped our understanding of the Scandinavian medieval runic corpus and the state of runic literacy in the Middle Ages — at least with regard to what has been preserved and discovered thus far.

---

[1] The inscriptions N288–N295 are published in the corpus edition of *Norges Innskrifter med de yngre Runer* (*NIyR*), see 'Hordaland fylke', ed. by Olsen, pp. 46–61.

Kristel Zilmer (kristel.zilmer@hvl.no) is Professor of Textual Studies at Western Norway University of Applied Sciences in Bergen. Her main research interests include runology, literacy studies, epigraphic media, and medieval textual cultures.

Moving Words in the Nordic Middle Ages: Tracing Literacies, Texts, and Verbal Communities, ed. by Amy C. Mulligan and Else Mundal, AS 8   BREPOLS ⬚ PUBLISHERS   (Turnhout: Brepols, 2019)
pp. 165–200   10.1484/M.AS-EB.5.116624

The general features of the Bryggen corpus are known thanks to the overviews provided in previous research.[2] One important aspect which has not received much discussion is that the corpus is more diverse than often perceived. Categorizations based upon type of object or inscription are useful as a means of organizing the material, yet such generalizations may not reveal the complexities and individualities of different inscriptions. This is important when exploring texts and artefacts jointly as vehicles of communication, which, in addition to content, also have a particular material form and outlook, and connect with different situational contexts.

The Bryggen inscriptions provide insight into the emergent literacy skills and writing habits of the men and women of Bergen, and into ways in which writing took place within a medieval town. *Literacy skills* in this context refer to the use of the written language but also to the adoption of particular media, tools of writing, and modes of communication used in producing, mediating, and understanding messages with distinct visual and material properties. The purpose of this chapter is to shed light on the features of selected Bryggen inscriptions as diverse and individual objects of historical textual culture, placing emphasis upon their nature as items of materialized communication. The approach is essentially an in-depth analysis of individual runic artefacts, according to the understanding that the script and the visual and material features of the objects work together complementarily. Recently, different scholarly disciplines have shown increasing interest in the materiality of communication and the forms and features of writing in historical settings.[3] Each rune-inscribed item of medieval Bergen may be described as a unique moment of materialized communication, though as historical media belonging within a common setting they naturally display shared features as well. This setting and the characteristic features of the corpus will serve as a suitable starting point. The chapter is introduced by a brief overview of runic writing in medieval Scandinavia, followed by a presentation of the Bryggen corpus. The next section turns to selected inscriptions to allow the inscribed and materialized words on medieval Bergen's runic items to speak for themselves. In order to give insight into the writing behaviour of some individuals in the town, the focus is on inscriptions that contain personal names.

---

[2] These include studies by Liestøl: see, e.g., 'Correspondence in Runes'; 'Runeninschriften von der Bryggen'; *Runer frå Bryggen*; 'The Runes of Bergen'; and 'Runic Voices from Towns'. See also Liestøl's articles on single inscriptions in the journal *Maal og Minne* in the 1960s. More recent studies are also referred to below.

[3] See, e.g., Enderwitz and Sauer, *Communication and Materiality*.

Writing Runes in Medieval Scandinavia

Regarding the main phases of runic writing in Scandinavia — from the early emergence of the runic script around the beginning of our era to its gradual disappearance as an actively used writing system during the late Middle Ages — it has been debated to what extent the preserved finds may document a widespread knowledge and active use of runes in different settings.[4] The medieval runic material shows that even after the introduction of roman script, runes did not vanish but continued to be used all over Scandinavia, in different environments and for various purposes. The relationship between runic writing and the roman alphabet, and their spheres of usage, have been central among research topics. Some have characterized runes and Roman letters as complementary writing systems connected with distinct domains, and, on a broader level, with different literacy cultures in medieval Scandinavia.[5] Others have traced instances of overlap and interaction;[6] and it has been suggested that the idea of separate domains for runic and Roman script literacy ought to be replaced by that of a continuum.[7]

Over 2600 medieval inscriptions are known from Scandinavia, connected to urban and rural, secular and ecclesiastical settings. The preserved artefacts with inscriptions seem to document a more varied, and perhaps more extensive, use of runes than in the preceding periods. The material can be grouped according to central types of inscription bearer, possible function, or context of usage, as a way of emphasizing the physical and situational features of inscriptions. The identification of main types has its limitations due to overlaps, uncertainties, and over-generalizations, and further problems arise from the wide dating frames — all that can be said in a number of instances is that the inscription is medieval, not earlier or later.

Nevertheless, from what can be determined, the dominant type of medieval runic find in Scandinavia consists of small loose artefacts, such as pieces of wood, bone, antler, metal, or stone (c. 40 per cent of the currently registered corpus).[8] Wood and bone in particular must have provided an available and

---

[4] Aspects of Viking Age (runic) literacy are discussed by Else Mundal in this volume, see the chapters 'Medieval Nordic Backgrounds' and 'From Oral to Written in Old Norse Culture'.

[5] See, e.g., Spurkland, 'Literacy and "Runacy" in Medieval Scandinavia'.

[6] Palm, 'Runkunskap under medeltid'; cf. also Palm, 'Runor och latinskrift'.

[7] Schulte, 'Pragmatic Runic Literacy in Scandinavia'.

[8] In the establishment of the medieval corpus, the *Samnordisk runtextdatabas* (*Scandina-*

accessible surface for writing, and many such artefacts gained their meaning and functions from the inscribed texts. This group of small portable artefacts is complemented by other loose items that had primary functions of their own. Inscriptions occur on a variety of practical items and tools, but also other articles (such as small crosses and the like) that may have served as personal amulets or objects of devotion.

The second main category consists of inscriptions that belong within or originate from the ecclesiastical context. Runes occur in stone and stave churches; inscriptions in church buildings account for around 25 per cent of the medieval corpus. This group is supplemented by inscriptions on ecclesiastical items and church inventory, as well as on other loose finds from churches. Inscribed grave stones are part of the ecclesiastical scene as well.

When it comes to regional concentrations in Scandinavia, some areas (most notably in Sweden and Denmark) are connected with different inscriptions, whereas others can be linked to a particular find type. In Sweden, Gotland and Västergötland display different types of inscription, whereas Småland has finds from the ecclesiastical context, and Uppland has rune-inscribed loose artefacts. In Denmark, Nørrejylland and Skåne emerge as regions for a variety of runic finds.[9] In Norway, a few regions, or more precisely the medieval towns of Bergen, Trondheim, Oslo, and Tønsberg, have finds of small runic artefacts; these differ from areas with the greatest number of extant inscriptions from the ecclesiastical setting.[10]

This picture is not representative of what may once have existed. Information on a number of lost inscriptions has been recorded, but otherwise we do not know what has disappeared or remains undiscovered. For instance, there may be numerous inscriptions on loose objects still hidden in the cultural layers of medieval towns. The overview highlights possible trends in the medieval use of

---

vian Runic Text Database) of the University of Uppsala <www.nordiska.uu.se/forskn/samnord. htm> was used, in combination with the corpus editions of Norwegian, Danish, and Swedish inscriptions (see the list of primary sources). A copy of a database of the Runic Archives, University of Oslo, containing data on unpublished Norwegian inscriptions in the A- and B-series, has been consulted (see the list of archival sources). The Danish material has been checked against the database *Danske Runeindskrifter* <http://runer.ku.dk/>. The number of inscriptions may be extended by new, unpublished finds that might be currently unknown to the author.

[9] The area of Skåne was part of the Danish kingdom during the Middle Ages.

[10] On the use of runes in Norwegian churches, see Zilmer, 'Words in Wood and Stone' (with references).

runes, and the areas that exhibit a variety of finds may indicate the presence of a textual culture that entailed different forms of writing behaviour. This would accord with the idea of runes as a tool of correspondence that could be used across different domains and social layers. At the same time, the general categories do not reveal enough about the potential diversities of the material.

Runic Inscriptions from Medieval Bergen

In the concluding chapter of a two-volume publication on medieval urban literacy, the editors state: 'One could argue that one of the main features of medieval urban literate behaviour was the coexistence of different forms and registers of literacy'.[11] Higher involvement of lay people (men and women) in literate activities is presumed to be characteristic of urban as opposed to non-urban environments, although no precise numbers can be established.[12]

In studies dealing with runic inscriptions from Bergen or other Scandinavian towns, the material is used as evidence of the practical and informal aspects of medieval literacy. When it comes to the role of runic writing in the everyday life of the medieval town, scholarly opinions and approaches differ, but some have characterized the Bryggen finds as proof of 'large-scale ephemeral literacy'.[13] The use of runes as a handy tool of correspondence has been brought to the fore, and the ways in which the inscriptions cast light upon the process of learning to write have been explored.[14] At the same time, the question has been raised as to what extent the inscriptions express a true literate mentality. It has thus been claimed that runic inscriptions were meant for silent reading, and that 'the addressee of most of the medieval runic inscriptions was not the collective but the individual'.[15] With large portions of the material consisting of personal notes or random scribblings, their role in 'extending and materializing the collective memory' would have been limited.[16] Others have emphasized that at least parts of this corpus — such as runic letters and inscriptions that reflect business transactions — undoubtedly indicate the existence of some form of

---

[11] Mostert and Adamska, *Uses of the Written Word*, p. 428.

[12] Mostert and Adamska, *Uses of the Written Word*, p. 428.

[13] Schulte, 'Pragmatic Runic Literacy in Scandinavia', p. 157.

[14] Knirk, 'Learning to Write with Runes'.

[15] Spurkland, 'Literacy and "Runacy" in Medieval Scandinavia', p. 342.

[16] Spurkland, 'Literacy and "Runacy" in Medieval Scandinavia', p. 342. For further discussion on the nature of runic literacy, see Spurkland, 'Viking Age Literacy in Runes'.

literate communities.[17] According to this view, 'literacy at a quite advanced level can probably be seen as part of the community of trade and tradesmanship'.[18] The argumentation depends upon how one defines literacy, and what is understood by literate mentality and literate communities. On the one hand, one may accentuate the existence of private writings and samples of practical correspondence — as evidence of the potential wide reach of runic writing on the level of individual people. On the other hand, one may examine aspects of runic literacy, which bear witness to the extended collective significance of the inscriptions and the artefacts as the material carriers of different acts of literacy.

What can be agreed upon is that the Bryggen material shows that runic writing could be used in a variety of ways, much in accordance with the idea of different forms and registers of urban literacy. When it comes to media, the practical and accessible nature of many items carrying runes is evident. The majority of inscribed objects from Bergen fall into the inclusive category of shaped pieces of wood when using their materiality as the defining criterion. In general surveys it is frequently highlighted that the principal find type consists of wooden (whittled or in some way fashioned) runic sticks. Some appear as casual or natural objects that did not require much preparation, whereas many others have one or more sides facetted to provide a plane surface for runes or other markings; their ends may be rounded or sharpened, and they may also have been shaped in other ways. This speaks of some intention and planning behind the act of making and inscribing different wooden artefacts and downplays the initial impression of spontaneity. Furthermore, the seemingly self-explanatory designations, such as *wooden stick* or *piece of wood*, relate in practice to different things; the dynamic and transecting properties of these and other inscribed artefacts thus require some critical examination.[19] The corpus also includes wooden household items, tools and utensils of various kinds; in such cases, writing is present on objects that had (primary) functions and uses of their own — though these could have been modified or altered through writing. In addition, there are some thirty-five inscribed artefacts made out of materials such as leather, stone, metal, bone, horn, or antler.[20]

---

[17] Hagland, 'Literacy and Trade in Late Medieval Norway'.

[18] Hagland, 'Literacy and Trade in Late Medieval Norway', p. 24.

[19] In a forthcoming study, I discuss such issues in more detail. See Zilmer, 'Runic Sticks and Other Inscribed Objects'.

[20] The number is based upon own assessment of the Bryggen corpus. An online database compiled in the 1990s provides an overview of some thirty objects, designated as 'artefacts other than wooden sticks', see Haavaldsen and Smith Ore, *Runes in Bergen*, electronic

Concerning the content of inscriptions, some common types include owner's tags and personal markers; *fuþork*-inscriptions; texts containing prayers, biblical quotes, and Christian (magic) formulas; letters and notes indicating business or other practical engagements; various private and informal messages; writing exercises and scribbles; carver's formulas; quotations of poetry; and even gossip, jokes, and obscenities. The groupings and descriptions may vary from study to study, but the customary distinctions remain the same. As, for instance, summed up by James E. Knirk:

> The largest group of inscriptions from Bryggen deals with mercantile transactions. Some 110 ownership tags have been identified by text or shape [...]. More than fifteen business letters and notes were uncovered, including accounting records and packing slips. [...] Several inscriptions consist of stereotyped carver's formulas or requests and prayers similar to ones cut into church walls, whereas others provide rare glimpses into private lives and human relationships. [...] Over thirty pieces of poetry written in runes, many very fragmentary, were unearthed. [...] The over sixty runic inscriptions in Latin include a taste of goliardic poetry.[21]

Content-based categorizations serve their general purpose but have their own problems of distinction and interpretation. When such categories are used in further study, there also arises the problem that one does not necessarily clarify the defining overarching criteria consistently. As a further alternative, one can systematize the inscriptions according to their linguistic and semantic features and different ways of making meaning with writing. The main distinction is between inscriptions that contain comprehensible texts or some lexically meaningful units (including proper names) in the vernacular (Old Norse) or in Latin (over 320/40 finds respectively).[22] The few inscriptions (*c.* ten instances) that

---

version (last updated 7 January 2003), <http://www.nb.no/baser/runer/ribwww/english/rune13.html> [accessed 27 January 2019]. The source is outdated, and the provided list does not comply fully with present data. As noted on the project's webpage, the database was not intended as a scholarly publication but as a 'generally available overview of all the material from the Bryggen excavations up until 1996'. Cf. also Haavaldsen and Smith Ore, 'Computerising the Runic Inscriptions'. During 2017, data on archaeological artefacts from Bryggen (including inscribed objects) have been made digitally accessible through the database of the Norwegian Archaeological Collection <http://www.unimus.no/arkeologi/forskning/index.php> [accessed 27 January 2019]. For critical perspectives concerning the use of information in different databases, see Zilmer, 'Runic Sticks and Other Inscribed Objects'.

[21] Knirk, 'Runes and Runic Inscriptions', pp. 553–54.

[22] The numbers are based upon own ongoing assessment of the Bryggen corpus and may differ from those presented in previous studies. Around fifty additional incomprehensible

combine elements from both languages can be considered a small group of their own or form a supplement to the vernacular and Latin varieties. The Latin group may further be expanded by some inscriptions that use formula words (which could be incorporated into the Church Latin texts) or contain elements reminiscent of pseudo-Latin.[23] Inscriptions with (parts of) the medieval *fuþork*, either alone or in combination with shorter or longer sequences of runes can be viewed as an independent group.[24] *Fuþork*-inscriptions may include personal names or other meaningful units, which means that there is some overlap with the vernacular group. More than eighty inscriptions with *fuþork* can be identified; when excluding those in the vernacular group, the number is close to fifty. A large group of Bryggen inscriptions (at least 170 instances) displays shorter or longer sequences of runes and on some occasions rune-like signs or other scribbles.[25] These inscriptions do not seem to mediate any lexical meaning, though some may no longer be intelligible due to their fragmentary state of preservation. Some inscriptions — for instance, those repeating similar units or rows of syllables — can be viewed in the context of writing exercises or imitations of writing. Yet others that follow an evident syllabic structure and even employ markers for word division may exhibit attempts at reproducing names and real or pseudo-words. Some inscriptions may perhaps represent forms of cryptic or playfully inventive writing that modern readers have not been able to decipher.[26]

---

inscriptions contain units that could be offered a possible lexical interpretation; however, due to various uncertainties, here they are not included in the main vernacular group. The Latin group comprises inscriptions that quote Church Latin (these may include Greek and Hebrew elements) or contain other formulations (for example poetic phrases).

[23] Forty-five inscriptions containing Latin text, phrases or presenting possible acquaintance with Latin, are published in *Norges Innskrifter*, vi.1, ed. by Liestøl and Sanness Johnsen. Further finds are discussed by Dyvik, 'Addenda Runica Latina'. See also Knirk, 'Runic Inscriptions Containing Latin in Norway'.

[24] On *fuþork*-inscriptions, see Seim, *De vestnordiske futhark-innskriftene*. The catalogue in the dissertation contains eighty-four inscriptions from Bergen. See also Seim, 'Var futharken en magisk formel'.

[25] Alternatively, all inscriptions that contain rune-like signs could be considered a separate group. However, it is not automatically evident how to distinguish consistently between attempts to carve a real rune vs a sign that is at best only rune-like. Occasionally, it also remains questionable whether some intended signs represent runes or roman characters (or imitations of these). In general overviews the material is more easily grouped together, but more specific treatments of particular parts of the corpus (and their features) are certainly needed as well.

[26] Inscriptions that use different types or systems of cryptic runes could also form a group of their own.

With these considerations in mind, a large proportion of the corpus still presents itself as incomprehensible. At the same time, even such items could arguably have had expressive and communicative meaning, such as through visual and material means. To this group we can add the over seventy inscriptions that consist of single runes (normally one or two runes, which may also appear as bind-runes), rune-like signs, traces of runes, or other marks that may imitate writing.[27] The presence of writing — or attempts at imitating or visualizing writing — on different objects is of interest in these cases as well.

Such ways of organizing the corpus cast light upon some of its characteristic features — with regard to items, textual content, linguistic and semantic features. However, the outlined distinctions can pose problems, and it is not certain how representative the chosen labels are. There occur overlaps between the groups, depending upon ways of assessing and interpreting the material. It is also not necessarily evident that inscribed sequences on different sides of one item are indeed connected. Alternatively, they could be grouped as separate instances of writing. Furthermore, there are inscribed items that demonstrate the fluid and to some extent arbitrary distinctions between (runic) writing and other forms of visual marks.[28] These and other complexities necessitate a look at the inscriptions as individual items of communication.

The Earliest Runic Finds from Bergen — Texts and Objects

A good starting point is examination of eight random inscriptions first known from Bergen: N288 (B6029a) was found in 1905; N289 (B6601a) in 1912; N290–N292 in 1919 (B7097b, B7097d, B7097e); and N293–N295 (B10266c, B10266b, B10266d) in 1950.[29] Is there anything remarkable about

---

[27] One could further distinguish between inscriptions that display one or two runes due to their damaged condition as opposed to those that clearly did not contain any more runes to start with.

[28] In the overview above, *inscription* has been applied as an overarching label for all forms of writing (or other visual markings) that occur on the same item.

[29] See 'Hordaland fylke', ed. by Olsen, pp. 46–61. Although there are some corrections and updated readings, the main data can be considered valid, and the texts are not reproduced here. The identification numbers in brackets (B6029a, etc.) refer to the accession numbers of the artefacts in the archives of the University Museum of Bergen, based upon the original field documentation of archaeological excavations. The catalogue entries on this material are now accessible digitally, through the abovementioned database of the Norwegian Archaeological Collection (cf. n. 20). From the scholarly perspective, however, the data registered there on

these objects and texts as a small sample of their own? And how do their features relate to the inscriptions that were found later?

Interestingly enough, this initial sample is of varied nature. There are different objects in bone and wood, including a gaming piece of whale bone (N288), an ornamented bone comb with a handle (N290), a wooden knife (N291), a wooden plane (N292), a specially shaped wooden stick with notches, possibly a rosary (N289), alongside a few more random-looking sticks and pieces of wood (N293–N295). The sizes vary, ranging from smaller items (the gaming piece is a flat circular disc of *c.* 5.5 cm in diameter) to longer objects (the wooden knife measures *c.* 25 cm). The sticks measure somewhere between 10 to 20 cm in length, as typical of much of the later found material. Some objects display decorative and ornamental details. The upper part of the gaming piece, for example, carries a series of concentric circles. Crosses or other visual markings occur; these may be integrated with the runic text.

The inscriptions are of varying length. The small wooden plane N292 has four identifiable runes, the piece of wood N294 five,[30] and the gaming piece N288 six or seven.[31] Longer sequences occur on the 'rosary' stick N289, where the inscription fills three sides; on the wooden knife N291, with both sides covered with runes; and on the piece of wood N295. Some inscriptions have their segments divided among different sides of the item, as on the bone comb N290 and the stick N293. The shortest inscriptions, N292 and N294, contain the beginning of the runic row, **fuþo** and **fuþor** respectively. Longer versions appear on one side of N293, with a slightly diverted order **fuþork hnisa**, and on N290: **fuþork hnias t** (see Figure 9).[32]

the Bryggen artefacts needs to be individually and critically assessed; for instance, the database does not contain systematically corroborated or updated information on the inscribed artefacts — not the least with regard to describing their 'runic' content, which (when included) may be of deficient or erroneous nature.

[30] There is an additional incised line in front of the runes; it appears intentionally carved but does not seem to mark a runic character.

[31] The runes in N288 are read as **uikigr**, followed by two lines (staves), out of which the first one appears as more deeply (hence intentionally?) incised. It cannot, however, be ruled out that even the second, weaker, and slightly curving line was intended as a continuation of the inscription, which was never completed.

[32] Seim reads the final sign in N290 as a long-branch **s**-rune, instead of **s** and **t**; *De vestnordiske futhark-innskriftene*, p. 343. Based upon my own examination of the item with a stereo magnifier, I tend to support the reading in the corpus edition. The runic row was incised after the ornamentation was made; as many signs as could fit were cut into the handle of the comb. The *fuþork* has a casual appearance as compared to the deeply executed lines of ornamentation.

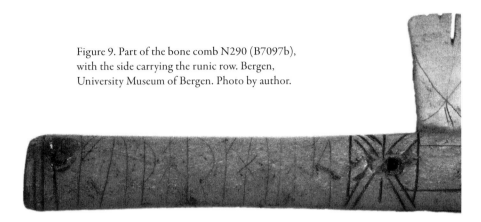

Figure 9. Part of the bone comb N290 (B7097b),
with the side carrying the runic row. Bergen,
University Museum of Bergen. Photo by author.

Both N290 and N293 carry one or several personal names.[33] Personal names
also occur in N288 (one name) and N291 (two names, as part of a carver's formula and an ownership claim). The long text on N289 is a vernacular invocation of Jesus Christ and Mary.[34] The damaged inscription N295 has a long row
of runes that appears lexically meaningless. Among specific features, we find
a cryptic rune on one side of N293. In N291 *á mik* (owns me) and *reist mik*
(carved me) both get repeated two times, turning the runes and the knife into
speaking agents.

What do these initial finds show? Personal names and *fuþork*s of varying
length are of interest, these are among the common elements in the known corpus today. The sample shows that names and *fuþork*s could occur on different
objects. Statements of ownership are recorded, without the items resembling
later discovered owner's tags. We also find a carver's formula and an extended
version of it in one inscription. In the present corpus only some twenty inscriptions mention the use of runes or the activity of writing or reading runes
(including some uncertain instances). Otherwise, the sample contains a longer
vernacular prayer; prayers and invocations are attested in the overall material,
but mostly as shorter quotations, and frequently in Latin. However, inscriptions in Latin are lacking among the early finds. With regard to characteristic

---

The line forming the **s** and the side-branch of **t** do not appear completely connected. The **t**-rune
does not reach a full length, which could indeed suggest the sign is **s**. At the same time, the stave
of the **i**-rune earlier in the runic row also appears slightly shorter than its neighbouring signs.

[33] The sequence containing personal names in N293 is discussed by Seim, 'Var futharken
en magisk formel', p. 286.

[34] See Spurkland, 'How Christian Were the Norwegians', pp. 189–92.

artefacts, we do not see any specially shaped owner's tags that can otherwise be located in the present corpus. In some ways, the early finds still point ahead to what was to be found later, though naturally not representative of the overall corpus. More importantly, the sample makes it easy to recognize the diverse features of sundry runic items in terms of their form, content, visual, and material properties. These features also relate to varying functions that may have been connected to everyday activities, religious devotion, entertainment, or the simple wish to scribble and express something in writing. Their evident individuality should be kept in mind when looking at other runic artefacts from Bergen.

'Gyrðir owns the key' and the Talking Objects of Medieval Bergen

In 1981 Ingrid Sanness Johnsen wrote about runic inscriptions from Norwegian towns that contain personal names: 'Behind every name there will be an individual, and this raises the question of the identity of the bearer. We would like to know who he might be, where he belonged.'[35] The focus here is not on what we can learn about the background of these rune-carving men and women. The meaning and materiality of individual runic items is brought to the fore, paying attention to their formal, textual, visual and physical features. Even in inscriptions that contain but one name and no further verbal information, the properties of the item may in various ways make the runes and the object work and talk together. The attention is hence on the act of writing one's name in runes on items that reflect various communicative situations.

Emphasis is given to inscriptions not yet published in *NIyR*;[36] and the variability of items commonly labelled as 'wooden sticks' or 'pieces of wood' is illuminated. The combination of these two aspects means that less attention is paid to some other, distinctive items of the Bryggen corpus, containing personal names. The group of owner's tags or labels was mentioned above, as related to the sphere of commerce and business transactions.[37] The presence of

[35] Sanness Johnsen, 'Personal Names in Inscriptions', p. 119.

[36] The inscriptions are identified by their preliminary registration numbers B + number, in the Runic Archives, University of Oslo as well as their BRM numbers which refer to their accession numbers in the archives of the University Museum of Bergen. I wish to thank Professor Emeritus James E. Knirk, University of Oslo, for a copy of the database of the Runic Archives (hereafter the Oslo runic database), containing general information, registered readings, and interpretations of the inscriptions. The transliterations and specific observations concerning the inscriptions and the items in this study are based upon my own examination of the artefacts at the Bryggen Museum.

[37] *Norges Innskrifter*, VI.2, ed. by Liestøl and Sanness Johnsen. Cf. also Sanness Johnsen,

personal names is evident on these items, where they stand alone or together with the verb 'owns', in some cases also specifying what it is one owns. In identifying particular runic objects as owner's tags and distinguishing these from other artefacts that display ownership claims, the material features of the item as well as their presumed functions and contexts of usage (with possible relations to other recovered artefacts) have been considered important. Common physical properties may include ways of shaping the object, with, for example, one end of a tag sharpened and made pointy, and/or the other end formed as a kind of neck or head. One or both ends could also be equipped with holes. This reflects the functionality of the items, which could then be attached to goods. Nevertheless, the recurring features and common purposes do not automatically indicate that the group is uniform. In further studies the individualities of owner's tags should be highlighted as well; not in the least with regard to the possible arbitrary lines of distinction between a 'standard' owner's tag and ownership statements or markings appearing on some other items.[38]

A captivating first example in the material studied here is B343 (BRM 0/31710, after 1198).[39] This nearly 18-cm-long rectangular stick has four clearly cut runes on the middle of one of its sides: þ, u, r, and finally an i- or e-rune.[40] One end of the stick is rounded and shaped as a simplistically carved man's head (see Figure 10).

'Die Runeninschriften über Handel und Verkehr'. In a series of studies, the possible origin or background of the people mentioned in some of the inscriptions on owner's tags has been discussed. Among recent contributions, the master's thesis by Elisabeth Magin, 'Die rúnakefli von Bryggen in Bergen', undertakes a runological, onomastical, and archaeological examination of the material.

[38] Some such ambiguities are discussed in Zilmer, 'Runic Sticks and Other Inscribed Objects'.

[39] The datings are based upon the find sites of runic items below, within or above fire-layers, which connect with historically known fires in Bergen. B343 was found above fire-layer 6, i.e., the fire in 1198, which indicates that it dates from after 1198. The archaeological datings of the inscriptions follow the information registered in the archives of the University Museum of Bergen, which have been updated during the 1990s and the first decades of 2000s. The information here is provided according to personal commentary from Professor Gitte Hansen, University Museum of Bergen, 20 May 2016. I am grateful to Professor Hansen for her expert help and for granting me access to the runic collection. For more information on the dating principles and limitations, see Herteig, *The Buildings at Bryggen*; Hansen, *Bergen c 800–c 1170*; Hansen 'The Bryggen Chronology'. See also Knirk, 'Tillegg om funntilhøve, brannlagsrelasjon og datering'.

[40] It is not evident whether the final rune is dotted or not; if dotted, the transliteration would be e (according to an alternative convention, the dotted i-rune is marked as ï). Terje

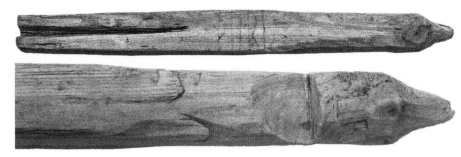

Figure 10. Details of the runic stick B343 (BRM 0/31710), shaped as a man.
Bergen, University Museum of Bergen. Photos by author.

The front part of the head, that is, the face with eyes, nose, and mouth/
beard is visible on the side opposite to the inscription. The side with runes has a
c. 7 cm long split that may similarly be an element of the carving. If considering
the whole stick as a rough figure of a man, the split may be his legs.[41] Holding
the stick up vertically, we see that the four runes appear on the man's lower back
as a possible naming label. The suggested interpretation is an oblique case form
of the male name *Þórir*, that is, *Þóri* (To Þórir). Alternatively, as proposed by
Markali,[42] **þure** stands for the name *Þóri*.[43] The latter form has been explained
as a derivation from the original *Þórir* or a shortened form of compound names
including *Þór-* by Fellows-Jensen in the analysis of Scandinavian names in
England.[44] In connection with B343, the difference between interpreting the

Spurkland has read this as an **i**-rune in *En fonografematisk analyse av runematerialet*, pp. 126,
297. Based upon my own examination, I support the identification of the rune as dotted.

[41] This possibility is also mentioned in the Oslo runic database.

[42] See Markali, 'Personnavnsmaterialet i runeinnskriftene fra Bryggen', p. 59. In her thesis,
Markali identified 157 (more or less) certain personal names and 289 name-bearers (with additional twenty-one uncertain instances). These numbers would have to be modified today, in the
light of alternative evidence as well as updated readings and interpretations. While beyond the
focus of the present study, this warrants further detailed discussion on future occasions.

[43] Spurkland has argued that **þuri** (which does not have to relate to the carved face) may
also stand for female names *Þóríðr* or *Þuríðr*, see *En fonografematisk analyse av runematerialet*,
p. 126. Various female names occur on items from Bryggen. The recorded form (with comparable occurrences in other Scandinavian runic inscriptions) in the meantime does not make the
interpretation *Þóríðr/Þuríðr* that evident.

[44] Fellows-Jensen, *Scandinavian Personal Names*, p. 295. According to Peterson in *Nordiskt
runnamnslexikon*, p. 232, a secondary weak form of the name *Þórir* would have been under
formation already in the Viking Age, whereas medieval forms without -r may be directly based

four runes as a case form of *Þórir* or the name *Þóri* influences the ways we attach meaning to the inscription and the object. Is the text on the man-headed item turning to a man called Þórir? Or is it supposed to identify somebody as Þóri? Is the item with the name meant to refer to the sender, the recipient, or somebody else? Whose voice is talking to us through the four runes and the carved face? Is the inscribed stick itself the man who is saying something to its maker or perhaps an intended reader/viewer? We do not know the answers, but the fact that the item with its simple text raises such varied questions is significant. When looking for potential comparative clues in the Bryggen material, it is by far most common to find personal names used as identifying labels in the nominative case, the case for naming. In letters, but from time to time also in short lists or labels, names can appear in the oblique case, as a way of addressing the people or speaking about them.[45]

What could have been the purpose behind a runic stick like B343? Does it reflect someone practising a craft and making a gift or a toy or perhaps starting to carve a wooden gaming piece with a human head? Is this a case of simple entertainment or does the object have a deeper meaning? The approaches of different scholars would certainly deviate here, ranging from practical explanations to seeking magic or ritualistic reasons behind puzzling items. Another example from Bryggen, B584 (BRM 83/4311, early fourteenth century, possibly before 1332), is telling. This 25 cm long, rectangular stick also has a face carved into one of its ends. The runic text running along the back of the item says: 'Sezt niðr ok ráð rúnar, rís upp ok fís við' (Sit down and interpret the runes, stand up, and fart). In addition, one of the sides between the back with runes and the front with the face is covered with a tight row of incised parallel lines. Viewing these features jointly, one may wonder whether the carved man is inviting and challenging a potential recipient to make sense of what is scribbled on the item. That this effort (perhaps expected to be fruitless and end in frustration and stomach pain) could have been intended to involve more than making sense of the runic text, may explain the side with the long row of incisions. 'Are you able to "read" these as well?', the man-faced stick may be asking. As pointed out by Jonas Nordby in a study on inscriptions containing the appeal *ráð þat* (Interpret that/this!), one could in a playful manner change ways of writing on different runic items, for instance writing upside down or in

upon other names with the element *Þór-*.

[45] See, e.g., the runic stick B122 (BRM 0/17701, after 1248 or before 1332), with the names *Ingiríði, Ingu* (?) (To Ingiríð, to Inga).

opposite directions.[46] Perhaps we witness an even more creative way of changing the idea of writing in B584?

This item thus serves to remind us of the potential entertainment or experimental value of medieval runic artefacts. It could be seen in the context of having fun with runes. It could also be argued that the very idea of what writing and reading might involve is challenged here, through the inclusion of the meaningless row of lines. The intricacies connected to the item are at the same time signified by the fact that 'Sezt niðr ok ráð rúnar, rís upp ok fís við' is in its essence a well formulated metrical inscription, with alliteration and internal rhyme. Both in the case of B584 and B343, the motives behind the inscriptions may thus have been varied; when looking for possible explanations we need to consider the item as a whole.

What we do know is that one's name is among the first words that a person would learn to read and write. Regarding the emergent literacy skills in the Bryggen material, it is not surprising that personal names are among the most frequently recorded elements. Over 260 runic items contain inscriptions in which one or more personal names can be identified (including some uncertain and debatable cases).[47] There are additional instances where otherwise incomprehensible sequences of runes display units that remind of names or attempts at rendering names.[48] The discussion here is in the meantime based upon these roughly 260 inscriptions that can be considered more definite evidence of names.

Around three-fourths of these runic items carry one name, either alone as we saw in the case of B343, or in combination with other text or runic sequences. The presence of two or more names on the same item is also well documented. Occasionally, whole lists of names occur — with ten or more names being recorded on one object. One of the most significant examples is B599 (BRM 0/87909, before 1248), a roughly 16 cm long stick that was at some point

---

[46] Nordby, '*Ráð þat*, If You Can!', p. 87.

[47] Only the names denoting (supposedly) real persons are considered here, leaving out references to saints, evangelists or other biblical (or occasional mythological) figures. The number is based upon runic items, which may be inscribed on one or more sides. The inscriptions containing personal names may appear on one side or continue from one side to the other. Some inscriptions may not be connected with each other, though appearing on the same object. Within the limitations of this study, the item forms an acceptable general criterion.

[48] Other inscriptions display different ways of marking oneself in writing, e.g., by using initials, personal monograms, or abbreviations of names. Such inscriptions will be the focus of a forthcoming study by the author.

during its existence broken into two parts (now repaired by conservators). Its three sides are covered with runes; in its present state, the inscription contains twenty-six names. One end of the stick is damaged, with traces of runes still visible, which makes it likely that it originally included a few more names. These are all male names; the list contains some of the most frequently recorded names in the Bryggen corpus, such as Sigurðr, Árni, Ólafr, Jón. Three names — Jón, Ólafr, and Erlendr — are repeated two times each, whereas Sigurðr occurs three times (once on each side of the stick). With the inscription presenting a detailed list of men, for instance a crew or companionship of some sort, it is likely that in each case a different person is meant. Some of the repeated names display small deviations in rune forms or spelling. This could be a personalizing trait, but it could also result from accidental variation. Variations in rune forms are otherwise visible throughout the inscription. It is of further interest that whereas most names are carved with runes in single lines, a few have runes in double incision. It is nevertheless not evident that different names would have been carved by different hands. The impression of a list is strengthened by the fact that throughout the inscription, there are separation markers in the form of (mostly) two vertically positioned small incisions between the names. Most of the names include one (some also two) bind-runes, i.e. ligatures where two or more runes have been written together sharing the same stave.[49] This may have been an economical way of writing to make sure that all the names would fit on the stick, although one longer name like Sigurðr is in all three instances carved in full: ᛌᛁᚴᚴᚢᚱᚦᚱ (see Figure 11).[50] The graphic visuality of each unit is evident, especially in shorter names that contain one or several bind-runes. In cases when there is an **a**-rune ᛆ or **o**-rune ᚮ in front of an **r**-rune, the formation of a bind-rune is almost obligatory. These and other features — from rune forms to contextual considerations — show the levels of variability in each runic item.

A different Bryggen item that carries two names is worth a closer look. B128 (BRM 0/18052, from the late fourteenth or early fifteenth century,

[49] The exceptions are Finnr (**finþr**), the second mention of Jón (**ion**), all three mentions of Sigurðr (**sikkurþr**), and possibly Þórr (**þorr**), though in the last name the final rune may be a bind-rune, combining **e** and **r**, in which case this unit could be repeating the name Þórir. Note that the transliteration of the second occurrence of **ion** (without a bind-rune) differs from the database registrations, which mistakenly have recorded a bind-rune there.

[50] The standardized runic font Futhark used here does not show the actual variability of rune forms. The **r**-runes within the name Sigurðr in B599, for instance, vary to some extent in all three recorded cases.

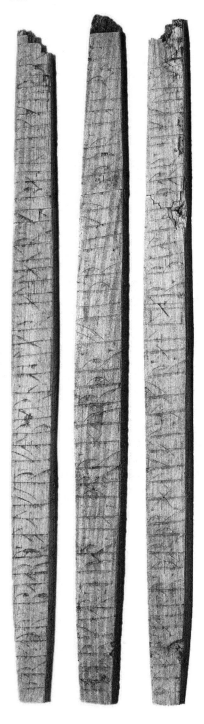

Figure 11. The runic inscription of B599
(BRM 0/87909). Bergen, University
Museum of Bergen. Photos by author.

around 1413), a nearly 17 cm long piece
of wood, has a wedge-like shape. With
wood being a material for everyday
medieval usage, it is to be expected that
the inscribed objects from Bergen also
include diverse practical tools and household objects. The availability of such
items was part of the medieval writing
environment. At the same time, not all of
the inscribed objects that share the features of particular tools may have ended
up being used as such. B128 is rounded,
but the side carrying runes has a flat-
tened surface, as if prepared for writing.
Ten runic signs can be identified, out
of which (at least) three are bind-runes
(here marked with ⁀), that is, **haluarþr ⦂
hauar**.[51] Two units emerge, separated by
three dots in the middle of the inscription. Whereas the first part is incised
using ordinary runes, the second one has
double-contoured runes, each with small
dots inside, which are of similar size and

[51] There also occurs a row of tiny lines, almost
looking like a visual pattern on the back side of
B128. The pattern appears especially clearly when
examining the item with a magnifier. Similar patterns are visible on other (runic) items from Bryggen
(including the abovementioned B343). They do
not look intentional and do not reflect the original
meaning and use of the objects, but rather result
from ways of handling the items, probably having
appeared during the conservation process. This is
confirmed by Gitte Hansen, personal commentary
(11 May 2016), who suggests that this was caused
by a metal net that the items were lying upon.

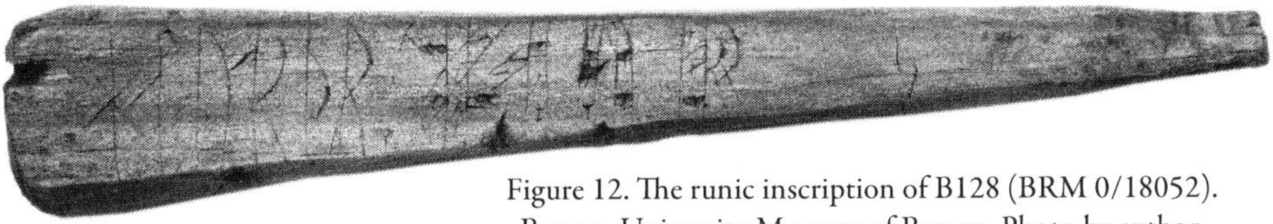

Figure 12. The runic inscription of B128 (BRM 0/18052).
Bergen, University Museum of Bergen. Photo by author.

appearance as the incisions forming the separation mark. Their number inside the main staves alternates between three and four, with additional ones occurring in the side branches. The exception is the final $\widehat{ar}$; the bowl and the leg of **r** are left empty. Another specific feature of this bind-rune is that the side branch indicating **a**-rune is incised diagonally inside the main stave, which also displays three dots (compare the appearance of the same bind-rune in the first unit, see Figure 12).

The double-lined runes make the two components of the inscription appear visually different. This type of runes, with or without the added pricks, occurs in other Bryggen inscriptions as well, perhaps as a way of adding decorative visual elements to the writing.[52] The decorative use of double-lined runes on parts of leather shoes is of interest, showing that writing, in a broad sense, could also mean making patterns and embroidering signs. Runes with contours also appear on other items, among which a flat rectangular piece of wood B465 (BRM 0/43110) carrying a love text is an especially fine example. In this inscription, triple-contoured runes of almost ornamental appearance are used. An interesting comparison to B128 is an around 38 cm long piece of wood B172 (BRM 0/20315) that carries three sequences of runes. The item has an irregular shape that bears rough visual resemblance to a wedge, as one end is wide, whereas the other end narrows in. The inscription starts with double-contoured runes, with dots inside, which is followed by a part with vaguely visible ordinary runes. Close to the right end of the stick, three additional ordinary runes appear upside down in relation to the rest of the inscription. B172 has not received a definitive interpretation, but it is of interest to note its partial visual and material resemblance to B128.[53]

---

[52] Regarding early runic inscriptions, it has been suggested that double-lined runes may connect with 'the technique of inlaying runes with silver thread or niello, such as can be gathered from the now empty impressions of once inlaid runes [...]. These contours may have been the source of inspiration for the creation of double-lined runes and thus go back to a technique used by (weapon)smiths'. See Looijenga, *Texts and Contexts*, p. 132.

[53] The two longer sequences of runes in B172 may conceal personal names.

In B128 the distinctive form of runes marks the object with some recogniz-able properties. The inscription is interpreted as containing two male names, *Hallvarðr* and *Hávarr*.[54] Regarding the sequence **hau͡ar**, Kjersti Markali men-tions a possible occurrence of a spelling mistake in the name, as **l**- and **u**-runes would appear rather alike, in particular as double-lined runes. The second sequence could be considered a mistaken repetition of **ha͡lua͡rþr**, though it does not contain any **þ**-rune either.[55] Markali hence asserts that the use of double-lined runes — being a more unusual way of writing — does not suggest spelling mistakes in the text; in her opinion the name must be *Hávarr* (otherwise not attested in the Bryggen material).

Additional arguments can support either case. The use of single- and dou-ble-lined runes could have been a technique to mark two names. The visual form would have strengthened the distinction between the names, which may otherwise resemble each other. Other features, however, suggest that the same name might be repeated. As noted above, the bind-rune **a͡r** has its left branch inside the double-contoured stave. It could be argued that the double-lined sec-tion of the inscription contains additional bind-runes, with two or more runes integrated through one shape. The shape of the double-lined **u**-rune may in its essence mark both **l** and **u**. Furthermore, the final bind-rune may combine three runes: **a**, **þ**, and **r**. As previously described, only the main stave there is marked with internal dots, whereas the branch indicating **a** as well as the bowl and the leg of **r** are without — possibly these elements were meant to be recognized as three distinctive entities. In this case, we could see the bowl of **r** also as contain-ing the **þ**-rune, resulting in **ha͡lua͡rþ**.

This latter reading of the inscription remains of uncertain character. Nevertheless, possible deviances and individualities in writing names and other lexical units in runic inscriptions should not automatically be approached from the perspective of spelling errors or faulty analysis on the part of rune-carvers.[56]

---

[54] Markali, 'Personnavnsmaterialet i runeinnskriftene fra Bryggen', pp. 34–35.

[55] Cf. also Knirk's comment in the Oslo runic database: *Hallvarðr Ha(ll)var-*(?).

[56] In a series of studies going back to the end of 1980s, Swedish runologists have reassessed these so-called spelling errors, by examining the actual variations in the Swedish runic inscrip-tions from the Viking Age, and explaining these as results of alternating individual sound analy-sis. See, e.g., Lagman, 'Till försvar för runristarnas ortografi'; Williams, *Åsrunan*. The complex relationships between speech and writing, and the notable synchronic and stylistic variation in some transitional runic inscriptions from *c.* AD 600, are discussed by Schulte, 'Stylistic Varia-tion in Runic Inscriptions?'. Schulte argues for the inclusion of textual-stylistic parameters of variation when studying runic inscriptions.

Judgements based upon some expected standard or common norm are not representative of how medieval (or earlier) rune-carving individuals could have practised, approached, and understood writing, especially during the process of learning to write. Though there exist some traceable conventions in runic writing, the many irregularities in the inscriptions may, among other aspects, result from casual variation and experiments with writing. The variations in rune-carvers' writing products may not necessarily reflect particular graphophonological or linguistic features, but could have also depended upon recurring visual patterns or individual designs.[57] This is relevant in connection with names, which as identifying labels could have been endowed with recognizable graphic forms as well as other visual features.

The final considerations here concern the practical or perhaps extended meanings attached to the runic item B128. It has one thicker end and one pointed end, and the runes run from the thicker end towards the narrow one. Thinking of its shape and possible applications, the wedge-like item could be fitted into a space and used as a tool of tightening or applying pressure. Possibly it could also separate two things stuck together, or mark a kind of division of space. A wedge as a tool for both tightening and separation in its own way accords with the distinct visual forms of the two names on the item — regardless of whether these are recordings of the same name or different ones. At the same time, it is possible that the item never served as an actual tool; perhaps its handy appearance with the pointed end was suitable for turning it into a kind of ownership marker.[58] The presence of two visually separated units on this particular item may be accidental. Nevertheless, the alternate techniques of incising runes would have had their own expressive and communicative potentials.

That one name could be repeated on the same item is attested to by other runic objects from Bergen, and it is of interest to explore cases in which the name is reproduced in a somehow variant manner. To name one example, B38 (BRM 0/10668, *c.* 1120–*c.* 1170), a rectangular and flat stick, with runes on two sides, repeats the name Grímr on one of its wide sides (see Figure 13). The

---

[57] In a broader perspective, it could be of interest to relate the seemingly random or deviating features of runic writing to some of the hypotheses tested within modern research into emergent literacy skills among young children. Among other factors, such approaches emphasize the visual understanding that young learners have of written language and its possible patterns, even before they can read or write.

[58] Note that *ownership marker* is here used as an inclusive designation. It can refer to different types of item that display ownership claims, in addition to the specifically shaped owner's tags and labels, as mentioned above.

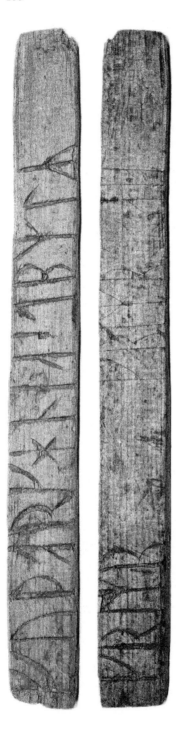

Figure 13. The two sides of B38 (BRM 0/10668).
Bergen, University Museum of Bergen. Photos by author.

spelling is the same (**grimr**), but the visual form differs, since the runes in the first unit (when following the order of elements on the item) are cut more deeply and clearly, using double incision.[59] Another significant case is B266 (BRM 0/29217, after 1248), a nearly 34 cm long piece of wood of somewhat irregular appearance. The side with runes has a complete *fuþork*, with the name Þórðr incised in front. The last runes in the name get crowded, which makes it look like an addition to the runic row. Following the *fuþork*, with some space left in between, is a sequence of five cryptic runes, which mediate the same name Þórðr. Here we do not only find a visually different rendering of the name, but its appearance in ordinary and cryptic runes seems to broadcast the skills of the writer and/or challenge an intended reader. There are other inscriptions in Bergen and elsewhere in Scandinavia that conceal personal names (or parts of names) in cryptic runes.[60] The key to understanding

[59] There is an additional unit of three runes (possibly another name) on the same side of the stick; spaces are left between all the three elements. On the opposite side, a complete *fuþork* is carved in double incision. Note that double incision is not the same as double-contoured runes; the lines making up the runes are cut in repeatedly and appear deepened, but they are not turned into contours with empty space in between.

[60] Jonas K. Nordby has identified a system of cryptic writing, which appears for example in B89 (BRM 0/15955). The inscription on one side shows that two male names were written both in ordinary

the type used in B266 lies in knowing the order and placement of signs in the runic row. The carving of the whole *fuþork* on the stick might hence have served as the logical first step. It then became a helpful tool for writing a person's name in ordinary and cryptic runes. Possibly this item was intended to function as a teaching tool.[61] This might even explain the less prepared appearance of the stick; it was used in a situation where the preparation of the surface for writing and the shaping of the item could have been considered less important.

A third item to mention is B245 (BRM 0/27173, possibly after 1332). This rectangular stick is around 13 cm long, and the inscription runs from one end to the other. Another side of the stick displays a small split (*c.* 1.5 cm) at one end, whereas the side opposite to the inscription shows some five short incisions along one edge as well as other possible markings.[62] The inscription consists of a repeated ownership statement: 'Einarr Síkr á mik' (Einarr Síkr owns me). The man's name is combined with a byname, which probably refers to a fish.[63] If the item is seen in conjunction with the text, one might associate the split in the stick with a rough imitation of an open mouth of a fish. At the same time, its practical purpose could have been to provide a way of attaching the stick to something the man owned; though small, the split would have provided enough space to fit a piece of rope around the stick. Such interpretations of the functionalities of the item presume that the inscription and the shaping of the stick were more or less contemporaneous and related to each other. It is, however, possible that they represent different stages during the production

---

runes and a type of code that is called *jötunvillur*. On the other side, abbreviated names of week days are given. Regarding this Bryggen inscription as well as others that use different systems of cryptic writing, see Nordby, 'Lønnruner. Kryptografi i runeinnskrifter fra vikingtid og middelalder'.

[61] Parallels can be drawn to B287 (BRM 0/29888, after 1248) — a roughly 20 cm long, flat rectangular tablet of wood that carries inscriptions on its two wide sides. Jointly, the two sides display various ways of writing runes, using different cryptic runes, same-stave runes, and abbreviations. The visuality of cryptic writing is brought to the fore, as on one side of the item the runes are shaped as fish and faces with beards.

[62] In the Oslo runic database these are explained as traces from possible runes. The last incision may be reminiscent of a runic shape, but the other small lines do not have to indicate runes. They can be compared to similar incisions on other Bryggen items (see below).

[63] See Markali, 'Personnavnsmaterialet i runeinnskriftene fra Bryggen', p. 89. The translation in the Oslo runic database is 'Einarr Whitefish owns me'. *Síkr* is included in the overview of Old Norse bynames; see Finnur Jónsson, 'Tilnavne i den islandske Oldlitteratur'. On male names identical with names of fish in the Swedish runic material, see Williams, 'Det inledande personnamnet'.

and use of the item (the order of which we cannot determine) — in this manner revealing the multiple layers of meaning that could connect with one artefact.

The runic text reads: **æinar · sikr · amek ainarsikre·mak**. The first part of the inscription has ordered the elements into three units with separation markers and small spaces in between the personal name, the byname, and the ownership formula **amek**. The name and the byname stand here as two separate elements. The rest of the inscription contains one marker within the ownership formula;[64] otherwise, the visual impression is that of a continuous row of runes.

An interesting feature is the possible marking of different vowels in the name and the ownership formula, compare: **æinar/ainar** and **amek/emak**. The personal name is carved using ⊦ (**æ**-rune) and then ⊦ (**a**-rune), at least judging from the identifiable forms. This could be understood as different ways of analysing the initial sound and expressing this in writing.[65] However, it could be argued that the divergence results from casual carving; in one case the side branch cuts through the main stave of the rune, in the other case not. The sequence **emak** for *á mik*, which has the order of vowels changed, could from a linguistic point of view be explained as a metathesis. Or rather, **amek/emak** may represent attempts at reproducing the statement in writing, resulting in what looks like metathesis.[66] According to Terje Spurkland, **emak** could reflect graphotactic spoonerism, that is, an exchange error in writing.[67] From a different perspective, a play or experiment with sounds or rather, with visual graphic forms that included dots and side branches, is another possibility to consider. First the statement was written one way, and then it was written (copied) with a few small modifications — as a kind of exercise or visual alteration. There are a few notable graphic differences when comparing rune forms in the first and the second part; this concerns, for instance, **r**-runes and **m**-runes. This and the somewhat differing visual set-up of the components of the inscrip-

[64] My reading differs from the previously registered one; in the Oslo runic database and the *Samnordisk runtextdatabas*, this final separation marker is in between the byname and the ownership formula.

[65] Cf. however Spurkland, *En fonografematisk analyse av runematerialet*, p. 94, who considers the two parts as written by different hands, the second one being a copy.

[66] Whether or not this should be considered metathesis also depends upon the definition of 'metathesis'. See, e.g., Meijer, 'Metathesis in Viking Age Runic Inscriptions'. Meijer defines metathesis as 'the inversion of the order of two — generally neighbouring — phonemes', adding that not all instances of deviating order necessarily qualify as such, but may also be the rune-carvers' attempts at 'reproducing as well as they could the sounds as they heard them' (p. 29).

[67] See Spurkland, *En fonografematisk analyse av runematerialet*, p. 94.

tion could indeed suggest that a different hand carved part 2. However, the Bryggen material in general demonstrates considerable variation in the use of rune forms and separation markers within one and the same inscription. Therefore, minor deviations are not necessarily decisive in themselves — especially when critically considering the (mostly) limited number of incised signs forming a given inscription, as these may not provide sufficient evidence for different arguments. In the case of B245, one person could still have written both sequences on the item, knowingly or unknowingly changing some features the second time.

The inscriptions B38, B266, and B245 have demonstrated, each in their own way, that the same name could be repeated on one item, and that the inscribed versions could vary — with different purposes in mind. The repeated ownership statement in B245 further highlighted that personal names could be accompanied by characterizing bynames. In other inscriptions, we find personal names alongside patronyms or occupational labels. In a well-executed inscription on a roughly 15.5 cm long flat stick, B403 (BRM 0/37208, dating to between 1248 and 1332), one *Sigurðr prestr* is mentioned. The text inscribed on one of the wide sides, is as follows: 'Guð, er alt má, blessi Sigurð prest, er mik á' (May God who is almighty bless Sigurðr the priest who owns me). The runic stick has been turned into a talking person, whose voice is used to humbly ask for God's blessing. The stick is nicely shaped, with the ends slightly rounded. The runes are clearly cut, and that also concerns the dotted runes ᚵᛂᛒ (transliterated as **g**, **e**, and **p**); even the **s**-runes ᛁ appear dotted. Throughout the inscription, separation markers are inserted and these have the shape of two dots, except for the single mark in between the final **mek** and **a**. At the end of the stick, three lines are incised next to and partly over the final **a**-rune, running diagonally from left down to right. This may have been a way of marking the completion of the (religious) statement. Additional features highlighting the skills of the rune-carver (possibly Sigurðr the priest himself) have to do with the almost poetic impression of the text. Though this may be accidental, the formulation even displays end rhyme. The item uses a slightly altered ownership formula, 'er mik á'. In this context, the text thus serves as a reminder that the motivation for writing a statement like this could have differed from one situation to another.

B403 and some of the examples discussed earlier illuminate the use of names in combination with different textual elements. The overall Bryggen material has personal names recorded in a variety of settings; in addition to ownership formulas they appear in letters, requests, prayers, carver's formulas, and various informal and personal messages (even including gossip). The previously discussed B38 and B266 directed attention towards the presence of names together with *fuþork*s. The combination of *fuþork* with personal names is a recurring feature. In the studied material approximately twenty-three such instances can be identified. Personal names are combined with shorter and longer versions of *fuþork*; they may be placed on the same side with the *fuþork*, or the item may display some division of content between its different sides.[68] Such inscriptions could be explained as writing exercises or a demonstration of the fact that after one had gained some runic knowledge in the form of the runic row, the next step would be to write one's name, or vice versa. However, the situational contexts behind different runic items certainly varied, and the features of each item need to be examined in detail.

A flat rectangular stick that measures around 16 cm, B66 (BRM 0/12777, dating from the second half of the thirteenth or the beginning of the fourteenth century), has a complete *fuþork* followed by four units, each distinguished by separation markers: ⠸ **asa** ⠸ **ion** ⠸ **sigriþ** ⠸ **þok**. There are four dots in front of **asa** and the final **þok**, and three in front of **ion** and **sigriþ**. The interpretation is: 'Ása, Jón, Sigríðr, þǫkk (?)', that is, the names of a woman, a man, another woman, and possibly the word 'thanks'.[69] The three names can be considered certain. The rune forms have the same regular appearance throughout the inscription. Concerning carving technique, the side branches to the left of the staves are incised with some more pressure — this has resulted in the branches looking more distinct in relation to the thinly incised main staves. Such features may speak in favour of one person having carved the whole inscription.

The final **þok** is puzzling. With several names listed after the *fuþork*, it would be logical to expect a name here as well. The use of four dots in front of **þok** does not necessarily single it out as an element separate from other names. The alteration between three and four dots — if even having any significance — could be a number connected to each name. Considering that first *Ása* and *Jón* are mentioned, one might expect a man's name after *Sigríðr*, but no apparent solutions can be offered. A different option would be to consider this as an absolute byname, that is, a byname occurring alone, or as a byname connected to *Sigríðr*. From mythological sources, Þǫkk is known as a giantess (Loki in disguise) who in the myth of Baldr's death refuses to weep, stating that she

---

[68] See also the discussion of *fuþork*-inscriptions with accompanying personal names, in Seim, *De vestnordiske futhark-innskriftene*, pp. 217–21. According to her, some names may be independent additions, documenting the reuse of one runic item, but there are also inscriptions where the integration of *fuþork*s and names is evident (see pp. 220–21).

[69] This interpretation is marked as uncertain in the Oslo runic database and subsequently also in the *Samnordisk runtextdatabas*.

would only cry dry tears.[70] Alternatively, if this is an absolute byname indicating a man, connections could be drawn to the poetic name Þekkr (also recorded as Þokkr), known as a dwarf name or the name of *Óðinn*. These mythological alternatives, however, do not provide any sufficient grounds for identifying a particular type of byname in B66.

Arguing from a different perspective, we could still place emphasis upon the three personal names being distinguished from the other segments of the inscription by having four dots marked in front of the first name and then again after the third one.[71] In this manner, **þok** would also visually stand as a concluding statement. It could signal an agreement (interpreted either as *þokk* 'thanks' or possibly connected to the verb *þokka*, 'to think (well) of, to like' or the noun *þokki* 'liking, satisfaction'), perhaps to the liking of the person writing. It could also be seen as an expression of gratitude towards or approval of those mentioned (i.e., the sender's 'thanks' to them), or alternatively, an indication that the three people themselves owed their 'thanks' to someone. Or perhaps the writer noted down the names of the people, adding a reminder to himself, using the singular imperative form of the verb, i.e. *þokk*: 'Think well (of them)!'. How the initial *fuþork* in B66 should be regarded is hard to establish. The fact that the whole inscription appears on one side of the stick, and seems to be executed by the same carver, does not necessarily show that its components are connected in meaning. Other Bryggen items display small collections of inscriptions that may originate from separate occasions or reflect alternative purposes. It is, however, possible to regard the initial *fuþork* in B66 and other similar inscriptions as a kind of introduction to what follows. The runic row may have also functioned as a visual tool to have in front of one's eyes when incising the subsequent record.

A different set-up of personal names, including the name of one woman, is found in B215 (BRM 0/24348, from around mid-thirteenth century, either before or after 1248). This 14.5 cm long stick narrows slightly down towards both ends, which gives it a rounded appearance. Runes appear on its two opposite broad faces. One of these (here called A) is almost completely filled with runes: **heþen : ræit : runa : þorbiorh : þorer :**. The other side (B) has seven runes by its left end: **þoralte**. On side A, different units have separation

---

[70] Cf. Seim, 'Var futharken en magisk formel', p. 286.

[71] It should nevertheless be kept in mind that runic inscriptions display varied and random ways of using separation markers. Such markings do not automatically qualify as word dividers either, but they may have had alternative purposes — from strategies of decoration and visualization to marking a spot where to pause in writing/reading.

markers in between; with one exception, these are all two dots. The overall impression is one of a well-executed inscription; the runes, including the dotted ones, are clearly cut. The text is introduced by a carver's formula, followed by two names, whereas a third name is found on the opposite side: 'Heðinn reit rúna(r). Þorbjǫrg, Þórir, Þóraldi' (Heðinn wrote the runes. Þorbjǫrg, Þórir, Þóraldi). If seeing the recorded names as connected sequences, one could argue that the last name did not fit on the same side with the rest and had to be carved separately. As previously mentioned, explicit references to carving runes in the Bergen material are not many, though some interesting texts occur. Of interest here is the verb *ríta* (write); the customary variant would be the strong verb *rísta* (pret. *reist*), or the weak verb *rista* (pret. *risti*), both meaning 'carve' or 'incise'.[72] According to Spurkland, the use of the strong verb *ríta* in runic inscriptions could signal a meaning parallel to 'carve'.[73]

The normalized rendering of the phrase *reit rúnar* (*rúnar* marks accusative plural of the word *rún*) is in B215 recorded as **ræit : runa**, thus lacking the final **r**-rune in **runa**. Varied recordings of this common component of the carver's formula are well attested in the overall Scandinavian runic material. As previously discussed, deviations (or rather variations) are a natural feature of many inscriptions and can be caused by several factors. In the medieval Norwegian material, the final **r**-rune is present in most cases where the word *rúnar* appears recorded, sometimes as a bind-rune **a͡r**. There is one inscription on a piece of bone from Oslo, A36, which includes the phrase: 'Ann sá þér, es risti rúnar þessar, Þordís' (He who carved these runes loves you, Þordís!). *Risti rúnar þessar* appears as: **risti × runaþesar**; in this case **runa** is followed by **þesar**.

The set-up of carver's formulas can vary, and the mention of 'runes' as the object for the act of writing is not compulsory: the name and the verb are sufficient in themselves. Although the most apparent interpretation of **heþen : ræit : runa** is that it is a statement about Heðinn writing runes, it is of some interest that **runa** is followed by three personal names. What could be the meaning of the stick carrying this text? If considering the item a personal note, it may be a list of people that had some importance to the one writing runes — perhaps members of his family or some other fellowship collective. The names all con-

---

[72] Among medieval Norwegian inscriptions, a carved bone from Oslo, A198, says 'Þórðr reit í rúnar'. A runic stick from Trondheim, A162 (identified as N825 in the forthcoming volume VII of *NIyR*), dated to the thirteenth century, provides another example of the verb. Cf. also two church inscriptions from the Atrå stave church in Telemark, N150 and N151.

[73] See Spurkland, 'Måtte Herren hjelpe den mann', p. 6. The weak form of the verb is attested in the Old Norse vernacular writing in manuscripts.

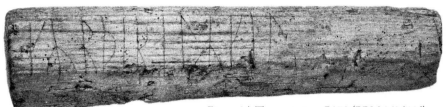

Figure 14. The runic item B379 (BRM 0/34556).
Bergen, University Museum of Bergen. Photo by author.

tain the element Þor-, as possible evidence of a naming practice within one kin. From this perspective, **runa** could relate to the list of persons, identifying them as members of a fellowship; compare the Old Norse noun *rúni* (m., 'a friend, counsellor', with accusative and genitive forms *rúna*) or *rúna* (f., 'a female friend', possibly pointing to Þorbjǫrg).[74] The text could suggest that Heðinn was recording the names of a group of people close to him, opening up the possibility of understanding the message in different ways.

A different interpretation could also be proposed. As noted, the three names Þorbjǫrg, Þórir, and Þóraldi all start with **þ**. The item may present a writing exercise, and the names might not even have to refer to real persons. This may be a way of writing runes, when interpreting the first part in the straightforward manner as 'Heðinn wrote the runes (or possibly: a row of runes)'. On a different runic stick, B604 (BRM 0/95056), one has used the names of runes to mediate a person's name, that is 'ár sól maðr úr nauð týr reið' = Ásmundr.[75] In B215, the list of personal names could be seen as highlighting that the rune Þ (or the sequence ÞᛆR) was repeated three times as an element producing different names. The hypotheses outlined above serve as a reminder that each runic item had its individual features, operational in specific writing situations, which need not follow an expected common pattern.

Compared to some of the inscriptions and items discussed above, the final example among this selection seems straightforward. This is B379 (BRM 0/34556, earlier than 1198, see Figure 14), with the text 'Gyrðir á lykil' (Gyrðir owns the key), quoted in the title.

The runes appear in one clearly cut row **kyrþiralykil** on one side of a wooden item that measures *c.* 12 cm. No word dividers are inserted, and there are no spaces left between the elements of the inscription. The runes start by one end

---

[74] Parallels could also be drawn to the female name *Rūna* (nom.) in Runic Swedish (recorded in inscriptions on a few Viking Age rune-stones); see, e.g., Williams, *Åsrunan*, pp. 69–70.

[75] See the Oslo runic database.

and run from left to right, covering a bit more than half of the item. The rune forms are ordinary, but the potential visual distinctiveness of twelve neatly incised signs should not be ignored. For an accustomed rune-reader, the row would divide itself into meaningful units; for someone else, it would appear as a visual sequence, with some notable inner symmetry in the form of repeated ᚼ **y**-, ᚱ **r**- and ᛁ **l**-runes: ᚴᚢᚱᚦᛁᚱᛁᛏᛆᚴᛁᛏ.

The male name *Gyrðir* appears here on an item of everyday importance, marking somebody as an owner of a key. The item has been previously registered as half a key shaft, which would suggest a fitting correspondence between the text and the artefact.[76] According to Gitte Hansen,[77] it does not seem to be a shaft of any kind, nor does it appear to be part of a key. Thus, the item's appearance in itself does not provide us insight into its potential original use. Occasionally, we find additional clues through other properties of runic items, also looking at what appears on the sides that do not carry runes. In the case of some owner's tags or labels, for instance, a visual division of the runic text and other markings (such as crosses, personal monograms or the like) may occur between two different sides of the object, suggesting that both sides could communicate in their own ways. The back of B379 has a deep dark line running across the item, which looks like a burnt-in groove. However, this may not have had anything to do with the purpose and use of the object in its original setting.

What we do observe on this piece of wood is that where the runic message ends, there appear some additional visual markings: namely, four small incisions or cuts close to the bottom edge of the side that carries runes. Incised lines, cuts, and even more pronounced notches occur frequently along the edges and/or on different sides of the runic items from Bryggen, as commented above. Their presence can be explained practically. In the case of systematically executed rows of notches (which may also appear as divided into small groups) on items like owner's tags, business and transaction notes, the finds have usually been explained as tally-sticks for tracking and counting goods. It is possible that comparable practices of keeping record or tallying something explain the occurrence of cuts and incisions on other runic items, regardless of their textual content and physical form. At the same time, these features may have had a visual and individualizing effect, marking the object in ways that did not depend upon skills of writing.

---

[76] See, e.g., the Oslo runic database.

[77] Personal communication, 11 May 2016.

In this light, the thick inscribed piece of wood stating 'Gyrðir owns the key' could have functioned as an ownership marker or a personal reminder, utilizing various modes of communication. The explicit purpose is to document who owned a particular key. Perhaps we witness here a weighty form of a medieval post-it note, meant to record a piece of information one might otherwise have been forgotten or confused. The item could have been connected to a particular key; broadly put, it could also have mediated that through the key Gyrðir (or whoever was using the key) had access and control over something that others did not, such as some space, building or items. This small artefact with its twelve runes expresses a clear message that was most likely not only intended for the one who wrote it, but others as well. The runic item would have been easy to produce and carry around, perhaps together with the key. As such, it forms one of the many fascinating examples of the materialized — but also moveable — moments of medieval communication from the town of Bergen.

Conclusions

This chapter has dealt with medieval runic inscriptions from Bergen, as evidence of individual products of writing. At the centre of attention have been a selection of runic items that document the act of writing one's name in runes; the varied formal, textual, visual, and material features of these runic media have been brought to the fore, and the alternating communicative practices and purposes they may reflect have been discussed.

Although the overall runic corpus from Bryggen shares common features and originates from the same urban environment, the present discussion has hopefully shown the need to go beyond general ways of organizing this material. As an alternative, it is important to look at single artefacts as individual items of communication. It has thus been discussed how labels like *wooden (fashioned) sticks* and *pieces of wood* can connect with objects of various shapes and sizes, also displaying visual and physical features that add distinct qualities to each item. Similarly, the seemingly uniform or recurring textual elements on these items may — especially when viewed in combination with other properties — mediate alternating messages.

The analysis has highlighted the features of inscriptions containing personal names, through their different modes of communication, and from the perspective of both senders and intended or potential recipients. Although the great bulk of the material can be characterized as expressing a kind of informal writing behaviour — including casual scribbling, and practical and personal notes — this does not mean that such runic artefacts were somehow non-communicative. The inscriptions discussed here have shed light upon the diversity of the Bryggen items. This moderates the initial impression of spontaneous, spur-of-the-moment scribbling and rather guides our attention towards the various ways in which a runic item could say or show something meaningful, which was perhaps not only meant for the eyes of one rune-carving individual. Even the items carrying but one person's name, perhaps jotted down as a casual exercise, could and would communicate something: being an expression of the need to write something.

Specific properties on the level of rune forms and chosen techniques of writing and visualization, in addition to the preparation and shaping of items, further show that some intention and planning went into the making of many a runic item. Naturally, these qualities should not be over-emphasized, but it is important to acknowledge the potential variability in the meanings attached to different runic objects, especially when hypothesizing about their original meaning and contexts of usage.

The presented inscriptions form only a small fraction of the overall Bryggen material, but they serve as examples of the functionality and communicative potential of runic writing in the setting of a medieval town. The very presence of runes — as an identifiable script and a visual tool — illuminates how writing could become an integrated part of different objects. To conclude with one such piece of materialized communication, we once again turn to the item, carrying the text 'Gyrðir owns the key'. This shaped piece of wood with its runes, visual, and physical features emerges as an artefact that reminds us of various aspects of medieval communication. Its possible practical uses were discussed above. Its symbolic meaning in the eyes of modern experiencers of runes is extended, as it also presents itself as one of the many keys we can use to try to gain some insight into the lives, habits and skills of medieval individuals. Gyrðir and other named or unnamed men and women of Bryggen are the ones who *own* the keys, but the self-mediating presence of these talking medieval runic items grants modern scholars and other interested readers and viewers with some access into their world as well.

Works Cited

Archival Sources

A + number = preliminary registration number in the Runic Archives of the University of Oslo, of the runic inscriptions found from Norway (except Bergen)

B + number = preliminary registration number in the Runic Archives of the University of Oslo, of the runic inscriptions found in the Bryggen area in Bergen

B + number + letter; BRM + number = accession number of the artefacts registered in the Archives of the University Museum of Bergen

Primary Sources

Danske Runeindskrifter, Database of the National Museum of Denmark and the Department of Scandinavian Research, University of Copenhagen <http://runer.ku.dk/> [accessed 4 August 2017]

Danmarks Runeindskrifter, ed. by Lis Jacobsen and Erik Moltke (Copenhagen: Ejnar Munksgaard, 1941–42)

'Hordaland fylke', ed. by Magnus Olsen, in *Norges Innskrifter med de yngre Runer*, IV: *Hordaland fylke. Sogn og Fjordane fylke. Møre og Romsdal fylke*, ed. by Magnus Olsen and Aslak Liestøl (Oslo: Norsk Historisk Kjeldeskrift-Institutt, 1957), pp. 1–78

NIyR = Norges Innskrifter med de yngre Runer, ed. by Magnus Olsen and others, 6 vols to date (Oslo: Norsk historisk Kjeldeskriftinstitutt, 1941–)

Norges Innskrifter med de yngre Runer VI.1: *Bryggen i Bergen*, ed. by Aslak Liestøl (Oslo: Norsk Historisk Kjeldeskrift-Institutt, 1980)

Norges Innskrifter med de yngre Runer, VI. 2: *Bryggen i Bergen*, ed. by Ingrid Sanness Johnsen and James E. Knirk (Oslo: Norsk Historisk Kjeldeskrift-Institutt, 1990)

Samnordisk runtextdatabas, Institutionen för nordiska språk, Uppsala Universitet (*Scandinavian Runic Text Database*, Department of Scandinavian Languages, Uppsala University) <http://www.nordiska.uu.se/forskn/samnord.htm> [accessed 4 August 2017]

Sveriges Runinskrifter, 15 vols to date (Stockholm: Kungl. Vitterhets Historie och Antikvitets Akademien, 1900–) <https://www.raa.se/kulturarvet/arkeologi-fornlamningar-och-fynd/runstenar/digitala-sveriges-runinskrifter/digitala-sveriges-runinskrifter-publicerat/> [accessed 4 August 2017]

Secondary Studies

Dyvik, Helge, '*Addenda Runica Latina*: Recently Found Runic Inscriptions in Latin from Bryggen', in *The Bryggen Papers: Supplementary Series II*, ed. by Knut Helle, Asbjørn Herteig, and Svein Indrelid (Bergen: Norwegian University Press, 1988), pp. 1–9

Enderwitz, Susanne, and Rebecca Sauer, eds, *Communication and Materiality: Written and Unwritten Communication in Pre-Modern Societies*, Materiale Textkulturen, 8 (Berlin: de Gruyter, 2015)

Fellows-Jensen, Gillian, *Scandinavian Personal Names in Lincolnshire and Yorkshire*, Navne-studier udg. af Institut for Navneforskning, 7 (Copenhagen: Akademisk forlag, 1968)

Finnur Jónsson, 'Tilnavne i den islandske Oldlitteratur', *Aarbøger for nordisk Oldkyndighed og Historie*, 22 (1907), 161–381

Haavaldsen, Anne, and Espen Smith Ore, 'Computerising the Runic Inscriptions at the Historical Museum in Bergen', in *Runeninschriften als Quellen interdiszipli-närer Forschung: Abhandlungen des Vierten Internationalen Symposiums über Runen und Runeninschriften in Göttingen vom 4.–9. August 1995*, ed. by Klaus Düwel, Er-gänzungsbände zum Reallexikon der germanischen Altertumskunde, 15 (Berlin: de Gruyter, 1998), pp. 117–26

——, *Runes in Bergen: Preliminary Report from the Project 'Computerising the Runic Inscriptions at the Historical Museum in Bergen'* (last updated January 7, 2003) <http://www.nb.no/baser/runer/ribwww/english/rune13.html> [accessed 4 August 2017]

Hagland, Jan Ragnar, 'Literacy and Trade in Late Medieval Norway', *Journal of Northern Studies*, 1 (2011), 29–37

Hansen, Gitte, *Bergen c 800–c 1170: The Emergence of a Town*, Bryggen Papers: Main Series, 6 (Bergen: Fagbokforlaget, 2005)

——, 'The Bryggen Chronology: New Light upon the Dating of the Periods before Fire V', in *Medieval Fires in Bergen — Revisited*, ed. by Ingvild Øye, Bryggen Papers: Sup-plementary Series, 6 (Bergen: Fagbokforlaget, 1998), pp. 81–127

Herteig, Asbjørn E, *The Buildings at Bryggen: Their Topographical and Chronological Dev-elopment*, Bryggen Papers: Main Series, 3. 1–2 (Bergen: Norwegian University Press, 1990–91)

Knirk, James E, 'Learning to Write with Runes in Medieval Norway', in *Medeltida skrift-och språkkultur: Nio föreläsningar från ett symposium i Stockholm våren 1992*, ed. by Inger Lindell, Runica et Mediævalia: Opuscula, 2 (Stockholm: Sällskapet Runica et Mediævalia, 1994), pp. 169–212

——, 'Runes and Runic Inscriptions, Paragraph 3: Norway', in *Medieval Scandinavia: An Encyclopedia*, ed. by Phillip Pulsiano and others (London: Garland, 1993), pp. 553–54

——, 'Runic Inscriptions Containing Latin in Norway', in *Runeninschriften als Quellen interdisziplinärer Forschung: Abhandlungen des Vierten Internationalen Symposiums über Runen und Runeninschriften in Göttingen vom 4.–9. August 1995*, ed. by Klaus Düwel, Ergänzungsbände zum Reallexikon der germanischen Altertumskunde, 15 (Berlin: de Gruyter, 1998), pp. 476–507

——, 'Tillegg om funntilhøve, brannlagsrelasjon og datering', in *Norges Innskrifter med de yngre Runer*, VI.2: *Bryggen i Bergen*, ed. by Ingrid Sanness Johnsen and James E. Knirk (Oslo: Norsk Historisk Kjeldeskrift-Institutt, 1990), pp. 245–248

Lagman, Svante, 'Till försvar för runristarnas ortografi', in *Projektet: De vikingtida runin-skrifternas kronologi. En presentation och några forskningsresultat*, ed. by Lennart Elmevik and Lena Peterson, Runrön 1 (Uppsala: Uppsala Universitet, 1989), pp. 27–37

Liestøl, Aslak, 'Correspondence in Runes', *Mediaeval Scandinavia*, 1 (1968), 17–27

——, 'Runeninschriften von der Bryggen in Bergen (Norwegen)', *Zeitschrift für Archäo-logie des Mittelalters*, 1 (1973), 129–39

——, *Runer frå Bryggen* (Bergen: Det midlertidige bryggemuseum, 1964)

——, 'The Runes of Bergen: Voices from the Middle Ages', *Minnesota History*, 40.2 (1966), 49–58

——, 'Runic Voices from Towns of Ancient Norway', *Scandinavica. An International Journal of Scandinavian Studies*, 13.1 (1974), 19–33

Looijenga, Tineke, *Texts and Contexts of the Oldest Runic Inscriptions*, The Northern World, 4 (Leiden: Brill, 2003)

Magin, Elisabeth, 'Die rúnakefli von Bryggen in Bergen: Möglichkeiten und Grenzen des Materials' (unpublished master's thesis, Georg-August-Universität Göttingen, 2014)

Markali, Kjersti, 'Personnavnsmaterialet i runeinnskriftene fra Bryggen i Bergen' (unpublished master's thesis, Universitetet i Oslo, 1983)

Meijer, Jan, 'Metathesis in Viking Age Runic Inscriptions', *Amsterdamer Beiträge zur älteren Germanistik*, 41 (1995), 29–36

Mostert, Marco, and Anna Adamska, eds, *Medieval Urban Literacy*, II: *Uses of the Written Word in Medieval Towns*, Utrecht Studies in Medieval Literacy, 28 (Turnhout: Brepols, 2014)

Nordby, Jonas K, '*Ráð þat*, if You Can!', *Futhark: International Journal of Runic Studies* 3 (2012/13), 81–88

Nordby, Jonas K, 'Lønnruner. Kryptografi i runeinnskrifter fra vikingtid og middelalder' (unpublished doctoral thesis, Universitetet i Oslo, 2018)

Palm, Rune, 'Runkunskap under medeltid — en analysemodell och några resultat', in *Till Barbro: Texter och tolkningar tillägnade Barbro Söderberg den 23 september 1997*, ed. by Roger Andersson and Patrik Åström, Meddelanden från Institutionen för nordiska språk vid Stockholms universitet, 45 (Stockholm: Institutionen för nordiska språk, Stockholms universitet, 1997), pp. 87–105

——, 'Runor och latinskrift: runorna under medeltid', in *Den medeltida skriftkulturen i Sverige: Genrer och texter*, ed. by Inger Larsson and others, Runica et Mediævalia: Scripta Maiora, 5 (Stockholm: Sällskapet Runica et Mediævalia, 2010), pp. 21–51

Peterson, Lena, *Nordiskt runnamnslexikon* (Uppsala: Institutet för språk och folkminnen, Uppsala Universitet, 2007)

Sanness Johnsen, Ingrid, 'Personal Names in Inscriptions from Towns of Medieval Norway', in *Proceedings of the First International Symposium on Runes and Runic Inscriptions*, ed. by Claiborne W. Thompson, Michigan Germanic Studies, 7 (Michigan: University of Michigan, 1981), pp. 119–28

——, 'Die Runeninschriften über Handel und Verkehr aus Bergen (Norwegen)', in *Untersuchungen zu Handel und Verkehr der vor- und frühgeschichtlichen Zeit in Mittel- und Nordeuropa*, IV: *Der Handel der Karolinger- und Wikingerzeit: Bericht über die Kolloquien der Kommission für die Altertumskunde Mittel- und Nordeuropas in den Jahren 1980 bis 1983*, ed. by Klaus Düwel and others, Abhandl Akad Wiss Göttingen, Phil-Hist Kl Dritte, 156 (Göttingen: Vandenhoeck & Ruprecht, 1987), pp. 716–44

Schulte, Michael, 'Pragmatic Runic Literacy in Scandinavia c. 800–1300: With a Particular Focus on the Bryggen Material', in *Epigraphic Literacy and Christian Identity: Modes of Written Discourse in the Newly Christian European North*, ed. by Kristel

Zilmer and Judith Jesch, Utrecht Studies in Medieval Literacy, 4 (Turnhout: Brepols, 2012), pp. 155–82

——, 'Stylistic Variation in Runic Inscriptions? A Test Case and Preliminary Assessment', *Arkiv för nordisk filologi*, 123 (2008), 5–22

Seim, Karin Fjellhammer, 'Var futharken en magisk formel i middelalderen? Testing av en hypotese mot innskrifter fra Bryggen i Bergen', in *Proceedings of the Third International Symposium on Runes and Runic Inscriptions: Grindaheim, Norway, 8–12 August 1990*, ed. by James E. Knirk, Runrön, 9 (Uppsala: Uppsala Universitet, 1994), pp. 279–300

——, *De vestnordiske futhark-innskriftene fra vikingtid og middelalder: Form og funksjon* (Trondheim: Institutt for nordistikk og litteraturvitenskap, Norges teknisk-natur-vitenskapelige universitet, 1998)

Spurkland, Terje, *En fonografematisk analyse av runematerialet fra Bryggen i Bergen* (Oslo: Universitetet i Oslo, 1991)

——, 'How Christian Were the Norwegians in the High Middle Ages? The Runic Evidence', in *Epigraphic Literacy and Christian Identity: Modes of Written Discourse in the Newly Christian European North*, ed. by Kristel Zilmer and Judith Jesch, Utrecht Studies in Medieval Literacy, 4 (Turnhout: Brepols, 2012), pp. 183–200

——, 'Literacy and "Runacy" in Medieval Scandinavia', in *Scandinavia and Europe, 800–1350: Contact, Conflict and Coexistence*, ed. by Jonathan Adams and Kathrine Holman, Medieval Texts and Cultures in Northern Europe, 4 (Turnhout: Brepols, 2004), pp. 333–44

——, '"Måtte Herren hjelpe den mann som ristet disse runer og likeså han som leser dem!" Et mentalitetshistorisk blikk på "skrive" og "lese" i norsk middelalder', *Norsk lingvistisk tidsskrift*, 2 (1994), 3–16

——, 'Viking Age Literacy in Runes — A Contradiction in Terms?', in *Literacy in Medieval and Early Modern Scandinavian Culture*, ed. by Pernille Hermann, The Viking Collection: Studies in Northern Civilization, 16 (Viborg: University Press of Southern Denmark, 2005), pp. 136–50

Williams, Henrik, *Åsrunan: Användning och ljudvärde i runsvenska steninskrifter*, Runrön, 3 (Uppsala: Uppsala Universitet, 1990)

——, 'Det inledande personnamnet på en av runstenarna i Danderyds kyrka, U 129', *Amsterdamer Beiträge zur älteren Germanistik*, 67 (2011), 79–90

Zilmer, Kristel, 'Runic Sticks and Other Inscribed Objects from Medieval Bergen: Some Problems of Study' (unpublished manuscript, Bergen, 2017)

——, 'Words in Wood and Stone: Uses of Runic Writing in Medieval Norwegian Churches', *Viking and Medieval Scandinavia*, 12 (2016), 199–227

Moving Lists:
Enumeration between Use and Aesthetics, Storing and Creating

Lucie Doležalová*

A list is, on the one hand, perhaps the most archaic form of writing, and is thus closely linked to the 'arrival of writing' proper. On the other hand, it is restricted neither to the realm of practical use nor to that of literature but is present wherever writing appears. It is a form that easily escapes attention for it is often conceived of as linear and unimaginative. Yet, the very opposite — as I shall attempt to show — is true. The list is a very simple form; it is in fact perhaps too simple, and thus none of the definitions succeed in covering all the ways in which it is practised. An enumeration of possible types of list is never exhaustive either. Three important monographs dedicated to lists — Robert E. Belknap's *The List: The Uses and Pleasures of Cataloguing*,[1] Francis Spufford's *The Chatto Book of Cabbages and Kings: Lists in Literature*, and

* Research leading to this study was supported by a two-month research fellowship at the Centre for Medieval Studies at the University of Bergen, as well as through European Regional Development Fund – Project KREAS (no. CZ.02.1.01/0.0/0.0/16_019/0000734) and Charles University Research Development Program Progress Q7 'Centre for the Study of the Middle Ages' undertaken at the Faculty of Arts. I am grateful to Amy Mulligan for her very kind help and corrections.

[1] After a detailed general discussion, the author concentrates on analysing lists in Ralph Waldo Emerson, Walt Whitman, Herman Melville, and Henry Thoreau.

Lucie Doležalová (Lucie.Dolezalova@ff.cuni.cz) is Associate Professor of Medieval Latin at Charles University in Prague. She has published monographs and edited collected volumes on the art of memory, mnemonics, reception, and transmission of obscure texts, including retellings of the Bible.

Moving Words in the Nordic Middle Ages: Tracing Literacies, Texts, and Verbal Communities, ed. by Amy C. Mulligan and Else Mundal, AS 8   BREPOLS PUBLISHERS   (Turnhout: Brepols, 2019)
pp. 201–225
10.1484/M.AS-EB.5.116625

Umberto Eco's *La Vertigine della Lista*[2] — each include a theoretical discussion, but they all nonetheless demonstrate the variety of possibilities the form offers rather than proposing a lucid definition.[3] It seems that the list defies an easy grasp. This study does not offer a new definition either; instead, it defines the basic features of the form before moving to a presentation of specific ancient and medieval lists and the way they are received in scholarship, and concludes with a brief comparative discussion.

Defining the List's Features

Salient features of the list — namely, the unifying idea; itemization; number of items, selection, and order of items; overall structure, formal and visual organization, and contextualization; and function and reception — are important to identify before moving into further discussion regarding lists in the medieval North. The list is unified by a concept or a theme behind the whole; it is a list *of something* — things to buy in a shop, best films of the year, the contents of one's pocket, and so forth. Arguably, the uniting idea might only emerge with the list itself — a list that is compiled ad hoc on the basis of mundane association may reveal a deeper meaning upon its completion.[4]

   The list is composed of distinct and easily distinguishable items. They might share the same structure, or each item may have a structure of its own. There are a variety of ways of forming items. There may be simple, one-word items, long complex items, or a mix of different types in a list. There is a certain number of items on a list.[5] Sometimes the number of items is required by the list-type (e.g., top-ten rankings), and other times it is decided upon by the author, with certain quantities more popular among list-makers than others (3, 7, 10, 100). There are also very long lists, some compiled, in fact, not to be read but to be searched, others made up in order to torture the readers or to experiment with the limits of their patience (e.g., those by François Rabelais or Laurence

---

[2] In English as *The Infinity of Lists: An Illustrated Essay*. In addition, there are several articles on the topic, for example a creative discussion by Gass, 'And'.

[3] A simple definition is proposed by Ivan M. Havel, but in my opinion it is not easily applicable in a literary environment. See Havel, 'Time in Lists'.

[4] I treated this topic in '*Ad hoc* Lists of Bernard Itier'.

[5] As far as the minimum number of items necessary for a list to be identified as such, definitions vary. Most frequently, scholars require three items, but, for example, for Havel it is zero while for Elizabeth Minchin it is five (Minchin, 'The Performance of Lists').

Sterne). A list's items are selected in a meaningful way from a certain group. The set of potential items might be small and well defined (e.g., in a list of shortlisted candidates for a job), rather broad (e.g., in a shopping list, the set comprises all possible goods), or absolutely extensive (e.g., the full vocabulary of a language), and this relationship between the potential and actually selected items can impact on a list's meaning. For a hopeful applicant, the meaning of a list might lie in answering the question: is a specific item (e.g., my name) on the list? Some lists strive (or pretend) to be exhaustive: that is, not to be based on the act of selection but to include all the items from the potential set relevant to the list's subject. If the subject (uniting idea) of the list is introduced at its beginning, certain expectations are raised, a specific set of possibilities comes to the reader's mind, and reading the list might include comparing the potential with the actual set. In this way, the author of a list may creatively play with the expectations by violating them (as, e.g., Jorge Luis Borges does ingeniously in his Chinese encyclopaedia).[6] The order of items is sometimes imposed by an external principle (alphabet, chronology, geography), other times it is a result of the decision of the list's author. The order of the items might be crucial to the list's meaning (e.g., exam results). It might be prepared with a recoverable underlying principle (chronological, geographical, etc.), or its logic might result from unconscious associations.

The overall structure, as well as the formal and visual organization of a list, tells us a great deal. Some lists are highly unified in their form and include items of identical type (nouns, or adjectives plus nouns, etc.), while others display greater variety through combining variously structured items. Some lists are in prose, others are in verse. The requirements of verse further influence the structure of a list — the items might be interconnected in a variety of ways. A number of possible visual markers may immediately indicate the existence of a list and make it easier to use, perhaps even pointing to the ad hoc character of the list (quick scribbles on a scrap of paper); however, a lack of visual markers can obscure a list's presence (for instance, by integrating it inconspicuously within another text).

Contextualization, thus, is important. A list may be free-standing or included in another textual structure. Its topic may be explicitly introduced, briefly or at length, and it may have a clear conclusion. It may appear among other lists. It may be carefully wrapped up in an explanatory narrative which makes its meaning clear, or it may be left by itself. Finally, function and recep-

---

[6] Borges, 'The Analytical Language of John Wilkins', p. 231.

tion, or the way a list operates within a particular environment, might form part of its meaning, too. Dealing with medieval lists, we are always in the position of outsiders trying to access the original function and reception on the basis of fragmentary clues.

Is it Literature? Practical vs Poetic Lists, Use vs Aesthetics

The list can be described simply as a sequence of words which do not have any syntagmatic relationship among themselves except for the linear flow imparted by their order. Every text is in the first place a list. But 'normal' texts feature, in addition, a complex set of relationships among these units. As texts lacking these, lists can be easily seen as a more primitive form than 'real' texts. Such considerations, together with the fact that lists seem to be the earliest type of writing, and appear widely across all ancient cultures, led Wolfram von Soden to suggest the idea of *Listenwissenschaft* (the science of lists)[7] as a primitive way of organizing knowledge and approaching reality. His condescending supposition that the Sumerians and Babylonians were scientifically unable to go beyond the list has been successfully challenged by a number of scholars. Niek Veldhuis, for example, argued persuasively that ancient lists on cuneiform tablets were meant to facilitate learning cuneiform script rather than presenting scientific learning; the list was a form deliberately chosen to serve a particular purpose.[8]

These lists were undergoing various transformations but were continuously used in scribal schools for over three thousand years.[9] Nevertheless, these early lists, as well as the list as a type, continue to be just marginally deemed literature: lists are commonly perceived as primarily monotonous and therefore boring. The reviews of Eco's book on lists show this: very few of the reviewers were persuaded by Eco's excitement, and one even suggested that Eco was not serious when promoting lists.[10] Eco himself seems to have anticipated this view:

---

[7] Von Soden, 'Leistung und Grenze'.

[8] Veldhuis, *Elementary Education*, p. 137. For a more detailed discussion of the reception of von Soden's Listenwissenschaft, see Visi, 'A Science of Lists?'.

[9] Green, 'Early Cuneiform', pp. 54–55. For an edition of these texts, see Englund and Nissen, *Die lexikalischen Listen*. See also the 'Digital Corpus of Cuneiform Lexical Texts' <http://oracc.museum.upenn.edu/dcclt> [accessed 6 February 2019].

[10] 'My own nagging worries are rather different. Has Eco actually succeeded in breathing life into the list? And is he entirely serious anyway? Going back to the Homeric catalogue, even after Eco's enthusiastic analysis, I still found it very hard going. But when I discovered him, in an interview, choosing the Telephone Directory as his *Desert Island* book, I wondered whether

he created a distinction between 'practical' list and 'poetic' list, and while he denounced the former, he was enchanted and fascinated by the latter. Practical lists are those that exclude and control, they are final and authoritative, and they seem objective and non-negotiable. Poetic lists are open and playful, and for Eco they express the 'poetics of the *etcetera*'. Practical lists (rankings, inventories, itineraries, timetables, telephone directories, etc.) are rarely considered to hold any aesthetic value or generate interpretative interest. They are usually stores of information organized according to an easily graspable principle, selected from a clearly defined set of items, and unified in form. Their point is to order information and make it easily accessible: readers should be able to scan a list quickly in order to note or retrieve its elements — they are not expected to actually *read* it but rather to *use* it. Poetic lists are different: they often play with the notion of a practical list and the expectations of organization, objectivity, and exhaustiveness that it raises. Thus, they often combine items of different forms and sets, and they take pride in confusing and misinforming the reader.

Yet, the distinction between the two types of list cannot be made so easily. There are no features of form or content that would securely distinguish a practical list from a poetic one: the only difference lies in context and reception. The author of the poetic list transfers the form from the practical context to that of the artistic or literary but otherwise maintains its structure. It is similar to parody, which copies the form and content of its model while making a subtle contextual shift. Thus, unless we can document the list author's intentions and/or the circumstances of the text's origin, its overall aim may be disputable.

In addition, even seemingly practical and objective lists do not always fulfil the general expectations:[11] they might not convey accurate information but instead promote their own hidden agendas. A list does not necessarily just *reflect* reality: it may, rather, be an attempt at *constructing* it. It is exactly its aura of objectivity that makes a list an especially successful means of manipulation. Apt medieval examples are lists of rulers. These lists appear to provide a chronological sequence of rulers over a particular area, yet it is manifestly clear that lists of rulers repeatedly exclude or include particular persons regardless of historical accuracy.[12]

---

the whole project was not, after all, slightly tongue-in-cheek. Perhaps the joke is on the reader for taking Eco's eulogy of the list seriously'; Beard, 'The Infinity of Lists'.

[11] See, for example, Leonardi, Morelli, and Santi, *Fabula in Tabula*.

[12] See, for example, Bláhová, 'Středověké katalogy'; Bláhová, 'Středověké dějiny'; or Bak, 'Lists in the Service'.

Alastair Fowler also argues that the division between 'practical' and 'poetic' lists (although he does not call them such) is not entirely clear:

> Originally, it [a list] may have been a social acknowledgement of the auditors and their kin, but its subsequent value has been formal and expressive [...] [he mentions other functions]. Probably no literary catalogue is entirely devoid of such expressive values. Now it is true that lists of practical character are among the earliest writings that have survived. But we are not entitled to assume that there were not even earlier oral and nonfunctional catalogues.[13]

Thus, early lists should not be simply placed into the category of dull pragmatism. Like other texts, lists almost invariably possess both utility and aesthetic value, and it is exactly the mixture of these two aspects that makes the form dynamic.

Ancient Greek — Homer's Catalogue of Ships

During Greek antiquity, lists were frequently used in epic poetry.[14] Approaches to the form are exemplified by the most celebrated ancient list: the catalogue of the ships in Homer's *Iliad* (Book ii, vv. 494–760). This section opens with the author asking the Muses to help him remember how many came to Troy. The list that follows is long, dense with the names of people and locations, and certainly does not advance the plot. It is typically skipped over by modern readers,[15] but is also omitted in a number of medieval manuscripts of the *Iliad* as well as a third-century CE papyrus. Michael Haslam suggests it was omitted because it was found to be boring rather than considered a fake, that is, a later addition to the *Iliad*. But because Porphyry records that schoolchildren in some cities were required by law to learn the catalogue by heart, Haslam concludes that 'at all periods there is a strong sense of each poem [i.e., Iliad and Odyssey]

---

[13] Fowler, *Kinds of Literature*, p. 153.

[14] See, for example, Gaardsøe, 'Skjolde, Stjerner, Dage', concentrating on the discussion of the lists in the *Illiad* (the shield of Achilles), Hesiod's *Work and Days*, and Aratus on the stars; Kühlmann, 'Katalog und Erzählung' (consulted thanks to the kind help of Jacob Klingner).

[15] See, e.g., Beard, 'The Infinity of Lists': 'Even the most ardent lovers of ancient literature tend to steer clear of one section of Homer's *Iliad*. This is the poem's second book, which is euphemistically known as "The Catalogue of Ships" — but is in fact dominated by a 350-line list of the various Greek forces that made up the "coalition of the willing" in the invasion of Troy. ("Fierce Ajax led the Locrian squadrons on [...] Euboea next her martial sons prepares" and so on, and on.) Most readers find it hard going, and skip it'.

as a whole, and this was not compromised by their physical fragmentation'.[16] Indeed, including the catalogue is exactly in keeping with the poet's strategy of equally illuminating the whole story, for what else should have been addressed in detail if not the participants of the great adventure?[17]

The general consensus is that the list formed part of the *Iliad* 'as early as the late seventh century BC'.[18] What might have been its charm? Kirk states:

> The effect of the catalogue as a whole is somewhat daunting for most modern read-ers, or for all in fact who are not connoisseurs of ancient political geography; but ancient audiences and readers must have been fascinated in different ways by the document's coverage, conciseness and virtuosity of expression, quite apart from its mythical and patriotic relevance [...]. It might be felt that the catalogue, or anything resembling it, could only be accommodated in such a monumental epic, and cannot have been part of the regular oral tradition about the heroic past, the Troy saga in particular; for it would swamp any normal short song, and could not stand as such a song on its own. Similarly it is extremely unlikely to have been composed *ex nihilo* for its present place. These are important factors in the debate over whether its source was ultimately a 'real' list, versified or not, which originated close to the time of the Trojan War itself (and when we use that phrase we have to remember the possibility that the expedition might have been very seriously exag-gerated, created almost, in the poetical tradition).[19]

Most scholars working on the list see its value as a historical source for the polit-ical situation in Greece in the seventh (or possibly the eighth) century BCE, and concentrate on identifying the place names with real locations.[20] As a histori-cal reality, the list curiously gives prominence to Boeotians who are otherwise not important within the epic,[21] presents unlikely relationships and extents of some domains, does not strictly follow the conspicuous geographical order, and

---

[16] See Haslam, 'Homeric Papyri', p. 59.

[17] As identified, e.g., by Erich Auerbach who argues that anything mentioned in the poem is elucidated in detail and with the same care, which results in a lack of perspective and tension. See Auerbach, 'Odysseus' Scar'.

[18] Kirk, *The Iliad*, p. 169.

[19] Kirk, *The Iliad*, p. 169.

[20] For example, Simpson and Lazenby, *The Catalogue of Ships*; further references are to be found in Kirk. Jachmann, *Der homerische Schiffskatalog*, is unique in suggesting that the cata-logue is a post-Homeric pastiche.

[21] This is usually explained that the expedition was assembled at Aulis in Boeotia, or that there was supposedly a Boeotian school of catalogue poetry which is thus alluded to.

seems to omit some information. This observation usually leads to the supposition that the catalogue includes information from various periods.[22]

The 266 verses list twenty-nine contingents of varying size but usually around two thousand men (forty ships, each with fifty men); every area had some six cities. There is minimal formal variation in the general syntactical structure of presenting the leaders and places, and the numbers assigned to many of the units as well as the epithets for place names seem conventional or even arbitrary. What is the actual difference between presenting this list and saying that there were many who came to Troy? By extending over numerous lines of the poem and making the reader spend time working through them, the full list is a literal reproduction of the multitude: upon finishing it, the readers truly *know*, because they have the actual experience of the *many* who came to Troy.

Another importance lies, of course, in the particular names mentioned. This list is long but still selective: it may have functioned to distinguish an elite — being on the list meant being important and thus one would read it with curiosity and rejoice when a familiar name appeared.[23] It is most likely that knowledge of the names and places helped the ancient audience (unlike us) enjoy the list.

But why does the author invoke the Muses at the beginning? In the Lattimore translation, the author says:

> Tell me now, you Muses who have your homes on Olympos.
> For you, who are goddesses, are there, and you know all things,
> and we have heard only the rumour of it and know nothing.
> Who then of those were the chief men and the lords of the Danaans?
> I could not tell over the multitude of them nor name them,
> not if I had ten tongues and ten mouths, not if I had
> a voice never to be broken and a heart of bronze within me,
> not unless the Muses of Olympia, daughters
> of Zeus of the aegis, remembered all those who came beneath Ilion.
> I will tell the lords of the ships, and the ships numbers.[24]

He explicitly says that he would not be able to enumerate the numerous heroes without the help of the Muses.[25] Does the author indeed ask for the Muses' help

---

[22] Kirk, *The Iliad*, p. 238.

[23] See Spufford, *The Chatto Book*, pp. 8–9.

[24] Homer, *The Iliad*, trans. by Lattimore, II.484–93. The translation is a widespread one, faithful to the Greek original line by line.

[25] In Ian Johnston's translation, the poet says he would never be able to enumerate all the

in order to ensure the list is accurate and exhaustive, and that no one is forgotten? That does not seem to be the only point in invoking the Muses — the list is also a poem.[26] While in modern translations it is rendered rather plainly,[27] older translations preserve more of its aesthetic qualities. For example, in Alexander Pope's reserved translation (1715) it begins:

> The hardy warriors whom Boeotia bred,
> Penelius, Leitus, Prothoenor, led:
> With these Arcesilaus and Clonius stand,
> Equal in arms, and equal in command.
> These head the troops that rocky Aulis yields,
> And Eteon's hills, and Hyrie's watery fields,
> And Schoenos, Scholos, Graea near the main,
> And Mycalessia's ample piny plain;[28]

Thus the poet possibly asks the Muses for help in writing a difficult poem. And perhaps the ancient audience did appreciate it as a poem and derived aesthetic pleasure from it, a kind of pleasure that may be alien to a contemporary reader with different expectations.[29]

There is yet another crucial issue raised by Elizabeth Minchin. She states that Homer 'is using his invocation to inform his audience that this will be no ordinary performance. To sing this catalogue-song would be beyond the resources of ordinary mortals'.[30] Using comparative evidence from contemporary singers, Minchin points out that while to read a list is tedious, to listen to a list-song is quite a different experience. The audience knows of the extensive skills required by the singer to remember such a song and appreciates a flawless

---

soldiers so he will concentrate only on the leaders ('It would be impossible for me to tell | the story of or name those in the common mass, | not even with ten tongues, ten mouths, an untiring voice [...]|. But I shall list the leaders, | commanders of the ships, and all the ships in full', ll. 487–89, 492–93).

[26] Pratt, *Lying and Poetry*, pp. 12–17 and 48–49, who, in spite of such passages that call upon the Muses for 'information', argues more broadly that the primary function of Achain poetry was aesthetic, rather than to offer access to some notion of 'truth'.

[27] For example, Ian Johnston's translation opens with: 'Peneleus, Leitus, and Arcesilaus | led the Boeotians, with Clonius and Prothoenor. | Their men came from Hyria, rocky Aulis, | Schoenus, Scolus, mountainous Eteonus' (ll. 494–97).

[28] Lines 494–501. See also, e.g., George Chapman's very eloquent version.

[29] The difference between oral and textual — heard and read poetry—is certainly a crucial element here.

[30] Minchin, 'The Performance of Lists', p. 11.

performance. In addition, Minchin writes, for the audience 'even a brief list of six or seven entries will serve a practical function — a diversion from the task of tracking the narrative. A longer list will do more, offering listeners the pleasure of listening for the sake of listening'.[31]

Surely, it is in no small part due to the very different context in which we encounter the catalogue of the ships — that is, as a written text consisting of completely unfamiliar items — that arguments for the list's later origin keep appearing. The list is now typically deemed too boring to have been original to the *Iliad*, the great epic, and the contextual shift in how we experience the list is perhaps now too vast for us to be able to put ourselves into the shoes of the original listeners. This is relevant to medieval lists, which we approach in a textual rather than oral environment, too.

Old Norse Contexts — Þulur *and Integrated Wisdom Lists*

At the end of *Skáldskaparmál* (The Language of Poetry), the second part of Snorri Sturluson's *Edda*, some medieval manuscripts include over a hundred stanzas of the so-called *þulur*, versified lists of poetic synonyms.[32] It is not certain that Snorri intended them to form part of his *Edda*. In fact, *Skáldskaparmál* also contains *heiti*, poetic synonyms for proper names, and abounds in prose lists of partly overlapping contents. The relationship between the prose lists within *Snorra Edda* and the *þulur* is therefore not completely clear. While Anthony Faulkes suggests that the *þulur* were the sources for the prose lists of names for bears, stags, the moon, and so forth,[33] Finnur Jónsson believes that the *þulur* were written separately and added to *Skáldskaparmál* later.[34] In addition to the complexities of the inclusion of semantically similar prose and poetry lists within *Snorra Edda*, the *þulur* are clearly related to other Old Norse texts, too, for example, *Grímnismál* and *Rígsþula*; the lists of weapon and ship names are likely derived from the sagas, particularly *fornaldarsǫgur*; and the lists of kings also include legendary names.[35] The foreign words (Latin, French,

---

[31] Minchin, 'The Performance of Lists', p. 16.

[32] Reykjavík, Stofnun Arna Magnússonar, GkS 2367 4to (R); Reykjavík, Stofnun Arna Magnússonar AM 748 II 4to (C); Utrecht, University Library, MS no. 1374 (Codex Trajectinus) (T); and more in Reykjavík, Stofnun Arna Magnússonar, AM 748 I b 4to (A), and Reykjavík, Stofnun Arna Magnússonar, AM 757 a 4to (B).

[33] Snorri, *Edda*, ed. by Faulkes, pp. xv–xvi.

[34] *Edda Snorra Sturlusonar*, ed. by Finnur Jónsson, pp. xlviii–xlix.

[35] Snorri, *Edda*, ed. by Faulkes, pp. xvi–xvii.

Greek) that are included are usually understood as a sign of the learned character of the *þulur*, and thus possibly mark an origin later than the twelfth century
to which they are usually dated.[36]

Faulkes explains the *þulur*'s often confusing combinations of listed items
as 'due partly to the vagueness of these categories in Norse mythology generally, and partly to the random way in which lists of these kinds of beings were
compiled'.[37] However, Margaret Clunies Ross argues for their overall thematic
arrangement and structure, which she describes as covering:

- supernatural and legendary beings (gods, sea kings,
  kings, giants, female trolls, and dwarves);
- men and women, war and war gear;
- waters and their denizens;
- earth, animals, and trees;
- heavens, heavenly bodies, fire, air (storms and winds),
  and moon and day;
- animals and birds;
- and, in one version (A), miscellaneous items.

Clunies Ross also suggests that the organization of the *þulur* is linked to that
of early medieval encyclopaedic literature, namely, to Isidore of Seville's *Etymo-
logiae*.[38] Later, she notes:

> Though *þulur* were of most use to skaldic poets, the extant examples use eddic verse
> forms. The evolution of the *þula* is speculative, but in all probability is attributable
> to the need oral poets felt to have access to versified aide-mémoires which func-
> tioned somewhat like rhyming dictionaries.[39]

The *þulur* are indeed normally perceived as a kind of repository for poetic
expressions, as raw material for the poet to use in the creative process of composition. If so, these lists do not strive to be beautiful poems but use the verse
form primarily for the sake of memorization. The main aim is to provide oppor-

---

[36] Snorri, *Edda*, ed. by Faulkes, pp. xv; Amory, 'Things *Greek* and the Riddarasogur'; Clunies Ross, *A History of Old Norse Poetry*, p. 31.

[37] Snorri, *Edda*, ed. by Faulkes, p. xvii.

[38] Clunies Ross, *Skáldskaparmál*, pp. 80–91, esp. pp. 87–88; see also some disagreement
with her conclusions in Nordal, *Tools of Literacy*, pp. 232–35.

[39] Clunies Ross, *A History of Old Norse Poetry*, p. 31.

tunities: the lists would not be used in their entirety, and only individual items would be selected, taken out and employed for other purposes. Thus, as far as their form is concerned, the *þulur* are more lists than poems: although they use rhyme and alliteration, they attempt as far as it is possible to exclude any other words than the items on the list. Unlike Homer's ship catalogue, no further epithets are added.

Since the *Snorra Edda* is a manual for poets, and *Skáldskaparmál* consists in large part of an annotated list of kennings, *heiti*, and other catalogues, the *þulur*, placed at the end may be seen as a kind of a mnemonic summary. If they serve as a summary, however, then it is a very unsystematic one — the *þulur* do not cover all of the subjects, and they do not order them in the same way as the main text of *Skáldskaparmál*. As far as their mnemonic function is concerned, the *þulur* usually contain more items than the celebrated 'seven, plus or minus two' number of items or 'bits' the human memory can hold at one time.[40] Yet, since each *þula* consists of eight brief lines, we can make it conform to the demands of memory easily by considering each line a 'bit'.

A different perspective on *þulur* was introduced by Elena A. Gurevič, who divided them into the categories of mythological, heroic, and skaldic based on their content.[41] Mythological *þulur* operate as abbreviated versions of myths — the names of mythical characters listed work as triggers to memory, eliciting whole stories. At the same time, Gurevič points out that, for example, a substantial number of Óðinn's names or river-names are not documented outside these lists and seem to have been invented specifically for the *þulur*. The heroic *þulur* often mix legendary and historical items, and the skaldic *þulur* were regarded as a natural form of learned poetic lexicology by the skalds. A number of items in the *þulur* at the end of *Skáldskaparmál*, Gurevič argues, were completely unsuitable for use in poetry and were indeed never employed. As it turns out, Gurevič concludes, poetic synonyms could not be generated by the same process of mythological name-giving, the skaldic *þulur* were a kind of a dead end, and, through them, the system of skaldic *heiti* was deformed.

We also find a great number of Old Norse poetic lists that, unlike the *þulur*, are integrated within larger works. Detailed attention was given to these poetic lists by Elizabeth Jackson, who persuasively shows that the lists are composed in a very complex and conscious way and contain mnemonic features.[42]

---

[40] Miller, 'The Magical Number Seven'.

[41] Gurevič, 'Zur Genealogie der Þula'.

[42] '[...] repetition, verbal balancing, the pairing of items using *oc* and *enn*, and the expansion of the final item to fill the whole line' (Jackson, 'Some Contexts', p. 138).

Jackson demonstrates how particular lists previously considered corrupt or interpolated, actually make perfect sense as they are.[43] She concludes:

> The qualities revealed by a close analysis of their structure, content, and contexts enable us both to appreciate the conventions which governed their composition and to conclude that the intentions of the literate poets who incorporated such lists into their poems may have been better preserved in the extant manuscripts than has been generally believed.[44]

Elsewhere Jackson also argues that the three final sections (lists) of *Hávamál* were intended to be read together as one unit, having all been addressed to Loddfáfnir on the same occasion,[45] that the list of gods' homes in *Grímnismál* was carefully crafted by the same author as the rest of the text and should not be considered corrupt,[46] and so on.[47] In short, Jackson identifies the list makers' specific strategies to argue for coherence where previous scholarship could only see corruption.[48] As she maintains, 'Listing was a fundamental activity of early poets, having its roots in the need for the efficient organization of information that had to be stored in the memory, as well as in the mnemonic requirements of oral delivery'.[49] Listing techniques are thus relevant to the study of the poems

---

[43] For example, at the beginning of her discussion of the Old Norse ordering lists, she states: 'Critics and commentators in the past have tended to see the lists as interruptions, not always appropriate and often of doubtful literary value. Indeed, some have gone so far as to dismiss certain lists entirely, regarding them as clumsy interpolations' (Jackson, 'Some Contexts', p. 111).

[44] Jackson, 'Some Contexts', p. 138.

[45] Jackson, 'A New Perspective'.

[46] Jackson, 'The Art of the List-Maker'. Again, she concludes: 'What emerges from the analysis in this article is a complex and elegant catalogue, composed by a list-maker whose talents, and even whose methods and goals, have gone unrecognized by generations of readers. De Vries' perplexity when faced with the task of making sense of its composition was due entirely to the fact that the art of the eddic list-maker has been forgotten. It is time to re-discover it, to lay to rest de Vries' sadly deficient *Bearbeiter*, and to restore to his place a master list-maker who was also, it is surely reasonable to suppose, the poet of Grímnismál' (p. 36).

[47] For example, she shows that *Vǫluspá* 20 is very sophisticated (Jackson, 'Scáro á scíði ørlǫg seggia'), as are lines 138–40 of Maxims I (Jackson, 'From the Seat of the "Þyle"?', concluding: 'This paper suggests a different approach: that we see the list as a remnant of ancient lore, part of the mass of inherited material passed on orally from generation to generation and preserved as long as it still had some use or maintained some valued connection with the past', p. 191).

[48] Jackson, 'Eddic Listing Techniques'.

[49] Jackson, 'Eddic Listing Techniques', p. 82.

in the *Poetic Edda* and useful 'as a supplement to metrical criteria when the integrity of the text is in question', because, 'regularity of meter is not an over-riding goal; rather, meter is a tool that may be used by the list maker to achieve other objectives'.[50] Indeed, understanding the list and gaining an appreciation of its form is 'enhanced by regarding it as composed with two recipients in mind: a listening audience and a reciter who needs to be able to memorize it accurately [...] a list is more difficult and requires greater concentration than a narrative'.[51] Jackson here too concludes with an argument for the primacy and importance of the lists.[52] In other studies Jackson goes on to introduce a comparative perspective by applying her conclusions from the lists in the *Poetic Edda* to Old English lists,[53] and rightly notes that the comparison often opens the questions of mutual influences or common roots of the early literate cultures, which is much disputed ground.[54] Although some of Jackson's observations might be seen as over-interpretative, it is nonetheless worth considering their relevance to other ancient and medieval lists.

Late Medieval Latin Contexts — Lists, Mnemonics, and the Art of Memory

Late medieval culture abounds in all kinds of lists — it is the time of concordances, indices, word-lists, tables of contents, and other means of structuring and organizing information.[55] This development is surely due to the rise of the universities and a general information boom, and a number of these lists, very simple in form and thus as a rule quite different from the sophisticated Old Norse lists, are closely connected to memory and meditation.[56] The art of memory is an ancient technique of memorizing public speeches, which is described in most detail in *Rhetorica ad Herennium*, an anonymous treatise from *c.* 80 CE which medieval readers ascribed to Cicero. It is based on a system of places

[50] Jackson, 'Eddic Listing Techniques', p. 83.

[51] Jackson, 'Eddic Listing Techniques', p. 85.

[52] Jackson, 'Eddic Listing Techniques', p. 106.

[53] Jackson, '"Not Simply Lists"'.

[54] For examples of such studies with contrasting conclusions, see Cross, 'The Old English Poetic Theme', pp. 66–70; Russom, 'A Germanic Concept of Nobility'; Dawson, 'The Structure of the Old English'.

[55] Cf. Rouse and Rouse, '*Statim invenire*'.

[56] The section below is partly based on my study 'Ordnen des Gedächtnisses', pp. 42–57.

(*loci*) and images (*imagines*). The places, usually houses, form a set structure in one's mind, which is filled with particular images dependent on the material to be remembered. There are many specific rules for the places (e.g., not too big and not too small, not too dark and not too light, dividable, sufficiently varied) and for the images (they must be striking and surprising, even bloody). Yet, the art remains personal: one should always select such places and images that fit one's memory.

It was in the late Middle Ages (*c.* 1420–1530) that the art of memory became very widely used, especially by university students and preachers.[57] By this time, the original context changed substantially: rather than speeches at a law court, and so forth, medieval people were using the art of memory to remember sermons or information learnt at the university. This period brought a number of innovations and changes in the character of the art of memory, in the ways both the places and the images were to be created. As far as places are concerned, instead of building architectural spaces (house, church, cloister, etc.) in one's mind, many of the late medieval treatises suggest using the body as a place, so that images would be placed on the head, limbs, and belly of a man, woman, or an animal.[58] But yet another possibility for creating a set structure of mnemonic places was making a list of one hundred words. Such a list would function as a permanent space to be occupied with temporary images. Adding the images in such a case did not mean hanging them on the walls, placing them in vaults or corners as before, but combining the image of the word from the place list with the image representing the thing to be remembered (which was to be 'placed' there) — again, as in the art of memory in general — in a striking and memorable way. However impractical this may seem, the word-list structure in fact became the most popular way of using the arts of memory during the fifteenth century.

Creating the lists of one hundred places was carried out in various ways. Usually the words on the list were divided into groups of five that always shared an aspect or characteristic. Thus, there are alphabetical lists in which every word within the group of five begins with the same consonant followed by a different vowel (e.g., Ba, Be, Bi, Bo, Bu), and there are thematic lists in which the words within every group of five belong to the same category (things to write with, or kitchen utensils, etc.), or, for example, one of the five words is an artisan and the other four are animals surrounding him. In addition, there are

---

[57] Cf. Kiss, 'Introduction'.

[58] See Rischpler, 'Spätmittelalterliche Mnemotechnik'.

other, more specific ways of creating these lists: for example, there is the unfinished list within a Hussite art of memory treatise with burning monks, violated sepulchres, snatched vessels, and so forth.[59]

Structuring one's memory around a (rather long) list of words is quite different from building castles and monasteries in the mind. When working with a list of words instead of places, the items on the list are most frequently visualized and visually combined with the images placed there. For example, in the anonymous Hussite art of memory mentioned above, illustrations of such combinations are provided: for example, if the place is a cat, and the image is a bird, one should put them together by imaging a cat eating a bird.[60] We do not learn from the treatises whether the lists of places were perceived more as words or as images: they definitely come down to us as words, but when they were placed into one's mind and reused as the set place structure, they would probably gradually become more and more visual. The lists as places of memory seem of little aesthetic value: they are not versified, and have invariably one hundred items divided into groups of five. They are designed to be used rather than to please. Yet, they are not random. They provide a unique insight into late medieval processes of association.

One case of a late medieval mnemonic list poem I have discussed elsewhere in detail is that of a biblical mnemonic aid usually called the *Summarium biblicum*,[61] which is a list of words, each representing one chapter of the Bible. The words in the list are selected in such a way as to form hexameters, and the entire Bible is thus presented in just over two hundred nonsense verses usually accompanied by interlinear glosses providing further context for the individual keywords. The *Summarium* seems to have been very popular during the late Middle Ages: more than 350 copies survive. There are many other biblical mnemonic aids created in a similar but not such extreme way — they typically dedicate several words, a line, or two lines to each chapter of the Bible.[62] Mnemonic

---

[59] Prague, Národní knihovna, MS VIII E 3, fol. 142ʳ, cf. Doležalová, '*Fugere artem memorativam?*'.

[60] 'Sicut si haberes in loco catum at pronunciaretur unus auis vel coruus aplica minorem auem vel coruos quasi a cato manducarentur' (Prague, Národní knihovna, MS VIII E 3, fol. 140ᵛ; cf. Doležalová, '*Fugere artem memorativam?*', 232–33).

[61] See Doležalová, *Obscurity and Memory*.

[62] There are similar mnemonic aids designed in a visual way: each chapter of the Bible is represented by an image. There is such a picture Bible surviving in at least five manuscripts and five early prints discussed in detail by Susanne Rischpler (in her *Biblia sacra figuris expressa*; one of the manuscripts, Munich, Bayrische Staatsbibliothek, clm. 697 is available online <http://

aids of the very same type were created for other late medieval school texts, such as the *Decretalia* or Peter Lombard's *Sententiae*.

When included at the end of a biblical codex, the *Summarium* is reminiscent of a kind of table of contents to the Bible. However, the text of the *Summarium* is surprisingly corrupted in the manuscripts: there are many scribal mistakes heavily affecting the meaning, the order of the chapters and the number of the chapters is often changed, and there are many omissions and additions. While its practical usefulness as a biblical mnemonic aid can easily be questioned, the charm of condensing the Bible into several pages of verse obviously continued to attract medieval readers: lists exert real appeal.

Beside the strictly mnemonic lists, in which every item is designed to bring to mind a particular piece of information, there were other frequently copied lists of words that are also linked to memory but in a looser way, mnemonic-meditative lists. In these lists, there is not specific retrievable content hidden behind each item. One's mind is almost encouraged to entertain free associations triggered, but not restricted, by the list items. Examples of such mnemonic-meditative lists are the verses on the effects of the Eucharist, surviving in at least fourteen manuscripts. Prague, Národní knihovna, MS X G 11, fol. 320ᵛ reads:

> Inflammat, memorat, sustentat, roborat, auget
> Hostia spem purgat, reficit, vitam dat et unit;
> Confirmatque fidem, munit fomitemque repellit.
>
> (It lights up, brings to memory, supports, invigorates, extends
> the host purifies hope, restores, gives and unites life,
> and confirms faith, strengthens, and sends away prejudice.)[63]

Here, the keywords lead one through a complex subject and divide it into digestible pieces on which one is encouraged to chew.[64] But is it appropriate to call them 'mnemonic verses'? As it turns out, not only a unified version of the verses, but even an authoritative or a theological concept which should

---

daten.digitale-sammlungen.de> [accessed 6 February 2019]), and, for the Gospels, there is an anonymous block book often ascribed to Peter of Rosenheim in which the images for each chapter are placed on figures standing for the evangelists: angel, lion, ox, and eagle. They attempt the same as the *Summarium*: to create one simple trigger that would stand for a whole biblical chapter, one image that would have the power of recalling the gist of a substantial piece of text.

[63] The translation is mine. To my knowledge, the poem has not yet been edited. Cf. Walther, *Alphabetisches Verzeichnis*, nos 26 and 9326 notes four manuscripts; Rothschild, *Bibliographie annuelle*, no. 3651 notes one manuscript.

[64] I discuss these verses and their reception in 'Verses on the Effects'.

be remembered through them is missing. The actual effects (although mostly twelve in number) are different in each version of the verses. What is then to be remembered here? In my opinion, these texts are in reality not mnemonic but meditative. In other words, one should keep in mind some (any) effects of the Eucharist, as an efficient reminder of its prominent role in one's life. Rather than simply remembering the Eucharist's importance, a person is invited to ponder the individual effects enumerated and re-create the power of this sacrament in all its weight. In this way, the Eucharist becomes present much more vividly and may influence one's behaviour more thoroughly. In this type of list, the stress is not placed on selecting the best-fitting keyword but simply on offering thought-provoking hints. For this purpose, the more obscure the word selected, the better it might work. The verses could thus serve (and indeed did serve) both to create a specific space for private meditation and as the structuring device of a sermon or a treatise.

The material form of this type of text is actually only a small part of its larger existence: the 'texts' were to be preserved in memory rather than written down as static, independent items. If they were written down, they appeared among other notes as reminiscences for personal use, not as polished texts. Personal notes, by definition, concentrate on what keeps escaping memory, what is difficult or new, and they omit obvious and routine elements. What we find in the surviving manuscripts are glimpses of the oral texts, fragmentary, unfinished, and momentary, like photographs. Thus, they are not polished or concretized texts; they are rather reflections on paper or vellum of the scribe's gradual process of organizing useful material while placing it in his or her memory. Texts are often gathered here without distinguishing or prioritizing among them, the same material gets repeated, and only slightly adjusted. These lists may also be presented in a visual manner.[65] In fact, the scripted list becomes the means to organize the material in one's mind. It is the material text which often ends up being messy and unpolished while the memory itself structures and refines the list.

---

[65] For the late Middle Ages, there are several usual set structures of organizing lists visually, such as a tree, a tower, or Noah's ark. With the visualization, the list might lose its original linearity but gain hierarchy, grouping, and possible directions. Is it still a list then? Again, the dividing line may not be so clear. What is sure is that when a real list (linear, and therefore graspable, repeatable, and simple) is combined with an image, it becomes also striking, unique, and memorable, and thus, it is in fact a most efficient means for structuring memory. (This is also the case of a curious list-like meditation-mnemonic aid discussed in detail by Kiss, 'Memory, Meditation and Preaching'.)

These late medieval Latin lists have functions similar to the Old Norse lists discussed by Jackson but they are much less sophisticated in their form, which may (or may not) be linked to the fact that literary culture by this time was to a much greater degree written than oral. But it is certainly linked to their ad hoc character — most of these lists are created for the moment and for the particular person's — their author's — sake. They are expected to be used in practice but not to survive centuries. And, indeed, they are numerous but completely neglected as part of the literary culture of their time.

Common Aspects

As the examples discussed above show, even ancient and medieval lists designed to be stored in one's memory are not easy to grasp and do not follow specific rules: some are in the form of a poem, others are not; some are simple enumerations, other display complex interconnections. For some (the *þulur*, or the verses on the effects of the Eucharist), the order of listed items does not seem to matter and appears to be primarily determined by poetic form (although with differing degrees of sophistication), while in other cases (the *Summarium*) the sequence is a crucial part of the meaning. Yet for others (the mnemonic *loci* lists), the order reflects a personal chain of associations. The mnemonic *loci* lists form a particular set structure in the mind to be refilled according to one's needs, the meditative verses structure meditation, the *Summarium* should be memorized as a whole and linked to the text of the Bible for which it stands, the *þulur* should be stored in memory so that particular items can be retrieved and used for another, independent, composition. Thus, few overarching conclusions or all-encompassing patterns can be articulated.

Yet, several aspects reappear in the diverse examples included here. First, in all the lists mentioned, the lack of scholarly appreciation of the form is more frequent than its opposite. Lists are considered interruptions, later interpolations, or corrupted passages. They are neglected and overlooked, and repeatedly omitted from editions and translations of longer texts containing them.

Second, upon the rare closer examination, the originally oral verse lists reveal intricate and complex forms. Although Jackson might not go so far as to call it 'the art of the list', her work implies that it *is* a specific art with particular rules. For example, Jackson argues that the variant for *Vǫluspá* 20 in Hauksbók, which is usually considered to represent an independent record based on oral tradition, actually preserves a change to the written version (by a copyist directed by Snorri or Snorri himself), with the main aim to standardize, to cut anomaly or irregularity, so that the verse text could be used by Snorri without incongruity in his prose text. Thus, this was a kind of 'modernizing' of the text for reception by a literate culture. She concludes by asking: is it the case that 'Iceland's scholars had forgotten the function of oral listing devices?' and

> Did they see repetitions, for instance, as many modern scholars have done, as transmission errors or as evidence of interpolation? Or did they understand the techniques of the oral list-makers but feel that the device they used, their mnemonic function now obsolete, could be consigned to history?[66]

The late medieval Latin lists discussed here are, however, much less complex in their form than the Old Norse lists. Even when versified, they are linear enumerations lacking the intricate methods applied by the oral list-makers. There remains much work to be done in analysing the relationship between oral and written lists, especially the specific listing strategies used in oral composition. Tentatively, however, it might be suggested that, with gradually prevailing literacy and increasingly developed written culture, the form of the list became simplified.

Third, these lists show that our distance presents an insurmountable obstacle. A crucial aspect of medieval texts is that they often come down to us seriously corrupted, which makes any textual analysis problematic: the text we interpret may be very different from the original composition. Substantial intervention of scribes leading to greater textual obscurity was widespread during the Middle Ages but is especially visible in lists, which are more easily corrupted than narratives. List items presenting otherwise undocumented information leave us invariably in doubt as to whether our sources are fragmentary or whether the list is just made up. This applies to the ships in Homer, the *þulur*, but also to the late medieval meditational lists. Items could have appeared on a list basically for the sake of the meter, alliteration, or a momentary association. They might not necessarily reflect a way of organizing existing knowledge and putting order on reality, but simply sound nice. For these reasons, it is also difficult to judge whether Gurevič is right about the skaldic *þulur* being a dead end or not: the fact that we do not have skaldic poetry using most of these synonyms may or may not mean that it was not composed.

Today, many of the lists seem to include items too diverse and basically incompatible — among the well-known warriors there are some totally obscure, among Óðinn's familiar names there are unattested monikers, among well-known river names there are some that must simply have been invented, and so

---

[66] Jackson, "'Scáro á scíði ørlǫg seggia'".

forth. It is possible that we lack the necessary context, just as it is possible that some of the material was made up. If the poems in which the lists coalesce are precisely designed compositions (as Jackson very persuasively argues in case of the Old Norse lists), such invention reflects true creative force.

In any case, there is no list that would be purely practical and simply mirror reality. By constructing, selecting, and ordering the items, as well as by contextualizing the whole, the author of the list always makes conscious creative choices. The result is an almost magical invention with which the process of naming has always been associated. After all, the *þulur* — the wise men, perhaps magicians and composers of *þulur* — are believed to have had the ability to give the 'correct' names to things. Lists are thus creations of a specific universe: a universe that is charming but not always easy for us to enter.

Works Cited

Manuscripts

Munich, Bayerische Staatsbibliothek, Clm. 697
Prague, Národní knihovna, MS VIII E 3
——, MS X G 11
Reykjavík, Stofnun Arna Magnússonar, AM 748 I b 4to (A)
——, AM 748 II 4to (C)
——, AM 757 a 4to (B)
——, GkS 2367 4to (R)
Utrecht, University Library, MS No. 1374 (Codex Trajectinus, T)

Primary Sources

Edda Snorra Sturlusonar, ed. by Finnur Jónsson (Copenhagen: Gyldendal, 1931)
Homer, *Iliad*, trans. by Ian Johnston (Nanaimo, British Columbia, Canada, 2010), published online at <http://johnstoniatexts.x10host.com/homer/iliad_title.html> [accessed 6 February 2019]
Homer, *The Iliad of Homer*, trans. by Richard Lattimore (Chicago: University of Chicago Press, 1951)
Snorri Sturluson, *Edda. Skáldskaparmál*, I: *Introduction: Text and Notes*, ed. by Anthony Faulkes (London: Viking Society for Northern Research/University College of London, 1998)

Secondary Studies

Amory, Frederic, 'Things *Greek* and the Riddarasogur', *Speculum* 59 (1984), 509–23

Auerbach, Erich, 'Odysseus' Scar', in *Mimesis: The Representation of Reality in Western Literature*, trans. by Willard R. Trask (Princeton: Princeton University Press, 1953), pp. 3–23

Bak, János, 'Lists in the Service of Legitimation in Central European Sources', in *The Charm of a List*, ed. by L. Doležalová (Newcastle upon Tyne: Cambridge Scholars, 2009), pp. 34–45

Beard, Mary, 'The Infinity of Lists by Umberto Eco', *The Guardian*, 11 December 2009 <https://www.theguardian.com/books/2009/dec/12/umberto-eco-lists-book-review> [accessed 6 February 2019]

Belknap, Robert E., *The List: The Uses and Pleasures of Cataloguing* (New Haven: Yale University Press, 2004)

Bláhová, Marie, 'Středověké dějiny pražského biskupství jako pramen dějin církevní správy v Čechách' (Medieval History of the Bishopric of Prague as a Source for the History of the Church Administration in Bohemia), in *Vývoj církevní správy na Moravě* (Development of Church Administration in Moravia) (Prague: Filozofická fakulta Karlovy univerzity v Praze, 2003), pp. 77–90

——, 'Středověké katalogy českých knížat a králů a jejich pramenná hodnota' (Medieval Catalogues of Czech Counts and Kings and their Source Value), in *Średnowiecze polskie i powszechne 1*, ed. by Idzi Panic (Katowice: Wydawnictwo Uniwersytetu Śląskiego, 1999), pp. 33–63

Borges, Jorge Luis, 'The Analytical Language of John Wilkins', in *Other Inquisitions (1937–1952)*, trans. by Ruth L. C. Simms (Austin: University of Texas Press, 1964), pp. 229–32

Clunies Ross, Margaret, *A History of Old Norse Poetry and Poetics* (Cambridge: Brewer, 2005)

——, *Skáldskaparmál: Snorri Sturluson's Ars Poetica and Medieval Theories of Language* (Odense: Odense University Press, 1987)

Cross, James E., 'The Old English Poetic Theme of the Gifts of Men', *Neophilologus* 46.1 (1962), 66–70

Dawson, R. MacGregor, 'The Structure of the Old English Gnomic Poems', *Journal of English and Germanic Philology* 61 (1962), 14–22

Doležalová, Lucie, '*Ad hoc* Lists of Bernard Itier (1163–1225), Librarian of St Martial de Limoges', in *The Charm of a List: From the Sumerians to Computerised Data Processing*, ed. by Lucie Doležalová (Newcastle upon Tyne: Cambridge Scholars, 2009), pp. 80–99

——, '*Fugere artem memorativam*? The Art of Memory in Late Medieval Bohemia (A Preliminary Survey)', *Studia mediaevalia Bohemica* 2.2 (2010), 228–34

——, *Obscurity and Memory in Late Medieval Manuscript Culture: The Case of the 'Summarium Biblie'*, Medium Aevum Quotidianum, 29 (Krems: Institut für Realienkunde des Mittelalters und der frühen Neuzeit, 2012)

——, 'Ordnen des Gedächtnisses: Das Verzeichnis als Raum des Wissens in der Vormoderne', in *Wissenspaläste – Räume des Wissens in der Vormoderne*, ed. Gesine Mierke and Christoph Fasbender (= *Euros: Chemnitzer Arbeiten zur Literaturwissenschaft*, 2 (2013)), pp. 42–57

——, 'Verses on the Effects of the Eucharist: Memory and the Material Text in Utraquist Miscellanies', in *Religious Controversy in Europe 1378–1536: Textual Transmission and Networks of Readership*, ed. by Pavel Soukup and Michael van Dussen (Turnhout: Brepols, 2013), pp. 105–36

Eco, Umberto, *The Infinity of Lists: An Illustrated Essay*, trans. by Alastair McEwen (London: Maclehose, 2009)

——, *La Vertigine della Lista* (Milano: Bompiani, 2009)

Englund, R. K., and H. J. Nissen, eds, *Die lexikalischen Listen der archaischen Texte aus Uruk*, Archaische Texte aus Uruk, 3 (Berlin: Gebrüder Mann, 1993)

Fowler, Alastair, *Kinds of Literature: An Introduction to the Theory of Genres and Modes* (Oxford: Clarendon Press, 1982)

Gaardsøe, Roar Melgaard, 'Skjolde, Stjerner, Dage: Katalogisering i græsk episk digtning' (Shields, Stars, Days: Cataloguing in Greek Epic Poetry) (unpublished doctoral dissertation, Aarhus University, 2010)

Gass, William, 'And', in *Voicelust: Eight Contemporary Fiction Writers on Style*, ed. by Allen Wier and Don Hendrie Jr (Lincoln: University of Nebraska Press, 1985), pp. 101–25

Green, M. W. 'Early Cuneiform', in *The Origins of Writing*, ed. Wayne M. Senner (Lincoln: The University of Nebraska Press, 1991), 43–58

Gurevič, Elena A., 'Zur Genealogie der Þula', *Alvíssmál*, 1 (1992 [1993]), 65–98

Haslam, Michael, 'Homeric Papyri and Transmission of the Text', in *A New Companion to Homer*, ed. by Ian Morris and Barry Powell, Mnemosyne Supplementum, 163 (Leiden: Brill, 1997), pp. 55–100

Havel, Ivan M., 'Time in Lists and Lists in Time', in *The Charm of a List: From the Sumerians to Computerized Data Processing*, ed. by Lucie Doležalová (Newcastle upon Tyne: Cambridge Scholars, 2009), 9–11

Jachmann, G., *Der homerische Schiffskatalog und die Ilias* (Köln: Westdeutscher Verlag, 1958)

Jackson, Elizabeth, 'The Art of the List-Maker and the *Grímnismál* Catalogue of the Homes of the Gods: A Reply to Jan de Vries', *Arkiv för nordisk filologi*, 110 (1995), 5–40

——, 'Eddic Listing Techniques and the Coherence of "Rúnatal"', *Alvíssmál*, 5 (1995), 81–106

——, 'From the Seat of the "Þyle"? A Reading of "Maxims I," Lines 138–40', *Journal of English and Germanic Philology*, 99.2 (2000), 170–92

——, 'A New Perspective on the Relationship between the Final Three Sections of *Hávamál* and on the Role of *Loddfáfnir*', *Saga-book of the Viking Society for the Northern Research*, 24 (1994), 33–57

——, '"Not Simply Lists": An Eddic Perspective on Short-Item Lists in Old English Poems', *Speculum*, 73.2 (1998), 338–71

——, '"Scáro á scíði ørlǫg seggia": The Composition of *Voluspá* 20 and the Implications of the Hauksbók Variant', *Alvíssmál*, 9 (1999), 73–88

——, 'Some Contexts and Characteristics of Old Norse Ordering Lists', *Saga-book of the Viking Society for the Northern Research*, 23 (1992), 111–40

Kirk, G. S., *The Iliad: A Commentary. Vol. 1, Books 1–4* (Cambridge: Cambridge University Press, 1985)

Kiss, Farkas Gábor, 'Introduction', in *The Art of Memory in Late Medieval East Central Europe*, ed. by Lucie Doležalová, Farkas Gábor Kiss, and Rafał Wójcik (Budapest: L'Harmattan, 2016), pp. 9–26

——, 'Memory, Meditation and Preaching: A Fifteenth-Century Memory Machine in Central Europe (The Text *Nota hanc figuram composuerant doctores... / Pro aliquali intelligentia...*)', in *The Making of Memory in the Middle Ages*, ed. by Lucie Doležalová (Leiden: Brill, 2010), pp. 49–78

Kühlmann, Wilhelm, 'Katalog und Erzählung: Studien zu Konstanz und Wandel einer literarischen Form in der antiken Epik' (unpublished doctoral dissertation, Freiburg im Breisgau, 1973)

Leonardi, Claudio, Marcello Morelli, and Francesco Santi, eds, *Fabula in Tabula: Una storia degli indici dal manoscritto al testo elettronico. Atti del convegno di studio (Firenze 21–22 ottobre 1994)* (Spoleto: CISAM, 1995)

Miller, George A., 'The Magical Number Seven, Plus or Minus Two: Some Limits on Our Capacity for Processing Information', *Psychological Review*, 63.2 (1956), 81–97

Minchin, Elizabeth, 'The Performance of Lists and Catalogues in the Homeric Epics', in *Voice into Text: Orality and Literacy in Ancient Greece*, ed. by Ian Worthington (Leiden: Brill, 1996), pp. 3–20

Nordal, Guðrún, *Tools of Literacy: The Role of Skaldic Verse in Icelandic Textual Culture of the Twelfth and Thirteenth Centuries* (Toronto: University of Toronto Press, 2001)

Pratt, Louise H., *Lying and Poetry from Homer to Pindar* (Ann Arbor: University of Michigan Press, 1993)

Rischpler, Susanne, *Biblia sacra figuris expressa: Mnemotechnische Bilderbibeln des 15. Jahrhunderts*, Wissensliteratur im Mittelalter, 36 (Wiesbaden: Reichert, 2001)

——, 'Spätmittelalterliche Mnemotechnik im Kontext von Konzil und Melker Reform', in *Wissenspaläste – Räume des Wissens in der Vormoderne*, ed. Gesine Mierke and Christoph Fasbender (= *Euros: Chemnitzer Arbeiten zur Literaturwissenschaft*, 2 (2013)), pp. 10–41

Rothschild, Jean-Pierra, ed., *Auteurs et textes latins* (= *Bibliographie annuelle du Moyen Age tardif*, 11 (2001))

Rouse, Richard H., and Mary A. Rouse, '*Statim invenire*: Schools, Preachers, and New Attitudes to the Page', in *Renaissance and Renewal in the Twelfth Century*, ed. by Robert. L. Benson, Giles Constable, and Carol D. Lanham (Cambridge, MA: Harvard University Press, 1982), pp. 201–25

Russom, Geoffrey R., 'A Germanic Concept of Nobility in the Gifts of Men and Beowulf', *Speculum*, 53.1 (1978), 1–15

Simpson. R. Hope, and J. F. Lazenby, *The Catalogue of Ships in Homer's Iliad* (Oxford: Clarendon Press, 1970)

Soden, Wolfram von 'Leistung und Grenze sumerischer und babylonischer Wissenschaft', *Die Welt als Geschichte*, 2 (1936), 411–64; 509–57

Spufford, Francis, *The Chatto Book of Cabbages and Kings: Lists in Literature* (London: Chatto and Windus, 1989)

Veldhuis, Niek, *Elementary Education at Nipur: The Lists of Trees and Wooden Objects* (Groningen: Rijksuniversiteit Groningen, 1997)

Visi, Tamás, 'A Science of Lists? Medieval Jewish Philosophers as List Makers', in *The Charm of a List: From the Sumerians to Computerised Data Processing*, ed. by Lucie Doležalová (Newcastle upon Tyne: Cambridge Scholars, 2009), pp. 12–33

Walther, Hans, *Alphabetisches Verzeichnis der Versanfänge mittellateinischer Dichtungen* (Göttingen: Vandenhoeck & Ruprecht, 1959)

Talking Place and Mapping Icelandic Identity in *Íslendingabók* and *Landnámabók*

Amy C. Mulligan

Introduction

Þat er margra manna mál, at þat sé óskyldr fróðleikr at rita landnám. En vér þykjumsk heldr svara kunna útlendum mǫnnum, þá er þeir bregða oss því, at vér séim komnir af þrælum eða illmennum, ef vér vitum víst várar kynferðir sannar, svá ok þeim mǫnnum, er vita vilja forn froeði eða rekja ættartǫlur, at taka heldr at upphafi til en hǫggvask í mitt mál, enda eru svá allar vitrar þjóðir, at vita vilja upphaf sinna landsbyggða eða hvers<u> hvergi til hefjask eða kynslóðir.

(People often say that writing about the Settlements is irrelevant learning, but we think we can better meet the criticism of foreigners when they accuse us of being descended from slaves or scoundrels, if we know for certain the truth about our ancestry. And for those who want to know ancient lore and how to trace genealogies, it's better to start at the beginning than to come in at the middle. Anyway, all civilized nations want to know about the origins of their own society and the beginnings of their own race.)[1]

---

[1] *Landnámabók*, in *Íslendingabók; Landnámabók*, ed. by Jakob Benediktsson, pt 2, p. 336, n. 1 (henceforth *Landnámabók*); translation from *The Book of Settlements*, trans. by Hermann Pálsson and Edwards, p. 6 (henceforth *Book of Settlements*). The lines appear in the seventeenth-century Þórðarbók redaction of *Landnámabók*, and Jakob Benediktsson argues the lines may be taken from the lost medieval source (Styrmisbók), thus possibly preserving

Amy Mulligan (amullig2@nd.edu) is a Fellow of the Medieval Institute and Assistant Professor of Irish Language and Literature at the University of Notre Dame, Indiana, where she conducts research and publishes on the literatures of medieval Britain, Ireland, and Scandinavia, with particular emphasis on cultural exchange among peoples of the medieval North Atlantic.

Moving Words in the Nordic Middle Ages: Tracing Literacies, Texts, and Verbal Communities, ed. by Amy C. Mulligan and Else Mundal, AS 8   BREPOLS PUBLISHERS   (Turnhout: Brepols, 2019) pp. 227–253   10.1484/M.AS-EB.5.116626

This well-known opening to a late copy of *Landnámabók* shows Icelanders' awareness of the importance of words, both hearsay and more formalized written pronouncements, in dictating the origins and character of a people. For the group unified by their physical occupation of Iceland, it is nonetheless words, verbalized knowledge, branding, and statements circulated about a group's *landsbyggð* ('origins' or literally, 'land-settlement'), through which they become a unified *kynslóð* ('race', 'people') and one of the *vitrar þjóðir* ('wise nations', 'knowledgeable peoples'). This article traces the role of words, spatial descriptions, written statements and verbalized prophecies that frame the settlement of the Icelandic landscape and valorize a distinct Icelandic national identity or ethnicity.[2] As two texts deeply invested in geography, spatial knowledge, and movement as constitutive of Icelanders' history and identity, *Íslendingabók* and *Landnámabók* are the two main sources to be addressed in this essay. *Íslendingabók* (Book of the Icelanders), a history of Iceland from 870 to 1118 written by Ari Þorgilsson *inn fróði* ('the wise' or 'learned') sometime between 1122 and 1133, became a foundational account of Iceland's history, even national myth. *Landnámabók* (literally, 'Book of Land-Takings', though more conventionally 'Book of Settlements'), first compiled around 1125, is a textual record of the movements and actions of the first Icelanders in their new geography; this history of the Icelanders also devotes considerable attention to place and place-name origins.

Indeed, as Adolf Friðriksson and Orri Vésteinsson have eloquently pointed out, the prominence of named sites in early written sources like *Landnámabók* has unfortunately obscured the need for a more objective, materially driven Icelandic archaeology. The significant gaps between textual and archaeological records have led them to conclude that 'the overall view of *landnám* and Icelandic society in these early sources was clearly a scholarly construct' and that this representation of the past mediated by Ari and subsequent writers 'had very little to do with any "genuine" traditions about the *landnám* that may

---

Ari Þorgilsson's own attitudes. Hermann Pálsson and Paul Edwards note that this quote significantly provides 'the underlying suggestion that the study of Iceland's beginnings was stimulated by foreign misconceptions' (*Book of Settlements*, pp. 6–7). Many Icelandic scholars of the eleventh and twelfth centuries trained abroad in Germany, France, and England, and it thus appears that the creation of foundational Icelandic verbal narratives about place and national identity were intimately bound up with international perspectives on Iceland, words originating in European conversations, discourses, and texts.

[2] See the chapter 'Establishing an Ethnicity: The Emergence of the "Icelanders" in the Early Middle Ages', in Hastrup, *Island of Anthropology*, pp. 69–70.

have existed at that time. Instead, it was probably generated by the social and cultural needs of the Icelandic intelligentsia in the High Middle Ages'.[3] From a literary scholar's perspective I want to further develop arguments about the con-structedness of *landnám* accounts by pointing to the virtuality or imaginative nature of Icelandic geospatial writing. The authors, compilers, and composers of *Íslendingabók* and *Landnámabók* were skilled literary practitioners who under-stood the power of words: they used words to create, structure, and drive concep-tions of Icelandic geography, such that the settlement accounts in *Íslendingabók* and *Landnámabók* have as much to do with words and imagined spaces as real, physical landscape. My own avenue of entry into the discussion, therefore, is the *verbal or textual rendering* of these geographically transformative activities.

A few words on the logic and processes of literary cartography (also referred to as 'geocriticism'), a method for exploring and analysing the spaces presented by written texts, can clarify this approach. As Barbara Piatti, Anne-Kathrin Reuschel, and Lorenz Hurni explain in their statement on what cartography brings to literary studies,

> One of its [literary cartography's] traditional starting points is precisely the assumption that a large part of fiction indeed refers to the physical/real world, called geospace in the following, by using an almost infinite variety of options to do so. Among them is for instance the use of identifiable toponyms or the dense description of existing spaces and places [...]. Having said that, literature is also able to create any other space, without any limitations — imaginary realms, invented cities, countries, continents, entire stellar systems. Those are the chapters of lit-erature featuring no reference towards geospace at all. In-between, one can find various degrees of transformed settings, spaces and places in fiction which are still linked to an existing geospatial section but are alienated by using literary means such as re-naming, re-modeling or overlaying.[4]

Icelandic settlement narratives embody this topographical 'in-between' and demonstrate conscientious overlaying of verbal narratives onto recognizable, real Icelandic geographies. As Westphal put it, 'Literary space, in the end, is a real, material, geographical place, imagined and represented by language. The vocation of geocriticism is to interpret the manifestations of this spatial imagination, at the intersection of geography and literature'.[5] In this essay,

---

[3] Adolf Friðriksson and Orri Vésteinsson, 'Creating a Past', p. 141.

[4] Piatti, Reuschel, and Hurni, 'Literary Geography', p. 4.

[5] Westphal, *La géocritique mode d'emploi*, p. x. Quote cited and translated in Tally, 'On Literary Cartography', p. 10.

I take a geocritical approach to narratives about the settlement of Iceland and the development of a topographically-oriented Icelandic identity. Specifically, I want to tease out the act of writing or articulating arrival, settlement, and eventual rootedness in Iceland, the *verbal creation* of a layered, historicized Icelandic place. I contend that these written words drive and shape, even create, encounters with the 'real' geography itself. While these narratives, as archaeologists have pointed out, might have 'had very little to do with any "genuine" traditions about the *landnám*', they are all the more important for what they reveal about the goals of the Icelanders and the 'Icelandic intelligentsia in the High Middle Ages'.

Many Icelandic settlement accounts become in their own way virtual journeys or pilgrimages to nationally sacred and mythically rich sites, and through these texts an audience witnesses important ancestors speaking and performing foundational acts that constitute 'Icelandic-ness'. While Iceland is a clear focus, Icelandic identity is also international and is mapped out in terms of the larger North Sea and Irish Sea regions and beyond. The multi-layered Icelandic origin stories are verbal maps of Iceland and as discussed in further detail below, the Icelanders also use these topographically rich accounts to enlarge an understanding of themselves as valued members of an extensive learned Christian community. Scenes of Icelanders' movement and spatial practice within the Icelandic landscape can be more productively understood when we avoid considering Icelandic geospatial writing as a static record of events, people and places from the past; rather, Icelandic textual geographies can provide cognitive, felt experiences that allow admission to a world, its figures, and community in an Icelandic nation. Although set in the past, written Icelandic places, or 'place-worlds', are important sites or spaces verbally brought to life through story, and made inviting and accessible at every hearing or reading. As Keith Basso expresses it, successful 'instances of place-making consist in an adventitious fleshing out of historical material that culminates in a posited state of affairs, a particular universe of objects and events — in short, a *place-world* — wherein portions of the past are brought into being'.[6] Through the combination of reading or experiencing these texts, and living within the familiar, yet verbally reimagined landscape of Iceland (the 'place-world' combines both space and story), important lessons about Icelandic identity are modelled and experienced. Examination of *Íslendingabók* and *Landnámabók* demonstrates how these complex actions take place within Icelandic literary geographies, or place-worlds made of words.

[6] Basso, *Wisdom Sits in Places*, p. 6.

Íslendingabók

While it is not the earliest text written in the Icelandic language, *Íslendingabók*, composed by the historian Ari Þorgilsson sometime in the 1120s or 1130s, has been widely recognized as instrumental in terms of identity formation because it 'creates' the settlers of Iceland as a distinct people.[7] This is accomplished in several ways. It is the first extant vernacular text to use the term *Íslendingar* (Icelanders) to denote the Icelanders as a collective and distinct people. It is also the earliest text to date the settlement and conversion. Finally, as I argue here, through description of a range of carefully selected sites, characters, and events (political, social, and religious), *Íslendingabók* creates or narratively maps out a national landscape. This historiographic narrative is not as engaged in the minutiae of place as are other sources on this early period, and there is little of the place-name material that is so common in other treatments of arrival and settlement like *Landnámabók*. Ari did not, however, lack interest in locating Iceland and its people; rather, like the designers of the *mappae mundi*, Ari fixed his gaze on the larger picture and invested geographical attentions in the universal alongside the local. We can read *Íslendingabók* as an all-encompassing map of Iceland and its place in the world — when Ari's settlers arrive, they do not just land in Iceland, but they also 'arrive' (with the added sense of gaining a prestigious position, or status) in the medieval Christian world.[8] I contend that Ari creates an extensive literary cartography, a verbal map centred on Iceland, which allows the Icelanders to understand themselves as arriving in and inhabiting a unique place *in the world*.

When I write of Ari's 'literary cartography' of Iceland, my thinking is informed by medieval maps, the *mappae mundi*, and their logics. The goal of medieval mapmakers 'was as much historical as geographical', and the 'resulting documents blended concepts of both time and space as a context for under-

---

[7] While the writing of the laws is clearly an important moment in terms of social development as a distinct people, as Hastrup discusses, the laws lack explicit reference to the Icelanders as a distinct ethnic group, the population referred to as, variously, 'men', 'tenants', 'heirs', 'adulterers', or (in contrast to foreigners), 'men of this country', and 'as far as the inhabitants of Iceland were concerned, they had not yet appeared as a people when the laws were written down (in 1117–18), if, by a "people" we understand a group created through naming'; Hastrup, *Island of Anthropology*, p. 76.

[8] On Ari's development of a uniquely Icelandic Christian narrative, see Mundal, '*Íslendingabók*: The Creation of an Icelandic Identity'.

standing the Christian life'.[9] We see this clearly on many *mappae mundi* in which expulsion from the Garden of Eden, the fall of the Tower of Babel, the Crucifixion, and the Last Judgement are all concurrently depicted on the map's visual plane. *Mappae mundi* use geography to simultaneously represent events from the past, present and future: 'the *mappaemundi* were not snapshots of the world's geography at a given point in time, but a blending of history and geography, a projection of historical events on a geographical framework'.[10] My intention is not to suggest that Ari was envisioning a medieval world map when constructing his own literary geography in *Íslendingabók*, but rather, that his understanding of the power of layering places with narratives from various times was in line with other medieval thinkers as they represented these issues and Judeo-Christian identities in both maps and verbal geographies.[11]

How, then, does Ari map Iceland in *Íslendingabók*? Like the *mappae mundi* which typically place the site of their greatest interest in the centre of the map (usually Jerusalem), in Ari's verbal mapping Iceland ultimately occupies the focal position. Ari opens by recording that 'Ísland byggðisk first ýr Norvegi' (Iceland was first settled from Norway).[12] While Norway is clearly important in Ari's version of the settlement, a shift in the following sentences very quickly privileges Iceland as occupying the narrative centre of this verbal map: the Norwegian Ingólfr 'es sagt at fœri fyrst þaðan til Íslands' (is said to have travelled from there [Norway] to Iceland), while a great many people moved 'út hingat ýr Norvegi' (out here [Iceland] from Norway).[13] For Icelandic writers *út* (out) denoted movement from a centre to a periphery (as from Norway to Iceland), and *útan* charted travel from the periphery back to centre (from Iceland to Norway, or alternately, from Greenland to Iceland); the directional *vest* and *vestan* have parallel meanings.[14] Despite this geographic concept of Iceland being peripheral to Norway, Ari nonetheless uses other means to convince us that Iceland can be conceptualized as ideologically central. Indeed,

---

[9] Woodward, 'Reality, Symbolism, Time, and Space', p. 511.

[10] Woodward, 'Reality, Symbolism, Time, and Space', p. 514.

[11] The lack of medieval Icelandic world-maps is, however, suggestive of the idea that the work of mapping took place in verbal, rather than visual, media.

[12] *Íslendingabók*, in *Íslendingabók; Landnámabók* ed. by Jakob Benediktsson, pt 1, p. 4 (henceforth *Íslendingabók*).

[13] *Íslendingabók*, pp. 4, 5.

[14] For discussion of this, and several examples, see Mundal, '*Framveksten* av den islandske identiten, dei norske rettene og forholdet til Noreg', pp. 7–29.

Iceland's very geographic peripherality in the North Atlantic allows it a role as a 'purer' place where new beginnings are possible in contrast to the inherited conflicts and violent histories characterizing more trafficked, geographically central lands. Throughout the text, Iceland occupies the valorized conceptual position of 'here' while Norway is somewhere else, over 'there'. After introducing Norway into the picture, Ari informs us that because so many are keen to move to Iceland, Norway's King Haraldr forbade their migration from Norway 'af því at hónum þótti landauðn nema' (because he thought it would lead to depopulation of the land).[15] Ultimately, would-be Icelanders are permitted to travel to Iceland and settle if they pay the Norwegian king for the privilege, and we gain a clear sense that while Norway is on the map, that map has been recentred so that its focus, and the most desirable location of this verbal world, is Iceland itself.

The geographic centrality of Iceland is later reinforced by the description of the discovery and settlement, from Iceland, of Greenland and Vínland. Iceland maintains its superiority, and these lands, like Norway, come off as less desirable and slightly denigrated by Ari. While settlers will pay for the opportunity to come to Iceland, according to Ari, Greenland required a more strategic plan to entice settlers. Eiríkr rauði 'gaf nafn landinu ok kallaði Grœnland ok kvað menn þat myndu fýsa þangat farar, at landit ætti nafn gótt' (gave a name to the country and called it Greenland, and said that it would encourage people to go there that the country had a good name).[16] In its attention to the persuasive power of words, Ari's rhetorical framing distinguishes it from Adam of Bremen's more straightforward account that Greenland was so named because of the green colour of the sea.[17] Ari's description of the place-naming episode focuses on Eiríkr's need to 'brand' and advertise Greenland in a conscientiously constructed way in order to woo settlers to it. Ari suppresses signs of his own propagandizing in *Íslendingabók*, but his explicit identification of it in Eiríkr's situations might give us insight into Ari's conceptualization of his own project as a way of producing Icelandic-ness for successful marketing and consumption. Through Ari, we see how the 'medieval Icelandic intelligentsia' deftly harnesses the power of words to create winning identity products that have sold very well.

---

[15] English translation from *Íslendingabók; Kristni saga: The Book of Icelanders; The Story of the Conversion*, trans. by Grønlie (henceforth *Book of Icelanders*), p. 4; *Íslendingabók*, p. 5.

[16] *Íslendingabók*, p. 13. *Book of Icelanders*, p. 7.

[17] Adam of Bremen, *History of the Archbishops of Hamburg-Bremen*, trans. by Tschan, iv.397, p. 218.

Returning to the role of geographic centrality, marking the locations of Greenland and Vínland does the work of removing Iceland from the periphery and the unknown north-western extremes of the world. The juxtaposition is not only geographical, though, but has in-built cultural and religious overtones, and we glimpse the significance of the place-worlds created by these accounts. When the first settlers arrive, the land of Iceland has already been sanctified or 'baptized' as a Christian space by earlier visiting Christians.[18] While they have all departed with the arrival of the pagan Norsemen, in Ari's Iceland these early Christian anchorites, the Irish *papar*, bestow upon the Icelandic land-scape their sacred Christian objects, perhaps best described as 'relics', when they 'létu eptir bœkr írskar ok bjǫllur ok bagla' (left behind Irish books and bells and staffs),[19] this catchy alliterative triad perhaps best rendered in English as 'Irish books, bells and bachalls'. The archaeological record does not evidence the presence of this formulaic collection of Irish objects with much certainty, although two Icelandic graves have yielded some bronze bells that are similar to Irish ones, but which are likely produced by Norse craftsmen. Furthermore, several sceptical scholars 'have felt it unlikely that the monks would have left behind their sacred objects and suspect they may instead have been robbed, killed or enslaved'.[20] The lack of material evidence for these early Irish church-men is intriguing precisely because it allows us to consider how Ari uses words and descriptions of material objects in specific physical locations to conjure or imagine a positive Christian past for Iceland that may have had little to do with any kind of historic reality. Indeed, perhaps the formulaic aspect of this allit-erating triad ought to alert us to the fictionality of the Irish books, bells and bachalls. The version of Iceland's past created in words becomes, however, far more persuasive, important, and real than what might actually have happened in the real geographic space of Iceland, and Ari persuades us that Iceland was first visited by Christian monks. This is in stark contrast to what he tells us of Greenland and Vínland, which are far more peripheral, geographically and culturally. He records that Greenland also had evidence of human habitation (remains of skin boats and stone tools), leading to the conclusion that it had

---

[18] See Mundal, '*Íslendingabók* vurdert som bispestolskrønike', p. 71, and Hermann, '*Ís-lendingabók* and History' p. 25.

[19] *Book of Icelanders*, p. 4; *Íslendingabók*, p. 5.

[20] *Book of Icelanders*, p. 17, n. 19. On the bells, see Kristján Eldjárn, *Kuml og haugfé úr heiðnum sið á Íslandi*, pp. 330–32; and on the historical unlikelihood of their abandonment of sacred objects, see Hermann Pálsson, *Keltar á Íslandi*, p. 37.

been settled by the same people who settled Vínland, whom 'Grœnlendingar kalla Skrælinga' (the Greenlanders call *Skrælingar*).[21] As Lindow argues, with these references

> Iceland is situated inside a Christian area, surrounding which, to the north, east, and now west, there are pagans. There is also an obvious myth of cultural superiority here, and the mention of Vínland, where relations with the *Skrælingar* were decidedly hostile, indicates a feeble end point of the migratory track and moves Iceland even closer to the Norwegian center and away from the wild pagan periphery.[22]

Ari maps out a literary geography that develops Iceland as a proto-Christian space, ripe for the Conversion he later tells us of, which is centred and central in his verbal map along both geographical and religious coordinates.

Like the *mappae mundi* that are dotted with images of important places (Garden of Eden, Tower of Babel) and moments (Parting of the Red Sea, Resurrection), *Íslendingabók* also focuses on familiar, sacred places and local geographies. We see the enterprise of mapping Iceland's interior enacted within the text itself, and Ari creates compelling place-worlds which allow us to participate in foundational Icelandic events. For instance, when settlement was largely accomplished, and a law system had been introduced by the Easterner Úlfljótr, the task of charting the full dimensions and attributes of the new land is attended to.

> En svá es sagt, at Grímr geitskǫr væri fóstbróðir hans, sá es kannaði Ísland allt at ráði hans, áðr alþingi væri átt. En hónum fekk hverr maðr penning til á landi hér, en hann gaf fé þat síðan til hofa.

> (And it is said that his foster-brother was Grímr geitskor, who explored the whole of Iceland on Úlfljótr's recommendation before the Althing was held. And everyone in the country gave him a penny for that, and he later gave the money to the temples.)[23]

Other scholars have noted that it is no accident that the act of establishing the law is virtually simultaneous with gaining knowledge of the land, both important moments in the birth of a society.[24] What we see here is expression of the

---

[21] *Book of Icelanders*, p. 7; *Íslendingabók*, p. 14.

[22] Lindow, '*Íslendingabók* and Myth', p. 460.

[23] *Book of Icelanders*, pp. 4–5; *Íslendingabók*, p. 7.

[24] As Lindow writes of this scene, it creates 'together with the information about the primal settlers of the four quarters a chiastic structure in which spatial knowledge bookends the

belief that it is essential to know one's own land, where one is located, before a national identity can be constituted. Most interesting is how identifying the contours and specifics marking 'place' out of undifferentiated 'space' are presented as a community act. While exploration of the full territory of Iceland is undertaken by one individual, it is quickly transformed into a group practice. In a pagan prefiguration of the Christian tithing that Bishop Gizurr is praised for later in *Íslendingabók*, 'everyone in the country' places a high value on this land-mapping knowledge and pays Grímr for it. That money is then donated to the temples, which potentially figures this as a ritual of gratitude to local deities for jurisdiction over the land while also looking forward to the Christian practices of paying church tithes. The participants in this episode become, through shared investment in mapping the country, a unified community that has a distinct and newly articulated geography to orient themselves within and identify as 'Iceland', their shared home. As in the *mappae mundi*, historical and reimagined events and people are fused to extant and still-visited physical sites (the Alþing in particular). Furthermore, through Ari's textual creation of accessible Icelandic place-worlds in *Íslendingabók*, audiences from various times and places can also participate by watching and hearing events unfold. Ari's text thus allows the audience and readership to be transformed by those national moments.

The way that the Alþing is described gives us another parallel with medieval maps, and how they exaggerate 'the spread of time within their borders' and 'consist of historical aggregations or cumulative inventories of events that occur in space'.[25] In another statement of collective agreement, we read that 'Alþingi vas sett at ráði Ulfljóts ok allra landsmanna þar es nú es' (the Althing was established where it is now by the decision of Úlfljótr and *everyone in the country*).[26] The site, however, has a more violent past. Rare for Ari, this is recorded in an extended etymology of a place-name, in this case associated with acts of murder, outlawry, and fratricide, with a slain slave giving his name to the site: 'Við hann es kennd gjá sú es þar es kǫlluð síðan Kolgsjá, sem hræin fundusk' (The gorge that has since been called Kolgsjá, where the remains were found, is named after him).[27] This land is declared public property for common use, and henceforth is

legal knowledge with which it must be joined to create a society'; Lindow, '*Íslendingabók* and Myth', p. 457. See also Hastrup, *Island of Anthropology*, pp. 72, 80–81.

[25] Woodward, 'Reality, Symbolism, Time, and Space', p. 519.

[26] *Book of Icelanders*, p. 5; *Íslendingabók*, p. 8.

[27] *Book of Icelanders*, p. 5; *Íslendingabók*, p. 8.

used 'at viða til alþingis í skógum ok á heiðum hagi til hrossahafnar' (to provide the Althing with wood from the forests and pasture for grazing horses on the heaths).[28] Ari introduces the Alþing environs as an original site of strife, feud, and lawlessness which is finally, through law and group consensus, made into Iceland's most important locus of order and concord, Ari's many later references to events that occur at the Alþing's Law Rock continuing to develop these themes. The Alþing and Law Rock are, of course, real, familiar places physically experienced by numerous Icelanders on their annual pilgrimage to meet other countrymen. However, through Ari's verbal treatment, it is an altered, 'transformed setting' built up in memory with numerous foundational events, which irrevocably alters the way in which all Icelanders move through and behave in what becomes a multi-layered, politically sacred, or mythic place. While oral communications and storytelling about happenings at past gatherings must also prompt these imaginative 'remodellings' of the Alþing site, Ari provides a formalized, lasting literary structure through which this can be consistently enacted time and again. His words comprise new Icelandic geographies, situated between imagined and real places, for the audience to inhabit.

Íslendingabók does not only focus on local, Icelandic territory, however. Though he accomplishes it quietly, Ari also anchors Iceland within the cosmos in his literary cartography, giving it a knowledgeably determined position within the scheme of the universe. This is achieved very subtly, without a map or explicit references to the act of charting, but in a way that highlights the genius of some wise Icelanders and the measured approval of an intellectually engaged Icelandic populace. After Iceland has been fully settled (*c.* 930) and the Alþing has been established, which 'effectively transformed the community of settlers into a society',[29] Ari's pen turns to giving Iceland a geographic place that exists in harmony with the seasons and celestial bodies. The Icelanders are close readers of their environment and the heavens, and Ari tells us that, considering the year to have 364 days, they are troubled when the course of the sun seems to be out of sync with the seasons.[30] When Þorsteinn surtr from Breiðafjorðr proposes at the Alþing's Law Rock that a week be added to the summer every seventh year, 'þá vǫknuðu allir menn við þat vel, ok vas þá þat þegar í lǫg leitt' (everyone then welcomed the proposal warmly, and it was immediately made law').[31]

---

[28] *Book of Icelanders*, p. 5; *Íslendingabók*, p. 9.

[29] Hastrup, *Island of Anthropology*, p. 72.

[30] *Íslendingabók*, p. 5.

[31] *Book of Icelanders*, p. 6; *Íslendingabók*, pp. 10–11.

As Westphal argues, geography is 'a *discourse* of space; through its thought and speech, it creates or invents spaces by describing and differentiating them. It is a mode of understanding the human cosmos, of appropriating the world through language'.[32] This scene shows the Icelanders appropriating their place in the world in a collective, national act — it is embraced at the Law Rock at the Alþing. By describing this new method of time-reckoning that looks to the sun and the scientific logic underlying seasonal change, the text moves the audience's focus out from Iceland specifically and into the universe. What we might refer to here as Ari's 'discourse of space' claims and validates a much larger and more certain place for the Icelanders within the cosmos.

Notably, this scene is introduced through a dream, the performance framed and validated through prophetic vision and discourse. Þorsteinn surtr had dreamt that he was at the Law Rock, and when he was awake, the crowds slept; yet as he slept, they awoke. Another wise man, Ósvífr Helgason, interprets the dream as prophesying 'at allir men myndi þǫgn varða, meðan hann mælti at lǫgbergi, en síðan es hann þagnaði, at þá myndi alllir þat róma es hann hefði mælt' (that everyone would remain silent while he spoke at the Law Rock, but that when he fell silent, everyone would applaud what he had said).[33] This important national moment of adopting a new calendar is preceded by prophetic speech, which frames the exchange as powerful and perhaps divinely ordained.[34] Speech, as elsewhere, is critical to positive geographic mapping and comprehension. Furthermore, it is through Ari's own writing that later audiences and readerships can nonetheless imaginatively witness and participate in this event at which Iceland is mapped into the world and located within the cosmos: though they may be geographically and temporally removed from the place and time Ari depicts, his words nonetheless allow us to recreate the sounds of Þorsteinn's and Ósvífr's wise voices and the images of these historical moments at the Law Rock.

Finally, Ari's literary geography begins to resemble the *mappae mundi* even further as he moves into the Christian period and fixes Iceland in a constellation with other important medieval Christian places. When, for instance, the

---

[32] Westphal, *La géocritique mode d'emploi*, p. x. Quote cited and translated in Tally, *Literary Cartography*, p. 10.

[33] *Book of Icelanders*, pp. 5–6; *Íslendingabók*, p. 10.

[34] Lindow points out that this 'performance at the Alþingi is in part the result of a dream suggests a connection with knowledge that is not wholly of this world', which leads him to convincingly argue that there are situational parallels here with *Vǫluspá* (Lindow, '*Íslendingabók* and Myth', p. 458).

revered Bishop Gizurr dies, his death is synchronized with those of other significant Christians in holy places:

> Á því ári enu sama obiit Paschalis secundus páfi fyrr en Gizurr byskup ok Baldvini Jórsalakonungr ok Arnaldus patriarchia í Híerúsalem ok Philippus Svíakonungr, en síðarr et sama sumar Alexíus Grikkjakonungr

> (In the same year, Pope Paschal II died before Bishop Gizurr, as did Baldwin king of Jerusalem and Arnulf patriarch in Jerusalem, and Philip king of the Swedes [who died on pilgrimage abroad] and, later the same summer, Alexius king of the Greeks)[35]

Linking Bishop Gizurr's passing to the deaths of other international Christian leaders in Jerusalem and Greece extends the Icelandic 'map' out into the Christian world. Iceland is legitimated as a Christian nation, and its role as a blessed Christian place is reinforced further in the genealogy encompassing all of Iceland's history that closes the text. In the penultimate chapter of *Íslendingabók* we learn that each of the four quarters of Iceland (south, east, west, and north) yields a bishop, thus giving an organic church structure that grows from the very land of Iceland itself. As in medieval maps, religious order and concerns are depicted in geographic, mappable phenomena. Ari's *Íslendingabók* like the *mappae mundi* ultimately comprises an accessible geographic interface which 'blended concepts of both time and space as a context for understanding the Christian life'.[36] Ari uses geographic writing and place-making to layer important historical moments into the Iceland he creates in his *Íslendingabók*. While the title leads us to remember ancestral Icelanders, and their key speeches and acts, Icelandic place is one of the most important characters in Ari's origin story.

Landnámabók

Landnámabók, as its name suggests, describes the settlement of discrete parcels of land at specific points within Iceland, yet *Landnámabók*'s framing also attests to its national and international outlook. Here I will explore how *Landnámabók*, despite its localizing concerns, also promotes a national and international identity, and, through words, written and spoken, textual and prophetic, the productive settlement of Iceland is prefigured and performed. In

---

[35] *Book of Icelanders*, p. 13; *Íslendingabók*, p. 25.

[36] Woodward, 'Reality, Symbolism, Time, and Space', p. 511.

Landnámabók's settlement accounts, time and again words precede travel and action, with prophetic and proleptic utterances driving Icelandic movement to and settlement of this new landscape. Many of the examples in *Landnámabók* furthermore show how an agentive land invites and 'plants' these settlers in Iceland, the country depicted not so much as a space to be conquered but a powerful character who will only be successfully wooed by suitable settlers. Moving to the level of the effect of words, and the creation of 'in-between' geographies, *Landnámabók* overlays stories onto real landscapes, so that the physical Icelandic landscape fuses with territories of the imagination.

Landnámabók's opening continues the tradition established by *Íslendingabók* of mapping out Iceland on a larger, universally oriented scale. It suggests an Icelandic investment in the idea that 'Knowledge of place is therefore closely linked to knowledge of the self, to grasping one's position in the larger scheme of things.'[37] *Landnámabók* mediates between global and local views of an Icelander's place in the world, and the Christian North Atlantic in particular, and encodes important and oft-repeated lessons regarding Icelandic identity. Intriguingly, this account of what it is to be an Icelander and live in Icelandic space begins in Britain, with our first access to Iceland mediated through the written words of the Venerable Bede:

> Í aldarfarsbók þeiri, er Beda prestr heilagr gerði, er getit eylands þess, er Thile heitir ok á bókum er sagt, at liggi sex dœgra sigling í norðr frá Bretlandi
>
> (In this book *On Times* the Venerable Priest Bede mentions an island called *Thule*, said in other books to lie six days' sailing to the north of Britain)[38]

This verbal map gives us a view of Britain and the island of Thule, which, we are told, *vitrir menn* (learned men) identify as Iceland. *Landnámabók* then returns to Bede and the movements of the early medieval saints, scholars, and sailors of Britain and Ireland:

> En Beda prestr andaðisk sjau hundruð þrjátigi og fimm árum eptir holdgan dróttins várs, at því er ritat er, ok meir en hundraði ára fyrr en Ísland byggðisk af Norðmǫnnum. En áðr Ísland byggðisk af Nóregi, váru þar þeir menn, er Norðmenn kalla papa; þeir váru menn kristnir, ok hyggja menn, at þeir hafi verit vestan um haf,

---

[37] Basso, *Wisdom Sits in Places*, p. 34.

[38] *Landnámabók*, p. 31; *Book of Settlements*, p. 16. It should be noted that the edition cited here is based on Sturlubók, a thirteenth-century revised version of an earlier *Landnámabók*. See the detailed discussion of *Landnámabók* manuscripts below in the section entitled 'Introducing *Landnámabók*' in Ranković, 'Traversing the Space of the Oral-Written Continuum'.

því at fundusk eptir þeim bœkur írskar, bjǫllur ok baglar ok enn fleiri hlutir, þeir er þat mátti skilja, at þeir váru Vestmenn. Enn er ok þess getit á bókum enskum, at í þann tíma var farit milli landanna.

(According to written sources, Bede the priest died 735 years after the Incarnation of our Lord, and more than 120 years before Iceland was settled by the Norwegians. But before Iceland was settled from Norway there were other people there, called *Papar* by the Norwegians. They were Christians and were thought to have come overseas from the west, because people found Irish books, bells, croziers, and lots of other things, so it was clear they must have been Irish [*Vestmenn*]. Besides, English sources tell us that sailings were made between these countries at that time.)[39]

We do not get an independent date for Iceland's settlement: rather, the temporal scheme for settlement of Iceland centres on Bede, who is in turn dated by reference to Christ's birth. There is mention of the Norwegians, with the statement that Iceland was *byggðisk af Nóregi* (settled from Norway), but even here, the narrative shifts right back to the early Christian figures that had travelled *vestan um haf* (west over the sea), these *Vestmenn* (literally 'Westmen') carrying, as in *Íslendingabók,* their alliterative triad of 'bœkur írskar, bjǫllur ok baglar' (Irish books, bells, and bachalls). Norwegians and Norway are mentioned, but in these critical opening pages, it is Britain, Bede, and the Vestmenn with their Christian Irish relics that capture the imagination. Temporally, geographically, and authoritatively our encounter with Iceland in these framing pages is mediated through the renowned English monastic scholar, Bede, with the closing words pinpointing that 'bókum enskum' (English books) tell us there 'var farit milli landanna' (was ongoing movement between these lands). Appeal is made to the accounts written by the English, rather than the oral histories of settlers from Norway, to frame and give authority to the settlement.

We first glimpse Iceland through the words of an English scholar (and not an eyewitness, for Bede never travelled far from Wearmouth-Jarrow) who died in 735, almost 150 years before Icelandic settlement began in 870, and Iceland is thus first conjured largely through foreign eyes. Learned writing about Thule (Bede's own but also more anonymously that which 'á bókum er sagt' (is said in books)) is furthermore privileged in *Landnámabók* over oral histories from early travellers. These collectively accomplish the task of giving venerably learned, Christian authorization to Iceland and, I think, removing it from Norway's ambit. Iceland is linked to Britain and British people and situated in a larger Christian nexus, which has important implications for distancing this

[39] *Landnámabók*, pp. 31–32; *Book of Settlements*, p. 16.

land, nation, and identity, from Norway and the Norwegian king, under whose tyranny, several stories tell us, Icelanders refused to live. By beginning with Bede's statements and his death 'more than 120 years before Iceland was settled by Norwegians',[40] Bede is given pre-eminence in the account, as are the Irish *papar*. This opening maps Iceland in a very different way, as an island nation situated in a North Atlantic Christian network.

The next section continues to fix Iceland within a largely international constellation, much like the conclusion of *Íslendingabók*. Iceland's settlement is synchronized with the rule of contemporary leaders: the list begins with figures at the centre of Christendom, Pope Adrian, followed by Pope John the Fifth in Rome, Germany's emperor Louis, and ruling *yfir Miklagarði* (over Byzantium) are Leo and his son Alexander. We next encounter a list of Scandinavian rulers, including Haraldr hárfagri of Norway, Eiríkr Eymundarson and his son Bjǫrn of Sweden, and Gormr of Denmark. The text then transports us from Scandinavia and establishes wider horizons for Iceland, by then shifting to the British Isles, and citing King Alfred and his son Edward in England, Kjarvalr (Irish Cerball) of Dublin, and Sigurðr the Mighty, earl of Orkney.[41] As in *Íslendingabók*, the network of characters expands beyond Iceland and Scandinavia, to place Iceland in an international position and extensive Christian network as well.

The following geographic details continue to reinforce ideas of international spatial movement:

> Svá segja vitrir menn, at ór Nóregi frá Staði sé sjau dœgra sigling í vestr til Horns á Íslandi austanverðu, en frá Snæfellsnesi, þar er skemmst er, er fjǫgurra dœgra haf í vestr til Grœnlands. En svá er sagt, ef siglt er ór Bjǫrgyn rétt í vestr til Hvarfsins á Grœnlandi, at þá mun siglt vera tylft fyrir sunnan Ísland. Frá Reykjanesi á sunnanverðu Íslandi er fimm dœgra haf til Jǫlduhlaups á Írlandi (í suðr; en frá Langanesi á norðanverðu Íslandi er) fjǫgurra dœgra haf norðr til Svalbarða í hafsbotn.
>
> (According to learned men it takes seven days to sail from Stad in Norway westwards to Horn on the east coast of Iceland, and from Snæfellsness four days west across the ocean to Greenland by the shortest route. People say if you can sail from Bergen due west to Cape Farewell in Greenland, you pass twelve leagues south of Iceland. From Reykjaness in South Iceland it takes five days to Slyne Head in Ireland, four days from Langaness in North Iceland northwards to Spitzbergen in the Arctic sea.)[42]

---

[40] *Book of Settlements*, p. 15.

[41] *Landnámabók*, p. 32.

[42] *Landnámabók*, pp. 32–34; *Book of Settlements*, p. 16.

Repeating earlier phrasing regarding the *vitrir menn* who identify Thule with Iceland, this litany of routes and travel times to Iceland also privileges what 'Svo segja vitrir menn' (wise or learned men say) rather than sailors' practical knowledge (though the two are not of course incompatible).[43] Norway is mapped first in terms of how long it takes (seven days) to sail from Norway to Iceland. The text then curiously mentions that one sails close to Iceland — within twelve leagues or 65 kilometres — but does not actually intersect with Iceland when voyaging from Bergen to Greenland's Cape Farewell: Iceland is significantly not depicted as a stopping point that connects Norway and Greenland.[44] The distances between Iceland and other countries are given, and according to the text's mapping, Norway is depicted as farthest away; surprisingly, Iceland is spatially closer to Ireland, a link that is continually strengthened through *Landnámabók*'s repeated references to settlers, names, and narrative motifs from Ireland (along with Britain and the Scottish Isles).

It was well known that the Irish monks were voyagers, journeying first to the Scottish Isles and establishing monasteries in places like Iona, but also travelling on to locations suitable for anchoritic visits, with the settlement myths recording Iceland as one such site. Like the Irish books, bells, and bachalls which narratively serve to consecrate the pre-Settlement landscape of Iceland, holy travellers and early explorers of North Atlantic islands were evoked as precedents for Icelandic settlement in the origin legends of the Icelanders. As we know from the prefaces to historic accounts such as that cited at the essay's opening, early authors were anxious to dissociate themselves from slaves, scoundrels, and those far more destructive seafarers, the Vikings. By starting with 'Beda prestr heilagr' (the holy priest Bede), and the monastic voyagers that plant their Christian relics in Icelandic soil thus foreshadowing that Christianity will later grow there, the author of *Landnámabók* maps Iceland's story of its origins back to Britain through textual ties to its holy scholars and narrative ties to its seafaring saintly anchorites. Norwegians are mentioned, of course — in the opening line, we have clear reference to this — but priority is given to the relationship between Britain and Iceland, and for good reason.

Linking Iceland's settlement narratives to early Christian North Atlantic figures and more universal Judeo-Christian origins also occurs elsewhere in

---

[43] *Segja* does however, connote a speech act, though can also be used of written sources, and was quite flexibly used to invoke authority throughout the sources, as Slavica Ranković discusses in this volume.

[44] Despite the historic likelihood of ships halting in Iceland, our mental map has the Norwegian ships stay out of Icelandic territory — it remains absent as a stop on this trajectory.

Landnámabók, and settlement, even by pagan figures, parallels biblical models. For instance, Floki's journey evokes that of Noah, the great biblical voyager also seeking a new promised land:[45]

> Flóki hafði hrafna þrjá með sér í haf, ok er hann lét lausan enn fyrsta, fló sá aptr um stafn; annarr fló í loft upp ok aptr til skips; enn þriði fló fram um stafn í þá átt, sem þeir fundu landit. Þeir kómu austan at Horni ok sigldu fyrir sunnan landit.

> (Floki took three ravens with him on the voyage. When he set the first one free it flew back from the stern, but the second raven flew straight up into the air, and then back down to the ship, while the third flew straight ahead from the prow, and it was in that direction that they found land.)[46]

Textual exemplars, in this case a biblical narrative, were employed to lend authority to the Icelandic settlement and project its value and venerability to a medieval Judeo-Christian audience who had already internalized the story of Noah's settlement in the new promised land.

Wise words and Christian prophecy frame the account of Ørlygr Hrappsson, fostered by a holy bishop Patrick of the Hebrides. This extensive, detailed scene records that Ørlygr

> fýstisk at fara til Íslands ok bað, at byskup sæi um með honum. Byskup lét hann hafa með sér kirkjuvið ok járnklukku ok plenárium ok mold vígða, er hann skyldi leggja undir hornstafina. Byskup bað hann þar land nema, er hann sæi fjǫll tvau af hafi, ok byggja undir enu syðra fjallinu, ok skyldi dalr í hvárutveggja fjallinu; hann skyldi þar taka sér bústað ok láta þar kirkju gera ok eigna enum helga Kolumba [...]. Þeir Ørlygr létu í haf ok fengu útivist harða ok vissu eigi, hvar þeir fóru; þá hét Ørlygr á Patrek byskup til landtǫku sér, at hann skyldi af hans nafni gefa ørnefni, þar sem hann tœki land. Þeir váru þaðan frá litla hríð úti, áðr þeir sá land, ok váru komnir vestr um landit. Þeir tóku þar, sem heitir Ørlygshǫfn, en fjǫrðinn inn frá kǫlluðu þeir Patreksfjǫrð [...]. Ørlygr sigldi vestan fyrir Barð; en er hann kom suðr um Snæfellsjǫkul á fjǫrðinn, sá hann fjǫll tvau ok dali í hvárutveggja. Þar kenndi hann land þat, er honum var til vísat [...] bjó að Esjubergi. Hann lét þar gera kirkju, sem mælt var [...]. Þeir Ørlygr frændr trúðu á Kolumba.

---

[45] See discussions of Iceland as a promised land modelled on Old Testament accounts, in Clunies Ross, 'Textual Territory'; Grønlie, 'Introduction', p. xxi; Lindow, '*Íslendingabók* and Myth', p. 456; Mundal, '*Íslendingabók* vurdert som bispestolskrønike', p. 71; Sverrir Tómasson, *Formálar íslenskra sagnaritara á miðöldum*, pp. 282–83.

[46] *Landnámabók*, p. 36; *Book of Settlements*, p. 17.

(had a great desire to go to Iceland, and asked the bishop [Patrick] for guidance. The bishop provided him with church timber, an iron bell, a plenarium, and consecrated earth which Orlyg was to place beneath the corner posts of his church. The bishop told him to settle at a place where from the sea he could keep two mountains in view, each with its valley. He was to make his home below the southern mountain where he was to build a house and a church dedicated to Saint Columba [...]. Orlyg and his men put to sea, and had such a rough passage they'd no idea where they were. Then Orlyg made a solemn vow to Bishop Patrick that if they made land he'd name the place after him. Shortly afterwards, they sighted land, having drifted west to Iceland. They came ashore at a place now called Orlygshaven, but the fjord that cut into the land from there they called Patreksfjord [...]. Orlyg journeyed east round Bard, and once he'd gone beyond Snæfellsness Glacier and sailed into the bay he could see two mountains, each of them with a valley cutting into it. Then he knew this was the place he'd been guided to, so he made for the southern mountain [...] [he made] his home at Esjuberg where he built a church as he had promised [...]. Orlyg and his kinsmen put their faith in St Columba.)[47]

A Christian saint's visionary address provides the directions for land-taking as do the pagan high-seat pillars in other settlement episodes. However, Patrick's verbal description that maps a specific site in Iceland also shows that the holy bishops of the British Isles know Iceland's landscape and can furthermore even create or 'perform' Iceland's geographic contours with their prophetic words. Bishop Patrick's words predetermine where settlement is to take place, and the tableau of the land promised to Ørlygr is painted out in such verbal detail before he sets sail that when the spot is encountered, 'Þar kenndi hann land þat' (there he recognized that place). Patrick is the named figure who intervenes here, yet the extant sources do not provide details of a bishop Patrick in Scotland. As suggested by Craigie long ago, it may be that Saint Patrick was Ørlygr's patron saint and the account was slightly confused.[48] In that case, it is interesting that the figure invoked, Patrick, was well known as a Briton who also sailed from western Britain, initially under duress, to a new land where his main work was evangelism and the spreading of Christianity among a pagan people: this is a narrative which would have been meaningful for the Christian settlers of Iceland. The mention of *helga Kolumba* (holy Columba) in the same account reminds us of the well-known legends of Saint Columba's voyaging follower, Cormac, as recorded in Adomnán's *Vita*

---

[47] *Landnámabók*, pp. 52, 54; *Book of Settlements*, pp. 23–24.

[48] Craigie, 'The Gaels in Iceland', p. 251.

Columbae.[49] The outcomes of Cormac's own fraught journeys by boat, one of which was fourteen days sailing north of Scotland into the unknown northern-most waters, were prophesied by Columba, and Cormac's crew were saved from disaster when Columba's prayers from Iona quelled the storms and allowed safe landing. Cormac's dangerous, but ultimately blessed, voyage into north-ernmost waters from the Hebrides under an Irish saint's protection provides some interesting parallels for the Ørlygr episode in *Landnámabók*, and it is plausible that such accounts, circulating in texts as well as in verbally trans-mitted stories, might have influenced Icelandic-authored representations of Iceland's Christian settlers. The legendary early Irish *peregrini* or *papar*, who gave their name to various topographic sites in Iceland, thus might also have informed depictions of Christian figures like Ørlygr who migrated from Norse colonies in the Scottish Isles. The Ørlygr account demonstrates how words, spoken prophecy as well as potential hagiographic exemplars, are used to pre-ordain and structure accounts of Icelandic settlement and church building within what becomes the 'promised land' of Iceland.

Though I have focused on Hebridean and Christian examples here, we find several prophecy-driven accounts of settlement in *Landnámabók*, which also feature detailed anticipatory accounts of the land to be settled. In one case a merman provides a prophecy regarding inheritance of land,[50] and Ingimund, a Norwegian who had raided in the British Isles with a Hebridean partner, is twice foretold (by a seeress, and two Sami) of his move to a yet-undiscov-ered country in the west, the land he is to settle described in great detail so that when he arrives, 'þar kenndi Ingimundr lǫnd þau, er honum var til vísat' (there Ingimund recognized the land he'd been guided to).[51] That Icelandic spaces of settlement are proleptically conjured and virtually explored in ver-balized form suggests to us the importance and complexity of words, and specifically prophetic words, in settlement narratives and geospatial writing. The *Landnámabók* composers are invested in the idea that while settlement is physical and spatial, it is also verbal and conditioned by narrative, a geography simultaneously real and imagined.

---

[49] Adomnán, *Vita sancti Columbae*, ed. and trans. by Anderson and Anderson, II.42, pp. 440–47.

[50] *Landnámabók* features other accounts of prophecy dictating settlement and land tak-ing, as in the case of the merman who foretells where Thorir will take land. See *Book of Settle-ments*, pp. 37–38.

[51] *Landnámabók*, p. 218; *Book of Settlements*, pp. 83–84.

Landnámabók also showcases scenes in which an agentive land actively welcomes certain newcomers over others: this highlights some important components in the later Icelandic intelligentsia's conceptions of what an idealized Icelandic settler looked like. The land responds with particular enthusiasm to Christians in some cases, which gives the landscape a role in embracing members of the new faith, and laying the ground for a productive nationwide conversion to Christianity. In one scene with important implications for creating settlement space, the land reshapes itself to change boundaries. When Bjarni, son of Sturla the priest and grandson of a Hebridean called Kalman (Irish Colmán), thus providing another link with Britain and Ireland, promises to convert to Christianity, the Hvítá river alters its course to carve out a new channel, visible *nú* (now, today), so that Bjarni gains possession of disputed lands.[52] Early in the text we read of a figure called Ásólfr that 'Hann var kristinn vel ok vildi ekki eiga við heiðna menn ok eigi vildi hann þiggja mat at þeim' (He was a devout Christian and would have nothing to do with the heathen. He wouldn't even accept food from them).[53] This anchoritic personality receives support from the land, however, and

> En er menn gengu til lœkjar þess, er fell hjá skálanum, var hann fullr af fiskum, svá at slík undr þóttusk menn eigi sét hafa. En er heraðsmenn urðu þessa varir, ráku þeir hann á brutt ok vildu eigi, at hann nyti gœða þessa.

> (when they [the people of the area] came to the stream which flowed past the house it seemed to be teeming with fish, and people were amazed, never having seen anything like it. When the local farmers found out about it they drove Asolf away, not wanting him to reap the benefit of this abundance.)[54]

In response to the heathens' persecution of the hallowed settler Ásólfr, the landscape punishes them with environmental barrenness, and the fish vanish. At Ásólfr's new home the river again fills with fish, leading to another eviction, yet for the third time the land reacts to Ásólfr's presence by yielding a plenitude of food.[55] Paralleled with the Christian *papar* described in *Íslendingabók* who similarly move away from the pagan Northmen 'af því at þeir vildu eigi vesa hér

---

[52] *Landnámabók*, p. 81; *Book of Settlements*, p. 32.

[53] *Landnámabók*, p. 62; *Book of Settlements*, p. 26.

[54] *Landnámabók*, p. 62; *Book of Settlements*, p. 26.

[55] See the excellent discussion of Ásólfr and the Irish hagiographic motif of plentiful fish in Jesch, 'Early Christians in Icelandic History'.

við heiðna menn' (because they did not wish to stay here with heathens),[56] it is no surprise when Ásólfr relocates to a hut built aside on his kinsman's land, where he is fed and allowed to pursue his anchoritic lifestyle. He remains there until his death, a church is built over his grave, his body hallowing the ground, and he becomes famed as an extremely holy man. In this episode, the land both responds generously to the sanctity of a hermit who takes up residence in Iceland, and also punishes inappropriately behaving settlers by emptying its rivers. Finally, the passage concludes by not only providing a history of a Christian's engagement with Iceland, but also by constructing a temporally lay-ered place-world that provides access to all of these events and personages for a contemporary audience as well, by telling us that this is the site where 'stendur þar nú kirkja' (now a church is built), with his different establishments also charted out as eastern Asólfsskála, Miðskála, and western Asólfskála.[57] Ásólfr's progression across a responsive landscape is mapped onto physical space and into a narrative place-world. While *skála* denotes a hut or temporary dwell-ing, the use of language, and place-names specifically, makes Ásólfr's huts permanent features of the remembered, verbalized landscape of Iceland, that 'in-between' geography preserved in text. In the literary construction of these place-names and Icelandic place-worlds, the Icelandic composers include ele-ments of the landscape's embrace of their early Christian forebears and high-light a reciprocal and positive relationship between chosen Icelandic settlers and their promised land.

Finally, *Landnámabók* closes as it opened, by giving an overarching view of Iceland from abroad and re-establishing international networks with Britain. This larger North Atlantic map is not based on distances or first approaches but in terms of the movement of Iceland's Christian settlers from the British Isles to Iceland:

> Svá segja vitrir menn, at nǫkkurir landnámsmenn hafi skírðir verit, þeir er byggt hafa Ísland, flestir þeir, er kómu vestan um haf. Er til þess nefndr Helgi magri ok Ørlygr enn gamli, Helgi bjóla, Jǫrundr kristni, Auðr djúpauðga, Ketill enn fífl-ski og enn fleiri menn, er kómu vestan um haf, ok heldu þeir sumir vel kristni til dauðadags. En þat gekk óvíða í ættir, því at synir þeira sumra reistu hof ok blótuðu, en land var alheiðit nær hundraði vetra. (S399)

> (According to well-informed people some of the settlers of Iceland were baptized, mostly those who came from the British Isles. These are Helgi the Lean, Orlyg the

---

[56] *Íslendingabók*, p. 5; *Book of Icelanders*, p. 4.

[57] *Landnámabók*, p. 63; *Book of Settlements*, p. 26.

Old, Helgi Bjolan, Jorund the Christian, Aud the Deep-Minded, Ketil the Foolish, and a number of others who came from the west. Some of them kept up their faith till they died, but in most families this didn't last, for the sons of some built temples and made sacrifices, and Iceland was completely pagan for about 120 years.)[58]

It is perhaps interesting that the origin narrative does not provide a story of a continuous Christianity in Iceland extending from the *papar* and early Norse Christian settlers, with even a few of their descendants as well as the early-adopters of Christianity we know were present elsewhere in Scandinavia mentioned in order to provide a bridge to the official conversion to Christianity in *c.* 1000. Rather, the language of *Landnámabók* asserts that 'en land var alheiðit nær hundraði vetra' (the land was completely heathen for close to one hundred years). Namely, though the historical picture suggests much openness regarding religious practice, with the likelihood being that several types of religion were practised in one form or another, including Christianity, here the narrative and the words used to frame the origin story suggest that Christianity lapsed. The preference for this story, despite the interest elsewhere in *Landnámabók* for giving Iceland a Christian past, is in keeping with the idea of Iceland as an autonomous nation privileging thought, discussion, and consensus. It is thus perhaps more important for this origin legend to depict the Icelanders as a people who resolve later on at the Alþing, that communal decision-making space, to collectively embrace Christianity. This of course also allows the Icelanders to participate in the prestigious accounts of Scandinavian conversion and to honour holy figures such as Óláfr Tryggvason, whose cult and hagiographies had become extremely popular and important to the Icelanders. Again, the point is that in these origin stories, the composers use their words to create place-worlds that do significantly more than objectively represent historical truths or real geographic space — by fusing important, often highly crafted stories, to known places and events, *Landnámabók* structures persuasive and moving place-worlds for varied audiences to inhabit.

Conclusion

When approaching literary texts geocritically, 'what comes gradually into view is the (imaginary) space of literature, which has its own dimensions, which functions according to its own rules, but which is nevertheless anchored in

---

[58] *Landnámabók*, p. 396; *Book of Settlements*, p. 147.

the "reality" of existing spaces and places'.[59] As the first writers of Iceland's origins undertook the writing of arrival, establishing a simultaneously and symbiotically real and imagined Iceland in narratives and settlement myths, they harnessed the power of words and crafted literary geographies to transform familiar spaces into places of Icelandic identity formation. These literary geographies, or 'place-worlds' to use Keith Basso's term, are persuasive, inviting, and involving. In this kind of 'historical theatre' in which the past becomes immediate and 'long-elapsed events are made to unfold as if before one's eyes', the place-making writer is able 'to speak the past into being, to summon it with words and give it dramatic form, to *produce* experience by forging ancestral worlds in which others can participate and readily lose themselves'.[60] For the audiences of *Íslendingabók* and *Landnámabók*, something new is also created:

> Building and sharing place-worlds [...] is not only a means of reviving former times but also of *revising* them [...]. If place-making is a way of constructing the past, a venerable means of *doing* human history, it is also a way of constructing social traditions and, in the process, personal and social identities.[61]

This is a key concept. While Icelandic settlement histories evince an antiquarian interest in preserving venerable lore, each place-world constructed within their pages constitutes a fresh story. These Icelandic place-worlds, or 'images of the past that can deepen and enlarge awareness of the present',[62] provide thoughtfully revised ideas about being an Icelander, and model what Icelanders can aspire to, how they too can thrive in this land. *Íslendingabók* and *Landnámabók*, and their literary geographies, allow access to the places and characters that are foundational in the Icelandic settlement myths, and which drive a sense of Icelandic identity. As I hope to also have shown, however, these texts also place great emphasis on Icelanders as word-smiths, as a nation and a culture sensitive to, and extremely skilled in, the powerful use of words to shape thought, opinion, and even realities. The settlement accounts of Iceland rely on prophecy as well as early, prestigious accounts of pioneering Christian inhabitants, and these valorizing narratives show how important words and literary motifs were in creating a potent and unifying myth of Iceland and Icelandic identity. The verbal place-worlds in *Íslendingabók* and *Landnámabók* are as significant

---

[59] Piatti, Reuschel, and Hurni, 'Literary Geography', p. 10.

[60] Basso, *Wisdom Sits in Places*, pp. 33, 32.

[61] Basso, *Wisdom Sits in Places*, p. 7.

[62] Basso, *Wisdom Sits in Places*, p. 32.

as the material sites of Icelandic settlement and national history, but as the Icelanders realized, both the verbal place-worlds and the material geography become more powerful, more persuasive, more Icelandic, when they are fused together, when spatial and narrative practice are intertwined. In *Íslendingabók* and *Landnámabók* the Icelanders generated politically, geographically, and culturally 'moving words', and their transformative power is still felt today as one walks across the Icelandic landscape itself or meanders through the pages of its national histories.[63]

[63] This realization informs much Icelandic tourism, and most people visiting Iceland experience the landscape by looking through the varied lenses of the Icelandic settlement myth and the sagas of the Icelanders. Even those who only go on the 'Golden Triangle' tour visit medieval sites (Alþing), travellers beyond the Reykjavík area encounter much rich 'Saga Country' branding which again overlays stories from the medieval past on the landscape of today, and the Tourist Offices freely provide several excellent maps that overlay the sagas and foundation myths onto the map of Iceland itself. See, for instance, Oslund, *Iceland Imagined*, pp. 30–61.

Works Cited

Primary Sources

Adam of Bremen, *History of the Archbishops of Hamburg-Bremen*, ed. and trans. by Francis J. Tschan (New York: Columbia University Press, 2002)

Adomnán, *Vita sancti Columbae*, pub. as *Adomnán's Life of Columba*, ed. and trans. by Alan Orr Anderson and Marjorie Ogilvie Anderson (London: Nelson, 1961)

The Book of Settlements: Landnámabók, trans. by Hermann Pálsson and Paul Edwards (Winnipeg: University of Manitoba Press, 1972)

Íslendingabók; Kristni saga: The Book of Icelanders; The Story of the Conversion, trans. by Siân Grønlie, Viking Society for Northern Research Text Series, 18 (London: Viking Society for Northern Research, 2006)

Íslendingabók; Landnámabók, ed. by Jakob Benediktsson, Íslenzk fornrit, 1 (Reykjavík: Hið íslenzka fornritafélag, 1968)

Secondary Studies

Adolf Friðriksson and Orri Vésteinsson, 'Creating a Past: A Historiography of the Settlement of Iceland', in *Contact, Continuity, and Collapse: The Norse Colonization of the North Atlantic*, ed. by James H. Barrett (Turnhout: Brepols, 2003), pp. 139–61

Basso, Keith, *Wisdom Sits in Places* (Albuquerque: University of New Mexico Press, 1996)

Clunies Ross, Margaret, 'Textual Territory: The Regional and Genealogical Dynamic of Medieval Icelandic Literary Production', *New Medieval Literatures*, 1 (1997), 9–30

Craigie, William A., 'The Gaels in Iceland', *Proceedings of the Society of Antiquaries in Scotland*, 31 (1897), 247–64

Grønlie, Siân, 'Introduction', in *Íslendingabók; Kristni saga: The Book of Icelanders; The Story of the Conversion*, Viking Society for Northern Research Text Series, 18 (London: Viking Society for Northern Research, 2006), pp. vii–xlvi

Hastrup, Kirsten, *Island of Anthropology: Studies in Past and Present Iceland*, Studies in Northern Civilization, 5 (Odense: Odense University Press, 1990)

Hermann Pálsson, *Keltar á Íslandi* (Reykjavík: Háskólaútgáfan, 1997)

Hermann Pálsson and Paul Edwards, 'Translators' Introduction', in *The Book of Settlements: Landnámabók* (Winnipeg: University of Manitoba Press, 1972), pp. 1–13

Hermann, Pernille, '*Íslendingabók* and History' in *Reflections on Old Norse Myths*, ed. by Pernille Hermann, Jens Peter Schjødt, and Rasmus Tranum Kristensen, Studies in Viking and Medieval Scandinavia, 1 (Turnhout: Brepols, 2007), pp. 17–32

Jesch, Judith, 'Early Christians in Icelandic History — A Case-Study', *Nottingham Medieval Studies*, 31 (1987), 17–36

Kristján Eldjárn, *Kuml og haugfé úr heiðnum sið á Íslandi* (Reykjavík: Bókaútgáfan Norðri, 1956)

Lindow, John, '*Íslendingabók* and Myth', *Scandinavian Studies*, 69.4 (1997), 454–64

Mundal, Else, '*Framveksten* av den islandske identiten, dei norske rettene og forholdet til Noreg', *Collegium Medievale*, 10 (1997), 7–29

——, '*Íslendingabók*: The Creation of an Icelandic Identity', in *Historical Narratives and Christian Identity on a Northern European Periphery*, ed. Ildar Garipzanov, Medieval Texts and Cultures of Northern Europe Series, 26 (Brepols, 2011), pp. 111–21

——, '*Íslendingabók* vurdert som bispestolskrønike', *Alvíssmál*, 3 (1994), 63–72

Oslund, Karen, *Iceland Imagined: Nature, Culture and Storytelling in the North Atlantic* (Seattle: University of Washington Press, 2011)

Piatti, Barbara, Anne-Kathrin Reuschel, and Lorenz Hurni, 'Literary Geography — or How Cartographers Open Up a New Dimension for Literary Studies', in *Proceedings of the 24th International Cartography Conference* (Santiago: International Cartography Conference, 2009), pp. 1–12 <http://icaci.org/files/documents/ICC_proceedings/ICC2009/html/nonref/24_1.pdf> [accessed 12 January 2017]

Sverrir Tómasson, *Formálar íslenskra sagnaritara á miðöldum* (Reykjavík: Magnússonar, 1988)

Tally, Robert T., Jr, 'On Literary Cartography: Narrative as a Spatially Symbolic Act', *NANO: New American Notes Online*, 1 (2011) <https://www.nanocrit.com/issues/issue1/literary-cartography-narrative-spatially-symbolic-act> [accessed 10 January 2017]

Westphal, Bertrand, *La géocritique mode d'emploi* (Limoges: Presses Unversitaires de Limoges, 2000)

Woodward, David, 'Reality, Symbolism, Time, and Space in Medieval World Maps', *Annals of the Association of American Geographers*, 75.4 (1985), 510–21

Traversing the Space of the Oral-Written Continuum: Medially Connotative Back-Referring Formulae in *Landnámabók*

Slavica Ranković

T**he present study examines the use of the formulaic mirror phrases *sem fyrr er ritat* (as has been written before) and *sem fyrr er sagt/getit* (as has been said/mentioned before) in the five extant redactions of an early piece of Icelandic historiography — *Landnámabók*, or the 'Book of Settlements'. This is part of a larger undertaking that involves Old Norse literature in general and whose aim is to investigate whether, relative to the period in which the examined texts were composed, there are any patterns of preference emerging with regard to the employment of these phrases, given that one type connotes the written, and the other the oral medium of communication.

As my previous work on the sagas of Icelanders has shown,[1] chronology is not the only criterion to be taken into account in this context; rather, one must also be mindful of genre. Preliminary searches conducted on standard editions of various Old Norse texts available online suggest that historiographical works or the more didactically orientated texts (e.g., *Heimskringla*, the *Skáldskaparmál* part of *Snorra Edda*, and, as we shall see, *Landnámabók*) show more propensity for the formula in general and the written mode in particular. In contrast, those

---

[1] Ranković, 'In the Refracted Light'.

Slavica Ranković (slavica@milos-and-slavica.net) researches traditional formulae in Old Norse literature and South Slavic epic, and explores the relationships between the individual and communal memory and creativity in oral and orally derived literature in general. Dr Ranković is currently pursuing work on 'distributed reading' — a networked, digitally enhanced reading methodology <https://github.com/distributedreading/>.

Moving Words in the Nordic Middle Ages: Tracing Literacies, Texts, and Verbal Communities, ed. by Amy C. Mulligan and Else Mundal, AS 8   BREPOLS 🦫 PUBLISHERS   (Turnhout: Brepols, 2019)
pp. 255–278   10.1484/M.AS-EB.5.116627

in which the fictional aspect predominates (e.g., *fornaldarsǫgur*) more often either do not feature the formula at all or, when they do, they tend to employ the oral mode. Finally, regional and/or personal preferences of specific authors also play a role in the context of this research. Thus, for example, the sagas that were composed in the west of Iceland, within the cultural and power domains of the Sturlungs, contain the largest number of written mode formula instances (*Laxdœla saga* in particular), whereas the 'northern sagas' (e.g. *Reykdœla saga ok Víga-Skútu*) show a strong bias towards the oral mode.[2]

Being mindful of these parameters (i.e., chronology, genre, and regional/authorial preferences), the study of the medially connotative formulae might shed more light on the complex interface processes played out within the space of the oral-written continuum.[3] Just how bright this light would be depends on whether indeed it can be shown that, relative to the period of composition, the distinction between the two formula modes lingered or mattered enough to make an aesthetic difference in a given text, and be indicative of its writer's authority and social status.

Back-Referring Formulae and Orality-Literacy Interfaces

In Old Norse literature, *sem fyrr var ritat/sagt* types of phrases tend to occur in complex, multi-stranded narratives and they serve to remind the reader of previously mentioned events, actions, people, and various other details.[4] Appropriately, Alfred Jakobsen included them among what he termed *bako-vervisende formler* or the 'back-referring formulae'.[5] Their precise function and purpose are discussed in more detail in my previous work;[6] here, a few examples from *Landnámabók* will suffice to give an impression of the nar-

---

[2] For more detail, see Ranković, 'In the Refracted Light', especially pp. 310–14.

[3] Elsewhere, I offer detailed arguments as to why I consider space to be a more accurate way of conceptualizing the oral-written continuum than a simple line of progression implied in the commonly used phrase '*from* oral *to* written'. See Ranković, 'The Oral-Written Continuum as a Space'.

[4] In Ranković, 'In the Refracted Light', pp. 303–04, I point to the way in which these formulaic phrases differ from *svá er sagt* (so / it is said), *svá segja sumir menn* (some people say), and other such expressions that are of a more general nature and appear to refer to the material *outside* the text itself. The latter phrases and the degree to which they can be trusted to point to a genuine oral tradition are discussed by Andersson, 'Textual Evidence'.

[5] Jakobsen, 'Om "bakovervisende formler" i norrønt'.

[6] Ranković, 'In the Refracted Light', pp. 300–07.

rative context in which these phrases typically appear: 'Eyvindr sørkvir nam Blǫndudal, sem fyrr er ritat' (Eyvindr Sørkvir settled Blǫndudal, as has been written before);[7] 'Hans son var Eiríkr rauði, er byggði Grœnland, sem fyrr segir' (His son was Eiríkr the Red who settled Greenland, as has been said before);[8] 'Ǫndóttr kráka, er fyrr var getit, gerðisk ríkr maðr (Ǫndóttr Crow, who was mentioned before, became a powerful man).[9]

Jakobsen's Trondheim colleague, Jan Ragnar Hagland,[10] later pointed to the potential significance of this specific, medially connotative subset of the back-referring formulae for the study of the orality-literacy interfaces in medieval Iceland. Indeed, unlike other, semantically, functionally, and phraseologically cognate expressions such as *sem fyrr var greint* (as already described) or *sem fyrr var frá horfit* (that which was left off earlier), formulaic phrases such as *sem fyrr var sagt/ritat* directly reference the medium of communication. Far from being arbitrary or merely motivated by a need for variation, Hagland suggests that specific verb choices by medieval Icelandic authors and scribes — 'to say' or 'to write', and also 'to read' or 'to hear' — indicate varying degrees of the writers' awareness of their medium. This potentially offers important insights for the study of orality-literacy interrelationships in Old Norse literature and culture.

Similarly, scholars have noted that early medieval Icelandic book titles — the work discussed here, *Landnámabók*, being the case in point — tend to end in *bók* (book) or *skrá* (dry parchment, book), rather than *saga* (based on *segja*, 'to say'). Such conspicuous emphasis of the terms connected to writing, indicating expressly, Diana Whaley notes, 'something to be read, not to be heard',[11] is potentially suggestive of early authors' anxiety to distance themselves from oral tradition (even as they relied on it); instead, they foregrounded the special status of writing and their own proficiency in this still rare and socially desirable skill. Else Mundal further points out that, while this trend was current before 1200, the opposite became the norm 'from the beginning of the thirteenth century onwards',[12] when *saga* title endings began to dominate. Mundal explains that 'as the written culture developed and grew strong, it was perhaps

---

[7] *Íslendingabók. Landnámabók*, ed. Jakob Benediktsson, pt 2, pp. 223–24. Unless otherwise specified, the translations from Old Norse are mine.

[8] *Íslendingabók. Landnámabók*, ed. Jakob Benediktsson, pt 1, p. 197.

[9] *Íslendingabók. Landnámabók*, ed. Jakob Benediktsson, pt 2, p. 260.

[10] Hagland, '*Segia frá* eller *rita, lesa* eller *heyra* i kongesagalitteraturen'.

[11] Whaley, 'A Useful Past', p. 169.

[12] Mundal, 'Modes of Authorship', pp. 217–20.

not felt as necessary as before to underline the "writtenness" of the text by using titles containing words such as *bók* or *skrá*.[13] In other words, familiarity with the medium had slowly obviated an authorial need to draw special attention to the fact of writing as such, and there was likely less prestige to be gained from what had become a more widely spread activity. This new dynamic had, in turn, likely introduced the authors to a more metaphorical use of language and stylistic exploitation of the immediacy of the spoken word. Thus *sem fyrr var sagt* was not only taken to mean *sem fyrr var ritat* as a matter of course, but it was quite possibly coming to be perceived as stylistically less disruptive to the narrative flow than its more pedantic and literal, written mode counterpart.

This, of course, is not to say that the word *saga* was not used before the thirteenth century to denote a written text, nor that in very early texts *sem fyrr var sagt* was never used to mean *sem fyrr var ritat*. Indeed, as I have suggested elsewhere, there is no reason to believe that *both* types of phrase were not readily available to Icelandic authors from the very point of the introduction of writing.[14] As a matter of fact, the opening of *Landnámabók* (the first version of which is dated to the early twelfth century) features the phrase *á bókum er sagt* (it is *said* in the books). The contention here, however, is that even if early Icelandic authors encountered both formula modes in Latin textbooks and other foreign language literature, and had, moreover, occasionally employed both types of phrase themselves, writing was still a relative novelty for them and their social circles, a skill to be proud of, something worth an explicit mention. Thus at least in principle, it remains possible (and thus worth investigating) that the two modes of phrase were used discriminately, with earlier works (especially those with a more historiographical/didactic slant), showing some bias towards the literal, written mode of the back-referring formula.

A more serious problem is the very notion of an 'early work': however strong the reasons for a text's early dating, most of them (like *Landnámabók*) are accessible to us today only through their later redactions and often even later vellum and paper copies. And yet, while we must allow for the fact that scribes were bound to introduce some changes to the text during the intervening periods (in some cases perhaps even substantial changes), it is nevertheless unlikely that all the traces of earlier usages of our formula would have been completely

---

[13] Mundal, 'Modes of Authorship', p. 219.

[14] It must be remembered that the books the Icelanders encountered from the exporting cultures (where writing had been thriving for centuries and was thus already well internalized), most likely included both sorts of phrases. See discussion in Ranković, 'In the Refracted Light', pp. 304–05, and on 'interiorization of writing', see Ong, *Orality and Literacy*, pp. 56 and 82.

obliterated. If for no better reason than sheer copying inertia, earlier patterns of preference (or at least their remnants) are likely to have persisted in some of the later copies, patterns that might become discernible through a careful comparison of the results from the manuscripts that had relied on the same exemplars.

In addition to specific *sem fyrr er/var ritat/sagt* formulations, this chapter also considers their many variants. Alongside the already indicated variation in the tenses, the adverb *áðr* is sometimes used rather than *fyrr*, and the relative pronoun *er* instead of *sem*. In *Landnámabók*, we also encounter abbreviated and extended versions of the back-referring formula (e.g., *sem ritat er*; *sem fyrr var frá sagt*), and when it comes to its oral mode, the variation can involve an entirely different main verb.[15] As we shall see, in *Landnámabók* the verb *geta* (to mention) dominates over *segja*, and verbs such as *nefna* (to name), *tala* (to tell), and *mæla* (to speak), are also found, even if only seldomly. Although *geta* and *nefna* may not be as explicitly evocative of oral communication as the others, they are nevertheless also taken into account since they strongly allude to the oral context of remembrance/commemoration in the case of *geta* (the verb is often featured in skaldic verse and occasionally appears in runic inscriptions too) and the performative act of naming (as in naming witnesses in legal proceedings) in the case of *nefna*.[16]

Before proceeding to *Landnámabók*, a brief summary of my earlier analysis of the sagas of Icelanders will provide some useful points for comparison/contrast in the ensuing discussions.

Summary of the Results from the Sagas of Icelanders

The most conspicuous feature of the sagas in terms of the back-referring formula is the overwhelmingly greater number of the oral (110) in respect to the written mode instances (only nineteen).[17] Moreover, while the latter have more or less been ossified into the *sem fyrr var/er ritat* form, the use of oral

---

[15] The written mode of the formula in *Landnámabók* invariably involves the verb *rita*, although in other genres, e.g., bishops' sagas, one occasionally comes across *skrifa* too.

[16] To maintain focus on the back-referring formula, I will on this occasion not consider other kinds of phrases, such as the closely related 'forward-referring formula' (*sem enn mun ritat/sagt verða*, 'as will be written/said later'). While these and other such medially connotative phrases certainly warrant further study, preliminary considerations suggest that their inclusion would not have dramatically affected my conclusions here.

[17] Out of these 110, seventy-seven oral mode instances feature *segja* as the main verb, seventeen *geta*, thirteen *nefna*, and three *tala*.

mode phrases is far more flexible and varied; hence, they also appear to be more organic to the genre. This suggests that, by the time the sagas as we know them were first composed, writing had become well internalized as a technology. Even so, both the horizontal study of the formula instances across the standard Íslenzk fornrit editions of the sagas and the vertical manuscript study of the sagas that contain the majority of the written mode instances (*Laxdœla saga*,[18] *Eyrbyggja saga*, and *Egils saga*)[19] show a general compliance with the hypothesis that the earlier the text, the better the chance that it will contain written mode instances.

In addition to chronological development, genre also plays a vital role in understanding the sagas' preference for the oral mode. This most likely pertained to these narratives' intermediary position within the Old Norse generic system in which they are often seen to occupy the space somewhere between the more historically inclined kings' sagas and the more fictionally oriented *fornaldarsǫgur*. The oral mode of the back-referring formula allowed the saga authors to imbue their stories with a documentary, historiographic air, and at a lesser cost to the story's flow than its written mode counterpart. In other words, the oral mode struck a particularly good balance between the genre's scholarly and narrational demands.

As mentioned above, the personal preferences of writers and scribes, as well as the region in which they were based (or trained), were also important factors in terms of a predilection for one or the other formula mode. It is probably not coincidental that the three sagas with the largest number of written mode instances (see above) all originate in the west of Iceland, within the cultural domains of the Sturlungs. In particular, the examined manuscript evidence suggests that *Laxdœla saga* and *Eyrbyggja saga* had a stronger preference for the written mode of the formula and featured a larger number of them than can be gleaned from the standard editions. This is perhaps not so surprising, bearing in mind that these two sagas (often paired together in manuscripts on account of their overlapping events) are thought to originate from within the same geographical, literary, and power spheres as the works of the famous lawman and historian Sturla Þórðarson. That Sturla may have had a special fond-

---

[18] *Laxdœla saga* alone features nine out of the total nineteen instances and is the only saga in which the written mode outnumbers the oral (five instances with, four without *Bolla þáttr*).

[19] I have in addition thoroughly examined all the manuscripts available at <http://handrit.is/> [accessed 13 February 2019] of *Kormáks saga*, but have found no significant changes in the transmission of its two instances (one in each mode). For more detail, see Ranković, 'In the Refracted Light', p. 317.

ness for the written mode of the formula also seems supported by the evidence from *Landnámabók* (as we shall soon discover), and my preliminary searches of his *Íslendinga saga* show a marked difference of this work from others in the *Sturlunga saga* compilation due to its profuse employment of the formula in general and the written mode in particular.[20] Whether this was a simple idiosyncratic authorial quirk or an index of an archaizing tendency on his part — namely, an attempt at emulating the style of his predecessors — is a question that remains.

Last but not least, the manuscript evidence examined suggests that there were two waves of scribal attitudes towards the formula in the sagas of Icelanders. While early and late medieval scribes tend to both convert the written mode instances into oral mode ones and/or omit the formula, post seventeenth-century copiers either preserve the status quo or omit the formula altogether. I have argued that this is probably due to the new interface dynamic brought about by the rise of print culture with its content-insensitive manner of textual reproduction,[21] which resulted in the more reverent attitude towards authorship on the one hand, and a growing aversion to the formulaic on the other.

Introducing Landnámabók

Landnámabók or the 'Book of Settlements' is a piece of early Icelandic historiography covering the period *c.* AD 860–930. It describes the discovery and settlement of Iceland, while also often offering vivid sketches from the lives of early Icelandic settlers, their disputes about land, and various other dealings.[22] The origins and purpose of this work are thought to be closely connected with the introduction, in 1097, of the tithe system by the Bishop Gizurr Ísleifsson,[23] and the first basic version of *Landnámabók* is thought to have been compiled in the

---

[20] I have used the HTML version of *Sturlunga Saga*, ed. by Gudbrand Vigfusson.

[21] In 'Oral-Written Continuum as a Space' (especially pp. 45–52), I suggest that the distinction between content-sensitive and content-insensitive technologies of reproduction (i.e., those aiming to reproduce the content of a text and those aiming to reproduce its graphic signs) might be a more fruitful way of understanding the difference (and continuity) between the oral and the written. Also see Ranković and Ranković, 'The Talent of the Distributed Author'.

[22] For more detail about the content and purpose of this work, as well as its role in constructing Icelandic identity, see Mulligan's contribution to this volume.

[23] See, for example, Hermann Pálsson and Edwards's 'Translator's Introduction', p. 2.

early twelfth century by Ari Þorgilsson the Learned, the first Icelandic historian to write in the vernacular, and Kolskeggr the Wise.[24] A more elaborate version of *Landnámabók* was produced by Styrmir Kárason (Styrmisbók) *c.* 1220, which, although now lost, was in turn the source of the three medieval redactions that are extant today.[25] The oldest of the three, Sturlubók, was composed by Sturla Þórðarson *c.* 1275–80, while Hauksbók was written *c.* 1306–08 by the lawman Haukr Erlendsson who, in the epilogue to his work, cites Sturlubók and Styrmisbók as his direct sources.[26] Finally, the Melabók redaction was most likely authored *c.* 1300–10 by the lawman Snorri Markússon.[27]

In addition to these three, two later, seventeenth-century redactions are extant: a composite version of Sturlubók and Hauksbók by Björn Jónsson of Skarðsá, completed before the autumn of 1636 and known as Skarðsárbók; and Þórðarbók, a version that uses Skarðsárbók as its base text while also supplying divergent readings from Melabók. This latter was compiled by the priest Þórður Jónsson of Hítardalur, whose death in 1670 represents the *terminus ante quem* for this redaction. Given that only two leaves of the late fourteenth-early fifteenth-century manuscript of the Melabók redaction of *Landnámabók* now remain (in AM 445b 4to), we have Þórður Jónsson to thank for giving us an idea of what this version looked like, since he had access to this manuscript when it was mostly complete.[28]

Each of the three surviving medieval redactions can be claimed as 'the oldest', depending on the criteria. As mentioned above, Sturla was the first to compose his version of *Landnámabók*. However, things become less straightforward

---

[24] Haukr Erlendsson, one of the redactors of this work, mentions Ari and Kolskeggr in this context in the epilogue of his version, along with Sturla Þórðarson and Styrmir Kárason. Hermann Pálsson and Paul Edwards provide a translation of the relevant excerpt in the already mentioned 'Introduction', p. 4.

[25] The most thorough study of the relationship between *Landnámabók* archetypes and redactions is by Jón Jóhannesson, *Gerðir Landnámabókar*.

[26] See n. 24.

[27] This is judging by the fact that genealogical material is in this redaction strongly focused on the inhabitants of Melar, and it stretches to Snorri's parents and wife. The authors of Sturlubók and Hauksbók are similarly preoccupied with their own families. For more detail, see Finnur Jónsson, 'Indledning', esp. pp. iv–vii.

[28] For more detailed discussion of *Landnámabók* redactions, manuscripts, their dating and mutual relationships, consult Jakob Benediktsson's introduction ('Formáli') to the Íslenzk fornrit edition of the work in *Íslendingabók. Landnámabók*, ed. Jakob Benediktsson, esp. pp. cxliv–cliv.

when we take into account that our chief witness of Sturlubók (AM 107 fol.) is a paper manuscript dated to *c*. 1640–60. The exemplar used by its scribe, the priest Jón Erlendsson of Villingaholt, was a vellum manuscript (dated *c*. 1400 based on its orthography) that perished a few decades later, in the infamous Copenhagen fire of 1728, along with so many precious Icelandic parchments. Judging from comparison with Hauksbók, scholars believe that Jón's exemplar also represents an augmented version of the 'original' Sturlubók which Haukr had used as his source.[29]

Hauksbók can also be said to be the oldest in the sense that the earliest extant manuscript of Landnámabók is a fragment of the original Hauksbók, AM 371 4to.[30] Today, fourteen leaves in the author's own hand remain, a rare occurrence by medieval standards. In addition to preserving Sturlubók, Jón Erlendsson also saved the Hauksbók version of *Landnámabók* from the oblivion by making a fairly reliable copy in *c*. 1650–60 (AM 105 fol.) when the manuscript only lacked two leaves. And yet, it appears that the version which most closely resembles the lost source for all three redactions, Styrmisbók, is actually Melabók, since both Sturla and Haukr appear to have expanded upon their source, using the material from the sagas.[31] Thus, Melabók too can lay a claim on being the oldest version of *Landnámabók*.

Fascinating and instructive as this situation is, it also complicates an assessment of which of the three versions' instances of medially connotative back-referring formula should be taken to represent earlier and which later habits of usage. However, deciding on the issue at this point seems premature, as the comparison of the data gathered from the extant redactions might in fact help us to better illuminate and address this problem. Therefore, the next section presents the results yielded by my searches for the back-referring formula in *Landnámabók*.

---

[29] See for example, Finnur Jónsson, 'Indledning', p. iii.

[30] Strictly speaking, Hauksbók is a large encyclopaedic work that, in addition to *Land-námabók*, contained various other historical, religious, and scientific material. However, for the sake of expediency and unless otherwise specified, in this article Hauksbók refers exclusively to Haukr Erlendsson's version or *Landnámabók*.

[31] See Hermann Pálsson and Edwards, 'Introduction', p. 5, or Jakob Benediktsson, 'Formáli', p. liii (also pp. lviii–lx, regarding the saga material that appears in Sturlubók).

Landnámabók *Statistics: Number and Types of Formula Instances*

To keep the focus on the findings and avoid inundating the reader with too much technical detail, only the summary of my results is presented here (cf. the table below). However, for the more exacting readers (or simply those more involved with the topic), two appendices and a further discussion of the data and my methodological choices are made available online at <https://github. com/distributedreading/landnamabok]>. Appendix 1 is a table citing all the instances of oral and written modes of the formula found in two representative manuscripts (one chief witness, one late copy) of each of the five *Landnámabók* redactions. Appendix 2, on the other hand, comprises a further six tables, each focused on one of the main verbs employed (i.e., *rita, geta, segja, nefna, tala*, and *mæla*) and listing all the phrase variations per examined type of the formula, as well as their usage frequencies.

For the sake of clarity and convenience, in the ensuing discussion the following abbreviations will be used: S for Sturlubók, H for Hauksbók, M for Melabók, Sk for Skarðsárbók, Þ for Þórðarbók, and Þ(M) is used when Þórðarbók and Melabók are treated as a composite redaction, that is, when Þ's M readings are used to fill in the gaps in AM 445b 4to. In addition, to avoid repeating cumbersome phrases demarcating each formula instance such as, for example, 'the second oral mode instance (fifth of the *segja* variety)', 'the fourth oral mode instance (third of the *geta* variety)', or 'the seventh written mode instance,'[32] these too will be abbreviated and referred to as: '2o (5s)', '4o (3g)', '7w', etc. When the instances are preceded by H+, M+,[33] Þ (M)+, or Sk+, this means that they are unique to these respective redactions and have no counterparts in S, the *Landnámabók* redaction which was taken as the point of departure for my searches,[34] whereupon I would first identify its own formula instances and then proceed to track their fate in the other redactions.

Now that the terms for further discussion have been set, I will turn to the table below, which, as already mentioned, provides the summary of the results from Appendix 1 as they pertain to the number of formula instances per main

---

[32] Since in *Landnámabók* only the verb *rita* (and not *skrifa*, for instance) is used for the written mode instances, no need arises to specify its variety.

[33] These instances refer to those that can actually be located in the remaining two leaves of *Landnámabók* from the AM 445b 4to.

[34] My reasons for choosing S for this purpose are elucidated in the 'Instructions for Reading Appendices 1 and 2: Methodology' section available at <https://github.com/distributedreading/landnamabok>.

verb featured (the highest number of each type of instance is rendered in bold). With some reservation as to their usefulness,[35] the total numbers of instances per redaction are given in the final column, with further indication being given as to how many of these are in the written and how many in the oral mode.

L red. / verb	S	H	M	Þ	Sk
rita	14	11: 8S+3H	1<8: 1Þ(M)+7S?	8: 7S+1Þ(M)	12 (12S)
geta	8	8: 6S+2H	8<17: 1M+7Þ(M)+7S?+2H?	17: 7S+2H+1M+7Þ(M)	10 (8S+2H)
segja	1	1: 1H	2<4: 1M+1Þ(M)+1S?+1H?	4: 1S+1H+1Sk+1Þ(M)	3 (1S+1H+1Sk)
tala	2	1: 1S	<1: 1S?	1: 1S	1 (1S)
nefna	1	1: 1H	1<3: 1Þ(M)+1S?+1H?	3: 1S+1H+1Þ(M)	2 (1S+1H)
mæla	1	0	0	0	0
TOTAL	27: 14w+13o	22: 11w+11o	12<33: 1<8w+11<24o	33: 8w+24o	28: 12w+16o

In all cases except S,[36] each number is broken up so as to indicate how many of the instances subsumed under it are shared with other redactions and how many of them only appear in the redaction at hand. Thus, for example, of the eleven *rita* instances featured by H (second column, third row), eight are shared with S, and three seem to originate with H itself,[37] while of the three *nefna* instances in Þ (sixth column, fifth row), one is shared with S, one with H, and one comes from the part in which Þ follows M rather than Sk. Such instances are here, as elsewhere, marked as Þ(M).

For the purposes of the data analysis (see the next section), I have in this table tried to disentangle M data from Þ, as far as this was possible. As can be seen in Appendix 1, the instance M+ 1o(1s) that can be found in the extant M

---

[35] For example, it is not terribly surprising that Þ(M) comes up on top here, since it combines the instances from all the other redactions: S and H (as already conflated by Sk), and M.

[36] This is because, as already stated, S has been chosen as the point of departure.

[37] Alternatively, they were taken over from H's lost source, Styrmisbók, but were omitted in S.

fragment (*sem fyrr var sagt*, relating to the already conveyed information about the settlement of Ketill gufa) does not appear in Þ since Þórður Jónsson followed Sk (ultimately H) rather than M in this place. This instance thus reminds us that, even if Þ is our chief witness of M, it is also a redaction in its own right, privileging at times its other source, Sk,[38] over M. This presents us with the unenviable task of working out (or in the present case, estimating) how many instances featured in Þ can be taken to be M instances too. Apart from the two that survive in the extant M fragment itself, we can, with some degree of confidence also 'count in' the ten instances marked as Þ(M), since these come from the parts in which Þórður Jónsson followed M text.[39] Based on the earlier mentioned fact that Þórður omitted (or rather, neglected to remark upon) M+ 1o (1s), it is far from certain that these ten Þ(M) instances constitute all the divergent M readings.[40] There could have been a few more, though probably not *many* more. After all, while Þórður may be guilty of an occasional omission/ slip, there is no evidence to charge him with gross negligence. What is much less certain than the number of M divergences is how many of the instances that Þ shares with Sk (i.e., S and H), M shared too.[41] Of course, there are bound to be some overlaps between the three medieval redactions, since they had shared the same predecessor, Styrmisbók. It is, however, highly unlikely that all the twenty-one instances that Þórður copied from Sk were indeed also in M, since this number comes as a consequence of Sk's conflation of S and H. Thus instead of offering any round figures, I have resorted to suggesting number ranges for M instances, with the Þ(M) number treated as the minimum and Þ number as the maximum of instances per verb under scrutiny. Tentative as these figures are, they are not entirely arbitrary or uninformative. Unless M represents a sta-

---

[38] Another time when Þ(M) follows Sk concerns the latter's single unique instance, *sem fyrr segir* (see Sk+ 1o (1s) in Appendix 1).

[39] Out of these ten, seven come from the M parts of Þ, while three instances (1w, 6w, and 11w) probably also overlapped with S, but feature the verb *geta* in the place of S's *rita*. There are in addition six verifiable absences or 'negative instances' relating to S's 5w, 8w, 12w, 13w, 12o, and 13o (see the fourth column results for these in the Appendix 1 table). Of these six, one (12w) comes from M and the other five are derived from the M parts of Þ.

[40] Þórður Jónsson's particular interest in Melabók in general (and not just its *Landnámabók* text) is evident from the fact that he emended his son Þorsteinn's copy of the Vatnshyrna version of *Eyrbyggja saga* by supplying the Melabók version readings of the same saga. However, here too, Þórður was not completely thorough and had on two occasions neglected to supply divergent M readings of the back-referring formula. For more detail, see Ranković, 'In the Refracted Light', Appendix II: *Eyrbyggja saga*, instances 1o and 3w, p. 330.

[41] My uncertainty here is expressed by the question marks in the 'M' row of the table above.

tistical anomaly of some sort, at least one important pattern emerges from this partial evidence, and that is M's preference for the oral mode of the formula in general and the *geta* type in particular. The time has come, then, to move from the presentation to interpretation of the gathered data.

Data Analysis

A very detailed analysis of the gathered data would soon transcend the scope, and perhaps also defeat the purpose of this article; hence, I will only engage in discussion of the more prominent patterns emerging from the results in the above table and the two appendices. The single, most conspicuous pattern of this sort is that the formula instances featuring *rita* and *geta* as main verbs by far outnumber all the others, and also appear in the greatest variety of formulations (six per each verb; see Appendix 2). This is in sharp contrast with the sagas of Icelanders where the *segja* type rather than *geta* is the main oral mode counterpart to *rita* and where it predominates in general. (Compare the seventy-seven *segja* instances to only nineteen of *rita* and seventeen of *geta* in the entire saga corpus.) I will address the potential significance of this difference in due course; however, while maintaining the comparative dimension with regard to the sagas,[42] a more thorough consideration of the two formula modes as employed in *Landnámabók* will be offered now. The primary focus will be on the three medieval redactions or (especially in the case of M) what can be gleaned of them.

Written Mode Instances: Discussion

As the table above shows, of all the extant *Landnámabók* redactions, it is S, the one considered to be the oldest in terms of its estimated date of composition, that features the largest number of *rita* instances — fourteen, which is only five short of the total that can be found in the entire sagas of Icelanders corpus. What this slight difference in numbers means in real terms is that the frequency of application of the written mode of the formula is in S much greater — 21.85 times greater to be precise — than in the sagas, which is almost in direct opposite proportion to the sizes of the two respective corpora (the saga

---

[42] Unless otherwise specified, the term 'saga' in the present study always refers to the sagas of Icelanders or the family sagas genre (and not, for example, the kings' sagas or the bishops' sagas).

corpus is 29.65 times larger than the S version of *Landnámabók*).[43] Inasmuch
as this piece of early Icelandic historiography can be taken to predate the sagas
(at least in terms of its earliest versions), its proportionately significantly larger
number of *rita* instances works in favour of the proposed hypothesis about the
possible special predilection of the early and factually oriented texts for the
written mode of the formula.

The pattern that emerges at the level of comparison between the
Landnámabók redactions lends further support to this hypothesis. While, as
we have seen, S contains the largest number of *rita* instances (fourteen), M has
the lowest — up to eight, only one of which (Þ(M)+ 1w) is unique to it,[44]
while the remaining ones (however many of them there might have actually
been in M) are shared with S. In addition, in three other places where S and M
material overlaps, S features *rita* instances — 1w, 6w, and 11w — whereas in M
(as represented by Þ(M))[45] they are rendered as *geta* ones. This presents us with
a very interesting question: were these three *rita* instances later conversions
into *geta* ones by the fifteenth-century M scribe, or was it the other way around,
and it was Sturla (or some later copiers of his work) who did the replacing of
what were initially *geta* instances?

A number of facts speak in favour of the former scenario. As already noted,
S was compiled before M, and even though scholars have argued that the latter
is probably the version that is closest to the lost source for all three medieval
redactions, Styrmisbók, these claims are, as we have seen, first and foremost
made on the basis of M's *content*,[46] not the linguistic features. It is fully possible, then, that S and H preserved more conservative attitudes towards the
usage of our formula, even as they expanded upon the content of their source.

---

[43] The statistics are based on the number of written mode instances in the two corpora
relative to the number of words in the sagas (1,103,681) and the S version of *Landnámabók*
(37,220) respectively. The word count information is according to 'Málföng fyrir íslenzku', an
online Icelandic language resource created by Eiríkur Röngvaldsson at <http://www.malfong.
is/index.php?lang=en&pg=fornritin> [accessed 14 September 2017]. I have not been able to
work out the precise frequencies of formula application for H and M since I do not have the
word count for them. Still, even though they feature fewer instances than S (H eleven, M up to
eight), they are both also more concise than S, so their frequencies of usage with respect to the
sagas are more or less similar to S, especially when H is concerned.

[44] Due to textual difference, the need for the formula in this particular place does not arise
in S and H.

[45] The caveat expressed in the parenthesis is to stand for the remainder of the article. I will
not keep repeating it so as to avoid continually interrupting the flow of the discussion.

[46] See Jakob Benediktsson, 'Formáli', pp. xcvi–cvi.

And conversely, if, as my previous research suggests, the oral mode of the formula was indeed becoming more popular with the passing of time, it is conceivable that, in the intervening one hundred or so years between the composition of M (*c.* 1300–10) and its earliest extant manuscript (AM 445b 4ᵗᵒ, dated *c.* 1390–1425), some of the *rita* instances could have been converted to *geta* ones, at no cost to the content whatsoever.

Of course, an objection could be made that S as we have it now does not reach much further back into the past than the earliest representative of M since, as already mentioned, Jón Erlendsson's exemplar is itself dated no earlier than *c.* 1400.[47] However, eight of fourteen S *rita* instances are also preserved in Jón Erlendsson's copy of H (dated 1306–08), which means that these reflect the usage that predates by one hundred years that encountered in M, and are only some thirty-odd years removed from the composition of S itself (1275–80). Among these eight happen to be all the three instances under scrutiny, one of which, 11w, is moreover featured in the extant fragment of the original H (along with 7w). This and the fact that, as was already mentioned, M appears to exhibit a special fondness for the *geta* variety of the formula, give further weight to the proposition that what we are dealing with here is M's conversion of *rita* into *geta* instances.

To the eight S instances that can be backdated to H, one more could potentially be added: 13w. In the extant H fragment this instance reads as *sem fyrr er getit*, but even though H is the oldest surviving manuscript of *Landnámabók* that we have, there is reason to believe that Haukr inadvertently replaced the verb *rita* with *geta* while copying from S. This becomes more apparent when the sentence (or two consecutive sentences) in question is considered more closely, especially the fact that, rather unusually, two instances of a back-referring formula are featured in quick succession: 'Ǫnundr bíldr, *er fyrr var getit*, nam land fyrir austan Hróarslœk ok bjó í Ǫnundarholti; frá honum er margt stórmenni komit, *sem fyrr er ritat* [S] / *getit* [H]'. Considering that the two instances find themselves in such close proximity, it seems more likely that, for the sake of variety, different types of phrase would have been used originally, that is, as in S rather than H. It also strikes me as significant that both redactions agree with respect to the first instance but diverge in the second. This makes it plausible

---

[47] At least thirteen of the fourteen instances found in Jón's copy of S can be confidently traced to his exemplar. This is because twelve of these can also be found in Sk, and it is known that the latter's compiler, Björn Jónsson, relied on the same manuscript as Jón. See Jakob Benediktsson, 'Formáli', p. li (also pp. xci and cxliv). The one that Björn omits (7w) is in fact preserved in the extant original part of H.

that the mistake was made in the process of copying, so that, as the beginning of the phrase *sem fyrr er...* was correctly executed, *geta* was accidentally added instead of *rita* as the verb from the previous instance still lingered in the consciousness of the scribe (i.e., Haukr). The alternative — that some later scribe of S attempted to 'repair' this sentence stylistically by adding a variation — is of course also possible, but seems a bit more far-fetched as it asks us to imagine that first Styrmir committed the stylistic blunder and that subsequently both Sturla and Haukr let it stand.

Thus far, it has been possible to trace nine out of fourteen S *rita* instances back to the age of the earliest surviving *Landnámabók* manuscript, H, but there is an additional one, 10w, that scholars have traced all the way to the 1220 Styrmisbók.[48] Their arguments are based on the fact that this is the only place where Sturla appears to have employed the formula erroneously, since the information to which he refers here as something already conveyed (in ch. 86), he will actually only introduce later on (in ch. 95). Thus the most likely scenario is that this is an instance of mechanical copying on Sturla's part, that is, that the formula was carried over by inertia from the exemplar. If we accept that 10w may be a remnant from Styrmisbók, then the fact that its specific formulation — *sem fyrr er ritat* — happens to crop up most frequently in *all* the redactions of *Landnámabók* (see Appendix 2) potentially gains an entirely new meaning. In other words, the question opens up whether this particular phrasing might be indicative of Styrmir's personal preference. If so, then suddenly the number of candidate phrases for the 1220 dating jumps from one to potentially eleven (eight from S and three from H; see Appendix 1).

Of course, we must be careful not to attempt to make too much out of this one instance, which might perhaps reflect Sturla's rather than Styrmir's habit of usage. After all, the phrase is employed most frequently in S — eight times out of fourteen. This, however, does not explain the fact that all three 'extra' H *rita* instances, none of which can be found in S, are also of the *sem fyrr er ritat* kind. Moreover, in *Íslendinga saga* which is Sturla's original work, the past tense of the auxiliary verb *vera* is preferred, and *sem fyrr **var** ritat* is the dominant formulation. The difference here may be slight, but it is there nevertheless and it is constant. Hence, if in the first place we can entertain the notion that the frequency of employment of a particular phrase is not a mere accident but points to someone's habit of usage, it is not clear why that someone would have to be Sturla rather than his (and Haukr's) predecessor.

---

[48] See Jakob Benediktsson, 'Formáli', p. liv; also *Íslendingabók. Landnámabók*, pt 2, p. 332 n. 2.

To conclude, the written mode instances in H and S are not only more numerous than in M, but H's eleven and ten (out of fourteen) S instances can also be dated as far as the original H, or even further back into the past, to the early decades of the thirteenth century (10w). Consequently, the lower number of written mode instances in the fifteenth-century M, and the subsequent conversion of some of them into the oral mode ones suggests that M reflects a later stage in the usage of our formula.

Possibly an even later stage that concerns the already-mentioned habit of scribes to omit the formula and/or turn written mode instances into the oral mode ones can also be detected in Sk. The two instances Sk omits while copying S text (5w and 7w) both happen to be in the written mode, while its sole original formula instance ((Sk+ 1o(1s)) is rendered in the oral mode: *sem fyrr segir*. It may be of interest in this context that one of *rita* instances specific to H (H+ 1w) appears in this same passage. Of course, this may be a pure coincidence, especially as Sk follows S text here, and can thus not be directly accused of either omitting H+ 1w or of replacing it with its own *segja* variety. Still, considering that Sk is a conflation, it stands to reason that, while choosing between the relevant passages in S and H, Sk's compiler, Björn Jónsson, opted for the longer one from S, but had still drawn inspiration from H to employ the formula, substituting in the process H's written mode instance with his own oral one. Elaborate speculations aside, even if Björn's one-off decision to employ the formula of his own accord was indeed completely coincidental, his very choice of phrase nevertheless suggests which of the two modes felt more intuitive to him.

This order of things — that is, that S and H represent the earlier and M the later stage of formula application, with Sk potentially reflecting an even later set of scribal attitudes — complies well with the general hypothesis that, the earlier the text, the more likely that it will feature, and perhaps even show some preference for the written mode of the formula.

Oral Mode Instances: Discussion

The redaction with the lowest number of written mode instances, M, is conversely also the one that contains the highest number of oral mode ones — from eleven to twenty-four. This fact further suggests that M most likely reflects a later stage in the usage of the back-referring formula than do S and H. The latter two also frequently employ oral mode instances,[49] yet even the maximum

---

[49] In fact, in comparison with the sagas, S employs the oral mode 3.23 times more frequently, relative to the sizes of the two corpora.

number of their most favoured *geta* variety is only the same as M's minimum: eight. As has been noted, M's minimums only include instances in which it diverges from the other two redactions,[50] but if any at all were also shared — which must have been the case — then their number becomes significantly higher, and in the case of the *geta* type it potentially more than doubles.

Beyond what they seem to confirm about M, the figures are the least interesting aspect of usage of the oral mode of the formula in *Landnámabók*, and in terms of chronology, what constitutes 'a difference that makes the difference' is the employment of the written mode instances since, as noted at the outset of this study, the oral ones occur in *both* early and late texts. What *is* of great interest, however, is the mentioned dominance of the *geta* type in all the redactions of *Landnámabók*, in contrast to the *segja* variety which dominates in the sagas. A further difference between the two corpora in this context is that, in the sagas, the mirror phrases such as *sem fyrr var sagt/ritat/getit* are more or less applied interchangeably, whereas in *Landnámabók* there appears to be a clear division of labour between the *rita* and *geta* varieties. While the written mode type is used in the same general multipurpose way as in the sagas (i.e., with reference to people, their actions, events, etc.), the most frequently occurring *geta* formulation (see Appendix 2) is *[X], er fyrr var/er getit* ([X], who was/is mentioned before), with the relative pronoun *er* (who) replacing the adverb *sem* (as). In other words, the *geta* variety of the formula refers in *Landnámabók* almost exclusively to the already mentioned persons. Moreover, even when the formulation includes the adverb *sem* and not the relative pronoun *er*, as is the case with Þ(M)+ 1o(1g) and Þ(M)+ 6o(4g), the formula still refers to people — here to Grímr háleyski and the sons of Þorgeirr Vestarsson respectively. The single clear exception to this rule is the S instance 4o(3g), where *sem fyrr var getit* relates to the fact that, after the death of his father, a certain Vébjǫrn became unfriendly with Jarl Hákon and thus decided to emigrate to Iceland with his sister. Other three possible exceptions are H's equivalent of 13w, and M's of 1w and 6w (see Appendix 1). However, as argued in the previous section, these are all most likely later conversions of what originally were *rita* instances. With or without them, the evidence that the *rita* and *geta* varieties of the back-referring formula were used discriminately in *Landnámabók* is nevertheless overwhelming.

---

[50] Of these eight divergences, one can be found in the extant fragment of the earliest surviving M manuscript, 445b 4⁰, while another seven are derived from Þ. As we have seen, out of these seven, three most likely represent later conversions of the original *rita* instances.

One explanation for both the discriminate usage of the oral and written mode instances and for the preference of the *geta* over the *segja* oral variety could be that they represent the author's personal habits, most likely Styrmir's. Whatever there may have been in the first *Landnámabók* version that Ari and Kolskeggr compiled is far beyond our reach, and since the mentioned patterns are detectable across all three extant versions, it is unlikely that any of the redactors is responsible. Besides, the most likely candidate of the three, Sturla, seems to have preferred the *segja* rather than the *geta* variety of the oral mode, as can be attested from his *Íslendinga saga*. Still, even if we accept that what we are witnessing here are Styrmir's personal habits, the question of why we do not encounter such functional segregation between the two modes in the sagas remains. After all, they had authors too, and even if anonymous, they would have been prone to developing some stylistic habits. Another interesting question is whether it is possible that, in addition to arbitrary matters of taste, there was something particular about the *geta* variety that made it more appealing to Styrmir in the context of his historiographical work than the *segja* variety that dominates in the sagas.

Granted that we are not dealing in certainties here, I believe it is still possible to offer at least tentative answers to these questions, and they both revolve around the fact that the verb *segja* is medially more explicit than *geta*, that is, it alludes more conspicuously to the spoken word. Ingrained in the very term *saga*, the verb *segja* as part of the back-referring formula finds a natural place in these narratives whose roots in the oral tradition are so deep that, even as written literary creations, they were still conceptualized as the ultimate property of their heroes rather than their authors.[51] It is probably due to this close connection with the anonymous tradition that the saga authors remain largely anonymous in turn,[52] which is in sharp contrast with the *Landnámabók*'s writers and redactors, and even skaldic poets who were proprietorial about their oral creations, often weaving their own names into the tissue of their intricately crafted verses. Hence, we can assume that *segja* instances would have stood out less in this narrative-oriented genre than in an early historiographic work such as *Landnámabók* whose very title comprising the word 'book' and the open-

[51] See Mundal, 'Modes of Authorship', p. 224.

[52] A rare exception to this rule is *Egils saga*, credited by many scholars to the famous historian, poet, and politician Snorri Sturluson. (Of course, not all saga scholars adhere to this view. See Louis-Jensen, 'Dating the Archetype'.) Snorri's nephew and one of the *Landnámabók* redactors, Sturla Þórðarson, is, however, thought to have authored an early version of *Grettis saga*.

ing lines that hearken to the written works of the ultimate medieval *auctor*, the Venerable Bede, index its author's desire to firmly place his work within the domain of the budding literate culture. If we entertain the notion that early medieval Icelandic writers may initially have favoured the literal, written mode of the formula while gradually opening up to the more metaphorical, oral mode, it makes sense that they would then sooner opt for the softer, more unobtrusive *geta* variety that invokes the medially more amorphous context of memory/commemoration than for the one so ostentatiously evocative of oral speech, such as *segja*. *Geta* could even have acted as intermediary in the process of adopting the formula's oral mode. In this scenario, it further stands to reason that at these interface stages, the usage of the oral and written modes would have been more segregated, with each being assigned a separate function. Later on, when the fact of writing became so transparent as to appear invisible, it is easy to imagine that the two modes of the formula would be employed interchangeably, with the oral one eventually gaining the upper hand in the genres such as the sagas — more focused on storytelling yet also intent on maintaining the air of learnedness.

Concluding Remarks

To sum up, from the comparison of the data gathered respectively from the sagas of Icelanders and *Landnámabók*, the following main points emerge:

1. Even though the saga corpus is *c.* thirty times the size of *Landnámabók's* largest redaction, Sturlubók, the written mode of the formula is in the latter employed about twenty-two times more frequently than in the sagas. Relative to size, even the application of the oral mode is in Sturlubók triple that in the sagas. This staggering difference lends weight to the hypothesis that, the earlier the text and the more factually orientated it is, the more likely it is to feature the formula in general and the written mode in particular. One can appreciate that, with *Landnámabók* being such a heavily enumerative, information-laden text, the back-referring formula must have proven an especially useful navigational tool.

2. The state of affairs that emerges from this cross-generic 'macro' perspective is further mirrored at the scale of 'micro' study of the saga manuscripts and of the three *Landnámabók* redactions. As my previous work has shown, the highest number of *rita* instances found in the standard editions of some of the earliest specimens of the family saga genre — *Egils saga*, *Laxdæla saga*, and *Eyrbyggja saga* — increases even further when the evidence from their manu-

scripts is taken into account (especially in the case of the latter two). As far as *Landnámabók* is concerned, while being mindful of the different senses in which each of the three redactions can be considered to be the oldest, it still appears that it is Sturlubók — the first of the three to be compiled and the one that features the largest number of the written mode instances — that also preserves the earliest stage of the usage of the formula. Conversely, as argued above, the later stage is represented by Melabók, or rather by what can be gleaned from its earliest extant version (AM 445b 4to, compiled *c*. 1390–1425).

3. With regard to the oral mode, sagas show a distinct preference for the *segja* variety, while *Landnámabók* most regularly employs the *geta* type. Moreover, the latter type is functionally more circumscribed than the former, since it almost exclusively refers to the already mentioned people. This is also in sharp contrast to their written mode counterparts, the use of which is in *Landnámabók* far more versatile. That these patterns might reflect particular habits and personal preferences of Styrmir Kárason (or perhaps his predecessors) need not mean that they are also wholly idiosyncratic or arbitrary. Rather, I have suggested that, in the initial stages of adoption of the oral mode, it is possible that authors would have been more open to the *geta* variety since it is not as explicitly allusive of the spoken word as the *segja* type. Furthermore, assigning the written and the oral formula modes separate roles in a text is more likely to occur at a stage when the two media were likewise thought of in more distinct terms, and when writing still held enough fascination to be worthy of particular emphasis. Consequently, when the relative novelty of this medium wore off and it became too widely spread to warrant special mention, the two formula modes began to be used interchangeably, as we encounter in the sagas.

That we come across such patterns as described above means that the movement of the back-referring formula within the space of the oral-written continuum is far from random. And the more such patterns we discover, the clearer we can expect our understanding of the orality-literacy interfaces to become. As I hope the above discussion demonstrates, the fact that we have been able to compare and contrast the data from the sagas of Icelanders and *Landnámabók* has yielded more insights than would have been possible to gain had each set been treated separately. One only wonders, then, what riches await, once we are able to adjoin present findings to those that might emerge from studying the usage of the medially connotative back-references in the kings' sagas, or the contemporary sagas, or the grammatical treatises, or *Snorra Edda*. Did the latter's author, Snorri Sturluson, apply the back-referring formula in any special way, and was it from him that his nephew Sturla inherited what appears to be a special fondness for the written mode? Do the habits of these two western writers differ from the northerners who, at least where the sagas of Icelanders are concerned, seemed to have preferred the oral mode, or the southerners (such as the author of *Njáls saga*) who do not seem to have developed a taste for the formula in the first place? The results so far provide enough reason to hope that, as we study the patterns these 'moving words' make — the way they cooperate and collide in different corpora and at different times, the way they are wielded by different writers — the dark contours of the oral-written space they traverse will also inevitably become more illuminated.

Works Cited

Manuscripts

Reykjavík, Stofnun Árna Magnússonar í íslenskum fræðum, AM 104 fol.
——, AM 105 fol.
——, AM 106 fol. Þórðarbók
——, AM 107 fol.
——, AM 108 fol.
——, AM 110 fol.
——, AM 111 fol.
——, AM 112 fol.
——, AM 375 4to, Hauksbók
——, AM 445 b 4to, Melabók
Reykjavík, Landsbókasafn Íslands — Háskólabókasafn, ÍB 45 4to
——, JS 17 fol.
——, JS 18 fol.
——, Lbs 747 fol.
——, Lbs 748 fol.
——, Lbs 2328 4to
——, Lbs 3633 8vo

Primary Sources

Edda Snorra Sturlusonar <http://www.heimskringla.no/wiki/Edda_Snorra_Sturlusonar> [accessed 12 February 2019]
Fornaldarsögur Norðurlanda <http://www.snerpa.is/net/forn/forn.htm> [accessed 12 February 2019]
Heimskringla <http://www.snerpa.is/net/snorri/heimskri.htm> [accessed 12 February 2019]
Hauksbók: the Arna-Magnæan manuscripts, 371, 4to, 544, 4to and 675, 4to, ed. by Jón Helgason (Copenhagen: Munksgaard, 1960)

Íslendingabók. Landnámabók, ed. by Jakob Benediktsson, Íslenzk fornrit, 1 (Reykjavík: Hið íslenzka fornritafélag, 1968)

Íslendingasögur <http://www.snerpa.is/net/isl/isl.htm> [accessed 12 February 2019]

Íslendingaþættir <http://www.snerpa.is/net/isl/isl-th.htm> [accessed 12 February 2019]

Landnámabók (Sturlubók) <http://www.snerpa.is/net/snorri/landnama.htm> [accessed 12 February 2019]

Landnámabók I–III. Hauksbók. Sturlubók. Melabók, ed. by Finnur Jónsson (Copenhagen: Thieles bogtrykkeri, 1900)

Landnámabók. Melabók AM 106/12 fol., ed. by Finnur Jónsson (Copenhagen: Nordisk forlag, 1921)

Sturlunga Saga: Including the Islendinga Saga of Lawman Sturla Thordsson and Other Works, ed. by Gudbrand Vigfusson, 2 vols (Oxford: Clarendon Press, 1878); <https://archive.org/stream/sturlungasagainc01aronuoft/sturlungasagainc01aronuoft_djvu.txt> [accessed 12 February 2019]

Secondary Studies

Andersson, Theodore M., 'The Textual Evidence for an Oral Family Saga', *Arkiv för nordisk filologi*, 81 (1966), 1–23

Eiríkur Röngvaldsson, 'Fornritin', *Málföng fyrir íslenzku* <http://www.malfong.is/index.php?lang=en&pg=fornritin> [accessed 12 February 2019]

Finnur Jónsson, 'Indledning', *Landnámabók I–III. Hauksbók. Sturlubók. Melabók*, ed. by Finnur Jónsson (Copenhagen: Thieles bogtrykkeri, 1900), pp. i–lx

Hagland, Jan Ragnar, '*Segia frá* eller *rita*, *lesa* eller *heyra* i kongesagalitteraturen — fri variasjon, eller ulike perspektiv på overgang frå "orality" til "literacy"?' *Arkiv för nordisk filologi*, 117 (2002), 86–96

Hermann Pálsson and Paul Edwards, 'Translators' Introduction', in *The Book of Settlements: Landnámabók* (Winnipeg: University of Manitoba Press, 1972), pp. 1–13

Jakob Benediktsson, 'Formáli', in *Íslendingabók. Landnámabók*, ed. Jakob Benediktsson, Íslenzk fornrit, 1 (Reykjavík: Hið íslenzka fornritafélag, 1968), pt 1, pp. l–cliv

Jakobsen, Alfred, 'Om "bakovervisende formler" i norrønt', *Motskrift: Arbeidsskrift for språk og litteratur*, 2 (1983), 69–80

Jón Jóhannesson, *Gerðir Landnámabókar* (Reykjavík: Félagsprentsmiðjan, 1941)

Louis-Jensen, Jonna, 'Dating the Archetype: *Eyrbyggja saga* and *Egils saga Skallagrímssonar*', in *Dating the Sagas: Reviews and Revisions*, ed. by Else Mundal (Copenhagen: Museum Tusculanum Press, 2013), pp. 133–47

Mundal, Else, 'Modes of Authorship and Types of Text in Old Norse Culture', in *Modes of Authorship in the Middle Ages*, ed. by Slavica Ranković and others (Toronto: Pontifical Institute of Mediaeval Studies, 2012), pp. 211–26

Ong, Walter J., *Orality and Literacy: The Technologizing of the Word* (London: Methuen, 1982)

Ranković, Slavica, 'In the Refracted Light of the Mirror Phrases *sem fyrr var sagt* and *sem fyrr var ritat*: Sagas of Icelanders and the Orality-Literacy Interfaces', *Journal of English and Germanic Philology*, 115 (2016), 299–332

——, 'The Oral-Written Continuum as a Space', in *Along the Oral-Written Continuum: Types of Texts, Relations and their Implications*, ed. by Slavica Ranković and others (Turnhout: Brepols, 2010), pp. 39–71

Ranković, Slavica, and Miloš Ranković, 'The Talent of the Distributed Author', in *Modes of Authorship in the Middle Ages*, ed. by Slavica Ranković and others (Toronto: Pontifical Institute of Mediaeval Studies, 2012), pp. 52–75

Whaley, Diana, 'A Useful Past: Historical Writing in Medieval Iceland', in *Old Icelandic Literature and Society*, ed. by Margaret Clunies Ross (Cambridge: Cambridge University Press, 2000), pp. 161–202

Qrvar-Oddr's *Ævikviða* and the Genesis of *Qrvar-Odds saga*: A Poem on the Move

Helen F. Leslie-Jacobsen

Q*rvar-Odds saga* is one of the longest Old Norse legendary sagas (*fornaldarsǫgur*), and the text is rich both in manuscripts of independent textual value and in poetic stanzas. The saga begins with a prophecy and culminates with the death of the hero. The protagonist Oddr, at the beginning of the saga, is prophesied to have a prodigiously long life of three hundred years, then to be killed by his horse's skull. In order to try and escape the prophecy coming true, he kills his horse and buries it in a deep hole on his home island of Hrafnista in Norway. He does indeed live three hundred years, and the saga is concerned with recounting his travels and battles along the way. The action is set in a variety of different places, including Bjarmaland (often translated to English as Permia), Ireland, Sweden, Aquitaine, and Jerusalem, to name but a few. His companions die successively, since they have a normal lifespan. Towards the end of the saga, Oddr goes back to his native island three hundred years after he originally killed his horse. Over the centuries, the dusty soil has blown away, exposing the horse's head, and, as he is examining the bones, a snake crawls out of the skull and bites him, inflicting a fatal injury. During his lingering death he extemporizes a poem, known as his *ævikviða* (poem of a life story), of seventy-one stanzas in its longest preserved form, and commands that it be recorded. This kind of poem extemporized at death is often known as a

Helen Leslie-Jacobsen (helen.leslie@uib.no) is a researcher in Old Norse philology at the University of Bergen, Norway, where she works on eddic poetry, *fornaldarsǫgur*, and medieval law.

Moving Words in the Nordic Middle Ages: Tracing Literacies, Texts, and Verbal Communities, ed. by Amy C. Mulligan and Else Mundal, AS 8   BREPOLS 🕮 PUBLISHERS   (Turnhout: Brepols, 2019) pp. 279–296   10.1484/M.AS-EB.5.116628

'death-song'.[1] Oddr's death-song recounts the story of the protagonist's entire life and provides the whole story of the saga and summarizes the action. Oddr's travels are thus told twice: once in the saga prose and a second time in poetry at the end of the saga.

This essay examines the genesis of the prose *Qrvar-Odds saga*, one of the longest Old Norse legendary sagas, from its poetic roots, and in doing so highlights the importance of eddic poetry to the genre's formation and the likely oral prehistory of the text.[2] Previously, I have explored the role that the two eddic 'death-songs' found in the saga play in the narrative and form of the saga, focusing on one death-song in the saga belonging to the hero Hjálmarr.[3] Here, I would like to examine the second death-song in *Qrvar-Odds saga*, known as Qrvar-Oddr's death-song or *ævikviða*, more closely with respect to what it can tell us about the diachronic development of the prosimetric structure of the saga.[4] My argument hinges on the derivation of the body of the saga from this long poem found at its end. I suggest that the prosimetric employment of some of the death-song stanzas in the saga prose shows that the death-song was known in oral tradition as a whole poem. I also argue that this whole poem in oral tradition was similar in composition and substance to the transmitted poem before it came to be codified, the earliest evidence of which we have from the fourteenth century. The saga continued to develop after being committed to writing, which accounts for the various manuscript versions in existence (see below). By considering the death-song, we hold a key to understanding the trajectory of the development of the saga from prosimetric roots.

Before continuing to examine the *ævikviða* in more detail, it is worth briefly discussing the genre to which the saga belongs. *Qrvar-Odds saga* is a *fornaldarsaga* (plural *fornaldarsǫgur*), meaning a 'saga of ancient times', a subcategory of the Old Norse saga genre. The saga genre is considered a prose genre of Old Norse literature, although in reality many of the saga subgenres, the *fornaldarsǫgur* included, are largely prosimetric. As far as the *fornaldarsǫgur* are concerned, this mixture of prose and poetry reflects their origin in oral tradition, where contextual material about stories told primarily in verse was given

---

[1] For the death-song in general, see Lönnroth, 'Hjálmar's Death-Song', and Harris, 'Beowulf's Last Words'.

[2] For more on the importance of eddic poetry to the development of *fornaldarsǫgur*, see Leslie-Jacobsen, 'Genre and the Prosimetra of the Old Icelandic *fornaldarsögur*'.

[3] Leslie, 'The Death Songs of *Örvar-Odds saga*'.

[4] The term 'prosimetric saga' refers to a saga in a mixture of prose and verse.

in prose. When the *fornaldarsǫgur* came to be recorded later on in written tradition, this style persisted. Each saga must be examined on a case-by-case basis
to determine the nature of the relationship of the prose to the poetry, since it
is clear that the *fornaldarsǫgur* have differing developmental trajectories with
regards to the poetry they contain. Some, for example *Vǫlsunga saga*, employ
poetry mainly as evidence for what the prose narrates. In sagas like *Ketils saga
hængs*, the poetry and prose have a symbiotic relationship in terms of the saga's
structure. In *Ǫrvar-Odds saga*, a good deal of the prose is structured around
verses that lie behind it.[5]

The Role of the Ævikviða *in the Saga Prose*

The fact that verses from the *ævikviða* are found in the prose has been critically
discussed for over a hundred years, with opinions concerning the relationship
of the *ævikviða* to the prose stemming from three main sources: R. C. Boer,
Andreas Heusler and Wilhelm Ranisch, and Finnur Jónsson. Boer in 1888
argued that the one and a half stanzas found at the end of the fourteenth-century S version (for manuscripts and sigla, see below) are all that remains of an
'original' poem, and that those stanzas used prosimetrically were *lausavísur* that
did not come from this poem. Later, they were collected together and helped to
form an *ævikviða* that was interpolated into later manuscripts (ABE).[6] Heusler
and Ranisch in 1903 interpreted these *lausavísur* as parts of an older, lost poem
from the twelfth century and argued that these stanzas formed the basis of an
ævikviða that was not composed until the fifteenth century.[7] Finnur Jónsson in
1923 agreed with Boer, Heusler, and Ranisch that there was indeed an earlier
poem, but that the poem that is extant as the *ævikviða* was the 'original' poem
with interpolations, and that the stanzas in the prose derived from it.[8] My overarching argument is that the *ævikviða* as a whole stands behind the saga prose
as an invisible backbone, and that the written saga likely took this form from
a prosimetric *Ǫrvar-Odds saga* that existed in oral tradition. It is impossible to
determine the long form this poem would have had in oral tradition.

---

[5] See Leslie, 'Prose Contexts of Eddic Poetry' for a detailed examination of the prosimetra
of the *fornaldarsǫgur*.

[6] *Ǫrvar-Odds saga*, ed. by Boer, p. xvii.

[7] *Eddica Minora*, ed. by Heusler and Ranisch, p. xlvii.

[8] Finnur Jónsson, *Den oldnorske og oldislandske litteraturs historie*, II, 150–51.

In the introductory prose to the *ævikviða*, emphasis is placed on some men recording Oddr's poem. This is presumably meant to indicate that the reader should assume that the recorded poem is the one preserved in the saga tradition, and that it gave rise to the whole saga. This is the legendary context for the saga's genesis, although it is likely also to be the literal one. In S, the context is given in detail for the recording of the poem:

> 'sumir skulu þér sitja hjá mínar ok rísta eptir kvæði því er ek vil yrkja um athafnir mínar ok ævi'. Eptir þat tekr hann at yrkja kvæði, en þeir rísta eptir á speldi, en svá leið at Oddi, sem upp leið á kvæðit. Þessa vísu kvað Oddr síðast. (195.5–9).[9]

> ('some of you shall sit by me and carve the poem that I will compose about my activities and life-story'. After that he began to compose the poem, and they carved along on tablets, and Oddr reached his end as the poem reached its end. Oddr recited this stanza last.)

It is notable that in S the poem is carved with what could be runes on tablets as a way of remembering it. This is a rather idiosyncratic feature; more normal is the context that ABE gives, in which the poem is memorized by those chosen to do so (195, see variants). In M, no information about the recording of the poem is given: '"En þó skal ek áðr yrkja kvæði um ævi mína". Síðan tekr hann til kvæðis'. (But nevertheless I shall, before (I die), compose a poem about my life-story) (194. 13–14). In S then, the oldest version of the saga according to extant manuscript evidence, a written record may emphasize the veracity of the poetic text that the saga prose mediates.

A parallel ought to be drawn between the situation in S quoted above and the recording of *Sonatorrek* in *Egils saga*, and I suggest *Egils saga* has influenced the S version here. In *Egils saga*, Þorgerðr convinces her father Egill to compose the poem, and she says she will record it on a *kefli* (stick):

> 'Núvikda ek, faðir, at vit lengðim líf okkart svá at þú mættir yrkja erfikvæði eptir Bǫðvar, en ek mun rista á kefli, en síðan deyju vit, ef okr sýnisk. Seint ætla ek Þorstein son þinn yrkja kvæðit eptir Bǫðvar, en þat hlýðir eigi at hann sé eigi erfðr, því at eigi ætla ek okr sitja at drykkjunni þeiri at hann er erfðr'.
>
> Egill segir at þat var þá óvænt at hann mundi þá yrkja mega, þótt hann leitaði við, 'en freista má ek þess', segir hann.

---

[9] All citations from *Ǫrvar-Odds saga* refer to Boer. Page number and line number are specified, also stanza number when preceded by 'st.' All translations are my own.

('Now I want us to stay alive, father, long enough for you to compose a poem in Boðvarr's memory, and I shall carve it on a stick. Then we can die if we want to. I doubt whether your son Þorsteinn would ever compose a poem for Boðvarr, and it is unseemly if his memory is not honoured, because I do not expect us to be sitting there at the feast when it is'.

Egill said it was unlikely that he would be able to compose a poem even if he attempted to. 'But I shall try', he said.)[10]

Þorgerðr records the poem so that following her own anticipated death and that of her father, Egill, the poem honouring Egill's dead sons will be preserved. This too is the situation in *Qrvar-Odds saga*. Whilst skalds usually memorized their poems for recitation, both Egill and Oddr think they are about to die, so Oddr has his poetry recorded, and Þorgerðr similarly records the poem so Egill will not think the composition futile. In *Qrvar-Odds saga*, the final stanza and half of the poem are cited; in *Egils saga*, in the Möðruvallabók version, only the first stanza of *Sonatorrek* is quoted, showing that quotation of only part of a poem to trigger the whole was a common scribal device. We can also see the influence of *Egils saga* on the S version of *Qrvar-Odds saga* in what happens after the poems are finished: 'Egill tók at hressask svá sem fram leið at yrkja kvæðit' (Egill began to recover his spirits as he proceeded to compose the poem),[11] whereas in *Qrvar-Odds saga*, 'en svá leið at Oddi, sem upp leið á kvæðit' (and as the poem came to an end, so did Oddr) (195. st. 8–9). The poetry saves Egill's life, cheering him up sufficiently so that he aborts his suicide attempt, while in Oddr's case, as the poem proceeds, so does his death. The absence of this context from MABE shows that only the S version incorporated this influence from *Egils saga*, and that it is likely that *Egils saga* influenced *Qrvar-Odds saga*, rather than the other way around.

Although almost all the stanzas of the *ævikviða* are autobiographically retrospective, Oddr's poem contains stanzas at the beginning and end that frame the internal stanzas to give them context and to link them firmly with their immediate prose context. At the beginning of the poem, he starts with a call for a hearing by the warriors around him: 'Hlýði seggir, en [ek] segja munk | vígsvoldundum frá vinum mínum' (Listen men, and I will tell of the cause of battles, from among my friends). After this introduction, he launches straight into recounting his boyhood. In the last two stanzas of the *ævikviða*, he comments that there is yet more to say about his travels, 'fjold er at segja frá forum

---

[10] *Egils saga*, ed. by Bjarni Einarsson, p. 146; *Egils saga*, trans. by Scudder, p. 151.

[11] *Egils saga*, ed. by Bjarni Einarsson, p. 154; *Egils saga*, trans. by Scudder, p. 156.

mínum' (much there is to tell about my travels) (208. st. 70. 3), but since he is now very close to death, he closes the poem by expressing a wish to have his final greetings conveyed to his wife and their sons (208. st. 71).

The style of the *ævikviða* is concise, and if we compare how events are narrated in the prose and how they are recorded in the *ævikviða*, we can see that the poem seeks to capture only the essence of the episode. The provision of a place or personal name, for example, and the briefest of details is enough to reference a whole episode that the audience already knows; indeed, they know it because they have just heard or read the whole saga, if not for any other reason.

We can also understand certain episodes to be so well known that they need no elaboration in the poem. Such an episode takes place on the island of Sámsey, in which the death of the hero Hjálmarr is recounted. This famous scene was widely known, and appeared for example in *Hervarar saga*.[12] In this way, economy of description can be employed without any risk to loss of content. In the saga as we have it today, this is how the narrative functions. In the depictions and conceptualization of events, the poetry plays a secondary, supporting role. If, however, the prose is based on the verse, the poetry must have initially performed a vital role in encapsulating enough of the story to make episodes recognisable to audiences and transmitting the bare bones of an episode that the prose writers could interpret and expand upon. How likely is this?

Refuting the older assertions that much of the death-song is interpolation postdating the saga prose, my paper argues that the long poem of Ǫrvar-Oddr's death-song at the end of the saga has roots throughout the whole of the extant saga prose, and as such its stanzas form a backbone for the written saga's construction. I contend that the saga seems to be composed around and on the basis of this long death-song, and thus that it is possible that the poetry could be older than the prose. This early dating of the material that makes up the saga is supported by the existence of parallels between episodes in the saga and the *Gesta Danorum* of Saxo Grammaticus, a twelfth-century work thought to have been based in part on Icelandic oral tradition. The iteration of the events in the poem would have been a means to give structure to the prose saga, whilst the saga prose allowed for more expansive narration of the concise information provided in the verses, as I will demonstrate.

[12] For a fuller exploration of the episode, see Mitchell, 'The *fornaldarsǫgur* and Nordic Balladry'.

The Versions of Ǫrvar-Odds saga

A further dimension to this discussion is that *Ǫrvar-Odds saga* exists in several versions. The older versions of the saga do not record the long death-song at the end, only the final stanzas (S; for sigla, see below) or a reference to it (M), whereas the younger, longer versions record the full poem (ABE).

Ǫrvar-Odds saga is preserved in sixty-eight manuscripts in total, but there are three identifiable versions extant in five manuscripts of independent value, as identified by R. C. Boer in his still standard edition of 1888. The main versions of the saga are known as S, M, and ABE. Only the ABE versions record the full *ævikviða*. The manuscripts and their sigla are as follows:

– Holm Perg. 4to nr 7, Kungliga biblioteket, Stockholm (S): This vellum manuscript was written in Iceland at the beginning of the fourteenth century.[13] As it is the oldest manuscript, it has been considered by Boer to preserve the best text of the saga.[14] *Ǫrvar-Odds saga* is to be found on fols 43ᵛ2–57ʳ19.

– AM 344 a 4to, Reykjavík, Stofnun Árna Magnússonar í íslenskum fræðum (M): A short, vellum manuscript of twenty-four pages, written in the late fourteenth century.[15] It only contains *Ǫrvar-Odds saga*.

– AM 343 a 4to, Reykjavík, Stofnun Árna Magnússonar í íslenskum fræðum (A): An Icelandic vellum manuscript written 1450–75.[16] *Ǫrvar-Odds saga* can be found on fols 59ᵛ–81ᵛ.

– AM 471 4to, Reykjavík, Stofnun Árna Magnússonar í íslenskum fræðum (B): A vellum manuscript written 1450–1500 in Iceland and closely related to A.[17] *Ǫrvar-Odds saga* is on fols 61–96ᵛ. The beginning is defective since a page is missing (the saga in B thus begins at the equivalent of 4.7 in the edition).

– AM 567 IV 4to, Reykjavík, Stofnun Árna Magnússonar í íslenskum fræðum (C): consists of three leaves from the fifteenth century, of which leaves 2 and 3 (fols 2ʳ–3ᵛ) contain fragments of *Ǫrvar-Odds saga*.

[13] Dated thus in *Ǫrvar-Odds saga*, ed. by Boer, p. i.

[14] *Ǫrvar-Odds saga*, ed. by Boer, p. i.

[15] *Ǫrvar-Odds saga*, ed. by Boer, p. ii dates the manuscript to the second half of the fourteenth century; Kålund dates it to *c.* 1400 in *Katalog over den Arnamagnæanske Handskriftsamling*, ii, 579.

[16] Dated thus in *A Dictionary of Old Norse Prose*, p. 452.

[17] *Ǫrvar-Odds saga*, ed. by Boer, p. vi. Dated in *A Dictionary of Old Norse Prose*, p. 453.

– AM 173 I fol.,[18] Reykjavík, Stofnun Árna Magnússonar í íslenskum fræðum (E): Written by Ásgeir Jónsson, the manuscript is from *c.* 1700, and *Qrvar-Odds saga* is to be found on fols 17^r–65^v. This manuscript is the best representative of a group of paper manuscripts with a common exemplar close to that of the common exemplar of AB, but not identical to it.[19]

Boer shows the readings in M to be intermediary between S and ABE, as they often agree with ABE, and then deviate on important points to agree with S. Boer's readings also demonstrate that MABE form a group against S, and that MABE have a common original that they cannot share with S.[20] This results in the groups ABE, S, and M. Since C is a fragment, it is not possible to decide which group it most closely resembles, but the three stanzas it preserves are nevertheless relevant to this study.

The Ævikviða *as Interpolation*

Boer states that since the *ævidrápa* is lacking in SM, it can be considered as an interpolation in the other versions.[21] The implication of this is that the death-song as a whole is secondary to the extant prose saga, and thus that the poetry cannot have been used to provide the bones of the saga. However, there are reasons that Boer does not take into account that might explain why SM lack the full *ævikviða*. One possibility is that that the scribe of the M version did not cite any of the *ævidrápa* because he did not know it; more likely is the explanation that the scribe chose not to cite the *ævidrápa* even though he knew it. The full poem may have not been cited because it was generally known, and thus did not need to be written out, or because it was generally unknown and therefore the scribe decided that the poem may not have been of interest to his audience. Likewise, in S, only part of the *ævikviða* may have been cited because a) that was the part that the scribe knew; b) the scribe expected it to be unknown and so just gave a brief example; or c) the scribe expected the whole poem to be known, and thus felt it was unnecessary to give the whole poem, and just pro-

---

[18] AM 173 fol. is made up of two manuscripts; *Qrvar-Odds saga* is in the first part, denoted I. The second part, AM 173 II fol., contains only *Sturlaugs saga Starfsama*, fols 1^r–18^v. Boer does not make this distinction in his edition. See 'AM 173 fol.', *Handrit.is*.

[19] *Qrvar-Odds saga*, ed. by Boer, p. vi.

[20] *Qrvar-Odds saga*, ed. by Boer, pp. vii–xii.

[21] *Qrvar-Odds saga*, ed. by Boer, pp. xiv–xv.

vided the last stanza and a half. In the context of the wider saga tradition, the last option is most likely, since we have other examples where one or two stanzas of a poem are cited as a *pars pro toto* to trigger the audience to recall the stanza or to prompt the reader to recite it.[22] Usually these are the opening stanzas of the poem, so the citation of final stanza(s) is rather idiosyncratic in S. This is supported by the introduction to the stanzas that are quoted in S: 'Þessa vísu kvað Oddr síðast' (Oddr recited this stanza last) (195. 5–9), through which the scribe of the manuscript makes perfectly clear that there are stanzas that have gone before those recorded. Accordingly, the fact that the *ævikviða* is clearly referred to in both SM is reason enough to consider the poem present in these versions of the text, even if it is wholly or partly invisible.

Even in the SM versions of the saga that do not record the whole of Oddr's death-song, the sagas allude to and show knowledge of the longer poem by employing some of its stanzas prosimetrically in other parts of the prose saga. I suggest such visible employment of the stanzas shows that the death-song was known in oral tradition as a whole poem similar in composition and substance to that transmitted today, or as units that came to make up a whole poem, before it came to be codified, the earliest evidence of which we have from the fourteenth century.

The Emergence of the Ævikviða *in the Prose*

Although M does not cite the *ævikviða* at the end of the saga at all, it does include some stanzas from the poem interspersed among the prose earlier in the saga, as do SABCE. This also lends weight to the suggestion that the *ævikviða* is in evidence in SM, even though the long poem is not written out in the manuscripts. In ABM, stanzas 21, 22, 38, and 41 of the full *ævikviða* can be found towards the beginning of the saga used prosimetrically as *lausavísur*; E also includes all these stanzas near the beginning of the saga except stanza 22, and the fragment C has 38 and 41. The situation in S is slightly different and warrants a closer look.

---

[22] This phenomenon of first stanza quotation has been treated in convincing detail by Quinn, '"Ok er þetta upphaf"'.

The *Ævikviða* in the S Version

In addition to *ævikviða* stanzas near the beginning of the saga prose in common with MABE, S also includes five additional stanzas of the *ævikviða*, stanzas 53, 52, 64, 69, 68 (in that order), in the second half of the saga, and not in direct proximity to stanzas 70–71 (i.e., the location in the saga in ABE where the rest of the *ævikviða* is found). That S has five extra stanzas of the *ævikviða* in its prose near the end of the poem is particularly interesting, since it suggests that in this, the oldest version of the saga considered by Boer to have the best text, the *ævikviða* hovers closely behind the prose despite not being written out in full.

Stanzas 8 and 9 in the S version are stanzas 53 and 52, respectively, in the death-song in the ABE version of the saga, and the differing uses of the stanzas in the two locations shed some light on how these *ævikviða* stanzas could be used in saga prose. These two stanzas recount in quick succession a visit to Aquitaine and Jerusalem:

Þar kom hann fremst, er heitir Akvitanaland; þar réðu fyrir fjórir höfðingjar, ok þar átti Oddr orrostu mikla ok feldi þar alla þessa höfðingja ok mikit fólk annat. [...]. Þar um kvað hann þessa vísu:

> 'Þar kvamk útarst, es Akvitana
> bragna kinder borgom réþo;
> þar létk fjóra fallna liggja
> hrausta drenge, nú'mk hér komenn'

[...] Eptir þat siglir Oddr út til Jórsalalands, ok þá fekk hann storm svá mikinn ok grunnsævi, at þar braut skip hans öll. Þar týnduz ok menn hans allir, svá at einn komz hann á land [...]. Hér um kvað Oddr þessa vísu:

> 'Sigldom síþan suþr langt í haf,
> áþr [ek] grunnsæve grimmo møttak,
> svát einn saman en ǫllo firþr
> gumna sinne gekk ek annan veg'

Oddr er nú kominn á Jórsaland; hann snýr nú leið sinni út til Jórdánar.

(The furthest he came is a place called Aquitaine; there ruled four chieftains, and there Oddr had a great battle, and fell all these chieftains and a great many folk besides [...]. About that place he composed this stanza:

> I came furthest out there, cities in Aquitaine
> ruled men of a mighty race. There I killed
> four valiant men, now I am come here.

[...] After that Oddr sailed to Jerusalem, and then he encountered a storm so great and in shallow water so that all his ships broke up. There he also lost all his men, so that he came to land alone [...]. About here Oddr composed a stanza:

> I sailed far to the south across the sea before
> I encounted grim shallow waters, so that
> alone, bereft of men, I went another way.

Oddr now arrives at Jerusalem, he turns on his way out to the river Jordan.)

In the death-song, these two stanzas are presented in a different order (9 then 8, or 52 then 53), so the stanza about journeying to the south comes first, followed by a trip to Aquitaine, and this is then followed by a stanza about going to Jerusalem and bathing in the river Jordan. In the prose of the S version, the reversal of the stanzas allows the journey to the south and the great storm, which otherwise does not give any specific place name, to be linked to his trip to Jerusalem to provide more content for the prose story. The loss of all his men in the storm also provides an explanation as to why Oddr carries on alone from Jerusalem.

Of particular interest is the end of stanza 8 of S, which is stanza 53 in the long *ævikvíða* of the ABE version. Although used in a prosimetric context in the saga prose, the end of the stanza reads 'nú'mk hér komenn' ('now I am arrived here', or as translated by Hermann Palsson and Paul Edwards: 'take note how far now I have come').[23] Intriguingly, this part of the stanza seems to refer to the context of the stanza's composition, but in the death-song rather than in the prosimetric saga context. At this point, Oddr is addressing the men ordered to write down his poem. This stanza can thus only make sense if it were originally found in the context of the longer poem and has been redeployed from there to form part of the saga's prosimetric structure. This is a rare piece of evidence that directly supports the oft-made claim that *fornaldarsaga* prose was constructed around poetry. In this case, it shows that the long poem was primary to the body of saga prose as now recorded, and that in terms of the text as we currently have it, the content of the long poem and its narrative context predates the saga prose of the S version.

The S version offers evidence of units of stanzas from the *ævikvíða* preserved together in the saga prose. Stanzas 21 and 22, which occur in all the full manuscripts of the saga, form a unit, as does the grouping of *ævikvíða* stanzas 53 and 52 in S and 69, 68, 70, and 71 in the latter part of S only. *Ævikvíða* stanzas 53,

---

[23] *Arrow-Odd*, trans. by Edwards and Herman Pálsson, p. 118.

52, and 64 also form a group in S, since they are S stanzas 8, 9, and 10. Units of stanzas in the saga prose indicate that there likely was a version of the longer poem in existence in oral tradition, in which verses were grouped together to tell certain elements of the story, yet were flexible in their order (so 53, 52, and 69, 68 would be presented in the running order S 52, 53 then 68, 69 in the *ævikviða*). This concurs with similar evidence from other eddic poems that are found recorded in several variants, in which units of stanzas can move around.[24] Also of note here is that stanzas from a large part of the *ævikviða* are found presented in the saga prose, being drawn from a span of fifty stanzas.

In S, the extra stanzas quoted from the *ævikviða* in the body of the saga are clearly introduced as quotations:

> S8, Æ53: 'Þar um kvað hann þessa vísu' (117.6)
>
> S9, Æ52: 'Hér um kvað Oddr þessa vísu' (117.17–18)
>
> S10, Æ64: 'Hér um kvað Oddr þessa vísu' (135.5, 137.19)
>
> S36, Æ69: 'Þessa vísu kvað Oddr hér um' (173.10)
>
> S41, Æ68: 'Hér um kvað Oddr þetta' (185.11)

In comparison, the other stanzas of the *ævikviða* that are used in the saga prose in all of the manuscripts are not introduced as quotations, but rather are used as direct speech, for example S3, Æ21 is introduced with 'þá kvað Oddr' (then Oddr said) (48.8, 49.8). The introductory phrase, 'Oddr composed a stanza about this place', presents the verse as quotation used as evidence for the prose, rather than as verse composed especially to embellish that particular part of the narrative. The introduction of these stanzas as quotations acknowledges their status as excerpts of a long poem, which suggests that S, the oldest of the saga manuscripts, relied more heavily on the pre-existing death-song to construct its prose than the younger versions of the saga, which do not have these additional quotations from the *ævikviða*.

As mentioned above, the quotation of the last stanza and a half of the death-song at the end of S is an unusual move, since first stanza quotation is more typical in Old Norse sagas and is thought to bring to mind the whole poem by naturally starting at the beginning. In S, the last two stanzas of the death-song appear instead, which in this particular context makes sense. First, quoting only the last one and a half stanzas marks that the end of the saga has been reached

---

[24] Mundal, 'Oral or Scribal Variation in *Vǫluspá*'.

in the sense that the saga actually follows the poem actively in creating the saga structure, rather than using the poem as a simple summing-up device. The quotation of extra stanzas in S as the oldest version might point towards the saga being composed around the stanzas and following the poem chronologically, since the later stanzas appear towards the end of the saga. Second, stanzas 69 and 68 are quoted nearby in the saga prose, so repetition was unnecessary. Since these penultimate stanzas had already appeared, it made sense to move on to 70–71 at the end of the saga in place of the whole death-song.

The Development of the Prosimetric Saga

There are two main arenas of 'moving words' during the development of the prosimetric *Ǫrvar-Odds saga*. The first is from poetry into prose, and the second is from orality into writing. The movement of poetry into prose essentially concerns the origins of the prosimetric saga. There seems to have been the following stages of development concerning the death-song and the saga prose:

1. There existed an oral poem corresponding to what we now know as Oddr's *ævikviða*. This poem seems to have had a prose framework to connect and contextualize the stanzas, which would change with every telling. The poem itself was likely also subject to variation during to its oral transmission, but nevertheless units of stanzas were transmitted together in flexible sequences.

2. The prose framework of the death-song developed a more substantial saga form, employing some of the *ævikviða* stanzas prosimetrically, potentially under the influence of the *konungasögur*.

3. The narrative developed to the point that the saga form predominantly contained prose, and by this point, other substantial sections of poetry were linked to the saga, such as Hjálmarr's death-song and Ǫrvar-Oddr's drinking contest. Oddr's *ævikviða* was appended to the end of the saga.

4. Several redactions of the saga developed; first, the older, shorter form, which shows clear evidence of having being based upon the *ævikviða*, although it does not include it quoted in its entirety (evidenced in manuscripts SM); and second, a younger, longer, version, which quotes the whole *ævikviða* at the end of the narrative (ABE).

Judging by the quotations of the *ævikviða* in S that are not in the other manuscripts, we can see that the first twenty stanzas of the *ævikviða* as preserved in ABE are not used prosimetrically, and are therefore not in evidence, in the older versions SM. This might suggest that these stanzas that begin the *ævikviða* are not original to the poem as such, but were added to the poem during stage four of the saga's development. However, they may indeed have existed orally in some form, but have not found their way into the beginning of the saga to be used prosimetrically when the saga gained its written form. This could be because the saga writer employs other stanzas as dialogue during the opening sequences of the saga, such as during Oddr's encounter with the *vǫlva* when his death is prophesied (pp. 14–15). The quotation of a stanza from the *ævikviða* during which this event is reported (such as st. 4 of the *ævikviða*), would not be nearly so effective in the narrative as the prophecy actually taking place in verse. Further evidence for the beginning of the poem's existence in oral tradition is that if the poem did indeed start with the first stanza found prosimetrically, which would be stanza 21 about Gusir's gifts, then if the first twenty stanzas really were missing, the beginning of Oddr's life would not have been included in the poem, which seems unlikely.

One clear question here is at what point we can understand the text as having moved from oral tradition into writing. The three reasonable places to suppose this could have happened are either between stages two or three, during stage three itself, or during stage four. There is evidence to suggest that a long poem such as the *ævikviða* could indeed have been recited at the end of a saga in oral tradition. In *Þorgils saga og Hafliða*, we hear that 'Ingimundr prestr sagði sǫgu Orms Barreyjarskálds ok vísur margar ok flokk góðan við enda sǫgunnar, er Ingimundr hafði ortan' (Ingimundr the priest told the story of Ormr Barreyjarskáld and many verses and a good *flokkr* ['poem'] at the end of the saga, which Ingimundr had composed).[25] The transition between stages two and three and even the whole of stage three may therefore have happened in oral tradition. It could be therefore that it was during the transition from stage three to stage four that the saga found its way into writing.

Ǫrvar-Odds saga is dated in handbooks to the end of the thirteenth or beginning of the fourteenth century,[26] corresponding with the dating of the oldest manuscript S to the beginning of the fourteenth century (stage four in the development of the saga). This is therefore the dating of the saga in its written form; stage three may thus have happened in the later stages of the thirteenth century. Stage two of the development of the saga, the development of a more substantial prose framework, is thus likely to have taken place in the

---

[25] *Þorgils saga ok Hafliða*, ed. by Brown, chs 10, 18.

[26] For example, by Kroesen, 'Ǫrvar-Odds saga'.

course of the thirteenth century, whereas the origin of the *ævikviða* could be around the 1200s, although likely not much before.

It is also useful to consider what might have come before the *ævikviða*, that is, what came before stage one of the developmental history of the saga. I propose that the *ævikviða* itself is based on traditions that were gathered together to form a poem. There is nothing to suggest that the poem drew upon written sources or traditions. These traditions brought together in the poem were probably drawn from two related sources: the first, Oddr's connection with the other famous men of Hrafnista and their sagas (*Ketils saga hængs*, *Gríms saga loðinkinna*, and *Áns saga bogsveigis*), a deep-rooted connection that I have explored previously[27] and one that seems to have fed especially into the beginning of the *ævikviða* (and indeed the saga itself), which gives some of Oddr's background. The second source of tradition that made its way into the poem concerned Oddr's travels, which formed the body of the *ævikviða* and subsequently the body of the saga prose, too. This second source of tradition may be reflected in the prose by the line that other characters often use when encountering and recognizing Oddr for the first time: 'Ertu sá Oddr, er fór til Bjarmalands?' (52. 12).[28] These travels make up the body of the *ævikviða*.[29] The two sources of tradition are blended throughout the saga, and come together for the first time in Lopthœna's (Oddr's mother's) comment near the beginning of the saga after Oddr's birth 'þótti mér, sem hann rendi lítt ástaraugum til vár Hrafnistumanna' (7. 11) (it seemed to me that he had little love in his eyes for us people of Hrafnista). This rather oblique comment is hard to understand

---

[27] Leslie, "'The Matter of Hrafnista".

[28] This is the first occurance in the M version. In the same place in the S version, the viking Hálfdan instead asks him 'Fórtu til Bjarmalands fyrra sumar?' (53.14) (Did you travel to Permia last summer?). This line is also used to show the passing of time throughout the saga in accordance with Oddr's great age; later it becomes in the M version 'Ertu sá Oddr, er fór til Bjarmalands fyrir nǫkkurum vetrum?' (62.6–7) (Are you that Oddr who went to Permia some winters ago?), (in the S version ÷ Oddr; ABE nǫkkurum vetrum] skǫmmu). Even later in the narrative it becomes in the M version 'Ertu ei sá Oddr [...] er fór til Bjarmalands fyrir lǫngu?' (84.14–15) (Are you not that Oddr [...] who went to Permia a long time ago?); for similar, see also 89.20–21, 90.6, 168.19–20. In ABE, the question is also used in a long section about Oddr's adventures that SM lacks by Oddr's son Vignir to ensure he has the right person (130.17–18).

[29] Also of note are the traditions surrounding the companionship of Oddr and Hjálmarr death of Hjálmarr (see Leslie, 'The Death Songs of *Örvar-Odds saga*'), which can likely be safely grouped here with traditions related to Oddr's travels. This particular element is first attested in writing by Saxo Grammaticus in the twelfth century in Book v of the *Gesta Danorum*.

given the rest of the saga narrative in which Oddr returns to Hrafnista quite a few times, unless we understand it to mean the amount of travelling Oddr does is due to his wanderlust and love of battles, which keeps him away from Hrafnista for extended periods. The poem and saga both reflect a blending of the links between Hrafnista and Oddr's seafaring adventures, most famously his two visits to Permia.

Conclusion

I have argued that *Ǫrvar-Odds saga* seems to have been based around a long monologue-type poem. This could have been similar at the oral stage; before it was committed to writing, the prose of the oral saga helped set the poem into a storytelling tradition. The stanzas of the death-song that are quoted individually only occasionally break to the surface of the saga prose that floats on them. The prose story acted as context for the stanzas, which were then quoted as part of the narrative, usually as dialogue stanzas. The saga continued to develop after being committed to writing, although it still predominantly retained dialogue stanzas. It is natural that other stanzas were composed for the saga that were unrelated, as far as we are able to tell, to the *ævikviða*, as dialogue for both Ǫrvar-Oddr and for other characters, and the saga also drew in the traditional episode of Hjálmarr's death, also found in some versions of *Hervarar saga*. The inclusion of only the last stanza and a half in the oldest, short redaction of *Ǫrvar-Odds saga* suggests that the poem was well known enough not be included in its entirety. This conclusion is useful for the study of the *fornaldarsaga* saga subgenre because it provides evidence that attests to one way the legendary sagas developed and also sheds light on the workings of prosimetrum at the oral-written interface.

Works Cited

Manuscripts and Archival Sources

Reykjavík, Stofnun Árna Magnússonar í íslenskum fræðum, AM 173 I fol.
——, AM 343 a 4to
——, AM 344 a 4to
——, AM 471 4to
——, AM 567 IV 4to
Stockholm, Kungliga biblioteket, Holm Perg. 4to nr 7

Primary Sources

Arrow-Odd: A Medieval Novel, trans. by Paul Edwards and Herman Pálsson (New York: New York University Press, 1970)
Eddica Minora: Dichtungen eddischer Art aus den Fornaldarsögur und anderen Prosa-werken, ed. by Andreas Heusler and Wilhelm Ranisch (Dortmund: Ruhfus, 1903)
Egil's saga, trans. by Bernard Scudder, in *The Complete Sagas of the Icelanders*, 5 vols (Reykjavík: Leifur Eiríksson, 1997), I, 33–177
Egils saga, ed. by Bjarni Einarsson (London: Viking Society for Northern Research, 2003)
Ǫrvar-Odds saga, ed. by R. C. Boer (Leiden: Brill, 1888)
Þorgils saga ok Hafliða, ed. by Ursula Brown, Oxford English Monographs (London: Oxford University Press, 1952)

Secondary Studies

A Dictionary of Old Norse Prose: Indices/Ordbog over det norrøne prosaprog: Registre (Copenhagen: Den Arnmagnæanske kommission, 1989)
'AM 173 fol.', *Handrit.is* <http://handrit.is/en/manuscript/view/is/AM02–0173> [accessed 20 August 2017]
Finnur Jónsson, *Den oldnorske og oldislandske litteraturs historie*, 2nd edn, 3 vols (Copenhagen: Gades, 1920–24)
Harris, Joseph, 'Beowulf's Last Words', *Speculum*, 67 (1992), 1–32
Kålund, Kristian, *Katalog over den Arnamagnæanske Handskriftsamling*, 2 vols in 4 (Copenhagen: Gyldendal, 1889–94)
Kroesen, Riti, 'Ǫrvar-Odds saga', in *Medieval Scandinavia: An Encyclopedia*, ed. by Phillip Pulsiano, Garland Encyclopedia of the Middle Ages, 1; Garland Reference Library of the Humanities, 934 (New York: Garland, 1993), p. 744
Leslie, Helen F., 'The Death Songs of Örvar-Odds saga', in *Cartografies de l'ànima: indentitat, memòria i escriptura*, ed. by Isabel Grifoll, Julián Acebrón, and Flocel Sabaté (Lleida: Pagès editors, 2014), pp. 231–44
——, 'Genre and the Prosimetra of the Old Icelandic *fornaldarsögur*', in *Genre — Text — Interpretation: Multidisciplinary Perspectives on Folklore and Beyond*, ed. by Kaarina Koski and Frog (Helsinki: Finnish Literature Society, 2016), pp. 251–75

——, 'Prose Contexts of Eddic Poetry: Particularly in the *fornaldarsögur*' (unpublished doctoral thesis, University of Bergen, 2013)

——, 'The Matter of Hrafnista', *Quaestio Insularis*, 11 (2010), 169–208

Lönnroth, Lars, 'Hjálmar's Death-Song and the Delivery of Eddic Poetry', *Speculum*, 46 (1971), 1–20

Mitchell, Stephen, 'The *fornaldarsǫgur* and Nordic Balladry: The Sámsey Episode across Genres', in *Fornaldarsagornas struktur och ideologi: Handlingar från ett symposium i Uppsala 31.8–2.9 2001*, ed. by Ármann Jakobsson, Annette Lassen, and Agneta Ney (Uppsala: Uppsala universitet, 2003), pp. 245–56

Mundal, Else, 'Oral or Scribal Variation in *Vǫluspá*: A Case Study in Old Norse Poetry', in *Oral Art Forms and their Passage into Writing*, ed. by Else Mundal and Jonas Wellendorf (Copenhagen: Museum Tusculanum Press, 2008), pp. 209–27

Quinn, Judy, '"Ok er þetta upphaf" — First-Stanza Quotation in Old Norse Prosimetrum', *alvíssmál*, 7 (1997), 61–80

'Blood flying and brains falling like rain': Chivalric Conflict Gone Norse

Ingvil Brügger Budal

Introductions to editions of, and encyclopaedic entries about, the *riddarasǫgur*, chivalric stories translated from Old French to Old Norse during the thirteenth century, frequently state that dramatic passages have been given added emphasis in translation, either by means of expansion, or through omission and abbreviation of descriptions, monologues, emotive behaviour, and other less animated parts of the narrative. The common explanation for this textual turn is a translator or redactor's concern for the Norse audiences' lack of appreciation for the complex interplay of the chivalric protagonists. A recent approach to the shift of emphasis in these texts is found in Sif Rikhardsdottir's investigation of the translatability of literary representations of emotion across linguistic and cultural boundaries. Drawing on the *riddarasǫgur*-material, she concludes that textual content, whether this is the representation of emotions or the more dramatic passages of narration, is both 'culturally contingent and socially determined' as well as reflective of 'generic dispositions of an audience'.[1]

This essay addresses the issue of medieval translations and their dynamics by looking at one piece of the puzzle: namely, the *riddarasǫgur* as witnesses of textual variance. Do texts become native, or rather adapt to indigenous taste

---

[1] Sif Rikhardsdottir, 'Translating Emotion', p. 178.

Ingvil Brügger Budal (**Ingvil.Brugger.Budal@hvl.no**) is Associate Professor of Norwegian at Western Norway University of Applied Sciences in Bergen. She holds a PhD in Old Norse philology from the University of Bergen, and works on the *riddarasǫgur* and their sources, medieval translation and textual transmission.

Moving Words in the Nordic Middle Ages: Tracing Literacies, Texts, and Verbal Communities, ed. by Amy C. Mulligan and Else Mundal, AS 8   BREPOLS ⬛ PUBLISHERS   (Turnhout: Brepols, 2019)
pp. 297–318   10.1484/M.AS-EB.5.116629

and stylistic ideals in translation and transmission through the highlighting of elements characteristic of the target culture?

The assumption that Norse translators emphasized certain textual elements in the *riddarasǫgur* has hardly been questioned. Moreover, analyses of how these dramatic or violent passages were highlighted and altered, and what this could tell us of their process of translation and transmission, are scarce. This study will present some methodological considerations regarding the evaluation of these medieval translations, specifically by querying the common assumption that violence is emphasized in the translated *riddarasǫgur*. At the centre of this investigation stand three versions of *Elíss saga ok Rósamundar*: close comparative readings of these texts will provide examples of how specific textual elements are highlighted and altered. First of all, the relevant extant sources and their material contexts will be presented, as the manuscripts are the tangible representation of moving words. Focus then shifts to textual transmission with commentary on the shifts of genre and style that occur. Finally, comparison of important passages from these texts featuring conflict and violence illustrates how words move between languages, through space and time.

Moving in Manuscripts, Languages, Space, and Time: Three Versions of the Tale of Élie

This study is based on three versions of the story of the knight Élie;[2] the French *chanson de geste*, its fragmentary Old Norwegian translation, as well as a full Icelandic redaction of the text.

There is only one extant French manuscript of the *chanson de geste*, the *Élie de Saint-Gilles* of the manuscript Paris, Bibliothèque nationale de France, no. 25516.[3] The manuscript originates from northern France and is commonly dated to the second half of the thirteenth century. The editors, Richard Hartman and Sandra Malicote, suggest that the French text was brought to the Norwegian court by Matthew of Paris together with other texts translated into Old Norse.[4] Neither literary sources, nor historical or physical evidence, suggest this. A source text can hardly postdate its supposed translation, and the thirteenth-century manuscripts of the French and the Norse texts are in no way

---

[2] The protagonist of both tales will be referred to as Élie.

[3] I have used the excellent 2013 edition of Bernard Guidot, but with the occasional glance at Hartman and Malicote's edition and English translation from 2011.

[4] *Elye of Saint-Gilles*, ed. and trans. by Hartmann and Malicote, p. xiv.

source text and translation.[5] The *chanson de geste* immediately following *Élie de Saint-Gilles* in the manuscript, *Aiol*, tells the adventures of Élie's son Aiol, and these two form the so-called 'petit cycle de *Saint-Gilles*'.[6]

A fragmentary French manuscript of the tale of Élie was in the hands of a Norse translator by the mid-thirteenth century. The oldest manuscript of *Elíss saga ok Rósamundar*, the Old Norwegian translation of *Élie de Saint-Gilles*, is found in Uppsala, Uppsala Universitetsbibliotek, De la Gardie 4–7 4°, a Norwegian compilation dated to the latter half of the thirteenth century, most likely to 1250–70.[7] The introduction to the manuscript's facsimile states that this is 'the oldest and most important collection of so-called "courtly" literature in Norse translation,'[8] as the manuscript contains *Elíss saga* and versions of *Pamphilus* and the *Strengleikar*, that is, Marie de France's *lais* translated into Norse.

The manuscript is incomplete, due both to the lacuna of two leaves mid-manuscript and the translator's source text lacking the final leaves. Abbot Robert comments on its partial nature in the final lines of his translation:

> En huessu sem elis ratt þæim vandræðum. oc huessu hann kom hæim til frannz. með rosamundam. þa er ægi a bok þessi skrifat. en roðbert aboti sneri. oc Hakon konungr son Hakons. konungs. lét snua þessi nœrrœnu bok. yðr til skemtanar.[9]

> (And it is not written in this book about how Elis got out of these difficulties and how he came home to France with Rósamunda. But Abbott Robert translated and King Hákon, the son of King Hákon, had this Norse book translated for your entertainment.[10])

---

[5] Hartman and Malicote's assumption misleads a reviewer, who feels 'grateful that this captivating and fun example of romance epic has reached us through the tenuous journey of a sole manuscript that traveled to the court of Norway's king to be translated into Old Norse, then back again to the Flanders library and later the Bibliothèque Nationale. Eight hundred years later, it has been translated into English, accompanied by a critical apparatus that bring to life both the original text and its historical and literary context'; Kelly, 'Review', pp. 875–76.

[6] Paris, 'Élie de Saint-Gilles', p. 470.

[7] For a recent diplomatic edition of *Elíss saga ok Rósamundar*, see *Elíss saga ok Rósamundar: De la Gardie 4–7 4°*, ed. by Budal. The entire Norse manuscript is available in facsimile with a useful introduction *Elis saga, Strengleikar and Other Texts*, ed. by Tveitane. Kölbing's 1881 edition is good, but there are some issues with his introduction; see Meissner, *Die Strengleikar*. For a recent approach to the manuscript, mainly originating in material philology, see Eriksen, *Writing and Reading*.

[8] *Elis saga, Strengleikar and Other Texts*, ed. by Tveitane, p. 9.

[9] *Elíss saga ok Rósamundar*, ed. by Budal, 17^{rv}.

[10] My translation. Unless otherwise mentioned, any translations are my own.

A fragmentary French source, and thereby an unfinished tale, could have easily led to the text to being deemed unsuited for translation. The passage quoted above suggests that the translator of *Elíss saga ok Rósamundar* discovered the incomplete state of the text while working on it. The saga in De la Gardie 4–7 4° has no appended conclusion, and one might expect that a later redactor would append a conclusion as soon as possible. Thus, the lack of a conclusion might be an indication of this witness being close to the original translation, even possibly the original translation.

However, a transmitted text from the lacuna is known from a younger manuscript, Stockholm, Kungliga biblioteket, Holm perg 7 fol., a late fifteenth-century manuscript, featured alongside the text from De la Gardie 4–7 4° in the only printed edition of this *riddarasaga*.[11] At some point in the transmission of the Norse text, an Icelandic text redactor completed Élie's adventures, and Holm perg 7 fol. includes his newly composed conclusion to the tale. Even though this conclusion uses narrative matter and motifs from the translated part of the saga, and even plagiarizes an entire scene, it deviates significantly from the French text. In *Kulturhistorisk leksikon for nordisk middelalder*, Eyvind Fjeld Halvorsen considers this conclusion to be written by someone without knowledge of French literature, who has drawn on other parts of *Elíss saga* and other translated sagas such as *Karlamagnús saga*, a compilation of translated *gestes* related to Charlemagne, most notably the *Chanson de Roland*.[12]

The relative abundance of Norse manuscripts indicates that the story was both popular and widespread. Some of these forty-three manuscripts are full versions of the saga, others are fragments known through the transmission of a single vellum leaf, and a couple are simple summaries.[13] Whereas only the oldest manuscript, the De la Gardie 4–7 4° from the latter half of the thirteenth century, is of Norwegian origin, the saga had a long afterlife in Iceland, and handwritten manuscripts are known from a span of six hundred years, from the early fourteenth century until the early twentieth century.

When studying medieval texts, a cautious approach and attention to the variations, no matter how minute, among the manuscript witnesses is crucial. In the case of *Élie de Saint-Gilles* and the Norwegian *Elíss saga*, these are the closest representatives of the source and target text available to us; there is only

[11] *Elis saga ok Rosamundu*, ed. by Kölbing.

[12] Halvorsen, 'Elis saga ok Rosamundu', pp. 596–97. All translations from Norwegian from *Kulturhistorisk leksikon for nordisk middelalder* are my own.

[13] Kalinke and Mitchell, *Bibliography*, pp. 36–37.

one French witness of the text, and, considering the dating and content, the Norwegian text from De la Gardie 4–7 ° could be the original translation, or an early copy of an original translation. The later Icelandic redaction (Holm perg 7 fol.) fills the mid-manuscript lacuna and gives an indigenous ending to the tale, and thus serves as witness to an important step in the Norse transmission of this text.

Eyvind Fjeld Halvorsen briefly and damningly evaluates the three stages of the tale's evolution. He describes the original as 'one of the poorest *chansons de geste* ever written'; characterized by 'poor and stereotypical language, the story is banal, with tremendously exaggerated tests and battles, and without a trace of characterization'. Halvorsen thus finds that the Norse translator wasted his skills on such a mediocre text. However, Halvorsen writes that the endeavors of the translator give *Elíss saga* 'an abundantly nuanced, lyrical language'; this, how-ever, vanishes in Icelandic transmission, as 'the language in the Icelandic manu-scripts has lost much of the charm of the original *Elis saga*'.[14] Renewed scholarly interest has since emerged, both for the *riddarasǫgur* in general and for *Élie de Saint-Gilles* and *Elíss saga ok Rósamundar* in particular, and the assessment of their literary quality has changed significantly.[15] Twentieth-century critics of *Élie de Saint-Gilles* such as M. Delbouille and E. Melli have pointed out 'the compositional unity and integrity complemented by its extremely sophisticated rhetorical development',[16] whereas the Norse *riddarasǫgur* are no longer seen as imported literature of low quality, but as witnesses of textual transmission, of medieval translations and cultural dissemination, and examined as such, and this shift has led to different questions and assessments.[17]

Moving between Genres and Styles — A Brief Comment

Élie de Saint-Gilles is a *chanson de geste*, a narrative poem of heroic deeds, belong-ing to a genre originally presented in a musical performance by jongleurs. Some of the early *chansons* were probably transmitted orally and, as Simon Gaunt puts it, were 'addressed to a broad non-courtly audience'. Nevertheless, the lav-ish compilations preserving many of the texts were 'clearly commissioned for a

---

[14] Halvorsen, 'Elis saga', pp. 596–97. My translation.

[15] For an overview of the material, see Kalinke, *The Arthur of the North*.

[16] Quoted in *Elye of Saint-Gilles*, ed. by Hartman and Malicote, p. xiv.

[17] See for instance *Riddarasögur*, ed. by Johansson and Mundal, and *Francia et Germania*, ed. by Johansson and Flaten.

wealthy lay audience'.[18] The stanzas, called laisses, of the *chansons de geste* tend
to have a repetitive language and use stock phrases, facilitating an oral performance from memory. Joachim Bumke suggests that the minstrels performed for
an hour at a time, covering approximately a thousand verses, and that the performances of *chansons de geste* thus extended over several days.[19] Nevertheless,
the German adaptation of French literary aristocratic culture differed from the
Norse, and the *chansons de geste* did not become a 'powerful source in shaping
literary taste in Germany' until much later.[20] Bumke sees a partial explanation
for the weak influence of the *chanson de geste* in its very form and suggests that
the metrical form posed a 'nearly insoluble problem' to the translators.[21] As
Norse poetic genres rest upon intricate patterns of stressed syllables and alliteration rather than end-rhyme, Norse and German translators were facing the
same problems. Yet, as we shall see, the Norse translators approached the task
at hand by creating a new literary style and adapting foreign courtly texts for a
Norse audience.

The Old Norse prose genre of *riddarasǫgur* is composed of two subgenres
— translated *riddarasǫgur* and indigenous *riddarasǫgur* — a division mainly
resting on the geographical and linguistic origins of the texts. The courtly translations, instigated by the Norwegian king Hákon Hákonarson (1204–63), are
for the most part thirteenth-century prose translations of mainly French texts,
whereas the indigenous *riddarasǫgur* are fourteenth-century imitations of the
courtly translations which reuse characters and motifs, but are strikingly different in tenor.[22] However, the term *riddarasǫgur* tends to refer to the translated
ones, whereas the indigeneity demands to be pointed out. The *riddarasǫgur*,
the genre and the style discussed here, are limited to the translations.

The term *riddarasǫgur* implies in itself a corpus of texts having a series of
common traits. The texts are translated from French, and their subject matter
is related to chivalry or courtly culture, but they are a multifaceted material.
The translations are grouped together on the basis of being translated but originate from a variety of genres, from Marie de France's *lais* to *chansons de geste*
and *fabliaux*. In the process of translation to Old Norse, the target culture and
its expectations for these texts leave an imprint on them, but the fundamental

---

[18] Gaunt, 'Romance and Other Genres', p. 48.

[19] Bumke, *Courtly Culture*, p. 522.

[20] Bumke, *Courtly Culture*, p. 93.

[21] Bumke, *Courtly Culture*, p. 93.

[22] See the bipartite entry on *riddarasögur* in *Medieval Scandinavia*, ed. by Pulsiano and Wolf.

differences between the varied source texts are by no means erased in trans-lation. The *Strengleikar*, the Old Norwegian translations of Marie de France's *lais*, retain their romantic, at times delicate, enchantment, whereas the transla-tion of the *fabliau Le mantel mautaillé*, *Möttuls saga*, remains splendidly and explicitly entertaining, exposing rather vulgarly the sexual preferences of ladies of the aristocracy.

This translated literature falls within the so-called *høvisk stil*, that is, 'courtly style', found in its most successful form in the translations of French litera-ture, notably in *Elíss saga*, *Strengleikar*, and *Tristrams saga*.[23] The translated *riddarasǫgur* share certain stylistic features, but it is nevertheless an oversimpli-fication to consider them to be uniform. Their style is 'woven of three strands', the native saga style, the Latinate learned style, and the poetic language of the source texts.[24] Within Norse literature, end-rhyme is scarce, and the epic gen-res lack a substitute for the French use of fixed-syllable couplets, laisses, and their rhythmic effect. The translators, striving to transfer their source's poetic quality into Norse, but lacking the equivalent rhetorical features, therefore employ a variety of verbal, in particular semantic, parallelisms and frequently add alliteration to give a rhythmic quality to the prose narratives. The translat-ability of the style of the French texts is not evident, and it has been assumed that the play with sounds and synonyms could have been inspired by rigid and formulaic Old Norse poetry.

Translated texts go through manifold transformations. Indeed, the manu-script texts we have of the *riddarasǫgur* originated in an oral, sung performance in French, after which these *chansons de geste* were put down in writing. The translation from French to Old Norse moves the text from poetry to an elabo-rate prose, from one genre to another and to a new culture and geography, from France to Scandinavia. Once translated, the *riddarasǫgur* were most likely once again subject to a new oral performance, being read or recited aloud. The dif-fusion of these texts is thus both an oral performance, sometimes based on the recital of a written text, as well as a written transmission through the emer-gence of copies, adaptations, and translations.

The earliest oral performances of the Norse *riddarasǫgur* were in all prob-ability public readings for selected, limited audiences. The Old Norse audience was likely comprised of members of the higher classes, yet this audience would have had a completely different set of expectations than the original French

[23] Halvorsen, 'Høvisk stil'.

[24] Jónas Kristjánsson, *Eddas and Sagas*, p. 322.

audience. Nevertheless, over time these stories were embraced by a wider audience, were adapted, rewritten, and imitated, and their motifs and characters were combined with indigenous legends.

Moving between Audiences and their Preferences; or, How (not) to Measure Emphasis Given to Textual Elements

Is it at all possible to measure the emphasis given to certain elements of a text? There is of course the option of *counting* words and lines, and data comprised of hardcore numbers can be quite satisfying. However, do such measurable entities truly provide a sound and working foundation for comparisons? The use of numbers can reveal that acts of aggression, battle, or violence constitute a certain percentage of one text, and a different percentage of another. Even though this can be a valid approach for examining certain stylistic and rhetorical features — for instance, alliterations, present participles, or a selection of specific word derivations —[25] the means of adding emphasis to certain elements of a text cannot be reduced to numbers. The effect of specific passages is of course determined by the portion of the entire text granted to the motif, but perhaps even more by the actual vocabulary chosen and the use of, for instance, rhetorical figures. Sif Rikhardsdottir has discussed the 'translatability of literary representation of emotion across linguistic and cultural boundaries'. While drawing on neuroscience and psychology, she still emphasizes that the emotions of fictional characters are discursive or textual constructions; she discusses the 'generically determined signifiers of the emotive subtext'.[26] Elements of a text function as signifiers, not only emotional signifiers, but as elements that can and will add emphasis to certain motifs. Such emphasis occurs in the interconnected web of signifiers within the text and can hardly be measured in 'hardcore numbers'.

When it comes to battle and violence, would not a highly paced passage, written in the present rather than the past tense, with swift changes rather than long elaborate descriptions, highlight the actions described, rendering them more vivid? Stylistic ideals are dependent upon region, period, language, and, to some

---

[25] This approach to the *riddarasǫgur* has been done by, for instance, Hallberg, *Stilsignalement*; Tveitane and Cook, *Strengleikar*; and Budal; *Strengleikar og lais*, as well as 'A Translation and its Continuation'.

[26] Sif Rikhardsdottir, 'Translation Emotion'.

extent, an individual reader's taste and his or her training.[27] The effect of specific textual representations are also a question of 'literary precedence and cultural conventions'.[28] These, combined with the audience's experience, compose the horizon of expectation upon meeting the text. As Sif Rikhardsdottir points out when examining the translatability of emotions in *Ivéns saga*, there is a 'general and overall reduction in emotional vocabulary in the Norse translation when compared to the French text'.[29] She identifies specific modifications in how the emotive content is conveyed, revealing the process of cultural adaptation.

The emphasis on violence in these translations might also be the result of the continued presence of specific elements — and the absence of others. Sif Rikhardsdottir explores the absence — or reduced representation of emotions — in her study of *Ívens saga*, the Norse translation of *Yvain*. While exploring the 'cultural premise of emotional representation', she sees the tendency to reduce the display of emotions in the *riddarasǫgur* as a cultural adjustment to the habits and preferences of the text's target audience.[30] This audience, she argues, was accustomed to deducing the internal emotional life in fiction though 'acts (but not through gestures), through somatic indicators (but not through bodily behaviour) and through verbalisation (but not through verbal expression)'.[31]

The next point is the forever recurring concern of the transmission and lives of medieval texts — a concern that not only applies to translations but perhaps *in particular* applies to translations. Any scholar working with medieval texts and manuscripts will be aware of issues regarding lost sources, vanished original translations, and missing intermediary manuscripts; therefore, the implications of these issues will not be pursued further here.[32] Nevertheless, of particular interest to the Norse translations and their transmission is Marianne Kalinke's work on the eighteenth-century Icelandic paper copy of the first of the *Strengleikar*-stories, *Gvímars saga*.[33] Kalinke's comparison between the French

---

[27] It is worth considering if this expectation depends on my own status as a Nynorsk-speaking Norwegian, and thus a member of a linguistic and literary community whose stylistic ideals are short sentences, and simple, straightforward expression.

[28] Sif Rikhardsdottir, 'Translation Emotion', p. 167.

[29] Sif Rikhardsdottir, 'Translation Emotion', p. 166.

[30] Sif Rikhardsdottir, 'Translation Emotion', p. 161.

[31] Sif Rikhardsdottir, 'Translation Emotion', p. 177.

[32] For a useful discussion and further references, see Kalinke, *The Arthur of the North*, pp. 22–48.

[33] Kalinke, *Gvímars saga* from Reykjavík, Lbs. 840.

(thirteenth-century), the Norwegian (thirteenth-century), and the Icelandic (eighteenth-century) redactions demonstrates that the youngest redaction contains complementary readings of the translation, thus preserving elements of the original translation already lost in the thirteenth-century Norwegian manuscript, but for a long time believed to be the original translation. This is an excellent and convincing illustration of the dangers of dismissing the textual evidence in later copies of a text, even post-medieval manuscripts. A study of *Elíss saga ok Rósamundar* including more than the textual witnesses available in printed editions, the thirteenth-century De la Gardie-text, and the somewhat abbreviated late fifteenth-century Holm perg 7 fol., would increase our knowledge of the variance and stability of medieval texts in transmission.

Moving Words between Languages, Locations, and through Time: Some Examples from Élie de Saint-Gilles *and* Elíss saga ok Rósamundar

Not all of the translated *riddarasǫgur* contain a great deal of violence. The *Strengleikar*-stories and their French counterparts, the *lais*, contain in general very little explicit chivalric physical conflict, aggression, or violence. Most references made to such acts are brief, summarizing statements of what has taken place, quite neutrally referring to the actions. In the story of *Guigemar*, three little octosyllabic couplets suffice for the hero and his men to besiege a city, increase their number of followers, and subsequently let everyone in the city starve to death before conquering and destroying the castle, as well as killing its lord (Guigemar vv. 875–80):[34]

Harley 978	**Harley 978**
Guigemar ad la vile assise,	Guigemar besieged the town;
N'en turnerat si serat prise.	he won't leave until it has fallen.
Tant li crurent ami e genz	His friends and other troops increased so greatly
Que tuz les affamat dedenz.	that he was able to starve everyone inside.
Le chastel ad destruit e pris	He captured and destroyed the castle,
E le seignur dedenz ocis.	Killed its lord.
De la Gardie 4–7 4°	**De la Gardie 4–7 4°**
ok skipaði þa Gviamar liðinu um	Then Guiamar arranged his men around the
herfis borginna ok vill engom	town — he will under no terms leave until he
koste brott fyrr en hann have	has prevailed. Then his band increased greatly

---

[34] The French text is from Rychner's edition of Marie de France's *Les lais*. p. 32, and its translation *The Lais of Marie de France* by Hanning and Ferrante, p. 54. The Norse text is from *Strengleikar*, ed. and trans. by Tveitane and Cook, pp. 40–41.

sott En þa vox sva miok lið hans
frendr hans ok felagar ok toko
þæir viste alla fyrir þæim ok
svællto alla þa er i varo borgenne
ok kastalanom. Siðan tok
Gviamarr borgena ok kastalann
ok drap Meriadum er fyrir sat.

(his kinsmen and companions),
and they took away all the
provisions and starved all those
who were in the town and castle.
Then Guiamar took the town and
castle and killed Meriadus, who
was in charge.

The actual French text uses six octosyllabic lines, a total of forty-eight syllables, to describe this, far less than I did in my attempt to summarize it. The result of added details, as well as the adjustments needed when transferring a text from verse to prose, is a more voluminous, but not more vigorous Old Norse text. As in Hartmann and Malicote's English translation of *Élie de Saint-Gilles*, the Old Norse translation tends to replace pronouns with personal names, supposedly for increased textual clarity.

The point of view of the *Strengleikar* stories is a detached view from a castle window, and the genre, as Bjarne Fidjestøl so brilliantly puts it, 'takes a folkloristic product (the oral story) of nature (i.e. the people) and lifts it up into the cultural sphere (i.e. the court) through the refinement into a lais'.[35] Thus, when working with the manuscript De la Gardie 4–7 4°, I moved from the artistry of *Strengleikar* to *Elíss saga ok Rósamundar*, the saga preceding *Strengleikar* in the manuscript. My horizon of expectation was profoundly shaped by my recent reading of the *Strengleikar* stories. Yet, all of a sudden I found myself surrounded by fierce heathens, horseheads split in two, intestines falling out, and King Arthur leading an army of the undead. Although almost identical in the two Norse texts examined, as well as in an 1858 Icelandic paper copy (Reykjavík, Handritasafn Landsbókasafns Íslands, Lbs 2153 4°),[36] these differ from the corresponding French passage referring to King Arthur in BnF, fr. 25516, vv. 653–58. Four knights, including Guillaume d'Orange, have just been released from captivity and rush forward, all set to fight off the pagans.[37] This is the pagans' reaction — and the old man referred to in the French text is Bernart de Brubant, Guillaume d'Orange's brother:[38]

[35] Fidjestøl, 'Erotisk lesnad', p. 81.

[36] A photographic facsimile is available at <https://handrit.is/is/manuscript/view/Lbs04–2153>.

[37] For an interesting comparative approach to the use of 'Kampf', battle, as a structuring element of these stories, see Winst, 'Mittelalterliche Logiken'.

[38] Hartman and Malicote's translation is at times quite free, and thus occasionally flawed for the academic reader.

BnF, fr. 25516[39]

Dist Jossés d'Alixandre,
   'Cis viex est mervellous!
C'est Artus de Bretaigne
   u Gavain ses nevos,
U Pilate d'enfer
   u Mordrant l'aïrous,
Qui mangüent les homes
   .V. u .IV. en .I. jor.
Par le foi que vous doi,
   si fera il nous tous,
Car poignomes a l'ost,
   qu'il nous facent secor.'

BnF, fr. 25516[40]

Joshua of Alexandria said,
   'That old man's a wonder!
He's like Arthur of Brittany,
   or Gawain his nephew,
Or like Pilate of hell,
   or the angry Mordrant,
Who in one day
   ate up four or five men!
By the faith I owe you.
   He'll do the same to us all!
Let's ride quickly to the army,
   so that they can help us!'

De la Gardie 4–7 4°[41]

þa mællti Jose or Alexandre, hæiðingi:
Nu se ec, kuað h*ann*, kynlect folk: her er
nu komi*nn* Artur *konung*r or Bretlande,
hi*nn* frægi *konung*r *oc* hi*nn* sigrsæli, *oc*
með hono*m* Gafer hi*nn* sterki *oc* Margant hi*nn* ræiðlynde *oc* Gulafri hi*nn*
ǫðe, er etr V me*nn* eða VI at æínu mali.

Snum aftr sem skiotazt til liðs vars til
hialpar, þuiat þessom maun*n*om stan-
daz engi lifande m*enn*: þessir ero kappar
kristi*nn*a man*n*a, er longu voro dauðer,
oc ero nu upp risnir af dauða, at drepa
oss *oc* veria riki sitt firir oss.

De la Gardie 4–7 4°

Then Jose of Alexandria, the heathen, said:
Now I see, he said, wondrous people. King
Arthur has arrived here from Brittany. The
famous king, and the victorious, and with
him Gafer the strong and Margant the fierce,
and Gulafri the furious, who eats five or six
men for one single meal.

Let's return to our army for help as soon as
possible, because no living men can withstand
these men. These are Christian combatants
that have been dead for a long time. And they
have now arisen from the dead in order to kill
us and protect their kingdom from us.

The basic elements of this passage are identical: something is a wonder, Arthur and some of his followers are present in the texts: one of them is a cannibal, and it is considered wise to return to the army for help. Nonetheless, these elements are put together in a completely different manner in the two texts. The old man who in *Élie de Saint-Gilles* is a wonder who can be compared to Arthur, is turned into an army of strange or wonderful people risen from the dead, led by the resurrected King Arthur in the Norse text. The textual displacement could originate from a translator struggling with a rather complicated source text, and

---

[39] *Élie de Saint-Gilles*, ed. by Guidot, p. 179.

[40] *Elye of Saint-Gilles*, trans. by Hartman and Malicote, p. 43.

[41] *Elis saga ok Rosamundu*, ed. by Kölbing, p. 41.

even Bernard Guidot, the editor, comments on the BnF fr. 25516 as '(ne) pas d'une lecture delicate' (not a delicate/easy read), referring to the text itself, as well as the editorial challenges when dealing with a 'manuscrit unique' (single manuscript).[42] It is not obvious exactly who Joshua refers to before the end of the French verses quoted above. An Old Norse translator may have chosen to preserve basic elements from his source, interweaving these to the best of his abilities. If so, the final lines, referring to 'the Christian combatants who have been dead for a long time', 'arisen from the dead in order to kill us and protect their kingdom from us', could be an Old Norse redactor's addition to the text. Nevertheless, only in rare cases it is possible to determine whether such paragraphs are additions in translation and transmission, or remnants of a lost source.

Even though there are only minor differences between the thirteenth- and the fifteenth-century Norse versions of these lines, the passages above illustrate several types of textual changes in intralingual transmission. The 'Christian combatants', or 'kappar kristna manna' in the oldest manuscript, has by the fifteenth century been replaced by 'kæmpur kristinna manna'. The nouns *kappa* and *kempa* both refer to a 'strong and brave man, hero, warrior', but then again, should not be perceived as entirely synonymous, as the *Ordbog over det norrøne prosasprog*'s overview of their use indicates a stronger Christian and supernatural meaning in *kappa* than in *kempa*.[43] Nevertheless, it seems like *kappa* and *kempa* could be interchangeable, as this occurs in two fourteenth-century manuscripts of *Jómsvíkinga saga*.[44] The similarity in use, signification, and orthographic appearance may have led to scribes randomly switching between them, out of habit or for variation. *Kappa* and *kempa* are furthermore listed together in *Snorra Edda* in a run of synonyms for *menn* (men): 'kappar, kenpvr, garpar, *snillingar, hreystimenn, harðmenni, avarmenni, hetivr'.[45] King Arthur's knights are also referred to as *kæmpur* in the Swedish manuscript of *Själens tröst*.[46]

Returning to the two *riddarasǫgur* of De la Gardie 4–7 4°, the leap from *Strengleikar* to *Elíss saga* is a leap from the rather neutral descriptions of battle

---

[42] *Élie de Saint-Gilles*, ed. by Guidot, p. 34.

[43] *Ordbog over det norrøne prosasprog* is available online: <http://onp.ku.dk/> [accessed 15 February 2019].

[44] Stockholm, Holm perg 7 4°, *c.* 1300–25, in *Jómsvikinga saga*, ed. by Cederschiöld, p. 30, and Reykjavík, GKS 1005 fol., *c.* 1387–95, in *Flateyjarbok*, ed. by Guðbrandr Vigfusson and Unger, p. 174.

[45] Reykjavík, GKS 2367 4°, *c.* 1300–50, in *Edda Snorra Sturlusonar*, ed. by Finnur Jónsson, p. 187.

[46] Stockholm, Kungliga biblioteket, A 108, *c.* 1430: *Själens tröst*, ed. by Klemming, p. 2.

to a far more hands-on approach, placing the reader mid-battle, smelling the blood, seeing the enemy approach, and experiencing the injuries inflicted first hand. Nevertheless, the stereotypical repetitiveness of these scenes and the use of stock formulae decrease their effect as the story proceeds. Indeed, there are only so many horseheads, bodies, and helmets that can be split in two and fall to the ground before the novelty of these passages is lost, and eventually the scenes become predictable in their exaggerated violence.

The gore of battle as reflected in the title of this essay, 'The blood flying and brains falling like rain', originates from *Élie de Saint-Gilles*: 'Voler sanc et cervelle conme pleue qui court'.[47] The image differs from its Norse counterpart: 'at bloðras þæirra rann sem á væri' (so that their running blood poured as if it were a river). One could speculate that the translator's source read *fle(u)ve* (river), rather than *ple(u)ve* (rain). If the translator's source was a Continental French manuscript from around 1200, it was probably written in Gothic textura script, and a misreading of the descending <p> and ascending <f> is implausible.

However, the insular descending <f> was incorporated in Norse Gothic script, replacing the Caroline ascending version. In Icelandic Gothic script, this <f> was often closed with a bow. It is thus possible to suggest that a Norse translator reading *ple(u)ve* could have misinterpreted the <p> of the Gothic textualis for a closed-bow insular <f>, thereby reading *fle(u)ve*, and translating it into *á*, 'river'.[48] To my knowledge, no misidentifications of this type are known, rendering this a rather far-fetched explanation for a potential misreading.

A second, and quite probable, explanation for this discrepancy is that either a French scribe or the translator had the text read aloud, thus mistaking these quite similar sounding words, *fle(u)ve* and *ple(u)ve*, for each other. Contemporary examples of *fleuve* referring to rain as well as to a river exist, for instance, in Henri d'Arci's *Antechrist*, from the middle of the thirteenth century.[49] A French copyist could thus also have replaced *fle(u)ve* with the synonymous *ple(u)ve*. The origin of the alteration from 'conme pleue qui court' (falling like rain) to the 'rann sem á væri' (poured as if it were a river) could be oral, from the recital of the French text, or resulting from a French copyist's use of synonyms. In either case, it is unlikely that the alteration is the result of a Norse redactor adding emphasis to a dramatic passage.

---

[47] *Élie de Saint-Gilles*, ed. by Guidot, v. 650, p. 179.

[48] Haugen, 'Paleografi', pp. 229–30.

[49] Preman, 'Henri d'Arci: The Shorter Works'.

Leaving the moving letters behind, I will pass on to a close reading of the episode initiating Élie's period of testing. Even though the passage is chosen quite randomly from the 2762 verses of the French *chanson*, it illustrates several of the alterations these texts go through in translation and transmission, both medieval and modern. Élie meets his cousin, a mortally wounded messenger:

BnF fr 25516[50]

Si voit .I. messagier
    desous l'onbre d'un pin:
De .III. lances navrés
    malement fu baillis;
La cervele li saut
    par desous les sorci.

BnF fr 25516[51]

And he saw a messenger
    in the shade of a pine tree,
Wounded by three lances,
    he was in sad shape;
His brain was oozing out
    from under his eyebrows.

De la Gardie 4–7 4° (*c.* 1270)[52]

[...] oc sa liggia i skugga viðarins, er stoð hia veginum, mann æinn, og stoðu þriu spiot i licam hans, oc hafðe hogg i andliti sua / mikit, at sia matti hæilan i giongum brunir / hans

De la Gardie 4–7 4°

And (he) saw a man lying in the shadow of the forest that stood next to the road, and three spears stood in his body and he had such a huge blow in his face that one could see the brain through his eyebrows

Holm perg 7 fol.
(late fifteenth-century)[53]

ser hann mann liggiandi fyrir ser, ok hefir feingit III sár i gengum sitt lær af spiote; hann hafdi eitt haugg yfir þuert anlitit svo micit, at sea matti heilann i gegnum bryn-hautt hans.

Holm perg 7 fol.

He sees a man lying in front of him, and (he) has received three wounds through his thigh by a spear. He had such a great blow straight across his face, that one could see his brain through the hood of his coat of mail.

When comparing these three excerpts, some striking differences emerge. First of all, there is a change of tense from past to present between the 1270 and the late fifteenth-century Norse text: 'oc sa liggia' (and (he) saw lying) becomes 'ser hann mann liggjandi' (he sees a man lying). This is also the case of the translation from medieval French to modern English, and the modern translators see this alteration as an effort of elucidating the text by modifying the verb tenses

---

[50] *Élie de Saint-Gilles*, ed. by Guidot, p. 136, vv. 82–84.

[51] *Elye of Saint-Gilles*, trans. by Hartman and Malicote, p. 13.

[52] *Elis saga ok Rosamundu*, ed. by Kölbing, p. 16.

[53] *Elis saga ok Rosamundu*, ed. by Kölbing, p. 16.

'when it might disconcert the reader'.[54] Like the work of medieval redactors, Hartman and Malicote's translation is, to some degree, also a work of adaptation, where the intention is to facilitate access to the texts for a modern audience through textual adjustments eliminating discursive ambiguities. For an edition and translation of a medieval text intended for an academic audience, this approach to translation is not unproblematic. This is highlighted by the juxtaposed verses from the Guidot-edition with the Hartman and Malicote-translation above, where the 'under' in the translation v. 184 relies on the assumption of a scribal error, repeating the *desous* from v. 182. Hartman and Malicote emend this scribal error to *desus*,[55] whereas Guidot leaves the text as written in the medieval manuscript. Both solutions are the result of diverging editorial practices — Guidot rendering the text as is, Hartman and Malicote adjusting for logical clarity. Turning to the Old Norse texts for an additional reading of this verse, they are of no help as the *desous* or *desus*, the 'under' or 'over', is rendered as *i giongum*, 'through', in translation.

The level of precision in the medieval texts varies as well, and an increased level of precision though the addition of details is common. The excerpt above shows a movement in the details of the physical environment. The old French *pin* (pine tree) of v. 182 is expanded to a 'viðarins, er stoð hia veginum' (forest, that stood by the road), in the oldest Norse text. However, reference to the physical surroundings of the wounded messenger has disappeared from the youngest manuscript. While there can be an increased level of precision, there can be a decreased level as well. In translations, this is expected when the target language lacks the equivalent concept, and therefore a term for it, and it is thus a matter of cultural differences. For the translated *riddarasǫgur*, vocabulary of chivalry, courtly life, or what Sif Rikardsdottir calls 'available emotive vocabulary' could pose such problems in translation.[56] Alternatively, a decreased level of precision occurs when the translator's linguistic skills are deficient, and he chooses to replace a quite specific term with a more general one, and it is thus a matter of individual skills or lack of such. Returning to the excerpt above, the French messenger (*messagier*) becomes a man (*mann*) in both of the Norse texts. The concepts and vocabulary of messenger and man are basic, and it is unlikely that this decrease in the level of precision originates from cultural differences or a translator's lack of linguistic skills.

---

[54] *Elye of Saint-Gilles*, ed. and trans. by Hartman and Malicote, p. xix.

[55] *Elye of Saint-Gilles*, ed. and trans. by Hartman and Malicote, p. 186.

[56] Sif Rikhardsdottir, 'Translation Emotion', p. 163.

Through translation and transmission, the physical injuries inflicted upon the messenger change. In the French text, he is injured by three spears ('De .III. lances navrés'); in the oldest Norse, three spears are still stuck in his body ('ok stoðu þriu spiot i licam hans'); and in the youngest Norse text, three wounds in his thigh are inflicted by spears ('ok hefir feingit III sár i gengum sitt lær af spiote'). In the following lines, all three texts refer to the messenger's second injury, leading to some kind of exposure of his brain. The Old Norse addition of the wound thus being in the face (De la Gardie 4–7: 'i anliti'), or across the face (Holm perg 7 fol.: 'yfir þuert andlitit') seems superfluous, but the expansion adds to the graphic quality of this description. Both the French and the Norse thirteenth-century texts place this injury in the proximity of his eyebrows. The editors of the French text, Hartman and Malicote, suggest that the phrase 'par des(o)us les sorci' simply means at eye-level, more specifically the temple.[57] The corresponding Norse text places the wound 'i giongum brunir hans' (through his eyebrows); however, it seems like a later Norse redactor has turned the brow, *bryn*, into *brynhautt*, 'a hood of a coat of mail'. Such an alternation could be motivated by a redactor's desire to improve the logic of the image, or wanting to imply a more forceful blow as it has penetrated both the hood and the skull. It is tempting to play with the idea of a potential misreading of *brunir* to *brynhautt* due to abbreviations, but without examining several witnesses of the Norse text in transmission, this is too speculative.

The depiction of how the brain becomes visible varies greatly. The French 'La cervele li saut [...]' is translated as 'His brain was oozing out' by Hartman and Malicote. The verb *sauter*, and its corresponding noun *saut*, have a far more dynamic and energetic significance, leaning towards 'jump, leap, bounce', than what is reflected in this modern translation. The vigorous expression is not unique to *Élie de Saint-Gilles*, but a rather formulaic expression. Several similar verses are found in *Erec et Énide*, for instance 'li sans et la cervele en saut; | et cil chiet morz, li cuers li faut'.[58] Its Old Norse translation, *Erex saga*, only known from post-medieval manuscripts, is heavily reduced and rearranged in comparison to its French source, rendering any direct comparisons impossible. Nevertheless, a reading of this saga reveals that brains fall out on several occasions, all referred to by the combination of *heili*, 'brain', and *liggja*, the Norse verb for 'lie', that is, a static state.[59] Returning to *Elíss saga* and the translation of

---

[57] *Elye of Saint-Gilles*, ed. and trans. by Hartman and Malicote, p. 186.

[58] *Erec et Enide*, ed. by Roques, vv. 4418–22.

[59] *Erex saga*, in *Norse Romance*, ed. by Kalinke, pp. 238, 246, 248, and 250–52.

'La cervele li sait [...]', the brain in both of the Norse texts rests in place, as the blow to the messenger's head seems to leave a crack, leaving the brain visible: 'at sia matti hæilan' (could see the brain).

At this point we will leave the depictions of the effects of violence behind, and step into battle, side-by-side with Élie when he conquers a pack of thieves:

BnF fr 25516[60]

Venus est au laron .I.
   ruiste cop le fiert:
Le maistre os de la geule
   li a parmi brisiet,
Que mort l'a abatu,
   devant lui a ses piés.
Puis a pris en son poing
   le baston de pumier,
Si fort en feri l'autre,
   mort l'abat a ses piés.

BnF fr 25516[61]

He came up to the thief,
   struck him with a fierce blow
And the main bone of his throat
   he cracked in two.
Elye struck him so hard
   that he fell dead at his feet.
Then he picked up
   the apple-wood club,
And he violently smashed the other thief;
   he struck him dead at his feet

De la Gardie 4–7 4° (c. 1270)[62]

oc skaut hann þa fœti sinum. a hals þæim er haufðingi var þiofanna. oc varð hauggit sua þungt. at alldre kom hann suaurum upp siðan. þuiat halsbæínit var ísundr brotit. en annan þiofinn tok hann hondom. um armleginn. oc kipti honom at ser. Sua at hondin slitnaði af honom við ǫxlina oc hiartat með inny-flum. fell or buk hans.

De la Gardie 4–7 4°

and he plunged his foot at the neck of the leader of the thieves, and the blow was so heavy that he never again could give an answer, because his larynx was broken. And he put his hands around the upper arm of the other thief and pulled him towards himself in such a manner that the hand tore off him at the shoulder and the heart with the intestines fell out of his belly.

Holm perg 7 fol.[63]

ok skaut fœti sinum a hals hofdingia Þeirra so micit hogg, at hann quad all-dri ia sidan [...]

Holm perg 7 fol.:

and he plunged his foot at the neck of their leader such a great blow that he never again said yes [...]

When examining this passage, we will start out by comparing the two Norse texts as examples of stages in the transmission. Obviously, the passage is heav-

---

[60] *Élie de Saint-Gilles*, ed. by Guidot, p. 196 vv. 1156–60.

[61] *Elye of Saint-Gilles*, trans. by Hartman and Malicote, p. 176.

[62] *Elis saga ok Rosamundu*, ed. by Kölbing, pp. 63–64.

[63] *Elis saga ok Rosamundu*, ed. by Kölbing, pp. 63–64.

ily abbreviated in Holm perg 7 fol., compared to De la Gardie 4–7, and the graphic images of violence are omitted. Nevertheless, as our previous example illustrates the opposite, an expansion, this can hardly be said to be a general tendency in Norse transmission of these episodes.

In intralingual transmission, the two opponents, *hauðingi* (the chieftain), and the *annan þiofinn* (the other thief), are reduced to a single individual, the chieftain. The result of the blow to the chieftain's throat is 'at alldre kom hann suaurum upp siðan' (that he never again could give an answer), and this inability to answer is paraphrased in Holm perg 7 fol., where the chieftain 'quad alldri ia sidan' (never again said yes).

Moving on to the changes between two thirteenth-century witnesses of the tale, both the French and the Norse text have two opponents, the chief and the thief. The violence in *Élie de Saint-Gilles* is less graphic and more realistic than in the Norse text, with the act of aggression towards the second thief differing greatly. In the French text, he is hit so violently by a 'baston de pumier', an 'apple-wood club', that he falls dead to the ground. No object is used in the Norse text, where the result of a very hands-on attack is that the thief's arm is ripped off, and his 'hiartat með innyflum. fell or buk hans' (heart with intestines fell out of his belly).

In one of the previous examples, in which Élie ran into what he believed to be King Arthur with his army of undead, the comparison of the French and Norse text indicated that the twists and turns could be the result of a translator's effort to make sense of a challenging passage, while translating the words he understood. However, traces of this technique are not apparent in the passage quoted above. Thus, the discrepancy between these witnesses might indicate that the final lines of the translator's source differed from the extant text, and a verse or two has disappeared during transmission of the French text.

Some Concluding Remarks

Tveitane and Cook's edition of *Strengleikar* presents percentages of abbreviation of the Norse texts compared to their supposed originals;[64] this spurred my idea to measure the emphasis given to certain textual elements by looking at their ratio in several versions of the *riddarasǫgur* and their sources. Such a mechanical assessment of the importance given to specific narrative elements within a text or in comparison to different versions of it, regardless of language,

---

[64] *Strengleikar*, ed. and trans. by Tveitane and Cook, p. xxiii.

is, however, simply not fully productive. Instead of just counting words and verses to compare the numbers, a philologist can, and must, metaphorically weigh the elements through detailed close readings of multiple witnesses of a text placed in their cultural contexts. This method gives substantial insight into the transformations that take place in translation and transmission.

My readings of corresponding passages from a French source text, its Old Norwegian translation, and a later Icelandic redaction, illustrate a series of different textual alterations having taken place over time. These alterations demonstrate that a diachronic perspective truly shows how the textual witnesses are interlinked and that additional information from each single text, its redactors, provenance, and transformation can be revealed through comparison. The translated *riddarasǫgur* are moving words, not only moving across languages, borders, and cultures, but also moving back and forth between orality and literacy, as well as across genres and through time in transmission. The move is tangible when examining the physical material, but the move of words between languages and through time in translation and transmission is also a reflection of the rich accretions provided by different time periods, cultures, ideas, and preferences.

Works Cited

Manuscripts and Archival Sources

London, British Library, Harley 978
Paris, Bibliothèque nationale Française, MS 25516
Reykjavík, Handritasafn Landsbókasafns Íslands, Lbs. 840
Reykjavík, Stofnun Árna Magnússonar í íslenskum fræðum, GKS 1005 fol.
——, GKS 2367 4°
Stockholm, Kungliga biblioteket, A 108
——, Holm peg 7 fol.
——, Holm perg 7 4°
Uppsala, Uppsala Universitetsbibliotek, De la Gardie 4–7 4°

Primary Sources

Chrétien de Troyes, *Erec et Enide*, ed. by Mario Roques, Classiques français du Moyen Âge, 80 (Paris: Honoré Champion Éditeur, 1990)
Edda Snorra Sturlusonar, ed. by Finnur Jónsson (København: Gyldendal, 1931)

Élie de Saint-Gilles, nouvelle édition par Bernard Guidot d'après le manuscrit BnF n° 25516, ed. by Bernard Guidot, Classiques français du Moyen Âge, 171 (Paris: Honoré Champion Éditeur, 2013)

Elis saga ok Rosamundu: mit Einleitung, deutscher Übersetzung und Anmerkungen zum ersten Mal, ed. by Eugen Kölbing (Heilbronn: Henninger, 1881)

Elis saga, Strengleikar and Other Texts: Uppsala University Library, Delagardieska samlingen nos. 4–7 folio and AM 666 b quarto, ed. by Mattias Tveitane (Oslo: Selskapet til utgivelse av gamle norske håndskrifter, 1972)

Elíss saga ok Rósamundar: De la Gardie 4–7 4°, ed. by Ingvil Brügger Budal (Medieval Nordic Text Archive, 2015) <http://clarino.uib.no/menota/catalogue>

Elye of Saint-Gilles: A chanson de geste, ed. and trans. by A. Richard Hartman and Sandra Malicote (New York: Italica, 2011)

Flateyjarbok: En Samling af norske Konge-Sagaer med indskudte mindre Fortællinger om Begivenheder i og udenfor Norge samt Annaler, ed. by Guðbrandr Vigfusson and C. R. Unger (Kristiania, 1860–68)

Jómsvíkinga saga efter skinnboken 7, 4° på Kungliga Biblioteket i Stockholm, ed. by Gustaf Cederschiöld. Lunds Universitets Årsskrift, 2 (Lund: Afdelningen för Philosophi, Språkvetenskap och Historia, 1874–75)

Marie de France, *Les lais de Marie de France*, ed. by Jean Rychner, Classiques français du Moyen Âge, 93 (Paris: Honoré Champion, 1966)

Marie de France, *The Lais of Marie de France*, trans. by Robert Hanning and Joan M. Ferrante (Durham: Labyrinth, 1982)

Norse Romance, ed. by Marianne E. Kalinke, 3 vols (Cambridge: Brewer, 1999)

Själens tröst: tio Guds bud förklarade genom legender, berättelser och exempel, ed. by G. E. Klemming (Stockholm: Norstedt, 1871–73)

Strengleikar. An Old Norse translation of twenty-one Old French lais, ed. and trans. by Mattias Tveitane and Robert Cook (Oslo: Norsk historisk kjeldeskrift-institutt, 1979)

Secondary Studies

Budal, Ingvil Brügger, *Strengleikar og Lais: høviske noveller i omsetjing frå gammalfransk til gammalnorsk* (Bergen: Universitetet i Bergen, 2009)

——, 'A Translation and its Continuation: The Use of the Present Participle in *Elíss saga ok Rósamundar*', in *Bibliotheca Arnamagnæana* (Copenhagen: Reitzel, forthcoming)

Bumke, Joachim, *Courtly Culture: Literature and Society in the High Middle Ages* (Woodstock: Overlook Press, 2000)

Den Arnamagnæanske Kommission, 'Ordbog over det norrøne prosasprog', http://onp.ku.dk/

Eriksen, Stefka Georgieva, *Writing and Reading in Medieval Manuscript Culture: The Translation and Transmission of the Story of Elye in Old French and Old Norse Literary Contexts* (Turnhout: Brepols, 2014)

Fidjestøl, Bjarne, 'Erotisk lesnad ved Håkon Håkonssons hoff', in *Middelalderkvinner — liv og virke*, ed. by Ingvild Øye (Bergen: Bryggens museum, 1981), pp. 72–89

Gaunt, Simon, 'Romance and Other Genres', in *The Cambridge Companion to Medieval Romance*, ed. by Roberta L. Krueger (Cambridge: Cambridge University Press, 2000), pp. 45–60

Hallberg, Peter, *Stilsignalement och författarskap i norrön sagalitteratur: synpunkter och exempel* (Göteborg: Acta Universitatis Gothoburgensis, 1968)

Halvorsen, Eyvind Fjeld, 'Elis saga ok Rosamundu', in *Kulturhistorisk leksikon for nordisk middelalder*, 22 vols (Copenhagen: Rosenkilde og Bagger, 1956–78), III, 596–97

——, 'Høvisk stil', in *Kulturhistorisk leksikon for nordisk middelalder*, 22 vols (Copenhagen: Rosenkilde og Bagger, 1956–78), VII, 315–20

Haugen, Odd Einar, 'Paleografi', in *Handbok i norrøn filologi*, ed. by Odd Einar Haugen (Bergen: Fagbokforlaget, 2013), pp. 194–248

Jónas Kristjánsson, *Eddas and Sagas: Iceland's Medieval Literature* (Reykjavík: Hið íslenska bókmenntafélag, 2007)

Kalinke, Marianne E., *The Arthur of the North the Arthurian Legend in the Norse and Rus' Realms* (Cardiff: University of Wales Press, 2011)

——, 'Gvímars saga', in *Opuscula VII: Bibliotheca Arnamagnæana, XXXIV* (Copenhagen: Reitzel, 1979), pp. 106–39

Kalinke, Marianne E., and P. M. Mitchell, *Bibliography of Old Norse-Icelandic Romances* (Ithaca: Cornell University Press, 1985)

Kelly, Molly C. Robinson, 'Review of A. Richard Hartman and Sandra C. Malicote, eds and trans, *Elye of Saint-Gilles: A Chanson de Geste*', *Speculum*, 87.3 (2012), 874–76

Meissner, Rudolf, *Die Strengleikar: Ein Beitrag zur Geschichte der altnordischen Prosaliteratur* (Halle am Saale: Niemeyer, 1902)

Paris, Gaston, 'Élie de Saint-Gilles, Deuxième Article', *Journal des Savants* (1886), 469–80

Perman, R. C. D., 'Henri d'Arci: The Shorter Works', in *Studies in Medieval French Presented to Alfred Ewert in Honour of his Seventieth Birthday* (Oxford: Clarendon Press, 1961), pp. 279–321

Pulsiano, Phillip, and Kirsten Wolf, eds, *Medieval Scandinavia: An Encyclopedia*, Garland Encyclopedia of the Middle Ages, 1; Garland Reference Library of the Humanities, 934 (New York: Garland, 1993)

Sif Rikhardsdottir, 'Translating Emotion: Vocalisation and Embodiment in *Yvain* and *Ívens saga*', in *Emotions in Medieval Arthurian Literature: Body, Mind, Voice*, ed. by Frank Brandsma, Carolyne Larrington, and Corinne Saunders (Cambridge: Brewer, 2015), pp. 161–80

Winst, Silke. 2012. 'Mittelalterliche Logiken ders Erzählens in der altfranzösischen Chanson de geste *Élie de Saint-Gilles* und in der nordischen Adaptation *Elis saga ok Rósamundu*', in *Das Potenzial des Epos: Die altfranzösische Chanson de geste im europäischen Kontext,* ed. by Susanne Friede and Dorothea Kullmann (Heidelberg: Winter, 2012), pp. 349–72

From Oral to Written in Old Norse Culture: Questions of Genre, Contact, and Continuity

Else Mundal

Introduction

The arrival of writing reshaped the Old Norse 'literary' landscape in multiple ways. We have, of course, no direct access to the oral genres that existed in Old Norse cultures since these genres are known mainly through their later written equivalents, and we cannot determine with certainty how close to — or different from — each other oral and written forms of the same genres were. Nor can we be confident that all oral art forms that existed in an oral culture found their way into writing, since there are in fact indications of lost genres. It is, however, possible, on the basis of what we know about oral cultures and on the basis of later written forms of oral genres, to get some idea about how the earlier oral art forms sounded. Oral art forms that never made their way into writing may be mentioned in written sources, or in some ways reflected by written texts, with the result that we even possess some information about lost oral genres, though our knowledge about them is very fragmented.

We know much more about the literature that existed in Old Norse culture after the arrival of writing. The extant written texts must be regarded as very good sources for the form, content, and function of early written texts, even though the preserved manuscripts in most cases are considerably later than the

Else Mundal (else.mundal@lle.uib.no) is Professor Emerita of Old Norse Philology in the Department of Linguistic, Literary, and Aesthetic Studies at the University of Bergen. From 2003 to 2012, she was the leader of the Arrival of Writing research group at the Centre for Medieval Studies, University of Bergen.

Moving Words in the Nordic Middle Ages: Tracing Literacies, Texts, and Verbal Communities, ed. by Amy C. Mulligan and Else Mundal, AS 8   BREPOLS PUBLISHERS   (Turnhout: Brepols, 2019)
pp. 319–343   10.1484/M.AS-EB.5.116630

originals, and the majority of what once existed, especially from the earliest period of writing, has been lost.

The transition from an oral to a literate culture was a long process that could take slightly different forms in different cultures, and within the varied regions comprising the Old Norse area as well.[1] It is, however, important to bear in mind that the advent of written culture did not mean an end to earlier oral culture; rather, the two cultures, written and oral, continued to exist side by side and influence each other.[2] The form and content of written art forms were in many cases strongly influenced by — or even determined by — older oral art forms, and this happened at the same time as the new written culture in turn altered the framework conditions of the oral art forms in ways that may have led to changes of many kinds. European genres that were introduced together with written culture offered fresh stories and motifs that may have been taken up in oral storytelling. The literary form of new written genres as well as transformed framework conditions may also have led to some innovations in oral art forms. It is perhaps more important that the introduction of written culture no doubt led to changes in society which would have likely influenced the milieu that existed around the creation and performance of oral art forms. It is a question as to whether the introduction of writing had consequences for the prestige of oral art forms and for the prestige of the creators and performers of these art forms in comparison to written literature, authors, and people who could read. It is likely that written culture, which was introduced by the Church, was more easily accessed by men than women and thereby reduced women's opportunities to take part in the life of this new culture of writing in comparison to the earlier oral culture. It is, however, also possible that there were differences between various cultures concerning the possibility for women to access both written culture and education.

In this essay, both the changes in the literate landscape brought about by the arrival of writing, as well as changes in society that influenced the framework conditions of cultural activity, will be discussed. The aim is to give an overview of the development from oral to written culture in Old Norse society and to call attention to social conditions that may have influenced this development.

---

[1] The standard work describing the transition from an oral to a written culture is Clanchy, *From Memory to Written Record*.

[2] The scholar who particularly has emphasized the oral-written continuum is Ruth Finnegan: see Finnegan, 'How Oral Is Oral Literature'; Finnegan, *Oral Poetry*; and Finnegan, 'The How of Literature'.

New Written Genres and the Introduction of Practical Literacy

Christian culture brought new literary genres into Old Norse culture. These genres included the different types of literature needed by the Church; among them were liturgical texts and texts needed for preaching and edification, such as sermons and legends. We can observe that early in the Christianization period Christian genres had taken root in Old Norse culture. For instance, two skaldic poems recount miracles that are said to have occurred both in connection with the death of King Óláfr inn helgi and later at his grave. The two skaldic poems are *Glælognskviða* by Þórarinn loftunga (probably as early as 1032) and *Erfidrápa Óláfs helga* by Sigvatr skáld (from around 1040).[3] Miracles are short and stereotypical narratives that may have spread to the North in oral form, but most likely the miracles retold in skaldic stanzas reflect, directly or indirectly, readings and preaching in churches on the basis of imported books. From this very early example of impact from Christian texts, we can learn that Old Norse culture was open to literary impulses from abroad, and at the same time, Old Norse people had a remarkable ability to include new literary impulses in their own culture and art forms, and to make the new culture their own. Christian miracles incorporated into oral skaldic stanzas in the old traditional metres illustrate how the new culture was included in the old. It would, in time, change the old culture from within.

Imported liturgical books were in all likelihood the first books that existed in Old Norse culture, and their form and content were the same as in the areas from where they were imported (mostly England). Later, when such books were copied in Old Norse society, they would contain the same types of text as liturgical books elsewhere in the Christian world, but readings from legends of local saints would also be incorporated.

Sermons and legends were certainly imported in Latin form, but had to be translated to be used in Old Norse culture. Translated sermons originally written by authorities within the Church — or thought to have been written by them — were used for centuries, but some new sermons modelled on these old ones were also composed. Indeed, in Old Norse culture, sermons sometimes display adaptation to local problems or local culture (as, for example, *stavkyrkjepreika*, or stave church homily, in the *Old Norwegian Homily Book*). As soon as a cult of local saints was established in a newly Christianized area,

---

[3] *Den norsk-islandske skjaldedigtning* B I, ed. by Finnur Jónsson, pp. 300–01 and 239–45. Now see also the eight-volume series (published and forthcoming), of *Skaldic Poetry of the Middle Ages,* ed. Margaret Clunies Ross, for the most up-to-date editions of the skaldic poetry.

the ground was laid for legends to be written about the local saints, with some variation as to whether, or how soon, that happened. Norway received its own national saints shortly after Christianization. St Sunnifa, believed to be an Irish princess, was, according to later written sources, already venerated as a saint during the period of Christianization. That may not be true, but her cult, or rather the cult of the collective of people who fled from Ireland with her, must have begun early in the eleventh century. In addition, King Óláfr Haraldsson was killed in 1030, and it is documented in skaldic poetry that he was venerated as a saint a few years later. A third saint, Hallvarðr, a relative of Saint Óláfr, was killed in 1043, and his cult started around the middle of the century. The existence of such a cult as early as in the 1030s may have something to do with previous heathen culture. Kings and royalties, the descendants of the gods, had also been objects of cults in heathen times and had most likely a shorter path to sainthood than other people during the period of Christianization. The veneration of these early saints did not result in legends written about them immediately; their legends were first recorded in the second part of the twelfth century, though their miracles may have been written down earlier.

The first legendary texts to be written would likely be notes of miracles recorded at the saint's shrine. These collections of miracles were later added to the *vita/passio* of the saint. Legends about new saints from the Old Norse area were first written in Latin, the international language of the Church, but were soon translated into the vernacular — or a new version in the vernacular was written. Both legends about local saints and imported and translated legends in all likelihood functioned as entertainment as well as for purposes of edification, and spread to wider milieus than those connected to churches and monasteries.

It is no surprise that the introduction of Christianity led to the importation of liturgical texts, with these texts later copied in clerical milieus. Translation of texts needed by the Church, such as sermons and legends, must also be expected. The imported genres later functioned as models for new sermons and legends about local saints, and translation activity continued throughout the Middle Ages. How much legendary literature was translated and how widely this literature spread in society must, however, be seen in connection with local cultural conditions.[4]

According to later textual sources, laws were written down in Norway at a very early date, initiated by King Óláfr inn helgi (1015–28) or his son King Mágnús inn góði (1035–47).[5] Scholars have been sceptical about this very early

---

[4] See Mundal, 'Backgrounds for Written Culture in Oral Society' in this book.

[5] According to *Historia de antiquitate regum Norwagiensium* (ch. 16) from around 1180

dating of the first Norwegian written laws, and the peaceful period in the reign of King Óláfr kyrri in the last quarter of the eleventh century has been pointed to as a more likely period. For the writing of Icelandic laws, we have reliable sources. According to Ari's *Íslendingabók*, ch. 10, the laws were written down in the winter of 1117–18, though the tithe laws had been written down earlier. Even though it is uncertain when Norwegian laws were first committed to writing, we can say for certain that it was considerably earlier than in Sweden and Denmark. The early transcription of the laws in the vernacular may have meant a great deal for the development of written culture both in Norway and Iceland.

We do not know much about letter-writing in the first two decades after Christianization, but becoming a part of Christian Europe made written communication a necessity.[6] What seems to be unique to Old Norse culture is that the administrators of both the king and the Church wrote letters in the vernacular if the addressee lived within the Old Norse area. Furthermore, private persons used the vernacular in all types of letters including legal documents. Written letters replaced to some degree the need for dispatching oral communications via messenger and having oral agreements and contracts of all kinds witnessed. However, oral and written communications and the use of oral agreements, attested by witnesses and written legal documents, continued to exist side by side.

Written Genres Introduced in the Twelfth Century

In an Icelandic work from around 1150 known as the *First Grammatical Treatise*, the anonymous author mentions four different types of written texts in the vernacular that were to be found in Iceland at this time:

1. Laws

2. Genealogies

3. *Þýðingar helgar*

4. Ari's writing

and the prologue of *Passio et miracula beati Olavi* from the late twelfth century, King Óláfr inn helgi had laws in the vernacular written down. *Sverris saga* (ch. 117) and *Magnús saga góða* (ch. 16) in *Heimskringla* claim that Magnús inn góði had the laws of Frostathing, *Grágás*, written down.

[6] See the essay of Wellendorf in this book, and Melve's essay 'Letters, Networks and Public Opinion in Medieval Norway' in this book.

Laws and religious literature have already been mentioned. *Þýðingar helgar* could mean both 'translated religious literature' and 'learned religious texts'. Later, the word *þýðing* is used about learned religious literature, but in this early context it is perhaps more likely that the word denotes translated religious literature, since such literature must have existed in the time before the *First Grammatical Treatise*. Genealogies are probably short notices on family relations, texts that probably had the practical function of helping people remember to whom they were related. Genealogical knowledge was important in Old Norse society: you had to know whom you could marry, when you were entitled to an inheritance, when you were entitled to compensation if a relative had been killed, and when you had to pay compensation if a relative was the killer.

The fact that Ari is mentioned while other authors writing in the vernacular are not shows clearly that the literary boom that characterized Iceland two generations later, from around 1200, had not yet started around 1150. Ari's writings include *Íslendingabók*, a short history of Iceland from the settlement period and up to Ari's own time, which focuses on the foundation of Icelandic institutions: law, thing, and church/bishoprics. Also the first, now lost, *Landnámabók* may be included among Ari's works. We do not know for certain that Ari was the author, but it is very likely. Both these works are clearly connected to the history of Iceland and the very special status of Iceland among other countries in medieval Europe as a land of recent settlers who remembered the birth of their nation. Ari's *Íslendingabók* could be modelled, at least partly, on the European genre of the chronicle of bishoprics,[7] and for *Landnámabók* the Bible could offer a model or at least inspiration. However, in spite of the models to be found in Christian literature, both of these early Icelandic works demonstrate that Icelandic written culture from the very outset showed great independence and originality.

Nevertheless, the writing of chronicles about kings started in Latin both in Iceland and in Norway.[8] Chronicles about kings or bishops were popular genres in European literature, and while such texts were not translated into Old Norse as far as we know, the genre itself was imported. In Iceland, we know of a Latin chronicle about Norwegian kings written by Sæmundr fróði early in the twelfth century (Sæmundr died in 1133). This chronicle has been lost, but an anonymous skaldic poem which builds on Sæmundr's work, *Nóregs*

---

[7] See Mundal, 'Íslendingabók vurdert som bispestolskrønike'.

[8] On the Latin literature in the North, and particularly Latin chronicles, see Conti's article in this book.

konungatal,[9] indicates that what Sæmundr had to say about the kings focused on the same subject as older genealogical skaldic poems: namely, first and foremost how and where the kings died. This shows again that the Icelanders from the very outset used foreign models very freely and could identify models in their own oral genres as well.

From Norway we have two chronicles about Norwegian kings written in Latin in the late twelfth century, the anonymous *Historia Norwegie* from the period 1165–80,[10] *Historia de anticuitate regum norwagiensium*, written by a certain Theodoricus in the late twelfth century. We know of a third chronicle in Latin, *Cathalogus regum Norwagiensium*, which is mentioned by Theodoricus. All these works in Latin can be seen as a branch of the common European genre. The one very early Latin chronicle in Iceland[11] and three Latin chronicles in Norway later in the twelfth century probably indicate that the use of Latin had a stronger position in Norway than in Iceland, and that the Icelanders led the way in making the vernacular a literary language.

The vernacular was, nonetheless, put to use in writings about kings in the twelfth century in both countries. The development of the genre of kings' sagas was a common Icelandic-Norwegian undertaking, and the genre of European chronicles was gradually changed into *saga* with an emphasis on chronology, causal connection, and objective style.[12] The genre of kings' sagas has its roots

---

[9] *Den norsk-islandske skjaldedigtning* B I, 575–90.

[10] See Mortensen in *Historia Norvegie*, pp. 11–24.

[11] In addition to Sæmundr's lost chronicle, the monk Oddr Snorrason in Þingeyrar wrote about Óláfr Tryggvason in Latin around 1190, and another monk, Gunnlaugr Leifsson, wrote, also in Latin, about the same king a few years later. We do not know, but the Latin works about this king could perhaps be seen in connection with a wish to make Óláfr Tryggvason, the king who Christianized Iceland, an Icelandic saint. If that was the case, writing in Latin would be the only choice.

[12] Ari fróði says in the prologue of *Íslendingabók* that he wrote *Konunga ævi*. This text is not preserved, but it was in all likelihood very short and written in the chronicle style. The Icelander Eiríkr Oddsson wrote *Hryggjarstykki* about the period 1130–39 or 1130–64. *Hryggjarstykki* may have been written as early as *c.* 1150 if it ended with the death of Magnús blindi (1139), but if it ended with the death of Ingi Haraldsson (1164) it was written after that date. This work is only known from quotations. Most likely *Hryggjarstykki* was written in Norway. In the 1180s the Icelander Karl Jónsson started writing *Sverris saga* (or the part of it that was called *Grýla*) while king Sverrir overlooked his work, which means that he too was writing in Norway. Where or by whom the saga was completed is unknown. Around 1190 *Ágrip*, a work about the Norwegian kings from the time of Hálfdan svarti and probably up to the battle at Ré (1177), was written in Norway, most likely in Trøndelag. King Óláfr inn helgi was popular also

in the European genre chronicles about kings and also partly in the legends of the Church, both because King Óláfr Haraldsson became a saint and because literary patterns from the legends were known to the authors. The first authors who wrote about kings had to build on oral tradition, skaldic stanzas included, or if they wrote about the present, they could build on material from informants. Later on, they could utilize older written sources as well. The authors were dependent on oral tradition not only for content. Gradually, both the language and the style of oral storytelling seem to have influenced the authors. The so-called saga-style developed in sagas about kings in the late twelfth century, but reached its zenith in the thirteenth century in Snorri's sagas of kings and in the genre of sagas of Icelanders (see below). The saga style was dependent on the oral art forms which it imitated and at the same time these oral traditions provided authors composing for the page with the content of their works. In short, oral art forms were influential in both style and content.

The translation activity brought about by the needs of the Church in a society where the vernacular had a strong position formed a solid basis for the later production of literature in the North. The legends especially have been regarded as important for the development of the later saga genres.[13]

The introduction of Christian culture opened the Old Norse world to the importation of written texts from Christian Europe in addition to those texts that explicitly filled the needs of the Church. From late in the twelfth century onwards, the pseudo-historical works *Veraldar saga* (History of the World), *Gyðinga saga* (History of the Jews), *Trójumanna saga* (History of the Trojans), *Rómverja saga* (History of the Romans), *Alexanders saga* (History of Alexander), and *Breta sǫgur* (Histories of the Britons) were translated from Latin into Old Norse. *Veraldar saga*, written from a salvation history perspective, and *Gyðinga saga* both establish the background for Christian history. The texts selected for translation into the Old Norse vernacular were not chosen at random, and they demonstrate that it was deemed important to write the newly Christianized countries of the North into Christian history. Some of these sagas tell the story of great heroes of European history in the remote past, and as elsewhere in Europe, people in the North connected themselves to European history by tracing their ruling families back to the heroes of Troy. The exact dating of some of these works are disputed, but the first of them belong to the

---

in Iceland, and a saga about him known as *Eldste saga* (Oldest saga) was written there, probably late in the twelfth century.

[13] Turville-Petre, *Origins of Icelandic Literature*, p. 142.

twelfth century. In some cases, it is also uncertain as to whether the translation took place in Iceland or in Norway, but Iceland seems to be the most likely site of translation for most of these texts.

It is noteworthy that the majority of these works on Christian or European history are not merely translations but compilations synthesizing a large number of texts. This demonstrates that the translators, or compilers, took ownership of the foreign material and fused it with their own culture at the same time as they incorporated themselves and their own culture into the wider European and Christian context. The translation of European genres such as the pseudo-histories shows that there was an audience for such literature. If much literature was translated into a society's vernacular, the logical interpretation is that literacy had spread outside the circles of people who were familiar with Latin.

One factor that may be important when trying to explain the richness of Old Norse literary culture, especially in Iceland, is the remarkable growth of learned literature which started in the latter half of the twelfth century. The *First Grammatical Treatise*, already mentioned, is a remarkably original work discussing how many letters would be needed to reproduce the phonemes of the Icelandic language correctly. This first work was followed by others on different topics.[14] Snorri's *Edda* (from around 1220) and the grammatical treatises[15] show a strong will to combine foreign and indigenous culture, as when Óláfr hvítaskáld references skaldic stanzas instead of Latin poetry as examples of different phenomena in poetic language. In Norway, too, learned literature was translated and written. In some cases, it is disputed whether certain learned texts were translated in Norway or in Iceland,[16] but the *Speech against the Bishops* (probably from the late twelfth century) and *Konungs skuggsjá* (from the middle of the thirteenth century) show that Norway also had supportive environments for learned literature. It may be a coincidence, but both these works must have been written in milieus connected to the king's court.

---

[14] See Wellendorf, 'Lærdomslitteratur'.

[15] *The Second Grammatical Treatise* was written late in the thirteenth century, the *Third Grammatical Treatise* by Óláfr Þórðarson hvítaskáld dates from the middle of the thirteenth century, and the *Fourth Grammatical Treatise* from the fourteenth century.

[16] The circles around the Norwegian kings in the thirteenth and early fourteenth century may have promoted translation of learned literature in both Norway and Iceland. For example, according to the prologue of one of the manuscripts of *Stjórn* (translation of the Bible), King Hákon V. Magnússon (r. 1299–1319) is said to have commissioned translation of the Bible.

New Written Genres in the Thirteenth Century

Around 1200 Iceland experienced an extraordinary literary boom. The writing of kings' sagas was well underway in the twelfth century, but reached a peak in thirteenth-century Iceland. Kings' sagas were also still being written in Norway,[17] and there was a common market in both countries, with manuscripts being exported both ways.[18]

Around 1200 or shortly after, several new written genres developed in Iceland. Iceland gained its first national saints around 1200: Bishop Þorlákr was declared a saint by the Alþing in 1199, and Jón in 1200. Legends were written about these holy bishops, first in Latin, and were soon followed by vernacular sagas about other Icelandic bishops, a genre that was unique to Iceland.[19]

While sagas about bishops had a close parallel in legends about bishops, the other written genre that saw the light of day in the same years as the first sagas about (not saintly) Icelandic bishops, namely, the sagas of Icelanders, had no parallels in earlier written literature, neither in Iceland nor in any other place in Europe. The sagas belonging to this genre built upon oral tradition about the men and women who came to the island some hundred years previously, and the first generations of settlers. A tradition of this type could develop only in a new settlement, and had therefore to be unique to Iceland, but it was not a given that this oral tradition should give rise to a new written genre. The development of a new written genre without clear models in European literature,

---

[17] *Morkinskinna* was written in Iceland around 1220, and *Fagrskinna* was in all likelihood written in Norway around the same time. Snorri's compilation of sagas about the Norwegian kings, known as *Heimskringla*, was written in Iceland around 1230, and later Snorri's nephew Sturla Þórðarson wrote the saga about King Hákon Hákonarson (probably in 1264/65) during a stay in Norway, and later on, during a second stay in Norway in 1278 he wrote, or started to write, the saga about King Magnús lagabœtir (see Mundal, 'Sagaskrivarane og Bergen'). *Oldest saga*, already mentioned, was reworked in Norway, and this version is known as the *Legendary saga*. In Iceland Styrmir's now lost saga about Óláfr inn helgi is probably a later Icelandic version of *Oldest saga*. The sagas known as *Bǫglunga sǫgur* exist as two variants, the shorter covering the years 1202–10, and the longer covering the years 1202–17. Scholars seem to agree that the shorter version was written by an Icelander, but perhaps in Norway. Knut Helle has argued that the longer version was written by a man from the circles around the archbishop in Nidaros (see Helle, *Omkring Bǫglungasǫgur*).

[18] Export from Norway to Iceland is well evidenced by the fact that many works written in Norway now exist only in Icelandic manuscripts. On the export of books from Iceland to Norway, see Stefán Karlsson, 'Islandsk bogeksport'.

[19] For a possible explanation, see Mundal, 'Medieval Nordic Backgrounds: Written Culture in an Oral Society', above.

namely, realistic writings about farmers at a time when farmers normally existed only as comic figures in European texts,[20] demonstrates great originality, confidence in one's own culture, and it probably indicates that literacy in Iceland had spread so that people who had enjoyed listening to oral storytelling now also wanted to have these stories in written form. This does not, however, mean that Old Norse audiences wanted to change the performances of saga literature. There are a few descriptions of oral delivery of written sagas in Old Norse sources indicating that people wanted some types of sagas to be performed as before, not read, even though the speaker had a book to hand at hand.

Sturlu þáttr describes how Sturla Þórðarson provided entertainment on King Magnús lagabœtir's ship by telling a saga, obviously a *fornaldarsaga*, about a troll woman called Huld. From the context it is clear that he had a book, but the description of the performance is: 'sagði hann þá Huldar sögu betur og fróðlegar en nokkur þeirra hafði fyrr heyrt er þar voru' (he then told the saga about Huld better and with more details than anyone present had heard before).[21] The end of *Hákonar saga Hákonarsonar* records how the sick king had literature read to him. First, he had books in Latin read to him. To listen to Latin was, however, too much for the sick king, and he then had books in Norse read, first sagas about holy men and, following that, sagas about all the kings of Norway.[22] Here the word used to describe the performance is *lesa* (read). There are too few descriptions of oral performance on the basis of written texts to draw firm conclusions, but the examples we do have seem to indicate that the audiences wanted the sagas most dependent on oral tradition, such as *fornaldarsǫgur* and sagas of Icelanders, to be told, not read. This desire for performances of written sagas with a dramatic storytelling voice (as opposed to a reading or reciting voice) demonstrates the strength of the oral culture.[23]

---

[20] Exceptions are legends of the Church. In this literature people from all layers of society could be heroes and heroines.

[21] *Sturlunga saga*, ed. by Örnulfur Thorsson, II, 765.

[22] Sturla Þórðarson, *Hákonar saga Hákonarsonar*, ed. by Unger, p. 479. Stephen Mitchell mentions this episode in his article from 2001, 'Performance and Norse Poetry', pp. 187–91. He takes it for granted that the book existed only in the queen's mind. This is a possible interpretation. However, *Sturlu þáttr* was most likely written in the beginning of the fourteenth century, at a time when many sagas within different genres existed in written form. In my opinion, it is therefore very likely that the anonymous author of the *þáttr* models the scene staged upon the king's ship on saga performances with a book in hand, as he knew such scenes from his own time.

[23] On this subject, see Mundal, 'How did the Arrival of Writing Influence Old Norse Culture?'.

Around forty sagas of Icelanders remain from the thirteenth century and the first decades of the fourteenth century.[24] Most of these sagas, even long and complex sagas such as *Njáls saga*, *Laxdœla saga*, and *Egils saga Skalla-Grímssonar*, are clearly rooted in oral art forms.[25] All sagas within the genre have much in common concerning both content and style. The central theme of the genre is feud between two families, and the sagas are — with many variations — constructed according to what Theodore M. Andersson has called the 'feud pattern', consisting of introduction, conflict, climax, revenge, reconciliation, and aftermath.[26] The similarities among the written sagas within the genre were interpreted by Andersson as a result of a common structure that had developed during earlier periods that were predominantly oral. When one considers the relation between the oral and the written in Old Norse culture, it is significant that the written genre, which is regarded as the artistic climax, is so dependent on the previous oral art form.

Sagas about Icelandic chieftains in the twelfth and thirteenth century, more or less contemporary sagas, were also written early in the thirteenth century. These sagas were written over a relatively short period of time and cover the period 1117–1264. The longest of these sagas is *Íslendinga saga* written by Snorri's nephew Sturla Þórðarson, probably shortly before his death in 1284. The authors of the other sagas cannot be identified with certainty. These sagas are loaded with information about historical events, and they are good historical sources for a dramatic period in the history of Iceland when the mightiest families on the island struggled for power, a struggle that resulted in the end of the Free State and union with Norway in 1262/64. The contemporary sagas about Icelandic chieftains were written as individual sagas, but most of them are now preserved only in the compilation *Sturlunga saga* written around 1300. The redactor of *Sturlunga saga* split up the older sagas and put the pieces together to create a new chronological unity. Where he could choose between two texts, he would usually select the more detailed one. Therefore, these sagas in many cases cannot be reconstructed without lacunae.[27]

---

[24] In some cases the sagas may even be later, at least in the form we have them.

[25] The sagas of Icelanders are often divided into pre-classical, classical, and post-classical sagas. Since the age of many sagas is disputed, some sagas have been placed among the oldest (pre-classical) sagas as well as among the latest (post-classical) sagas. For a tentative division of the sagas of Icelanders into three groups partly based on their time of composition, see Vésteinn Ólason in Böðvar Guðmundsson and others, *Íslenzk bókmenntasaga*, ii, 42; and Mundal, 'Sagalitteraturen', p. 449.

[26] See Andersson, *The Icelandic Family Saga*.

[27] The manuscript Króksfjarðarbók (*c.* 1360) preserves the original redaction of *Sturlunga*

The contemporary sagas about Icelandic chieftains in the twelfth and thirteenth century are closer to the chronicle genre than sagas of Icelanders, but there are no models for these sagas in European literature. Icelandic authors living in this dramatic period may have found it necessary to document what happened, and since they had no king, the actors to whom the history of the nation had to be attached would of necessity be their chieftains and bishops.

Around the middle of the thirteenth century, one further written saga genre developed in Iceland. This genre was the *fornaldarsǫgur*, or the sagas about ancient times. This genre too builds on oral tradition, at least the older sagas, and like the sagas of Icelanders, the *fornaldarsǫgur* are all written by anonymous authors. Some of these sagas share their subject matter with heroic eddic poems, others can be characterized as Viking sagas, a third group shares some motifs with fairy tales, and many *fornaldarsǫgur* are a mixture of these types.[28] The events take place in the distant past, mostly before the time of King Haraldr hárfagri and the unification of Norway, and the sagas are therefore primarily set in Scandinavia. In the sagas that share subject matter with heroic poems, the action takes place on the Continent,[29] and also in other cases the action of these sagas partly takes place on the Continent, in England, and Ireland as well as in the land of trolls in the Far North.[30] The sagas about ancient times were put into written form only in Iceland, but as opposed to the sagas of Icelanders which in all likelihood were a well-kept Icelandic secret in the Middle Ages, some written sagas about ancient times may have been known outside Iceland: at least one manuscript, AM 344 a 4to, which contains the *fornaldarsaga Orvar-Odds saga*, existed in Norway in the Middle Ages. However, the tradition behind these sagas must also have been known in the rest of Scandinavia, at

---

saga and consists of *Þorgils saga ok Hafliða*, *Sturlu saga*, *Prestsaga Guðmundar góða*, *Guðmundar saga dýra*, *Hrafns saga Sveinbjarnarsonar*, *Íslendinga saga*, *Þórðar saga kakala*, and *Svinfellinga saga*. In the younger redaction Reykjarfjarðarbók (last quarter of the fourteenth century) *Þorgils saga skarða*, *Sturlu þáttr*, miracles connected to Bishop Guðmundr Arason, and *Árna saga biskups* are included. The younger redaction covers the period up to 1291. To connect the original sagas, the redactor of *Sturlunga saga* composed a few shorter texts, such as *Geirmundar þáttr* and *Haukdœla þáttr*.

[28] Examples of the first type are *Vǫlsunga saga* and *Hervarar saga*. *Ǫrvar-Odds saga* and *Ragnars saga loðbrókar* are examples of the Viking sagas. Examples of *fornaldarsǫgur* that share many motifs with fairy tales are *Illuga saga Gríðarfóstra and Egils saga einhenda*.

[29] Examples of such sagas are *Vǫlsunga saga* and *Hervarar saga*.

[30] *Orvar-Odds saga* and *Ragnars saga loðbrókar* are examples of sagas that are partly set outside Scandinavia, and *Illuga saga Gríðarfóstra* and *Egils saga einhenda* are examples of sagas that are partly set in the world of trolls.

least in Norway, and literary motifs known from the written *fornaldarsǫgur* can
be found in Scandinavian medieval ballads.[31]

While Icelandic literary milieux in the first decades of the thirteenth century seem to have been preoccupied with their own history and culture, those
of Norway were more extroverted. This difference should not be exaggerated,
but there is a difference nonetheless. The Norwegian court became the centre
of a new interest in European literature that arrived with chivalric texts. Such
literature may have been known and read by a few people in the North before
translation began — in most cases from Old French — but at the court of the
Norwegian king Hákon Hákonarson a magnificent translation effort seems to
have been initiated. In the thirteenth century, the Norwegian court functioned
as a literary centre through which European literature and culture were chan-
nelled to a wider Nordic audience. It has been a matter of discussion whether
the main function of chivalric literature in the North was to be entertaining or
didactic — I argue that in all likelihood both functions were simultaneously
important.[32] We should, however, note that the attribution of one chief function to chivalric literature in the North has implications for our understanding of medieval Norwegian attitudes towards Europe and European literature
and culture. If people in the circles around the Norwegian court intended the
main function of chivalric literature to be didactic, this suggests that they saw
their Norwegian countrymen as belonging to the less civilized periphery that
needed to learn from the civilized cultures of more central European countries.
Conversely, entertainment as the main function and appeal of the translations
does not place the Nordic cultures in an inferior, unlearned position in quite
the same way. Nonetheless, the intended function of this literature was not necessarily the same in the mind of the medieval Norwegians who initially had it
translated as in the minds of those who used it later on.

As the genre of kings' sagas developed, more and more emphasis was put on
documenting the truth of the story with the help of skaldic stanzas, and much
skaldic poetry has only been preserved because its stanzas are quoted in sagas.
In kings' sagas skaldic stanzas are normally used as documentation, though in
other saga genres they are more often quoted as integrated parts of the story.

---

[31] See Liestøl, *Norske trollvisor og norrøne sogor*.

[32] Geraldine Barnes has argued that the main function of chivalric literature was didactic
(see Barnes, 'Arthurian Chivalry in Old Norse; Barnes', 'Some Current Issues'; and Barnes, *Old
Icelandic Literature in Society*). Marianne Kalinke, on the other hand, has argued that this literature served as entertainment (see Kalinke, *King Arthur North-by-Northwest*; Kalinke, 'Norse
Romance'; and Kalinke, 'Riddarasögur, Fornaldarsögur').

The oldest extant skaldic poetry dates to the middle of the ninth century. This oral art form had flourished long before being written down, and skaldic poetry continued to thrive following the arrival of writing. Poetry in all cultures has a more stable form than prose. Skaldic poetry was a much more extreme form of memorized poetry than eddic poetry, and the skalds had to obey numerous, strict metrical rules dictating how a skaldic poem should be composed, though some skaldic metres were stricter than others. As is the case for poetry, it is very difficult, indeed nearly impossible, to separate skaldic stanzas composed in an oral tradition from stanzas composed by a literate skald.

While eddic poetry normally is preserved in whole and coherent poems, coherent skaldic poems are found only in exceptional cases. Strange as it may sound, this indicates that the preservation of skaldic poetry was not the main reason the poems were written down. Skaldic poetry is mostly preserved as integral parts of sagas, first and foremost sagas of Icelanders and sagas of kings, and skaldic poetry's passage into writing must be seen in connection with the writing of the sagas of which they formed an integral part. Skaldic stanzas in sagas of Icelanders were mostly so-called *lausavísur*. They formed part of the saga narrative so that in many cases they could not be separated from the prose text without disturbing the story's coherence. In the kings' sagas skaldic stanzas could be an integral part of the saga narrative, but more often skaldic stanzas were used to document the truth of what was described in the prose text. In such cases only parts of the whole poem were needed, and therefore skaldic stanzas are very often preserved only fragmentarily. The use of skaldic stanzas as documentation shows that skaldic poetry was regarded by scribal authors as the best evidence that could be found when written sources were lacking.

We are certain that eddic and skaldic poetry existed in the preliterate period. Eddic poetry, which is anonymous, is of course difficult to date, and the time of composition is in fact disputed for many — or even most — of the eddic poems.[33] Mythological eddic poems are perhaps most likely to have originated in the pre-Christian period, but the possibility that some of them were generated in a much later period, when earlier heathen culture was no longer felt as a threat but looked upon with antiquarian interest, cannot be dismissed. For the other type of eddic poetry, the heroic poems, Christianization did not represent a critical phase, and they may have been composed over a longer period of time. The majority of Old Norse heroic poems, which are related to the Sigurðr Fáfnisbani story cycle, share subject matter with literature from other

---

[33] See Fidjestøl, *The Dating of Eddic Poetry*.

Germanic areas. Furthermore, kennings in Old Norse poetic language referring to the story about Sigurðr Fáfnisbani indicate that at least older versions of poems or the stories behind them were known before the arrival of writing, if not the extant poems themselves.

Oral poetry is often described as memorized or improvised.[34] Memorized poetry was learned by heart, whereas improvised art forms were to a greater extent reshaped at every performance on the basis of formulas and stock phrases. Eddic poetry is characterized by most scholars as memorized poetry, but this does not mean that there were no changes to an eddic poem from one performance to the next, or that the person who first wrote an eddic poem down transcribed it exactly as he heard it performed by a single informant. In oral tradition wording of lines could shift, the number or stanzas to be included in a performance might vary, and the order of stanzas — and even of lines — could change as well.[35] When a poem was first written down, it is likely that the writer would have chosen from among variant lines and stanzas he knew, and perhaps also include all the stanzas familiar from oral tradition — this might have amounted to more stanzas than were normally included in an oral performance.

Some eddic poems, both mythological and heroic, may have been composed after written culture was well established, perhaps even in a milieu in which written culture flourished. However, the fact that it is difficult to separate old poems composed in the time before the arrival of writing from poems that probably were composed in a culture in which writing was used, indicate that the arrival of writing did not change this art form much. Oral poems which were written down had in principle the same form both before and after they were recorded, and poems composed by literate authors closely followed the model of earlier oral poems.

It was not a given that the eddic and skaldic poetry that existed in the oral culture should be written down. There is strong evidence that eddic poetry was used widely across Scandinavia, but as far as we know, this poetry was written down only in Iceland, which suggests unique conditions in Icelandic society. Iceland developed a stronger written culture than was to be found in the rest

---

[34] A good overview of oral theory in relation to eddic poetry is found in Acker, *Revising Oral Theory*. See also Thorvaldsen, 'Svá er sagt í fornum vísindum', especially the chapter 'Edda-digtningen i den norrøne poetiske tradisjon'.

[35] If the different versions of *Vǫluspá* (the Codex Regius version, the Hauksbók version, and the version quoted in Snorri's *Edda*) were written down independently from oral tradition these versions demonstrated examples of all these types of variation (see Mundal, 'Oral or Scribal Variation').

of Scandinavia; further, it is likely that in a society of settlers with strong links to their old homeland, old traditions were more carefully preserved than in other places. It is also a question as to whether we should see the writing down of eddic poetry in connection with the establishment of schools and the teaching of *grammatica*. *Ars poetica* was an integral part of classical grammar, and we know that in Iceland *ars poetica* was taught on the basis of Latin poetry as well as Old Norse poetry.[36] This demonstrates the very strong and prestigious position of the vernacular in Icelandic society. The use of native poetry in the vernacular in the schools may have promoted the writing down of such poetry.

Lost Oral Genres

Not all oral art forms which existed in Old Norse culture passed on into writing, and there may be different reasons for leaving some oral genres behind. While written culture came with Christianity, Old Norse oral genres had their background in heathenism, with some Old Norse oral genres so closely connected to heathen culture that Christian authors and scribes hesitated to transmit them to posterity. There may, however, also have been other reasons connected to the forms and function of oral genres which explain why there was no need to record the performed oral art in writing.

It should not come as a surprise that oral genres closely connected to earlier heathen culture died out or did not make it into written form. There are at least two genres which seem to have existed in Old Norse oral culture that never made it into written form, namely, female mourning songs and songs connected to fertility cults. In 1944 Jón Helgason launched the theory, based on his reading of the runic inscription on the Swedish Bällsta stones, that a song of mourning (*grátr*) had existed in Scandinavia.[37] His theory has been accepted by the majority of scholars. I have argued elsewhere that stanzas within some eddic poems recounting a woman's words after being told her beloved is dead, function as a mourning song, as a *grátr*, within the eddic poem;[38] these therefore give a relatively good picture of a lost genre.[39]

---

[36] See Guðrún Nordal, *Tools of Literacy*, p. 23. On Icelandic poetics, see Clunies Ross, *A History of Old Norse Poetry and Poetics*.

[37] See Jón Helgason, 'Bällsta-inskriftens "i grati"'.

[38] Such stanzas are *Guðrúnarkviða i*, 18, *Guðrúnarkviða ii*, 2, *Helgakviða ii*, 38.

[39] See Mundal, 'Female Mourning Songs', for a fuller discussion of female mourning songs in Old Norse culture.

There may be several reasons for the loss of this genre. New Christian burial ceremonies may partly explain why female mourning songs disappeared. Genuine mourning songs cannot be separated from the scenes at which they were first performed. They expressed the real grief of lamenting women and were not suitable for entertainment later on. These songs were improvised literature made up of more or less fixed lines and stock phrases that existed within the tradition and could be used in constantly new combinations. The mourning songs were thus never formalized as individual poems in the tradition. Rather, they were a one-off performance, and when the ceremonies they were connected to died out, the songs died out with them.

Poems closely connected to a heathen fertility cult had only a small chance of survival in a Christian culture. In Book IV, Chapter 27, scholion 141 of *Gesta Hammaburgensis ecclesiae pontificum*, Adam of Bremen mentions songs connected to offerings in Uppsala that were so obscene he cannot repeat them. Adam is not a very reliable source on what happened in the North, but there are several indications in Old Norse sources that improvised oral poetry of a type fitting Adam's description existed in Scandinavia in the Middle Ages and even later.[40] Poor documentation of the existence of this type of poetry can partly be explained by its improvised nature. In addition, the inappropriate content may have prevented the poetry from passing into writing, but in oral culture, at least in some areas, this type of poetry seems to have lived on for centuries. The poems did not disappear from the culture, yet they did not make it into the written record either.

The Situation after Three Hundred Years of Christianity and Writing

In the late Middle Ages we can observe a development towards texts being written without basis in historical events or oral tradition. Some of the youngest sagas of Icelanders, for example *Bárðar saga Snæfelsáss* and *Víglundar saga*, scarcely contain any historical truth, and whether they relied on oral tradition or not is uncertain. In its last phase, this genre, which started as an orally based genre with roots in history, began moving in the direction of fiction. The written *fornaldarsǫgur* also started as a genre based on oral tradition, and saga composition seems to have developed gradually by building on older saga models and authorial imagination. The shift towards fiction can, however, be most clearly seen in the Icelandic indigenous *riddarasǫgur*, which were partly mod-

---

[40] See Mundal, 'Holdninga til erotikk', and Mundal, 'Female Mourning Songs'.

elled on the translated *riddarasǫgur*, but borrowed motifs from other genres, especially from *fornaldarsǫgur*. In the movement towards fiction, or towards a fiction that expressed a consciousness of its own imaginative status and 'writtenness' which can be observed in several Icelandic genres in the late Middle Ages, written text freed itself from oral tradition; as such, this can be seen as a breakthrough for written culture.[41]

Another development that can be observed from the arrival of writing through the late Middle Ages is a tendency to gather more and more written texts in big collections. A typical example of this includes the contemporary sagas now found in *Sturlunga saga* which were first written as individual sagas but later collected to form a continuous presentation of Icelandic history from around 1120 onwards. Within the kings' sagas, the tendency to write new and bigger works, based at least partly on earlier written sagas, can be observed in Snorri's sagas of kings. The writing of new sagas ended with Sturla Þórðarson's saga about King Magnús lagabœtir, but after 1300, anonymous authors — or compilers — incorporated older material contained in Snorri's saga about Óláfr Tryggvason and his special saga about Óláfr inn helgi to create the so-called *Great Saga about Óláfr Tryggvason* and the *Great Saga about Óláfr inn helgi*. This tendency to gather older written texts into great compilations may also be represented by the creation of many large manuscripts containing sagas of the same type (for example, Möðruvallabók) or of different types (for example, Hauksbók). The great sagas incorporating many older texts and the collection of texts into big codices demonstrate the growing strength of the written culture.

In comparison to the literary landscape around the year 1000, the literary landscape around 1300 was considerably changed. Written texts and written genres had been imported, oral genres had been written down, and new written genres had developed, on the basis of oral art forms and foreign models. A new alphabet and a new language, Latin, had come as part of the package introduced by the Church. The changes that took place are of course closely connected to structural changes in society, of which the introduction of Christianity was the most fundamental. The change of religion in turn generated new institutions connected to the Church that were important for the growth of literacy and simultaneously altered the framework conditions for cultural life. Differences

---

[41] On the development of fiction and a consciousness of writing, see Glauser, 'Romance' and 'Staging the Text'; Kalinke, *Stories Set Forth with Fair Word*; and Barnes, *The Bookish Riddarasögur*.

among preliterate societies may have led to variation in how institutions important to the development of cultural life were organized, with the result that
framework conditions for the spread of literacy and a strong written culture
were better in some places than in others. As we have seen, the changes cata-
lysed by the arrival of writing resulted in varied developments within Old
Norse culture. Though not easy to explain, the differences found in preliterate
culture and in society at the time when literacy began to grow may cast some
light on why literacy spread more widely and was more innovative in Iceland
than in Norway and the other Scandinavian countries.[42]

To some degree it is possible to connect different types of literature to certain types of centres of writing and learning. The Norwegian court was in the
beginning the centre that introduced chivalric literature. Centres connected to
bishoprics and monasteries must have had the main responsibility for introducing, copying, and writing religious literature. We know that sagas of kings in
Iceland could be written both in a monastery like Þingeyrar, and at a *staðr*[43]
such as Snorri's Reykholt. In Norway, writing kings' sagas was at least sometimes directly connected to the court, as, for example, when Karl Jónsson wrote
Grýla with King Sverrir looking over him and his work. Where the anonymous
genres, sagas of Icelanders, *fornaldarsǫgur*, and indigenous *riddarasǫgur* were
written is an interesting question. It would probably be wrong to connect these
genres to one special type of centre. Authors interested in many different topics may have been found at centres of varying types, and authors also moved
between centres. For example, Styrmir for a long time lived at Reykholt, but
later became Abbot at the monastery in Viðey, and Sturla Þórðarson resided for
most of his life in Iceland (his farm Staðarhóll was a *staðr*) but also spent time
at the Norwegian court.

However, the strong position of written culture in Iceland should perhaps
also be seen in connection with the oral-written continuum, and not only in
connection with oral culture in the time before writing. It is important to recall
that the transition from oral to written was not a steady development where
oral art forms and oral culture were gradually replaced by written literature and
written culture. Old oral art forms continued to exist long after the arrival of
writing, and even new oral art forms sometimes developed, on basis of written texts, a long time after written culture was firmly established. The ballads,

---

[42] See Mundal, 'Medieval Nordic Backgrounds: Written Culture in an Oral Society' in
this book.

[43] For a definition of *staðr*, see p. 48 in this volume.

which were inspired from abroad, from France, probably via England and Scotland, took roots in Scandinavia, most likely as early as in the thirteenth century. For this oral genre the Norwegian court seems to have been one of the centres from which it started to spread.[44] In Iceland the *rímur*-genre that probably dates from the fourteenth century existed both as a written and oral genre. Seen in retrospect, oral art forms are hardly visible if they are not reflected or mentioned in written texts. Therefore it is difficult to say for certain how long skaldic and eddic poetry were productive as oral art forms, and how long they were transmitted orally. The oral tradition behind the sagas of Icelanders which were written in the thirteenth, and partly in the beginning of the fourteenth century, was still flourishing when these sagas were written and most likely for some time after that. The oral tradition behind the *fornaldarsǫgur*, which were probably written from the middle of the thirteenth century throughout the Middle Ages and even later, indicates that the oral tradition behind this saga genre continued to endure throughout the same period.

The co-existence of written and oral in medieval Nordic societies is, for several reasons, important for understanding the strength of written culture. Literate societies are normally thought of as more advanced than oral societies, and in many ways they were.[45] However, oral cultures did also have their advantages. The laws in Sweden and Denmark were written down considerably later than in Norway and Iceland, which has partly been seen in connection with the earlier consolidation of the kingdom in Norway than in the neighbouring countries. Perhaps there is another conclusion to draw from the late writing down of laws: namely, that oral laws, whatever they were, after all did work. Skalds, storytellers, and oral performers were in all likelihood recruited from wider social groups than authors of written texts, though of course, literate as well as illiterate people could cultivate oral art forms. Oral art forms continued to flourish both outside and inside learned centres of writing.

We do not know to what degree women took part in the creation and performance of oral art forms, but they were not excluded. We know of a few female skalds, especially from the pre-literary period,[46] the lost mourning songs were a female genre, and eddic poetry is often placed in the mouths of women. The few scenes in saga literature describing saga-telling show men in such scenes, but it is difficult to see why women should not be saga-tellers and

---

[44] See Jonsson, 'Kring Sophus Bugges balladuppfatning'.

[45] See the first part of Melve's article 'Literary Studies: Past, Present, and Future' in this book.

[46] See Mundal, 'Overgangen frå munnleg til skriftleg kultur'.

bearers of tradition, and they are in fact mentioned by some authors as sources for oral tradition.[47] Even though the great majority of skalds, saga-tellers, and performers of oral art forms in the Old Norse world were men, written culture excluded women to a much higher degree than did oral culture. Women did not get the same access to schools as men, and Old Norse gender roles did not give women much time for writing — a few nuns would be the exception. An oral society involved a larger part of the population in cultural activity than a literate society; therefore written culture would profit from the co-existence of an oral culture.

---

[47] Two well-known examples are Ari fróði's mentioning of his informant Þóríðr Snorradóttir in *Íslendingabók*, ch. 1, and the list of informants consisting of three men and three women found both in *Óláfs saga Tryggvasonar in mesta* and in one manuscript of Oddr Snorrason's *Óláfs saga Tryggvasonar*. See Andresson, *The Saga of Olaf Tryggvason*, p. 2.

Works Cited

Primary Sources

The First Grammatical Treatise, ed. by Hreinn Benediktsson, University of Iceland Publications in Linguistics, 1 (Reykjavík: University of Iceland, 1972)

Gesta Hammaburgensis ecclesiae pontificum, ed. by Bernhard Schneidler, Hamburgische Kirchengeschichte = Magisteri Adam Bremensis Gesta Hammaburgensis ecclesiae pontificum (Hannover: Hahn, 1917)

Historia Norwegie, ed. by Inger Ekrem and Lars Boje Mortensen (Copenhagen: Museum Tusculanum Press, 2003)

Íslendingabók. Landnámabók, ed. by Jakob Benediktsson, Íslenzk fornrit, 1 (Reykjavík: Hið íslenzka fornritafélag, 1968)

Den norsk-islandske skjaldedigtning: A.1–2, B.1–2, ed. by Finnur Jónsson (Copenhagen: Gyldendal, 1912–15)

Passio et miracula beati Olavi, ed. by Fredirick Metcalfe (Oxford: Clarendon Press, 1881)

The Saga of Olaf Tryggvason: Oddr Snorrason, trans. by Theodore M. Andersson (Ithaca: Cornell University Press, 2003)

Skaldic Poetry of the Middle Ages, ed. Margaret Clunies Ross and others, 8 vols (Turnhout: Brepols, 2009–)

Snorri Sturluson, *Heimskringla*, ed. by Finnur Jónsson (Copenhagen: Gad, 1911)

Sturla Þórðarson, *Hákonar saga Hákonarsonar*, in *Konunga sögur. Sagaer om Sverre og hans efterfølgere*, ed. by C. R. Unger (Christiania: Brøgger, 1873), pp. 239–484

Sturlu þáttr, in *Sturlunga saga*, ed. by Örnulfur Thorsson, 3 vols (Reykjavík: Svart á hvítu, 1988), pp. 759–69

Sturlunga saga, ed. by Örnulfur Thorsson, 3 vols (Reykjavík: Svart á hvítu, 1988)

Sverris saga, ed. by Þorleifur Hauksson, Íslenzk fornrit, 30 (Reykjavík: Hið íslenzka fornritafélag, 2007)

Theodoricus Monachus, *Historia de antiquitate regum Norwagiemsium*, ed. by David McDougall and Ian McDougall (London: Viking Society for Northern Research, 1998)

Secondary Studies

Acker, Paul, *Revising Oral Theory: Formulaic Composition in Old English and Old Icelandic Verse*, Garland Studies in Medieval Literature, 16 (London: Garland Publishing, 1998)

Andersson, Theodore M., *The Icelandic Family Saga: An Analytic Reading* (Cambridge, MA: Harvard University Press, 1967)

Barnes, Geraldine, 'Arthurian Chivalry in Old Norse', *Arthurian Literature*, 7 (1987), 50–102

——, *The Bookish Riddarasögur: Writing Romance in Late Mediaeval Iceland*, The Viking Collection Studies in Northern Civilizations, 21 (Odense: University Press of Southern Denmark, 2014)

—— 'Romance in Iceland', in *Old Icelandic Literature and Society*, ed. by Margaret Clunies Ross (Cambridge: Cambridge University Press, 2000), pp. 266–86

——, 'Some Current Issues in *Riddarasögur* Research', *Arkiv för nordisk filologi*, 104 (1989), 73–88

Böðvar Guðmundsson, Sverrir Tómasson, Torfi H. Tulinius, and Vésteinn Ólason, eds, *Íslenzk bókmenntasaga II* (Reykjavík: Mál og Menning, 1993)

Clanchy, M. T., *From Memory to Written Record: England, 1066–1307* (London: Edward Arnold, 1979)

Clunies Ross, Margaret, *A History of Old Norse Poetry and Poetics* (Cambridge: Brewer, 2005)

Fidjestøl, Bjarne, *The Dating of Eddic Poetry: A Historical Survey and Methodological Investigation*, ed. by Odd Einar Haugen, Bibliotheca Arnamagnæana, 41 (Copenhagen: Reitzel, 1999)

Finnegan, Ruth, 'How Oral Is Oral Literature?' *Bulletin of the School of Oriental and African Studies, University of London*, 37 (1974), 52–64

——, 'The How of Literature'. *Oral Tradition*, 20 (2005), 164–87

——, *Oral Poetry: Its Nature, Significance and Social Context* (Bloomington: Indiana University Press, 1992)

Glauser, Jürg, 'Romance (Translated *riddarasögur*)', in *A Companion to Old Norse-Icelandic, Literature and Culture*, ed. by Rory McTurk (Malden: Blackwell, 2005), pp. 372–87

——, 'Staging the Text: On the Development of a Consciousness of Writing in the Norwegian and Icelandic Literature of the Middle Ages', in *Along the Oral-Written Continuum: Types of Texts, Relations and their Implications*, ed. by Slavica Ranković with Leidulf Melve and Else Mundal, Utrecht Studies in Medieval Literacy, 20 (Turnhout: Brepols, 2010), pp. 311–34

Guðrún Nordal, *Tools of Literacy: The Role of Skaldic Verse in Icelandic Textual Culture of the Twelfth and Thirteenth Centuries* (Toronto: University of Toronto Press, 2001)

Helle, Knut, *Omkring Bǫglungasǫgur*, Historisk-antikvarisk rekke, 7 (Bergen: Universitetet i Bergen, 1958)

Jón Helgason, 'Bällsta-inskriftens "i grati"', *Arkiv för nordisk filologi*, 59 (1944), 159–62

Jonsson, Bengt R., 'Kring Sophus Bugges balladuppfatning', in *Eyvindarbók: Festskrift til Eyvind Fjeld Halvorsen 4. mai 1992*, ed. by Finn Hødnebø, Jon Gunnar Jørgensen, Else Mundal, Magnus Rindal, and Vésteinn Ólason (Oslo: Institutt for nordistikk og litteraturvitenskap, 1992), pp. 138–68

Kalinke, Marianne, *King Arthur North-by-Northwest: The 'matière de Bretagne' in Old Norse-Icelandic* Romances, Bibliotheca Arnamagnæana, 37 (Copenhagen: Reitzel, 1981)

——, 'Norse Romance (*Riddarasögur*)', in *Old Norse-Icelandic Literature: A Critical Guide*, ed. by Carol J. Clover and John Lindow, Islandica, 45 (Ithaca: Cornell University Press, 1985), pp. 316–63

——, '*Riddarasögur, Fornaldarsögur*, and the Problem of Genre', in *Actes de la Ve Conférence Internationale sur les Sagas: Toulon, Juillet 1982,* ed. by Régis Boyer (Paris: Presses de l'Université de Paris-Sorbonne, 1985), pp. 77–91

——, *Stories Set Forth with Fair Words: The Evolution of Medieval Romance in Iceland* (Cardiff: University of Wales Press, 2017)

Liestøl, Knut, *Norske trollvisor og norrøne sogor* (Kristiania: Norli, 1915)

Mitchell, Stephen A., 'Performance and Norse Poetry: The Hydromel of Praise and the Effluvia of Scorn', *Oral Tradition*, 16.1 (2001), 168–202

Mundal, Else, 'Female Mourning Songs and Other Lost Oral Poetry in Pre-Christian Nordic Culture', in *The Performance of Christian and Pagan Storyworlds: Non-Canonical Chapters of the History of Nordic Medieval Literature*, ed. by Lars Boje Mortensen and Tuomas M. S. Lehtonen with Alexandra Bergholm (Turnhout: Brepols, 2013), pp. 367–88

——, 'Holdninga til erotikk i norrøn dikting', in *Kjønn — Erotikk — Religion*, ed. by Einar Ådland and Kirsten Bang, Bergen Museums skrifter, 9 (Bergen: Universitetet i Bergen, 2001), pp. 28–40

——, 'How did the Arrival of Writing Influence Old Norse Culture?', in *Along the Oral-Written Continuum: Types of Texts, Relations and their Implications*, ed. by Slavica Rankovic with Else Mundal and Leidulf Melve, Utrecht Studies in Medieval Literacy, 20 (Turnhout: Brepols, 2010), pp. 163–81

——, 'Íslendingabók vurdert som bispestolskrønike', *Alvíssmál*, 3 (1994), 63–72

——, 'Oral or Scribal Variation in *Vǫluspá*', in *Oral Art Forms and their Passage into Writing*, ed. by Else Mundal and Jonas Wellendorf (Copenhagen: Museum Tusculanum Press, 2008), pp. 209–27

——, 'Overgangen frå munnleg til skriftleg kultur — Ei ulukke for kvinnene?', in *Förändringar I kvinnors villkor under medeltiden. Uppsatser framlaghda vid ett kvinno-historiskt symposium I Skálholt, Island, 22.–25. juni 1981*, ed. by Silja Aðalsteinsdóttir and Helgi Þorláksson, Ritsafn Sagnfræðistofnunar (Reykjavík: Sagnfræðistofnun Háskóla Íslands, 1983), pp. 11–25

——, 'Sagalitteraturen', in *Handbok i norrøn filologi: Andre utgåve*, ed. by Odd Einar Haugen (Bergen: Fagbokforlaget, 2013), pp. 418–62

——, 'Sagaskrivarane og Bergen', in *Fragment frå Fortida*, ed. by Geir Atle Ersland and Øystein Hellesøe Brekke (Oslo: Dreyers, 2013), pp. 174–99

Stefán Karlsson, 'Islandsk bogeksport til Norge i middelalderen', *Maal og Minne* (1979), 1–17

Thorvaldsen, Bernt Øyvind, 'Svá er sagt í fornum vísindum: Tekstualiseringen av de mytologiske eddadikt' (unpublished doctoral dissertation, Universitetet i Bergen, 2007)

Turville-Petre, Gabriel, *Origins of Icelandic Literature* (Oxford: Clarendon Press, 1953)

Wellendorf, Jonas, 'Lærdomslitteratur', in *Handbok i norrøn filologi: Andre utgåve*, ed. by Odd Einar Haugen (Bergen: Fagbokforlaget, 2013), pp. 302–55

INDEX

Entries beginning with *Þ/þ*, *Æ/æ*, *Ǫ/ǫ* and *Ø/ø* are found at the end of the index. Icelanders are indexed by first name. The editors would like to thank Laura Napran, who indexed this book, and the Institute for Scholarship in the Liberal Arts, College of Arts and Letters, University of Notre Dame, whose financial support made that possible.

ACTA SCANDINAVICA

All volumes in this series are evaluated by an Editorial Board, strictly on academic grounds, based on reports prepared by referees who have been commissioned by virtue of their specialism in the appropriate field. The Board ensures that the screening is done independently and without conflicts of interest. The definitive texts supplied by authors are also subject to review by the Board before being approved for publication. Further, the volumes are copyedited to conform to the publisher's stylebook and to the best international academic standards in the field.

Titles in Series

Medieval Christianity in the North: New Studies, ed. by Kirsi Salonen, Kurt Villads Jensen, and Torstein Jørgensen (2013)

The Nordic Apocalypse: Approaches to Vǫluspá and Nordic Days of Judgement, ed. by Terry Gunnell and Annette Lassen (2013)

New Approaches to Early Law in Scandinavia, ed. by Stefan Brink and Lisa Collinson (2014)

Minni and Muninn: Memory in Medieval Nordic Culture, ed. by Pernille Hermann, Stephen A. Mitchell, and Agnes S. Arnórsdóttir (2014)

Christian Oertel, *The Cult of St Erik in Medieval Sweden: Veneration of a Royal Saint, Twelfth–Sixteenth Centuries* (2016)

Studies in the Transmission and Reception of Old Norse Literature: The Hyperborean Muse in European Culture, ed. by Judy Quinn and Adele Cipolla (2016)

Theorizing Old Norse Myth, ed. by Stefan Brink and Lisa Collinson (2017)